Room Acoustics

Room Acoustics

Fourth edition

Heinrich Kuttruff
Institut für Technische Akustik, Technische
Hochschule Aachen, Aachen, Germany

Taylor & Francis
Taylor & Francis Group
LONDON AND NEW YORK

First published 1973
by Elsevier Science Publishers Ltd
Second edition 1979
Third edition 1991

Reprinted 1999
by Taylor & Francis

Transferred to Digital Printing 2006

Fourth edition published 2000 by Taylor & Francis
2 Park Square, Milton Park, Abingdon, Oxon, OX14 4RN

Simultaneously published in the USA and Canada
by Taylor & Francis
270 Madison Ave, New York NY 10016

Taylor & Francis is an imprint of the Taylor & Francis Group

Typeset in 10/12 pt Sabon by Graphicraft Limited, Hong Kong

British Library Cataloguing in Publication Data
A catalogue record for this book is available from the British Library

Library of Congress Cataloging in Publication Data
Kuttruff, Heinrich.
  Room acoustics/Heinrich Kuttruff.–4th ed.
    p. cm.
  Includes bibliographical references and index.
  1. Architectural acoustics. I. Title.

NA2800 .K87 2000
729'.29–dc21   00-021584

ISBN 0-419-24580-4

Contents

vi *Contents*

Preface to the fourth edition

Almost a decade has elapsed since the third edition and during this period many new ideas and methods have been introduced into room acoustics. I therefore welcome the opportunity to prepare a new edition of this book and to include the more important of those developments, while also introducing new topics which were not dealt with in earlier editions.

In room acoustics, as in many other technical fields, the digital computer has continued its triumphant progress; nowadays hardly any acoustical measurements are carried out without using a computer, allowing previously inconceivable improvements in accuracy and rapidity. Therefore, an update of the chapter on measuring techniques (Chapter 8) was essential. Furthermore, the increased availability of computers has opened new ways for the computation and simulation of sound fields in enclosures. These have led to better and more reliable methods in the practical design of halls; indeed, due to its flexibility and low cost, sound field simulation will probably replace the conventional scale model in the near future. Moreover, by simulation it can demonstrated what a new theatre or concert hall which is still on the drawing board will sound like when completed ('auralisation'). These developments are described in Chapter 9, which contains a separate section on auralisation.

Also included in the new edition are sections on sound scattering and diffuse reflection, on sound reflection from curved walls, on sound absorption by several special arrangements (freely hanging porous material, Schroeder diffusers) and on the measurement of diffuse reflections from walls.

As in the earlier editions, no attempt is made to list all relevant publications on room acoustics, and references are given only where I have adopted material from another publication, or to enable the reader to obtain more detailed information on a particular topic. I apologise for leaving many important and interesting publications unmentioned.

The preparation of a new edition offered the chance to present some subjects in a more comprehensive and logical way, to improve numerous text passages and formulae and to correct errors and mistakes that inevitably crept into the previous editions. I appreciate the suggestions of many critical readers, who drew my attention to weak or misleading material in the book. Most text passages, however, have been adopted from the previous editions without any changes. Therefore I want to express again my most sincere thanks to Professor Peter Lord of the University of Salford for his competent and sensitive translation. Finally, I want to thank the publishers for their cooperation in preparing this new edition.

Heinrich Kuttruff
Aachen

Preface to the first edition

This book is intended to present the fundamentals of room acoustics in a systematic and comprehensive way so that the information thus provided may be used for the acoustical design of rooms and as a guide to the techniques of associated measurement.

These fundamentals are twofold in nature: the generation and propagation of sound in an enclosure, which are physical processes which can be described without ambiguity in the language of the physicist and engineer; and the physiological and psychological factors, of prime importance but not capable of exact description even within our present state of knowledge. It is the interdependence and the equality of importance of both these aspects of acoustics which are characteristic of room acoustics, whether we are discussing questions of measuring techniques, acoustical design, or the installation of a public address system.

In the earlier part of the book ample space is devoted to the objective description of sound fields in enclosures, but, even at this stage, taking into account, as far as possible, the limitations imposed by the properties of our hearing. Equal weight is given to both the wave and geometrical description of sound fields, the former serving to provide a more basic understanding, the latter lending itself to practical application. In both instances, full use is made of statistical methods; therefore, a separate treatment of what is generally known as 'statistical room acoustics' has been dispensed with.

The treatment of absorption mechanisms is based upon the concept that a thorough understanding of the various absorbers is indispensable for the acoustician. However, in designing a room he will not, in all probability, attempt to calculate the absorptivity of a particular arrangement but instead will rely on collected measurements and data based on experience. It is for this reason that in the chapter on measuring techniques the methods of determining absorption are discussed in some detail.

Some difficulties were encountered in attempting to describe the factors which are important in the perception of sound in rooms, primarily because of the fragmentary nature of the present state of knowledge, which seems to consist of results of isolated experiments which are strongly influenced by the conditions under which they were performed.

We have refrained from giving examples of completed rooms to illustrate how the techniques of room acoustics can be applied. These are already in print, for example Beranek,[1] Bruckmayer,[2] and Furrer and Lauber.[3] Instead, we have chosen to show how one can progress in designing a room and which parameters need to be considered. Furthermore, because model investigations have proved helpful these are described in detail.

Finally, there is a whole chapter devoted to the design of loudspeaker installations in rooms. This is to take account of the fact that nowadays electroacoustic installations are more than a mere crutch in that they frequently present, even in the most acoustically faultless room, the only means of transmitting the spoken word in an intelligible way. Actually, the installations and their performance play a more important role in determining the acoustical quality of what is heard than certain design details of the room itself.

The book should be understood in its entirety by readers with a reasonable mathematical background and some elementary knowledge of wave propagation. Certain hypotheses may be omitted without detriment by readers with more limited mathematical training.

The literature on room acoustics is so extensive that the author has made no attempt to provide an exhaustive list of references. References have only been given in those cases where the work has been directly mentioned in the text or in order to satisfy possible demand for more detailed information.

The author is greatly indebted to Professor Peter Lord of the University of Salford and Mrs Evelyn Robinson of Prestbury, Cheshire, for their painstaking translation of the German manuscript, and for their efforts to present some ideas expressed in my native language into colloquial English. Furthermore, the author wishes to express his appreciation to the publishers for this carefully prepared edition. Last, but not least, he wishes to thank his wife most sincerely for her patience in the face of numerous evenings and weekends which he has devoted to his manuscript.

Heinrich Kuttruff
Aachen

1 Beranek, L.L. (1962). *Music, Acoustics and Architecture*. John Wiley, New York/ London.
2 Bruckmayer, F. (1962). *Schalltechnik im Hochbau*. Franz Deuticke, Wien.
3 Furrer, W. & Lauber, A. (1972). *Raum und Bauakustik, Lärmabwehr*, 3rd edn. Birkhäuser, Basel.

Introduction

We all know that a concert hall, theatre, lecture room or a church may have good or poor 'acoustics'. As far as speech in these rooms is concerned, it is relatively simple to make some sort of judgement on their quality by rating the ease with which the spoken word is understood. However, judging the acoustics of a concert hall or an opera house is generally more difficult, since it requires considerable experience, the opportunity for comparisons and a critical ear. Even so the inexperienced cannot fail to learn about the acoustical reputation of a certain concert hall should they so desire, for instance by listening to the comments of others, or by reading the critical reviews of concerts in the press.

An everyday experience (although most people are not consciously aware of it) is that living rooms, offices, restaurants and all kinds of rooms for work can be acoustically satisfactory or unsatisfactory. Even rooms which are generally considered insignificant or spaces such as staircases, factories, passenger concourses in railway stations and airports may exhibit different acoustical properties; they may be especially noisy or exceptionally quiet, or they may differ in the ease with which announcements over the public address system can be understood. That is to say, even these spaces have 'acoustics' which may be satisfactory or less than satisfactory.

Despite the fact that people are subconsciously aware of the acoustics to which they are daily subjected, there are only a few who can explain what they really mean by 'good or poor acoustics' and who understand factors which influence or give rise to certain acoustic properties. Even fewer people know that the acoustics of a room is governed by principles which are amenable to scientific treatment. It is frequently thought that the acoustical design of a room is a matter of chance, and that good acoustics cannot be designed into a room with the same precision as a nuclear reactor or space vehicle is designed. This idea is supported by the fact that opinions on the acoustics of a certain room or hall frequently differ as widely as the opinions on the literary qualities of a new book or on the architectural design of a new building. Furthermore, it is well known that sensational failures in this field do occur from time to time. These and similar anomalies add even more weight to the general belief that the acoustics of a room is beyond the scope of calculation or prediction, at least with any reliability, and hence the study of room acoustics is an art rather than an exact science.

In order to shed more light on the nature of room acoustics, let us first compare it with a related field: the design and construction of musical instruments. This comparison is not as senseless as it may appear at first sight, since a concert hall too may be regarded as a large musical instrument, the shape and material of which determine to a considerable extent what the listener will hear. Musical instruments – string instruments for instance – are, as is well known, not designed or built by scientifically trained acousticians but, fortunately, by people who have acquired the necessary experience through long and systematic practical training. Designing or building musical instruments is therefore not a technical or scientific discipline but a sort of craft, or an 'art' in the classical meaning of this word.

Nevertheless, there is no doubt that the way in which a musical instrument functions, i.e. the mechanism of sound generation, the determining of the pitch of the tones generated and their timbre through certain resonances, as well as their radiation into the surrounding air, are all purely physical processes and can therefore be understood rationally, at least in principle. Similarly, there is no mystery in the choice of materials; their mechanical and acoustical properties can be defined by measurements to any required degree of accuracy. (How well these properties can be reproduced is another problem.) Thus, there is nothing intangible nor is there any magic in the construction of a musical instrument: many particular problems which are still unsolved will be understood in the not too distant future. Then one will doubtless be in a position to design a musical instrument according to scientific methods, i.e. not only to predict its timbre but also to give, with scientific accuracy, details for its construction, all of which are necessary to obtain prescribed or desired acoustical qualities.

Room acoustics is in a different position from musical instrument acoustics in that the end product is usually more costly by orders of magnitude. Furthermore, rooms are produced in much smaller numbers and have by no means geometrical shapes which remain unmodified through the centuries. On the contrary, every architect, by the very nature of his profession, strives to create something which is entirely new and original. The materials used are also subject to the rapid development of building technology. Therefore, it is impossible to collect in a purely empirical manner sufficient know-how from which reliable rules for the acoustical design of rooms or halls can be distilled. An acoustical consultant is confronted with quite a new situation with each task, each theatre, concert hall or lecture room to be designed, and it is of little value simply to transfer the experience of former cases to the new project if nothing is known about the conditions under which the transfer may be safely made.

This is in contrast to the making of a musical instrument where the use of unconventional materials as well as the application of new shapes is either firmly rejected as an offence against sacred traditions or dismissed as a whim. As a consequence, time has been sufficient to develop well established empirical rules. And if their application happens to fail in one case or another, the faulty product is abandoned or withdrawn from service – which is not true for large rooms in an analogous situation.

For the above reasons, the acoustician has been compelled to study sound propagation in closed spaces with increasing thoroughness and to develop the knowledge in this field much further than is the case with musical instruments, even though the acoustical behaviour of a large hall is considerably more complex and involved. Thus, room acoustics has become a science during the past century and those who practise it on a purely empirical basis will fail sooner or later, like a bridge builder who waives calculations and relies on experience or empiricism.

On the other hand, the present level of reliable knowledge in room acoustics is not particularly advanced. Many important factors influencing the acoustical qualities of large rooms are understood only incompletely or even not at all. As will be explained below in more detail, this is due to the complexity of sound fields in closed spaces – or, as may be said equally well – to the large number of 'degrees of freedom' which we have to deal with. Another difficulty is that the acoustical quality of a room ultimately has to be proved by subjective judgements.

In order to gain more understanding about the sort of questions which can be answered eventually by scientific room acoustics, let us look over the procedures for designing the acoustics of a large room. If this room is to be newly built, some ideas will exist as to its intended use. It will have been established, for example, whether it is to be used for the showing of ciné films, for sports events, for concerts or as an open-plan office. One of the first tasks of the consultant is to translate these ideas concerning the practical use into the language of objective sound field parameters and to fix values for them which he thinks will best meet the requirements. During this step he has to keep in mind the limitations and peculiarities of our subjective listening abilities. (It does not make sense, for instance, to fix the duration of sound decay with an accuracy of 1% if no one can subjectively distinguish such small differences.) Ideally, the next step would be to determine the shape of the hall, to choose the materials to be used, to plan the arrangement of the audience, of the orchestra and of other sound sources, and to do all this in such a way that the sound field configuration will develop which has previously been found to be the optimum for the intended purpose. In practice, however, the architect will have worked out already a preliminary design, certain features of which he considers imperative. In this case the acoustical consultant has to examine the objective acoustical properties of the design by calculation, by geometric ray considerations, by model investigations or even by computer simulation, and he will eventually have to submit proposals for suitable adjustments. As a general rule there will have to be some compromise in order to obtain a reasonable result.

Frequently the problem is refurbishment of an existing hall, either to remove architectural, acoustical or other technical defects or to adapt it to a new purpose which was not intended when the hall was originally planned. In this case an acoustical diagnosis has to be made first on the basis of appropriate measurement. A reliable measuring technique which yields objective quantities, which are subjectively meaningful at the same time, is an indispensable tool of the acoustician. The subsequent therapeutic step is essentially the same as described above: the acoustical consultant has to propose measures which would result in the intended objective changes in the sound field and consequently in the subjective impressions of the listeners.

In any case, the acoustician is faced with a two-fold problem: on the one hand he has to find and to apply the relations between the structural features of a room – such as shape, materials and so on – with the sound field which will occur in it, and on the other hand he has to take into consideration as far as possible the interrelations between the objective and measurable sound field parameters and the specific subjective hearing impressions effected by them. Whereas the first problem lies completely in the realm of technical reasoning, it is the latter problem which makes room acoustics different from many other technical disciplines in that the success or failure of an acoustical design has finally to be decided by the collective judgement of all 'consumers', i.e. by some sort of average, taken over the comments of individuals with widely varying intellectual, educational and aesthetic backgrounds. The measurement of sound field parameters can replace to a certain extent systematic or sporadic questioning of listeners. But, in the final analysis, it is the average opinion of listeners which decides whether the acoustics of a room is favourable or poor. If the majority of the audience (or that part which is vocal) cannot understand what a speaker is saying, or thinks that the sound of an orchestra in a certain hall is too dry, too weak or indistinct, then even though the measured reverberation time is appropriate, or the local or directional distribution of sound is uniform, the listener is always right; the hall does have acoustical deficiencies.

Therefore, acoustical measuring techniques can only be a substitute for the investigation of public opinion on the acoustical qualities of a room and it will serve its purpose better the closer the measured sound field parameters are related to subjective listening categories.

Not only must the measuring techniques take into account the hearing response of the listeners but the acoustical theory too will only provide meaningful information if it takes regard of the consumer's particular listening abilities. It should be mentioned at this point that the sound field in a real room is so complicated that it is not open to exact mathematical treatment. The reason for this is the large number of components which make up the sound field in a closed space regardless of whether we describe it in terms of vibrational modes or, if we prefer, in terms of sound rays which have undergone one or more reflections from boundaries. Each of these components depends on the sound source, the shape of the room and on the materials from which it is made; accordingly, the exact computation of the sound field is usually quite involved. Supposing this procedure were possible with reasonable expenditure, the results would be so confusing that such a treatment would not provide a comprehensive survey and hence would not be of any practical use. For this reason, approximations and simplifications are inevitable; the totality of possible sound field data has to be reduced to averages or average functions which are more tractable and condensed to provide a clearer picture. This is why we have to resort so frequently to statistical methods and models in room acoustics, whichever way we attempt to describe sound fields. The problem is to perform these reductions and simplifications once again in accordance with the properties of human hearing, i.e. in such a way that the remaining average parameters correspond as closely as possible to particular subjective sensations.

From this it follows that essential progress in room acoustics depends to a large extent on the advances in psychological acoustics. As long as the physiological and psychological processes which are involved in hearing are not completely understood, the relevant relations between objective stimuli and subjective sensations must be investigated empirically – and should be taken into account when designing the acoustics of a room.

Many interesting relations of this kind have been detected and success- fully investigated during the past few decades. But other questions which are no less important for room acoustics are unanswered so far, and much work remains to be carried out in this field.

It is, of course, the purpose of all efforts in room acoustics to avoid acoustical deficiencies and mistakes. It should be mentioned, on the other hand, that it is neither desirable nor possible to create the 'ideal acoustical environment' for concerts and theatres. It is a fact that the enjoyment when listening to music is a matter not only of the measurable sound waves hitting the ear but also of the listener's personal attitude and his individual taste, and these vary from one person to another. For this reason there will always be varying shades of opinion concerning the acoustics of even the most marvellous concert hall. For the same reason, one can easily imagine a wide variety of concert halls with excellent, but nevertheless different, acoustics. It is this 'lack of uniformity' which is characteristic of the subject of room acoustics, and which is responsible for many of its difficulties, but it also accounts for the continuous power of attraction it exerts on many acousticians.

1 Some facts on sound waves, sources and hearing

In principle, any complex sound field can be considered as a superposition of numerous simple sound waves, e.g. plane waves. This is especially true of the very involved sound fields which we have to deal with in room acoustics. So it is useful to describe first the properties of a simple plane or a spherical sound wave or, more basically, the general features of sound propagation. We can, however, restrict our attention to sound propagation in gases, because in room acoustics we are only concerned with air as the medium.

In this chapter we assume the sound propagation to be free of losses and ignore the effect of any obstacles such as walls, i.e. we suppose the medium to be unbounded in all directions. Furthermore, we assume our medium to be homogeneous and at rest. In this case the velocity of sound is constant with reference to space and time. For air, its magnitude is

$$c = (331.4 + 0.6\Theta) \quad \text{m/s} \tag{1.1}$$

Θ being the temperature in centigrade.

In large halls, variations of temperature and hence of the sound velocity with time and position cannot be entirely avoided. Likewise, because of temperature differences and air conditioning, the air is not completely at rest, and so our assumptions are not fully realised. But the effects which are caused by these inhomogeneities are so small that they can be neglected.

1.1 Basic relations, the wave equation

In any sound wave, the particles of the medium undergo vibrations about their mean positions. Therefore, a wave can be described completely by indicating the instantaneous displacements of these particles. It is more customary, however, to consider the velocity of particle displacement as a basic acoustical quantity rather than the displacement itself.

The vibrations in a sound wave do not take place at all points with the same phase. We can, in fact, find points in a sound field where the particles vibrate in opposite phase. This means that in certain regions the particles are pushed together or compressed and in other regions they are pulled apart or rarefied. Therefore, under the influence of a sound wave, variations of gas density and pressure occur, both of which are functions of time and position. The difference between the instantaneous pressure and the static pressure is called the sound pressure.

The changes of gas pressure caused by a sound wave in general occur so rapidly that heat cannot be exchanged between adjacent volume elements. Consequently, a sound wave causes adiabatic variations of the temperature, and so the temperature too can be considered as a quantity characterising a sound wave.

The various acoustical quantities are connected by a number of basic laws which enable us to set up a general differential equation governing sound propagation. Firstly, conservation of momentum is expressed by the relation

$$\text{grad } p = -\rho_0 \frac{\partial \mathbf{v}}{\partial t} \tag{1.2}$$

where p denotes the sound pressure, $\mathbf{v}$ the vector particle velocity, t the time and ρ_0 the static value of the gas density.

Furthermore, conservation of mass leads to

$$\rho_0 \text{ div } \mathbf{v} = -\frac{\partial \rho}{\partial t} \tag{1.3}$$

ρ being the total density including its variable part, $\rho = \rho_0 + \delta\rho$. In these equations, it is tacitly assumed that the changes of p and ρ are small compared with the static values p_0 and ρ_0 of these quantities; furthermore, the absolute value of the particle velocity $\mathbf{v}$ should be much smaller than the sound velocity c.

Under the further supposition that we are dealing with an ideal gas, the following relations hold between the sound pressure, the density variations and the temperature changes $\delta\Theta$:

$$\frac{p}{p_0} = \kappa \cdot \frac{\delta\rho}{\rho_0} = \frac{\kappa}{\kappa - 1} \frac{\delta\Theta}{\Theta + 273} \tag{1.4}$$

Here κ is the adiabatic exponent (for air $\kappa = 1.4$).

The particle velocity $\mathbf{v}$ and the variable part $\delta\rho$ of the density can be eliminated from eqns (1.2) to (1.4). This yields the differential equation

$$c^2 \Delta p = \frac{\partial^2 p}{\partial t^2} \tag{1.5}$$

where

$$c^2 = \kappa \cdot \frac{p_0}{\rho_0} \qquad (1.5a)$$

This differential equation governs the propagation of sound waves in any lossless fluid and is therefore of central importance for almost all acoustical phenomena. We shall refer to it as the 'wave equation'. It holds not only for sound pressure but also for density and temperature variations.

1.2 Plane waves and spherical waves

Now we assume that the acoustical quantities depend only on the time and on one single direction, which may be chosen as the x-direction of a cartesian coordinate system. Then eqn (1.5) reads

$$c^2 \frac{\partial^2 p}{\partial x^2} = \frac{\partial^2 p}{\partial t^2} \qquad (1.6)$$

The general solution of this differential equation is

$$p(x, t) = F(ct - x) + G(ct + x) \qquad (1.7)$$

where F and G are arbitrary functions, the second derivatives of which exist. The first term on the right represents a pressure wave travelling in the positive x-direction with a velocity c, because the value of F remains unaltered if a time increase δt is associated with an increase in the coordinate $\delta x = c\delta t$. For the same reason the second term describes a pressure wave propagated in the negative x-direction. Therefore the constant c is the sound velocity.

Each term of eqn (1.7) represents a progressive 'plane wave': As shown in Fig. 1.1a, the sound pressure p is constant in any plane perpendicular to the x-axis. These planes of constant sound pressure are called 'wavefronts', and any line perpendicular to them is a 'wave normal'.

According to eqn (1.2), the particle velocity has only one non-vanishing component, which is parallel to the gradient of the sound pressure, to the x-axis. This means sound waves in fluids are longitudinal waves. The particle velocity may be obtained from applying eqn (1.2) to eqn (1.7):

$$v = v_x = \frac{1}{\rho_0 c}[F(ct - x) - G(ct + x)] \qquad (1.8)$$

As may be seen from eqns (1.7) and (1.8) the ratio of sound pressure and particle velocity in a plane wave propagated in the positive direction ($G = 0$) is frequency independent:

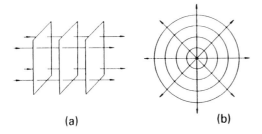

Figure 1.1 Simple types of waves: (a) plane wave; (b) spherical wave.

$$\frac{p}{v} = \rho_0 c \tag{1.9}$$

This ratio is called the 'characteristic impedance' of the medium. For air at normal conditions its value is

$$\rho_0 c = 414 \text{ kg m}^{-2} \text{ s}^{-1} \tag{1.10}$$

If the wave is travelling in the negative x-direction, the ratio of sound pressure and particle velocity is negative.

Of particular importance are harmonic waves in which the time and space dependence of the acoustical quantities, for instance of the sound pressure, follows a sine or cosine function. If we set $G = 0$ and specify F as a cosine function, we obtain an expression for a plane, progressive harmonic wave:

$$p(x, t) = \hat{p} \cos [k(ct - x)] = \hat{p} \cos (\omega t - kx) \tag{1.11}$$

with the arbitrary constants $\hat{p}$ and k. Here the angular frequency

$$\omega = kc \tag{1.12}$$

was introduced which is related to the temporal period

$$T = \frac{2\pi}{\omega} \tag{1.13}$$

of the harmonic vibration represented by eqn (1.11). At the same time this equation describes a spatial harmonic vibration with the period

$$\lambda = \frac{2\pi}{k} \tag{1.14}$$

This is the 'wavelength' of the harmonic wave. It denotes the distance in the x-direction where equal values of the sound pressure (or any other field quantity) occur. According to eqn (1.12) it is related to the angular frequency by

$$\lambda = \frac{2\pi c}{\omega} = \frac{c}{f} \tag{1.15}$$

where $f = \omega/2\pi = 1/T$ is the frequency of the vibration. It has the dimension second^{-1}; its units are hertz (Hz), kilohertz (1 kHz = 10^3 Hz), megahertz (1 MHz = 10^6 Hz) etc. The quantity $k = \omega/c$ is the propagation constant or the wave number of the wave.

A very useful and efficient representation of harmonic oscillations and waves is obtained by observing that $\cos x$ is the real part, and $\sin x$ is the imaginary part of $\exp(ix)$ with $i = \sqrt{-1}$. This is the complex or symbolic notation of harmonic vibrations and will be employed quite frequently in what follows. Using the aforementioned relation, eqn. (1.11) can be written in the form

$$p(x, t) = \mathrm{Re}\{\hat{p} \exp [i(\omega t - kx)]\}$$

or, omitting the sign Re:

$$p(x, t) = \hat{p} \exp [i(\omega t - kx)] \tag{1.16}$$

where $\hat{p} = |p(x, t)|$ is the amplitude of the pressure wave.

The complex notation has several advantages over the real representation (1.11). Any differentiation or integration with respect to time is equivalent to multiplication or division by $i\omega$. Furthermore, only the complex notation allows a clear-cut definition of impedances and admittances (*see* Section 2.1). It fails, however, in all cases where vibrational quantities are to be multiplied or squared. If doubts arise concerning the physical meaning of an expression it is advisable to recall the origin of this notation, i.e. to take the real part of the expression.

As with any complex quantity the complex sound pressure in a plane wave may be represented in a rectangular coordinate system with the horizontal and the vertical axis corresponding to the real and the imaginary part of the impedance, respectively. It is often depicted as an arrow pointing from the origin to the point which corresponds to the value of the impedance (*see* Fig. 1.2). The length of this arrow corresponds to the magnitude of the complex quantity while the angle it includes with the real axis is its phase angle or 'argument' (abbreviated arg p). In the present case the phase angle depends on time and on position:

$$\arg p = \omega t - kx$$

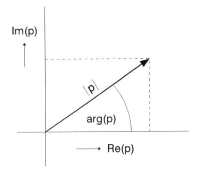

Figure 1.2 Representation of a complex quantity *p*.

This means, that for a fixed position the arrow rotates around the origin with an angular velocity ω, which explains the expression 'angular frequency'.

So far it has been assumed that the wave medium is free of losses. If this is not the case, the pressure amplitude does not remain constant in the course of wave propagation but decreases according to an exponential law. Then eqn (1.16) is modified in the following way:

$$p(x, t) = \hat{p} \exp (-mx/2) \exp [i(\omega t - kx)] \tag{1.16a}$$

We can even use the representation of eqn (1.16) if we conceive the wave number *k* as a complex quantity containing the attenuation constant *m* in its imaginary part:

$$k = \frac{\omega}{c} - i\frac{m}{2} \tag{1.17}$$

Another simple wave type is the spherical wave in which the surfaces of constant pressure, i.e. the wave fronts, are concentric spheres (*see* Fig. 1.1b). In their common centre we have to imagine some vanishingly small source which introduces or withdraws fluid. Such a source is called a 'point source'. The appropriate coordinates for this geometry are polar coordinates with the distance *r* from the centre as the relevant space coordinate. Transformed into this system, the differential equation (1.5) reads:

$$\frac{\partial^2 p}{\partial r^2} + \frac{2}{r}\frac{\partial p}{\partial r} = \frac{1}{c^2}\frac{\partial^2 p}{\partial t^2} \tag{1.18}$$

A simple solution of this equation is

$$p(r, t) = \frac{\rho_0}{4\pi r} \dot{Q}\left(t - \frac{r}{c}\right) \tag{1.19}$$

It represents a spherical wave produced by a point source at $r = 0$ with the 'volume velocity' Q, which is the rate (in m^3/s) at which fluid is expelled by the source. The overdot means partial differentiation with respect to time. Again, the argument $t - r/c$ indicates that any disturbance created by the sound source is propagated outward with velocity c, its strength decreasing as $1/r$. Reversing the sign in the argument of $\dot{Q}$ would result in the unrealistic case of an in-going wave.

The only non-vanishing component of the particle velocity is the radial one; it is calculated by applying eqn (1.2) to eqn (1.19):

$$v_r = \frac{1}{4\pi r^2}\left[Q\left(t - \frac{r}{c}\right) + \frac{r}{c}\dot{Q}\left(t - \frac{r}{c}\right)\right] \tag{1.20}$$

If the volume velocity of the source varies according to $Q(t) = \hat{Q}\exp(i\omega t)$, eqn (1.19) yields a harmonic spherical wave in complex notation

$$p(r, t) = \frac{i\omega\rho_0}{4\pi r}\hat{Q}\exp[i(\omega t - kr)] \tag{1.21}$$

while the particle velocity as obtained form eqn (1.20) is

$$v_r = \frac{p}{\rho_0 c}\left(1 + \frac{1}{ikr}\right) \tag{1.22}$$

This formula indicates that the ratio of sound pressure and particle velocity in a spherical sound wave depends on the distance r and the frequency $\omega = kc$. Furthermore, it is complex, i.e. between both quantities there is a phase difference. For $kr \gg 1$, i.e. for distances which are large compared with the wavelength, the ratio p/v_r tends asymptotically to $\rho_0 c$, the characteristic impedance of the medium.

A plane wave is an idealised wave type which does not exist in the real world, at least not in its pure form. However, sound waves travelling in a rigid tube can come very close to a plane wave. Furthermore, a limited region of a spherical wave may also be considered as a good approximation to a plane wave provided the distance r from the centre is large compared with all wavelengths involved, i.e. $kr \gg 1$, *see* eqn (1.22).

On the other hand, a point source producing a spherical wave can be approximated by any sound source which is small compared with the wavelength and which expels fluid, for instance by a small pulsating sphere or a loudspeaker mounted into one side of an airtight box. Most sound sources, however, do not behave as point sources. In these cases, the sound pressure depends not only on the distance r but also on the direction, which can be characterised by a polar angle ϑ and an azimuth angle φ. For distances exceeding a characteristic range, which depends on the sort of sound source and the frequency, the sound pressure is given by

$$p(r, \vartheta, \varphi, t) = \frac{A}{r} \Gamma(\vartheta, \varphi) \exp\left[i(\omega t - kr)\right] \tag{1.23}$$

where the 'directivity function' $\Gamma(\vartheta, \varphi)$ is normalised so as to make $\Gamma = 1$ for its absolute maximum. A is a constant.

1.3 Energy density and intensity, radiation

If a sound source, for instance a musical instrument, is to generate a sound wave it has to deliver some energy to a fluid. This energy is carried away by the sound wave. Accordingly we can characterize the amount of energy contained in one unit volume of the wave by the energy density. As with any kind of mechanical energy one has to distinguish between potential and kinetic energy density:

$$w_{pot} = \frac{p^2}{2\rho_0 c^2}, \qquad w_{kin} = \frac{\rho_0 |\mathbf{v}|^2}{2} \tag{1.24}$$

and the total energy density is

$$w = w_{pot} + w_{kin} \tag{1.25}$$

Another important quantity is sound intensity, which is a measure of the energy transported in a sound wave. Imagine a window of 1 m² perpendicular to the direction of sound propagation. Then the intensity is the energy per second passing this window. Generally the intensity is a vector parallel to the vector $\mathbf{v}$ of the particle velocity and is given by

$$\mathbf{I} = p\mathbf{v} \tag{1.26}$$

The general principle of energy conservation requires

$$\frac{\partial w}{\partial t} + \operatorname{div} \mathbf{I} = 0 \tag{1.27}$$

It should be noted that – in contrast to the sound pressure and particle velocity – these energetic quantities do not simply add if two waves are superimposed on each other.

In a plane wave the sound pressure and the longitudinal component of the particle velocity are related by $p = \rho_0 c v$, and the same holds for a spherical wave at a large distance from the centre ($kr \gg 1$, *see* eqn (1.22)). Hence we can express the particle velocity in terms of the sound pressure and the energy density and the intensity are

$$w = \frac{p^2}{\rho_0 c^2} \quad \text{and} \quad I = \frac{p^2}{\rho_0 c} \tag{1.28}$$

They are related by

$$I = cw \tag{1.29}$$

Stationary signals which are not limited in time may be characterised by time averages over a sufficiently long time. We introduce the root-mean-square of the sound pressure by

$$p_{rms} = \left(\frac{1}{t_a} \int_0^{t_a} p^2 \, dt \right)^{1/2} = \left(\overline{p^2} \right)^{1/2} \tag{1.30}$$

where the overbar is a shorthand notation indicating time averaging. The eqns (1.28) yield

$$\overline{w} = \frac{p^2_{rms}}{\rho_0 c^2} \quad \text{and} \quad \overline{I} = \frac{p^2_{rms}}{\rho_0 c} \tag{1.28a}$$

Finally, for a harmonic sound wave with the sound pressure amplitude $\hat{p}$, p_{rms} equals $\hat{p}/\sqrt{2}$, which leads to

$$\overline{w} = \frac{\hat{p}^2}{2\rho_0 c^2} \quad \text{and} \quad \overline{I} = \frac{\hat{p}^2}{2\rho_0 c} \tag{1.28b}$$

The last equation can be used to express the total power output of a point source $P = 4\pi r^2 I(r)$ by its volume velocity. According to eqn (1.21), the sound pressure amplitude in a spherical wave is $\rho_0 \omega \hat{Q}/4\pi r$ and therefore

$$P = \frac{\rho_0}{8\pi c} \hat{Q}^2 \omega^2 \tag{1.31}$$

If, on the other hand, the power output of a point source is given, the root-mean-square of the sound pressure at distance r from the source is

$$p_{rms} = \frac{1}{r} \sqrt{\left(\frac{\rho_0 c P}{4\pi} \right)} \tag{1.32}$$

1.4 Signals and systems

Any acoustical signal can be unambiguously described by its time function $s(t)$ where s denotes a sound pressure, a component of particle velocity, or the instantaneous density of air, for instance. If this function is a sine or cosine function – or an exponential with imaginary exponent – we speak of a harmonic signal, which is closely related to the harmonic waves as introduced in Section 1.2. Harmonic signals and waves play a key role in acoustics although real sound signals are almost never harmonic but show a much more complicated time dependence. The reason for this apparent contradiction is the fact that virtually all signals can be considered as superposition of harmonic signals. This is the fundamental statement of the famous Fourier theorem.

The Fourier theorem can be formulated as follows: let $s(t)$ be a real, non-periodic time function describing, for example, the time dependence of the sound pressure or the volume velocity, this function being sufficiently steady (a requirement which is fulfilled in all practical cases), and the integral $\int_{-\infty}^{+\infty} [s(t)]^2 \, dt$ have a finite value. Then

$$s(t) = \int_{-\infty}^{+\infty} S(f) \exp(2\pi i f t) \, df \qquad (1.33a)$$

with

$$S(f) = \int_{-\infty}^{+\infty} s(t) \exp(-2\pi i f t) \, dt \qquad (1.33b)$$

Because of the symmetry of these formulae $S(f)$ is not only the Fourier transform of $s(t)$ but $s(t)$ is the (inverse) Fourier transform of $S(f)$ as well. The complex function $S(f)$ is called the 'spectral function' or the 'complex amplitude spectrum', or simply the 'spectrum' of the signal $s(t)$. It can easily be shown that $S(-f) = S^*(f)$, where the asterisk denotes the transition to the complex conjugate function. $S(f)$ and $s(t)$ are completely equivalent representations of the same signal.

According to eqn (1.33a), the signal $s(t)$ is composed of harmonic time functions with continuously varying frequencies f. The absolute value of the spectral function, which can be written as

$$S(f) = |S(f)| \exp[i\psi(f)] \qquad (1.34)$$

is the amplitude of the harmonic vibration with frequency f; the argument $\psi(f)$ is the phase angle of this particular vibration. The functions $|S(f)|$ and $\psi(f)$ are called the amplitude and the phase spectrum of the signal $s(t)$. An example of a time function and its amplitude spectrum is shown in Fig. 1.7.

The Fourier theorem assumes a slightly different form if $s(t)$ is a periodic function with period T, i.e. if $s(t) = s(t + T)$. Then the integral in eqn (1.33a) has to be replaced by a series:

$$s(t) = \sum_{n=-\infty}^{+\infty} S_n \exp\left(\frac{2\pi i n t}{T}\right) \tag{1.35a}$$

with

$$S_n = \frac{1}{T}\int_0^T s(t) \exp\left(\frac{-2\pi i n t}{T}\right) dt \tag{1.35b}$$

If the signal is not continous but consists of a sequence of N discrete, periodically repeated numbers

$$\ldots, s_0, s_1, s_2, \ldots, s_{N-2}, s_{N-1}, s_0, s_1, \ldots$$

the Fourier coefficients are given by

$$S_m = \sum_{n=0}^{N-1} s_n \exp\left(-2\pi i\frac{nm}{N}\right) \tag{1.35c}$$

The sequence of these coefficients, which is also periodic with the period N, is called the Discrete Fourier Transform (DTF) of s_n.

The steady spectral function has changed now into discrete 'Fourier coefficients', for which $S_{-n} = S_n^*$ as before. Hence a periodic signal consists of discrete harmonic vibrations, the frequencies of which are multiples of a fundamental frequency $1/T$. These components are called 'partial vibrations' or 'harmonics', the first harmonic being identical with the fundamental vibration.

Of course all the formulae above can be written with the angular frequency $\omega = 2\pi f$ instead of the frequency f. Furthermore, a real notation is possible. It can be obtained simply by separating the real parts from the imaginary parts of eqns (1.33) and (1.35) respectively.

Equations (1.33) cannot be applied in this form to stationary non-periodic signals, i.e. to signals which are not limited in time and the average properties of which are not time dependent. In this case the integrals would not converge. Therefore, firstly a 'window' of width T_0 is cut out of the signal. For this section the spectral function $S_{T_0}(f)$ is well defined and can be evaluated numerically or experimentally. The 'power spectrum' of the whole signal is then given by

$$W(f) = \lim_{T_0 \to \infty}\left[\frac{1}{T_0} S_{T_0}(f) S_{T_0}^*(f)\right] \tag{1.36}$$

The determination of the complex spectrum $S(f)$ or of the power spectrum $W(f)$, known as 'spectral analysis' is of great theoretical and practical importance. Nowadays it is most conveniently achieved by using digital computers. A particularly efficient procedure for computing spectral functions is the 'fast Fourier transform' (FFT) algorithm. Since the description of this method is beyond the scope of this book, the reader is referred to the extensive literature on this subject (see, for instance, Ref. 1). A rough, experimental spectral analysis can also be carried out by applying the signal to a set of bandpass filters.

The power spectrum, which is an even function of the frequency, does not contain all the information on the original signal $s(t)$, because it is based on the absolute value of the spectral function only, whereas its phase has been eliminated. Inserted into eqn (1.33a), it does not restore the original function $s(t)$ but instead yields another important time function, called the 'autocorrelation function' of $s(t)$:

$$\phi_{ss}(\tau) = \int_{-\infty}^{+\infty} W(f) \exp{(2\pi i f \tau)}\, df = 2\int_{0}^{+\infty} W(f) \cos{(2\pi f \tau)}\, df \qquad (1.37)$$

The time variable has been denoted by τ in order to indicate that it is not identical with the real time. In the usual definition of the autocorrelation function it occurs as a delay time:

$$\phi_{ss}(\tau) = \lim_{T_0 \to \infty} \frac{1}{T_0} \int_{-T_0/2}^{+T_0/2} s(t)s(t + \tau)\, dt \qquad (1.38)$$

The autocorrelation function indicates the extent to which a signal is preserved over the time τ.

Since ϕ_{ss} is the Fourier transform of the power spectrum, the latter is also obtained by Fourier transformation of the autocorrelation function:

$$W(f) = 2\int_{0}^{+\infty} \phi_{ss}(\tau) \cos{(2\pi f \tau)}\, d\tau \qquad (1.39)$$

Equations (1.37) and (1.39) are the mathematical expressions of the theorem of Wiener and Khinchine: power spectrum and autocorrelation function are Fourier transforms of each other.

If $s(t + \tau)$ in eqn (1.38) is replaced with $s'(t + \tau)$, where s' denotes a time function different from s, one obtains the 'cross-correlation function' of the two signals $s(t)$ and $s'(t)$:

$$\phi_{ss'}(\tau) = \lim_{T_0 \to \infty} \frac{1}{T_0} \int_{-T_0/2}^{+T_0/2} s(t)s'(t + \tau)\, dt \qquad (1.40)$$

The cross-correlation function is a measure of the statistical similarity of two function s and s'.

In a certain sense a sine or cosine signal can be considered as an elementary signal; it is unlimited in time and steady in all its derivatives, and its spectrum consists of a single line. The counterpart of it is Dirac's delta function $\delta(t)$: it has one single line in the time domain, so to speak, whereas its amplitude spectrum is constant for all frequencies, i.e. $S(f) = 1$ for the delta function. This leads to the following representation:

$$\delta(t) = \lim_{f_0 \to \infty} \int_{-f_0}^{+f_0} \exp(2\pi i f t)\,df \tag{1.41}$$

It can easily be shown that the delta function has the following fundamental property:

$$s(t) = \int_{-\infty}^{+\infty} s(\tau)\delta(t - \tau)\,d\tau \tag{1.42}$$

where $s(t)$ is any function of time. Accordingly, any signal can be considered as a close succession of very short pulses as indicated in Fig. 1.3. Especially, for $s(t) \equiv 1$ we obtain

$$\int_{-\infty}^{+\infty} \delta(t)\,dt = 1 \tag{1.43}$$

The delta function $\delta(t)$ is zero for all $t \neq 0$; the relation (1.43) indicates that its value at $t = 0$ must be infinite.

Now we consider a linear but otherwise unspecified transmission system. Examples of acoustical transmission systems are all kinds of ducts (air ducts, mufflers, wind instruments, etc.) and resonators. Likewise, any two

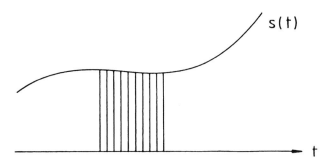

Figure 1.3 Continuous function as the limiting case of a close succession of short impulses.

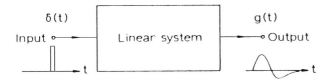

Figure 1.4 Impulse response of a linear system.

points in an enclosure may be considered as the input and output terminal of an acoustic transmission system. Linearity means that multiplying the input signal with a factor results in an output signal which is augmented by the same factor. The properties of such a system are completely character-ised by the so-called 'impulse response' $g(t)$, i.e. the output signal which is the response to an impulsive input signal represented by the Dirac func-tion $\delta(t)$ (*see* Fig. 1.4). Since the response cannot precede the excitation, the impulse response of any causal system must vanish for $t < 0$. If $g(t)$ is known the output signal $s'(t)$ with respect to any input signal $s(t)$ can be obtained by replacing the Dirac function in eqn (1.42) with its reponse, i.e. with $g(t)$:

$$s'(t) = \int_{-\infty}^{+\infty} s(\tau)g(t-\tau)\,\mathrm{d}\tau = \int_{-\infty}^{+\infty} g(\tau)s(t-\tau)\,\mathrm{d}\tau \tag{1.44}$$

This operation is known as the convolution of two functions s and g. A common shorthand notation of it is

$$s'(t) = s(t) * g(t) = g(t) * s(t) \tag{1.44a}$$

Equation (1.44) has its analogue in the frequency domain, which looks even simpler: let $S(f)$ be the complex spectrum of the input signal $s(t)$ of our linear system, then the spectrum of the resulting output signal $s'(t)$ is

$$S'(f) = G(f)S(f) \tag{1.45}$$

The complex function $G(f)$ is the 'transmission function' or 'transfer func-tion' of the system; it is related to the impulse response by the Fourier transformation:

$$G(f) = \int_{-\infty}^{+\infty} g(t)\exp(-2\pi \mathrm{i}ft)\,\mathrm{d}t \tag{1.46a}$$

$$g(t) = \int_{-\infty}^{+\infty} G(f)\exp(2\pi \mathrm{i}ft)\,\mathrm{d}f \tag{1.46b}$$

with $G(-f) = G^*(f)$ since $g(t)$ is a real function. The transfer function $G(f)$ has also a direct meaning: if a harmonic signal with frequency f is applied to a transmission system as shown in Fig. 1.4 its amplitude will be changed by the factor $|G(f)|$ and its phase will be shifted by the phase angle of $G(f)$.

1.5 Sound pressure level and sound power level

In the frequency range in which our hearing is most sensitive (1000–3000 Hz) the threshold of sensation and the threshold of pain in hearing are separated by about 13 orders of magnitude in intensity. For this reason it would be impractical to characterise the strength of a sound signal by its sound pressure or its intensity. Instead, the so-called 'sound pressure level' is generally used for this purpose, defined by

$$SPL = 20 \log_{10}\left(\frac{p_{\mathrm{rms}}}{p_0}\right) \text{ decibels} \tag{1.47}$$

In this definition, p_{rms} denotes the 'root mean square' pressure as introduced in Section 1.3. p_0 is an internationally standardised reference pressure and its value is 2×10^{-5} N/m^2, which corresponds roughly to the normal hearing threshold at 1000 Hz. The 'decibel' (abbreviated dB) is not a unit in a physical sense but is used rather to recall the above level definition. Strictly speaking, p_{rms} as well as the SPL are defined only for stationary sound signals since they both imply an averaging process.

According to eqn (1.47), two different sound fields or signals may be compared by their level difference:

$$\Delta SPL = 20 \log \frac{(p_{\mathrm{rms}})_1}{(p_{\mathrm{rms}})_2} \text{ decibels} \tag{1.47a}$$

It is often convenient to express the sound power delivered by a sound source in terms of the 'sound power level', defined by

$$PL = 10 \log\left(\frac{P}{P_0}\right) \text{ decibels} \tag{1.48}$$

where P_0 denotes a reference power of 10^{-12} W. Using this quantity, the sound pressure level produced by a point source with power P can be expressed as follows:

$$SPL = PL - 20 \log\left(\frac{r}{r_0}\right) - 11 \text{ dB} \quad \text{with } r_0 = 1 \text{ m} \tag{1.49}$$

1.6 Some properties of human hearing

Since the ultimate consumer of all room acoustics is the listener, it is important to consider at least a few facts relating to aural perception. More
information may be found in Ref. 2, for instance. One of the most obvious
facts of human hearing is that the ear is not equally sensitive to sounds of
different frequencies. Generally, the loudness at which a sound is perceived
depends, of course, on its objective strength, i.e. on its sound pressure level.
Furthermore, it depends in a complicated manner on the spectral composition of the sound signal, on its duration and on several other factors. The
loudness is often characterised by the 'loudness level', which is the sound
pressure level of a 1000 Hz tone which appears equally loud as the sound
to be characterised. The unit of the loudness level is the 'phon'.

Figure 1.5 presents the contours of equal loudness level for sinusoidal
sound signals which are presented to a listener in the form of frontally
incident plane waves. The numbers next to the curves indicate the loudness
level. The lowest, dashed curve which corresponds to a loudness level of
3 phons marks the threshold of hearing. According to this diagram, a
pure tone with a SPL of 40 decibels has by definition a loudness level of
40 phons if its frequency is 1000 Hz, its loudness level is only 24 phons at
100 Hz whereas at 50 Hz it would be almost inaudible.

Using these curves, the loudness level of any pure tone can be evaluated
from its frequency and its sound pressure or intensity level. In order to
simplify this somewhat tedious procedure, meters have been constructed
which measure the sound pressure level. The contours of equal loudness are

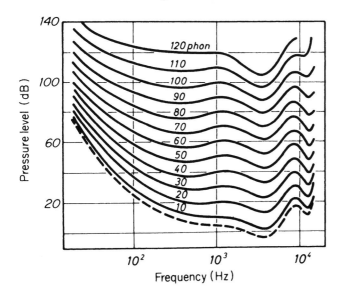

Figure 1.5 Contours of equal loudness level for frontal sound incidence.
The dashed curve corresponds to the average hearing threshold.

taken into account by electrical networks, the frequency-dependent attenuation of which approximates to the shape of these curves. Several attenuation functions are in use and have been standardised internationally; the most common of them is the A-weighting curve. Consequently, the result of such a measurement is not the loudness level in phons, but the 'A-weighted sound pressure level' in dB(A).

Whenever such an instrument is applied to a sound signal with more complex spectral structure, the result of measurement may deviate considerably from the true loudness level. The reason for such errors is the fact that, in our hearing, weak spectral components are partially or completely masked by stronger ones and that this effect is not modelled in the above-mentioned sound level meters. More reliable procedures for the measurement of loudness level which include some spectral analysis of the sound signal are avaliable nowadays, but they have not found widespread application so far.

The loudness level as defined above has a fundamental defect, namely that doubling the subjective sensation of loudness does not correspond to twice the loudness level as should be expected. Instead it corresponds only to an increase of about 10 phons. This fault is avoided by the loudness scale with the 'sone' as a unit. The sone scale is defined in such a way that 40 phons correspond to 1 sone and that every increase of the loudness level by 10 phons corresponds to doubling the number of sones. Nowadays instruments as well as computer programs are available which are able to measure or to calculate the loudness of almost any type of sound signal, taking into account the above-mentioned masking effect.

Another important property of our hearing is its ability to detect the direction from which a sound wave is arriving, and thus to localise the direction of sound sources. For sound incidence from a lateral direction it is easy to understand how this effect is brought about: an originally plane or spherical wave is distorted by the human head, by the pinnae and – to a minor extent – by the shoulders and the trunk. This distortion depends on sound frequency and the direction of incidence. As a consequence, the sound signals at both ears show characteristic differences in their amplitude and phase spectrum or, to put it more simply, at lateral sound incidence one ear is within the shadow of the head but the other is not. The interaural amplitude and phase differences caused by these effects enable our hearing to reconstruct the direction of sound incidence.

Quantitatively, the changes a sound signal undergoes on its way to the entrance of the ears can be described by the so-called 'head transfer functions' which characterise the transmission from a very remote point source to the ear canal, for instance its entrance. Such transfer functions have been measured by many researchers.[3] As an example, Fig. 1.6 shows head transfer functions for eleven lateral angles of incidence directions φ relative to that obtained at frontal sound incidence ($\varphi = 0°$); one diagram shows the magnitude expressed in decibels, and the other one the group delays,

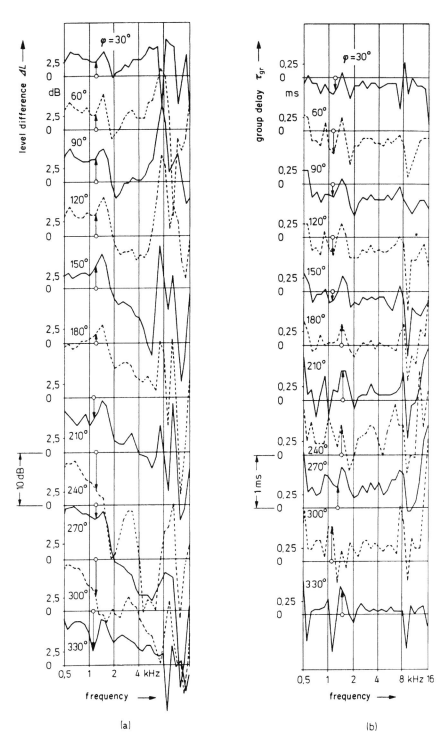

Figure 1.6 Head transfer functions for several directions of sound incidence in the horizontal plane, relative to that for frontal incidence, average over 25 subjects: (a) amplitude (in logarithmic representation); (b) group delay (after Blauert[3]).

i.e. the functions $d\psi(\omega)/d\omega$. By comparing the curves of $\varphi = 90°$ and $\varphi = 270°$, the shadowing effect of the head becomes obvious.

However, if the sound source is situated within the vertical symmetry plane, this explanation fails since then the source produces equal sound signals at both ear canals. But even then the ear transfer functions show characteristic differences for various elevation angles of the source, and it is commonly believed that the way in which they modify a sound signal enables us to distinguish whether a sound source is behind, above or in front of our head.

These considerations are valid only for the localisation of sound sources in a free sound field. In a closed room, however, the sound field is made up of many sound waves propagating in different directions, accordingly matters are more complicated. We shall discuss the subjective effects of more complex sound fields as they are encountered in room acoustics in Chapter 7.

1.7 Sound sources

In room acoustics we are concerned with three types of sound source: the human voice, musical instruments, and technical noise sources. (We do not consider loudspeakers here because they reproduce the sounds from other sources.)

It is a common feature of all these sources that the sounds they produce have a more or less complicated spectral structure – apart from some rare exceptions. In fact, it is the spectral content of speech signals (phonemes) which gives them their characteristics. Similarly, the timbre of musical sounds is determined by their spectra.

The signals emitted by most musical instruments, in particular by string and wind instruments including the organ, are nearly periodic. Therefore, their spectra consist mainly of many equally spaced lines (*see* Section 1.4), and it is the frequency of the lowest component, the fundamental, which determines what we perceive as the pitch of a tone. It is evident that our ear receives many harmonic components of quite different frequencies even if we listen to a single tone. Likewise, many speech sounds, in particular vowels and voiced consonants, have a line structure. As an example, Fig. 1.7 presents the time function and the amplitude spectrum of three vowels.[4] There are some characteristic frequency ranges in which the overtones are especially strong. These are called the 'formants' of the vowel.

For normal speech the fundamental frequency lies between 50 and 350 Hz and is identical to the frequency at which the vocal chords vibrate. The total frequency range of conversational speech may be seen from Fig. 1.8 which plots the long-time power spectrum of continuous speech, both for male and female speakers.[5] The high-frequency energy is mainly due to the consonants, for instance to fricatives such as | s | or | f |, or for plosives such as | p | or | t |. Since consonants are of particular importance for the intelligibility of speech, a room or hall intended for speech, as well as a public

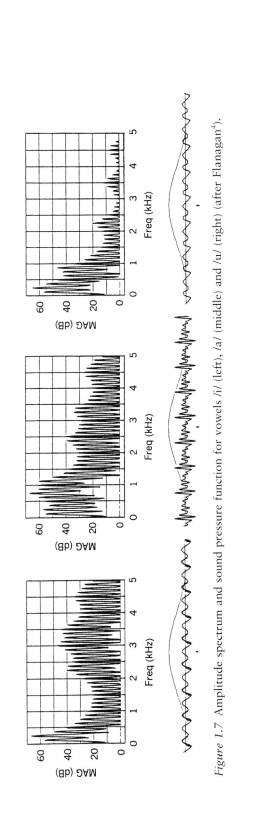

Figure 1.7 Amplitude spectrum and sound pressure function for vowels /i/ (left), /a/ (middle) and /u/ (right) (after Flanagan[4]).

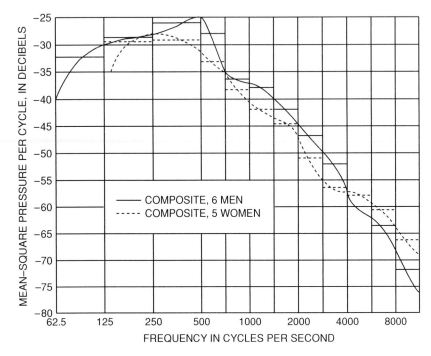

Figure 1.8 Long-time power density spectrum for continuous speech 30 cm from the mouth (after Flanagan[5]).

address system, should transmit the high frequencies with great fidelity. The transmission of the fundamental vibration, on the other hand, is less important since our hearing is able to reconstruct it if the periodic sound signal is rich in higher harmonics.

Among musical instruments, large pipe organs have the widest frequency range, reaching from 16 Hz to about 9 kHz. (There are some instruments, especially percussion instruments, which produce sounds with even higher frequencies.) The piano follows, having a frequency range which is smaller by about three octaves, i.e. by nearly a decade. The frequencies of the remaining instruments lie somewhere within this range. This is true, however, only for the fundamental frequencies. Since almost all instruments produce higher harmonics, the actual range of frequencies occurring in music extends still further, up to about 15 kHz. In music, unlike speech, all frequencies are of almost equal importance, so it is not permissible deliberately to suppress or to neglect certain frequency ranges. On the other hand, the entire frequency range is not the responsibility of the acoustical engineer. At 10 kHz and above the attenuation in air is so large that the influence of a room on the propagation of high-frequency sound components can safely be neglected. At frequencies lower than 50 Hz geometrical considerations are almost useless because of the large wavelengths of the sounds; furthermore, at these frequencies it is almost impossible to assess correctly the sound absorption by vibrating panels or walls which influences the reverberation, especially at low frequencies. This means that, in this frequency range too, room acoustical design possibilities are very limited. On the whole, it can be stated that the frequency range relevant to room acoustics reaches from 50 to 10 000 Hz, the most important part being between 100 and 5000 Hz.

The acoustical power output of the sound sources as considered here is relatively low by everyday standards. The human voice generates a sound power ranging from 0.001 µW (whispering) to 1000 µW (shouting), the power produced in conversational speech is of the order of 10 µW, corresponding to a sound power level of 70 dB. The power of a single musical instrument may lie in the range from 10 µW to 100 mW. A full symphony orchestra can easily generate a sound power of 10 W in fortissimo passages. It may be added that the dynamic range of most musical instruments is about 30 dB (woodwinds) to 50 dB (string instruments). A large orchestra can cover a dynamic range of 100 dB.

An important property of the human voice and musical instruments is their directionality, i.e. the fact that they do not emit sound with equal intensity in all directions. In speech this is because of the 'sound shadow' cast by the head. The lower the sound frequency, the less pronounced is the reduction of sound intensity by the head, because with decreasing frequencies the sound waves are increasingly diffracted around the head. In Figs 1.9a and 1.9b the distribution of the relative pressure level for different frequency bands is plotted on a horizontal plane and a vertical plane respectively. These curves are obtained by filtering out the respective frequency bands from natural speech; the direction denoted by 0° is the frontal direction.

Musical instruments usually exhibit a pronounced directionality because of the linear dimensions of their sound-radiating surfaces, which, in the interest of high efficiency, are often large compared with the wavelengths. Unfortunately general statements are almost impossible, since the directional distribution of the radiated sound changes very rapidly, not only from one frequency to the other; it can be quite different for instruments of the same sort but different manufacture. This is true especially for string instruments, the bodies of which exhibit very complicated vibration patterns, particularly at higher frequencies. The radiation from a violin takes place in a fairly uniform way at frequencies lower than about 450 Hz; at higher frequencies, however, matters become quite involved. For wind instruments the directional distributions exhibit more common features, since here the sound is not radiated from a curved anisotropic plate with complicated vibration patterns but from a fixed opening which is very often the end of a horn. The 'directional characteristics of an orchestra' are highly involved, but space is too limited here to discuss this in detail. For the room acoustician, however, it is important to know that strong components, particularly from the strings but likewise from the piano, the woodwinds and, of course, from the tuba, are radiated upwards. For further details we refer to the exhaustive account of J. Meyer.[6]

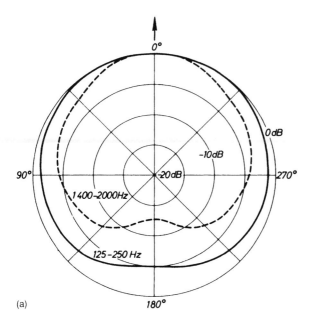

(a)

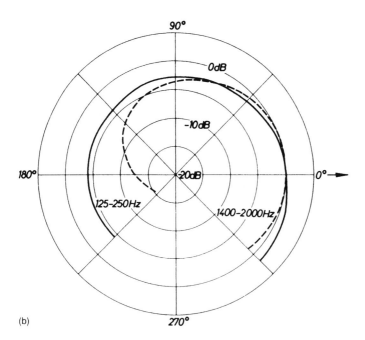

(b)

Figure 1.9 Directional distribution of speech sounds for two different frequency bands. The arrow points in the viewing direction. (a) in a horizontal plane; (b) in a vertical plane.

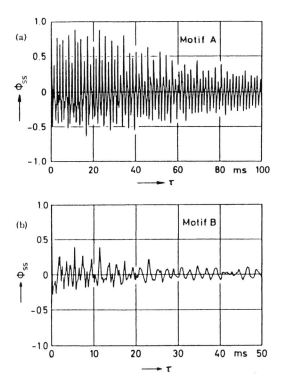

Figure 1.10 Examples of measured autocorrelation functions: (a) music motif A; (b) music motif B (both from Table 1.1) (after Ando[8]).

In a certain sense, the sounds from natural sources can be considered as statistical or stochastic signals, and in this context their autocorrelation function is of interest as it gives some measure of a signal's 'tendency of conservation'. Autocorrelation measurements on speech and music have been performed by several authors.[7,8] Here we are reporting results obtained by Ando, who passed various signals through an A-weighting filter and formed their autocorrelation function according to eqn (1.38) with the finite integration time $T_0 = 35$ s. Two of his results are depicted in Fig. 1.10. The effective duration of the autocorrelation function is defined by the delay τ_e, at which its envelope is just one-tenth of its maximum. These values are indicated in Table 1.1 for a few signals. They range from about 10 to more than 100 ms.

The variety of possible noise sources is too large to discuss them in any detail. A common kind of noise in a room is sound intruding from adjacent rooms or from outside through walls, doors and widows, due to insufficient sound insulation. A typical noise source in halls is the ventilation or air conditioning system; some of the noise produced by the machinery propagates in the air ducts and is radiated into the hall through the air outlets.

Table 1.1 Duration of autocorrelation functions of various sound signals (after Ando[8])

Motif	Name of piece	Composer	Duration τ_e (ms)
A	Royal Pavane	Gibbons	127
B	Sinfonietta opus 48, 4th movement (Allegro con brio)	Arnold	43
C	Symphony No. 102 in B flat major, 2nd movement (Adagio)	Haydn	65
D	Siegfried Idyll; bar 322	Wagner	40
E	Symphony KV551 in C major (Jupiter), 4th movement (Molto allegro)	Mozart	38
F	Poem read by a female	Kunikita	10

References

1 Bracewell, R.N., *The Fourier Transform and its Applications*, McGraw-Hill, Singapore, 1986.
2 Zwicker, E. and Fastl, H., *Psychoacoustics – Facts and Models*, Springer-Verlag, Berlin, 1990.
3 Blauert, J., *Spatial Hearing*, MIT Press, Cambridge, Mass., 1997.
4 Flanagan, J.J., Speech communication, in *Encyclopedia of Acoustics*, ed. M.J. Crocker, John Wiley, New York, 1997.
5 Flanagan, J.J., *Speech Analysis Synthesis and Perception*, Springer-Verlag, Berlin, 1965.
6 Meyer, J., *Acoustics and the Performance of Music*, Verlag Das Musikinstrument, Frankfurt am Main, 1978.
7 Furdujev, V., Proceedings of the Fifth International Congress on Acoustics, Liege, 1965, p. 41.
8 Ando, Y., *J. Acoust. Soc. America*, **62** (1977) 1436. Proceedings of the Vancouver Symposium, Acoustics and Theatres for the Performing Arts, The Canadian Acoustical Association, Ottawa, Canada, 1986, p. 112.

2 Reflection and scattering

Up to now we have dealt with sound propagation in a medium which was unbounded in every direction. In contrast to this simple situation, room acoustics is concerned with sound propagation in enclosures where the sound conducting medium is bounded on all sides by walls, ceiling and floor. These room boundaries usually reflect a certain fraction of the sound energy impinging on them. Another fraction of the energy is 'absorbed', i.e. it is extracted from the sound field inside the room, either by conversion into heat or by being transmitted to the outside by the walls. It is just this combination of the numerous reflected components which is responsible for what is known as 'the acoustics of a room' and also for the complexity of the sound field in a room.

Before we discuss the properties of such involved sound fields we shall consider in this chapter the process which is fundamental for their occurrence: the reflection of a plane sound wave by a single wall or surface. In this context we shall encounter the concepts of wall impedance and absorption coefficient, which are of special importance in room acoustics. The sound absorption by a wall will be dealt with mainly from a formal point of view, whereas the discussion of the physical causes of sound absorption and of the functional principles of various absorbent arrangements will be postponed to a subsequent chapter.

Strictly speaking, the simple laws of sound reflection to be explained in this chapter hold only for unbounded walls. Any free edge of a reflecting wall or panel will scatter some sound energy in all directions. The same happens when a sound wave hits any other obstacle of limited extent, such as a pillar, a listener's head or a wall irregularity which is not very small compared with the sound wavelength. Since scattering is a common phenomenon in room acoustics we shall briefly deal with it in this chapter.

Throughout this chapter we shall assume that the incident, undisturbed wave is a plane wave. In reality, however, all waves originate from a sound source and are therefore spherical waves or superpositions of spherical waves. The reflection of a spherical wave from a plane wall is highly complicated unless we can assume that the wall is rigid. More on this matter may be found in the literature (*see*, for instance, Ref. 1). For our discussion it may be sufficient to assume that the sound source is not too close to the reflecting wall or to the scattering obstacle so that the curvature of the wave fronts can be neglected without too much error.

2.1 Reflection factor, absorption coefficient and wall impedance

If a plane wave strikes a plane and uniform wall of infinite extent, in general a part of the sound energy will be reflected from it in the form of a reflected wave originating from the wall, the amplitude and the phase of which differ from those of the incident wave. Both waves interfere with each other and form a 'standing wave', at least partially.

The changes in amplitude and phase which take place during the reflection of a wave are expressed by the complex reflection factor

$$R = |R| \exp(i\chi)$$

which is a property of the wall. Its absolute value as well as its phase angle depend on the frequency and on the direction of the incident wave.

According to eqn (1.28), the intensity of a plane wave is proportional to the square of the pressure amplitude. Therefore, the intensity of the reflected wave is smaller by a factor $|R|^2$ than that of the incident wave and the fraction $1 - |R|^2$ of the incident energy is lost during reflection. This quantity is called the 'absorption coefficient' of the wall:

$$\alpha = 1 - |R|^2 \tag{2.1}$$

For a wall with zero reflectivity ($R = 0$) the absorption coefficient has its maximum value 1. The wall is said to be totally absorbent or sometimes 'matched to the sound field'. If $R = 1$ (in-phase reflection, $\chi = 0$), the wall is 'rigid' or 'hard'; in the case of $R = -1$ (phase reversal, $\chi = \pi$), we speak of a 'soft' wall. In both cases there is no sound absorption ($\alpha = 0$). The latter case, however, very rarely occurs in room acoustics and only in limited frequency ranges.

The acoustical properties of a wall surface – as far as they are of interest in room acoustics – are completely described by the reflection factor for all angles of incidence and for all frequencies. Another quantity which is even more closely related to the physical behaviour of the wall and to its construction is based on the particle velocity normal to the wall which is generated by a given sound pressure at the surface. It is called the wall impedance and is defined by

$$Z = \left(\frac{p}{v_n}\right)_{surface} \tag{2.2}$$

where v_n denotes the velocity component normal to the wall. For non-porous walls which are excited into vibration by the sound field, the normal component of the particle velocity is identical to the velocity of the wall vibration. Like the reflection factor, the wall impedance is generally complex and a function of the angle of sound incidence.

Frequently the wall impedance is divided by the characteristic impedance of the air. The resulting quantity is called the 'specific acoustic impedance':

$$\zeta = \frac{Z}{\rho_0 c} \tag{2.2a}$$

The reciprocal of the wall impedance is the 'wall admittance'; the reciprocal of ζ is called the 'specific acoustic admittance' of the wall.

As explained in Section 1.2 any complex quantity can be represented in a rectangular coordinate system (*see* Fig. 1.2). This holds also for the wall impedance. In this case, the length of this arrow corresponds to the magnitude of Z while its inclination angle is the phase angle of the wall impedance:

$$\mu = \arg(Z) = \arctan\left(\frac{\operatorname{Im} Z}{\operatorname{Re} Z}\right) \tag{2.3}$$

If the frequency changes, the impedance will usually change as well and also the length and inclination of the arrow representing it. The curve described by the tips of all arrows is called the 'locus of the impedance in the complex plane'. A simple example of such a curve is shown in Fig. 2.8a.

2.2 Sound reflection at normal incidence

First we assume the wall to be normal to the direction in which the incident wave is travelling, which is chosen as the x-axis of a rectangular coordinate system. The wall intersects the x-axis at $x = 0$ (Fig. 2.1). The wave is coming from the negative x-direction and its sound pressure is

$$p_i(x, t) = \hat{p}_0 \exp\left[i(\omega t - kx)\right] \tag{2.4a}$$

The particle velocity in the incident wave is according to eqn (1.9):

$$v_i(x, t) = \frac{\hat{p}_0}{\rho_0 c} \exp\left[i(\omega t - kx)\right] \tag{2.4b}$$

The reflected wave has a smaller amplitude and has undergone a phase change; both changes are described by the reflection factor R. Furthermore, we must reverse the sign of k because of the reversed direction of travel. The sign of the particle velocity is also changed since $\partial p/\partial x$ has opposite signs for positive and negative travelling waves. So we obtain for the reflected wave:

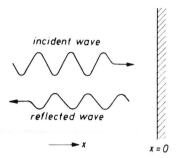

incident wave

reflected wave

x

$x = 0$

Figure 2.1 Reflection of a normally incident sound wave from a plane wall.

$$p_r(x, t) = R\hat{p}_0 \exp [i(\omega t + kx)] \tag{2.5a}$$

$$v_r(x, t) = -R \frac{\hat{p}_0}{\rho_0 c} \exp [i(\omega t + kx)] \tag{2.5b}$$

The total sound pressure and particle velocity in the plane of the wall are obtained simply by adding the above expressions and by setting $x = 0$:

$$p(0, t) = \hat{p}_0(1 + R) \exp (i\omega t)$$

and

$$v(0, t) = \frac{\hat{p}_0}{\rho_0 c}(1 - R) \exp (i\omega t)$$

Since the only component of particle velocity is normal to the wall, dividing $p(0, t)$ by $v(0, t)$ gives the wall impedance:

$$Z = \rho_0 c \frac{1 + R}{1 - R} \tag{2.6}$$

and from this

$$R = \frac{Z - \rho_0 c}{Z + \rho_0 c} = \frac{\zeta - 1}{\zeta + 1} \tag{2.7}$$

A rigid wall ($R = 1$) has impedance $Z = \infty$; for a soft wall ($R = -1$) the impedance will vanish. For a completely absorbent wall the impedance equals the characteristic impedance of the medium.

Inserting eqn (2.7) into the definition (2.1) gives for the absorption coefficient:

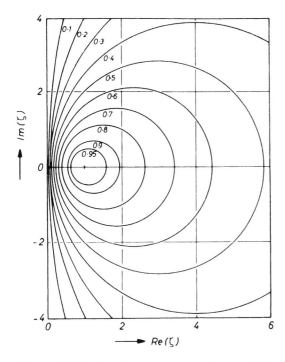

Figure 2.2 Circles of constant absorption coefficient in the complex wall impedance plane. The numbers denote the magnitude of the absorption coefficient.

$$\alpha = \frac{4 \operatorname{Re} (\zeta)}{|\zeta|^2 + 2 \operatorname{Re} (\zeta) + 1} \tag{2.8}$$

In Fig. 2.2 this relation is represented graphically. The diagram shows the circles of constant absorption coefficient in the complex ζ-plane, i.e. abscissa and ordinate in this figure are the real and imaginary part of the specific wall impedance, respectively. As α increases the circles contract towards the point $\zeta = 1$, which corresponds to complete matching of the wall to the medium.

The distribution of sound pressure in the standing wave in front of the wall is found by adding eqns (2.4a) and (2.5a), and evaluating the absolute value

$$\hat{p}(x) = \hat{p}_0 [1 + | R |^2 + 2| R | \cos (2kx + \chi)]^{1/2} \tag{2.9}$$

Similarly, for the particle velocity we find

$$\hat{v}(x) = \frac{\hat{p}_0}{\rho_0 c} [1 + | R |^2 - 2| R | \cos (2kx + \chi)]^{1/2} \tag{2.10}$$

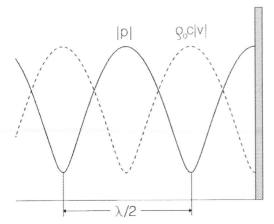

Figure 2.3 Standing sound wave in front of a plane surface with real reflection factor $R = 0.7$. ——— magnitude of sound pressure; - - - - magnitude of particle velocity.

The time dependence of the pressure and the velocity is taken into account simply by multiplying these expressions by $\exp(i\omega t)$. According to eqns (2.9) and (2.10), the pressure amplitude and the velocity amplitude in the standing wave vary periodically between the maximum values

$$p_{max} = \hat{p}_0(1 + |R|) \quad \text{and} \quad v_{max} = \frac{\hat{p}_0}{\rho_0 c}(1 + |R|) \tag{2.11a}$$

and the minimum values

$$p_{min} = \hat{p}_0(1 - |R|) \quad \text{and} \quad v_{min} = \frac{\hat{p}_0}{\rho_0 c}(1 - |R|) \tag{2.11b}$$

but in such a way that each maximum of the pressure amplitude coincides with a minimum of the velocity amplitude and vice versa (*see* Fig. 2.3). The distance of one maximum to the next is $\pi/k = \lambda/2$. So, by measuring the pressure amplitude as a function of x, we can evaluate the wavelength. Furthermore, the absolute value and the phase angle of the reflection factor can also be evaluated. This leads to an important method of measuring the impedance and the absorption coefficient of wall materials (*see* Section 8.6).

2.3 Sound reflection at oblique incidence

In this section we consider the more general case of sound waves whose angles of incidence may be any value Θ. Without loss of generality, we can assume that the wall normal as well as the wave normal of the incident wave lie in the x–y plane of a rectangular coordinate system. The new situation is depicted in Fig. 2.4.

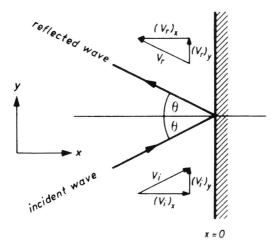

Figure 2.4 Sound reflection at oblique incidence.

Suppose we replace in eqn (2.4a) x by x', the latter belonging to a coordinate system, the axes of which are rotated by an angle Θ with respect to the $x-y$ system. The result is a plane wave propagating in a positive x'-direction. According to the well-known formulae for coordinate transformation, x' and x are related by

$$x' = x \cos \Theta + y \sin \Theta$$

Inserting this into the previously mentioned expression for the incident plane wave we obtain for the latter

$$p_i = \hat{p}_0 \exp \left[-ik(x \cos \Theta + y \sin \Theta) \right] \tag{2.12a}$$

(In this and the following expressions we omit, for the sake of simplicity, the factor $\exp(i\omega t)$, which is common to all pressures and particle velocities.) For the calculation of the wall impedance we require the velocity component normal to the wall, i.e. the x-component. It is obtained from eqn (1.2) which reads in the present case:

$$v_x = -\frac{1}{i\omega\rho_0} \frac{\partial p}{\partial x}$$

Applied to eqn (2.12a) this yields

$$(v_i)_x = \frac{\hat{p}_0}{\rho_0 c} \cos \Theta \exp \left[-ik(x \cos \Theta + y \sin \Theta) \right] \tag{2.12b}$$

When the wave is reflected, as for normal incidence, the sign of x in the exponent is reversed, since the direction is altered with reference to this coordinate. Furthermore, the pressure and the velocity are multiplied by the reflection factor R and $-R$, respectively:

$$p_r = R\hat{p}_0 \exp\left[-ik(-x \cos \Theta + y \sin \Theta)\right] \tag{2.13a}$$

$$(v_r)_x = -\frac{R\hat{p}_0}{\rho_0 c} \cos \Theta \exp\left[-ik(-x \cos \Theta + y \sin \Theta)\right] \tag{2.13b}$$

The direction of propagation again includes an angle Θ with the wall normal, i.e. the reflection law well known in optics is also valid for the reflection of acoustical waves.

By setting $x = 0$ in eqns (2.12a) to (2.13b) and by dividing $p_i + p_r$ by $(v_i)_x + (v_r)_x$ we obtain

$$Z = \frac{\rho_0 c}{\cos \Theta} \frac{1 + R}{1 - R} \tag{2.14a}$$

and from this

$$R = \frac{Z \cos \Theta - \rho_0 c}{Z \cos \Theta + \rho_0 c} = \frac{\zeta \cos \Theta - 1}{\zeta \cos \Theta + 1} \tag{2.14b}$$

The resulting sound pressure amplitude in front of the wall is given by

$$p(x, y) = \hat{p}_0[1 + |R|^2 + 2|R| \cos(2kx \cos \Theta + \chi)]^{1/2} \exp(-iky \sin \Theta) \tag{2.15}$$

This pressure distribution again corresponds to a standing wave, the maxima of which are separated by a distance $\lambda/2 \cos \Theta$ and which moves parallel to the wall with a velocity

$$c_y = \frac{\omega}{k_y} = \frac{\omega}{k \sin \Theta} = \frac{c}{\sin \Theta}$$

Of special interest are surfaces the impedance of which is independent of the direction of incident sound. This applies if the normal component of the particle velocity at the wall surface depends only on the sound pressure in front of a wall element and not on the pressure in front of neighbouring elements. Walls or surfaces with this property are referred to as 'locally reacting'.

In practice, surfaces with local reaction are rather the exception than the rule. They are encountered whenever the wall itself or the space behind it is unable to propagate waves or vibrations in a direction parallel to its surface. Obviously this is not true for a panel whose neighbouring elements

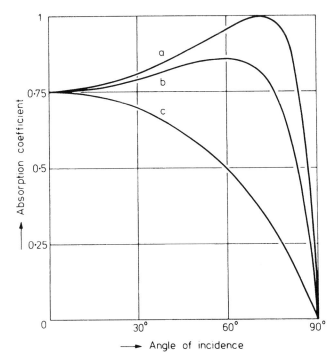

Figure 2.5 Absorption coefficient of walls with specific impedance: (a) $\zeta = 3$; (b) $\zeta = 1.5 + 1.323i$; (c) $\zeta = 1/3$.

are coupled together by bending stiffness. Moreover, this does not apply to a porous layer with an air space between it and a rigid rear wall. In the latter case, however, local reaction of the various surface elements of the arrangement can be brought about by rigid partitions which obstruct the air space in any lateral direction and prevent sound propagation parallel to the surface.

Using eqn (2.14*b*) the absorption coefficient is given by

$$\alpha(\Theta) = \frac{4 \operatorname{Re}(\zeta) \cos \Theta}{(|\zeta| \cos \Theta)^2 + 2 \operatorname{Re}(\zeta) \cos \Theta + 1} \tag{2.16}$$

Its dependence on the angle of incidence is plotted in Fig. 2.5 for various values of ζ.

2.4 A few examples

In this section we consider as examples two types of surface which are of some practical importance as linings to room walls.

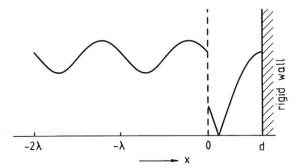

Figure 2.6 Sound reflection from a porous layer with a distance *d* from a rigid wall. The plotted curve is the pressure amplitude for $r = \rho_0 c$ and $d/\lambda = 5/16$.

The first arrangement consists of a thin porous layer of fabric or something similar which is stretched or hung in front of a rigid wall at a distance *d* from it and parallel to it. The *x*-axis is normal to the layer and the wall, the former having the coordinate $x = 0$. Hence, the wall is located at $x = d$ (*see* Fig. 2.6). We assume that the porous layer is so heavy that it does not vibrate under the influence of an incident sound wave. Any pressure difference between the two sides of the layer forces an air stream through the pores with an air velocity v_s. The latter is related to the pressures *p* in front of and *p'* behind the layer by

$$r_s = \frac{p - p'}{v_s} \tag{2.17}$$

r_s being the flow resistance of the porous layer. We assume that this relation is valid for a steady flow of air as well as for alternating air flow.

In front of the rigid wall but behind the porous layer there is a standing wave which, for normal incidence of the original sound wave, is represented according to eqns (2.4a) to (2.5b) by

$$p'(x) = \hat{p}'\{\exp[-ik(x - d)] + \exp[ik(x - d)]\}$$
$$= 2\hat{p}' \cos[k(x - d)] \tag{2.18}$$

$$v'(x) = \frac{\hat{p}'}{\rho_0 c}\{\exp[-ik(x - d)] - \exp[ik(x - d)]\}$$

$$= -\frac{2i\hat{p}'}{\rho_0 c} \sin[k(x - d)] \tag{2.19}$$

(In the exponents *x* has been replaced by $x - d$ since the rigid wall is not at $x = 0$ as before but at $x = d$.) The ratio of both expressions at $x = 0$ is the 'wall' impedance of the air layer of thickness *d* in front of a rigid wall:

$$Z' = \left(\frac{p'}{v'}\right)_{x=0} = -i\rho_0 c \cot(kd) \tag{2.20}$$

If the thickness of the air space is small compared with the wavelength, i.e. if $kd \ll 1$, then we have approximately

$$Z' \approx \frac{\rho_0 c}{ikd} = \frac{\rho_0 c^2}{i\omega d} \tag{2.20a}$$

Because of the conservation of matter, the particle velocities in front of and behind the layer must be equal to each other, and to the flow velocity through the layer:

$$v(0) = v'(0) = v_s \tag{2.21}$$

Therefore the definition of the wall impedance of the whole arrangement (layer plus air space plus rigid wall) yields

$$p(0) = Zv_s \tag{2.22}$$

whereas eqn (2.20) now reads

$$p'(0) = -i\rho_0 c v_s \cot(kd) \tag{2.23}$$

Substitution of both these expressions into eqn (2.17) results in

$$Z = r_s - i\rho_0 c \cot(kd) \tag{2.24}$$

Hence the impedance of the air space behind the porous layer is simply added to the flow resistance to give the impedance of the complete arrangement.

In the complex plane of Fig. 2.2, this wall impedance would be represented by a vertical line at a distance $r_s/\rho_0 c$ from the imaginary axis. Increasing the wave number or the frequency is equivalent to going repeatedly from $-i\infty$ to $+i\infty$ on that line. As can be seen from the circles of constant absorption coefficient, the latter has a maximum whenever Z is real, i.e. whenever the depth d of the air space is an odd multiple of $\lambda/4$. Introducing $\zeta = Z/\rho_0 c$ from eqn (2.24) into eqn (2.8) yields the following formula for the absorption coefficient of a porous layer in front of a rigid wall:

$$\alpha(f) = \frac{4r'_s}{(r'_s + 1)^2 + \cot^2(2\pi fd/c)} \tag{2.25}$$

with $r'_s = r_s/\rho_0 c$.

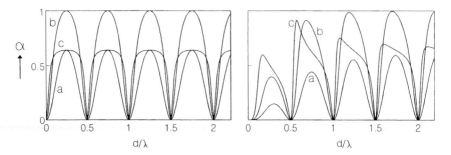

Figure 2.7 Absorption coefficient of a porous layer in front of a rigid surface.
(a) $r_s = 0.25\ \rho_0 c$, (b) $r_s = \rho_0 c$, (c) $r_s = 4\rho_0 c$. Left: $r_s d/M_s c = 0$ (i.e. layer kept at rest);
right: $r_s d/M_s c = 4$.

In Fig. 2.7a the absorption coefficient of this arrangement is plotted as a function of the frequency for $r_s = \rho_0 c/4$, $r_s = \rho_0 c$ and $r_s = 4\rho_0 c$. Beginning from very low values, the absorption coefficient assumes alternate maximum and minimum values. Minimum absorption occurs for all such frequencies at which the distance d between the porous layer and the rigid rear wall is a multiple of half the wavelength. This can be easily understood since, at these distances, the standing wave behind the porous layer has a zero of particle velocity in the plane of the layer, but energy losses can take place only if the air is moving in the pores of the layer.

In reality a porous layer will not remain at rest in a sound field as assumed so far but will vibrate as a whole, due to its finite mass. Then the total velocity in the plane $x = 0$ of Fig. 2.6 consists of two components, namely that due to the porosity of the material, $v_s = (p - p')/r_s$, and the velocity of the layer as a whole which is $v_m = (p - p')/i\omega M_s$ where M_s is the mass of the layer per unit area (see eqn (2.26) with $r_s = 0$). Hence, the ratio of the pressure difference between both sides of the layer and the velocity $v_s + v_m$ is no longer r_s but

$$Z_r = \left(\frac{1}{r_s} + \frac{1}{i\omega M_s} \right)^{-1} = \frac{r_s}{1 - i\omega_s/\omega} \tag{2.17a}$$

where the characteristic frequency $\omega_s = r_s/M_s$ has been introduced. Accordingly, r_s in eqn (2.24) – but not in eqn (2.25)! – must be replaced by Z_r. It is left to the reader to work out a modified formula corresponding to eqn (2.25). Fig. 2.7b demonstrates the influence of the finite mass on the absorption coefficient of the arrangement.

In practical applications it may be advisable to provide for a varying distance between the porous fabric and the rigid wall in order to smooth out the irregularities of the absorption coefficient. This can be done by hanging or stretching the fabric in deep folds.

To this arrangement we now add a second layer or sheet which is not porous and which is placed immediately in front (as seen by the incident sound wave) of the porous layer, but in such a way that there is no contact between the two layers. Under the influence of a sound wave, it can vibrate in the direction of its normal. Its motion is merely controlled by its mass: if there is a pressure difference Δp between its faces this is related to v_s by

$$\Delta p = M\frac{dv_s}{dt} = i\omega M v_s$$

where M is the mass of the non-porous sheet per unit area. We denote the pressure behind the porous layer by p' and the pressure in front of the non-porous layer by p, i.e. at the surface of the whole construction, then, instead of eqn (2.17), we now obtain

$$\frac{p - p'}{v_s} = r_s + i\omega M \tag{2.26}$$

Hence the wall impedance which is determined in a manner similar to that used before is

$$Z = r_s + i\left(\omega M - \frac{\rho_0 c^2}{\omega d}\right) \tag{2.27}$$

As in the preceding example, this impedance is represented in the complex plane as a vertical with distance r_s from the imaginary axis (*see* Fig. 2.8a). But now the locus moves only once from $-i\infty$ to $+i\infty$ if the frequency is varied from zero to infinity. When it crosses the real axis, the absolute value of the wall impedance reaches its minimum. Since $Z = p/v_s$, a given sound pressure will then cause a particularly high velocity of the impervious sheet. According to eqn (2.27), this 'resonance' occurs at the angular frequency:

$$\omega_0 = \left(\frac{\rho_0 c^2}{Md}\right)^{1/2} \tag{2.28}$$

where $f_0 = \omega_0/2\pi$ is the 'resonance frequency' of the system. As may also be seen from Fig. 2.8a and Fig. 2.2, in resonance the absorption coefficient of the system assumes a maximum.

In Fig. 2.8b the corresponding resonance curve is depicted, i.e. the velocity amplitude for a given pressure amplitude as a function of the sound frequency

$$|v_s| = \frac{\omega\hat{p}}{M[(\omega^2 - \omega_0^2)^2 + 4\delta^2\omega^2]^{1/2}} \tag{2.29}$$

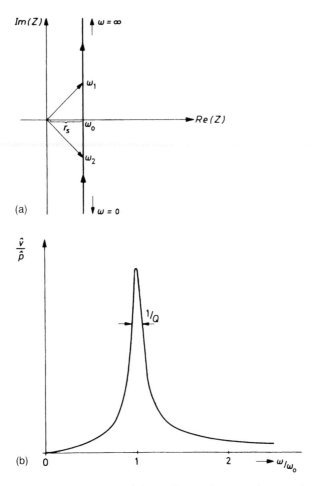

Figure 2.8 (a) Locus of the wall impedance in the complex impedance plane for resonance system. (b) Ratio of velocity to pressure amplitude as a function of the driving frequency for a resonance system.

where the damping constant

$$\delta = \frac{r_s}{2M} \qquad (2.30)$$

has been introduced.

Assuming that δ is small compared with ω_0,

$$\omega_{1,2} = \omega_0 \pm \delta$$

are the angular frequencies for which the phase angle of the wall impedance becomes $\pm 45°$. At the same time the value of the velocity amplitude at these frequencies is below the maximum value $\hat{p}/2\delta M$ by a factor $(2)^{1/2}$. The difference $\Delta\omega = \omega_1 - \omega_2$ is the 'half-width' of the resonance system or, divided by the resonance angular frequency ω_0, the 'relative half-width', which is the reciprocal of the 'quality factor' or 'Q-factor' Q:

$$\frac{\Delta\omega}{\omega_0} = \frac{1}{Q} = \frac{2\delta}{\omega_0} \qquad (2.31)$$

All these quantities may be used to characterise the sharpness of the resonance.

Using eqns (2.8) and (2.27), the absorption coefficient is obtained as

$$\alpha = \frac{4r_s\rho_0 c}{(r_s + \rho_0 c)^2 + [(M/\omega)(\omega^2 - \omega_0^2)]^2}$$

$$= \frac{\alpha_{max}}{1 + Q_\alpha^2(\omega/\omega_0 - \omega_0/\omega)^2} \qquad (2.32)$$

Here we have introduced the maximum absorption coefficient α_{max} and the 'quality factor' concerning the frequency dependence of the absorption, Q_α:

$$\alpha_{max} = \frac{4r_s\rho_0 c}{(r_s + \rho_0 c)^2} \qquad (2.33)$$

$$Q_\alpha = \frac{M\omega_0}{r_s + \rho_0 c} \qquad (2.34)$$

The physical meaning of Q_α is similar to that of Q; it is related to the frequencies at which the absorption coefficient has fallen to half its maximum value. It takes into account not only the losses caused by the porous sheet but also the loss of vibrational energy due to re-radiation (reflection) of sound from the surface of the whole arrangement.

Practical resonance absorbers will be discussed in Chapter 6.

As a last example we consider the 'open window', i.e. an imaginary, laterally bounded surface behind which free space extends. This concept played an important role as an absorption standard in the early days of modern room acoustics, since by definition its absorption coefficient is 1.

When a plane sound wave strikes an open window at an angle Θ to its normal, the component of the particle velocity normal to the 'wall' is $v \cos \Theta$, where v is the particle velocity in the direction of propagation. Hence the wall impedance is given by

$$Z = \frac{p}{v \cos \Theta} = \frac{\rho_0 c}{\cos \Theta} \qquad (2.35)$$

Thus the area does not react locally; its impedance depends on the angle of incidence. By inserting this into eqns (2.14*b*) and (2.16) it is easily shown that $R = 0$ and $\alpha = 1$ for all angles of incidence.

We can enforce local reaction by filling the opening of the windows with a large number of parallel tubes with thin and rigid walls whose axes are perpendicular to the plane of the window. The entrances of these tubes are flush with the window opening; the tubes are either infinitely long or their opposite ends are sealed by a perfect absorber. In each of these tubes and hence on the front face of this 'wall' we can apply

$$\frac{p}{v_n} = \rho_0 c = Z$$

where v_n is the velocity component parallel to the tube axis. This expression leads to

$$R(\Theta) = \frac{\cos \Theta - 1}{\cos \Theta + 1} \tag{2.36a}$$

$$\alpha(\Theta) = \frac{4 \cos \Theta}{(\cos \Theta + 1)^2} \tag{2.36b}$$

The absorption is perfect only at normal incidence; at grazing incidence its value approaches zero. If the absorption coefficient is averaged over all directions of incidence (*see* Section 2.5), a value of 0.912 is obtained, whereas if the lateral subdivision of the window opening is absent, the mean absorption coefficient is of course 1.

2.5 Random sound incidence

In a closed room, the typical sound field does not consist of a single plane wave but is composed of many such waves each with its own particular amplitude, phase and direction. To find the effect of a wall on such a complicated sound field we ought to consider the reflection of each wave separately and then to add all sound pressures.

With certain assumptions we can resort to some simplifications which allow general statements on the effect of a reflecting wall. If the phases of the waves incident on a wall are randomly distributed one can neglect all phase relations and the interference effects caused by them. It is sufficient then just to add or to average their energies which are proportional to the squares of the pressures of the elementary waves. Furthermore we assume that the intensities of the incident sound are uniformly distributed over all possible directions, hence each solid angle element carries the same energy per second to the wall. In this case we speak of 'random sound incidence', and the sound field associated with it is referred to as a 'diffuse sound field'.

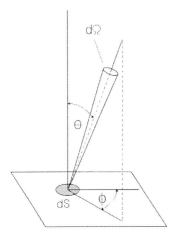

Figure 2.9 Spherical polar coordinates.

This type of sound field plays the role of a standard field in room acoustics, and the reader will frequently encounter it in this book.

In the following it is convenient to use a spherical polar coordinate system as depicted in Fig. 2.9. Its origin is the centre of a wall element dS, the wall normal is its polar axis. We consider an element of solid angle dΩ around a direction which is determined by the polar angle Θ and the azimuth angle Φ. Expressed in these angular coordinates, the solid angle element is d$\Omega = \sin \Theta\, \mathrm{d}\Theta\, \mathrm{d}\Phi$.

First we calculate the dependence of the energy density, which is essentially equal to the square of the sound pressure amplitude, on the distance from the wall which, for the moment, is assumed to be perfectly rigid ($R = 1$). For this case, according to eqn (2.15), the square of the pressure amplitude with respect to a wave incident at angle Θ is

$$|p|^2 = 2\hat{p}_0^2[1 + \cos(2kx \cos \Theta)] \tag{2.37}$$

Multiplied by dΩ this represents the contribution to the total square pressure due to the solid angle element with polar angle Θ. By averaging eqn (2.37) over all directions on one side of the wall we obtain

$$\langle|p|^2\rangle = 2\hat{p}_0^2 \frac{1}{2\pi} \int_0^{2\pi} \mathrm{d}\Phi \int_0^{\pi/2} [1 + \cos(2kx \cos \Theta)] \sin \Theta\, \mathrm{d}\Theta$$

$$= 2\hat{p}_0^2 \left[1 + \frac{\sin(2kx)}{2kx}\right] \tag{2.38}$$

This quantity, divided by $|p_\infty|^2 = 2\hat{p}_0^2$, is plotted in Fig. 2.10 (solid curve) as a function of the distance x from the wall. Immediately in front of the wall

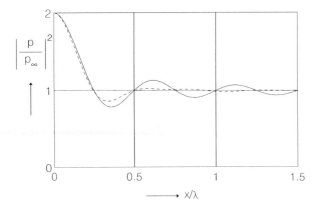

Figure 2.10 Squared sound pressure amplitude in front of a rigid wall, for random sound incidence. ———— sine tone, ------- random noise of one octave bandwidth.

fluctuations of the square pressure occur, as they do in every standing wave. With increasing distance, however, they fade out and the square pressure approaches a constant limiting value which is half of that in front of the wall. A microphone which is sensitive to the sound pressure indicates a pressure level which is higher by 3 dB at the wall than at some distance from it. For the same reason, the sound absorption of an absorbent surface adjacent and perpendicular to a rigid wall is higher near the edge than at a distance of several wavelengths from the wall.

Experimentally it may prove to be difficult to confirm eqn (2.34). The reason for this is not so much the difficulty of establishing a sufficiently diffuse sound field but rather the impossibility of realising the independence of phases among the various components, at least at one single frequency, as assumed in our derivation. When a room is acoustically excited by a sinusoidal signal, the resulting steady state sound field is made up of a number of 'characteristic vibrations' or normal modes (*see* Chapter 3), the phases of which are inter-related in a well-defined way. These inter-relations may be destroyed to a certain extent by replacing the sinusoidal signal with random noise with a limited bandwidth. But then the pressure distribution must also be averaged with respect to frequency over the exciting frequency band. Experimentally, this averaging could be performed by exciting a relatively large room with random noise which has passed a band-pass filter. As an example, the dotted curve of Fig. 2.10 plots the result of averaging $\langle |p|^2 \rangle$ over an octave band, i.e. a frequency band with $f_2 = 2f_1$ where f_1 and f_2 denote the limiting frequencies of the band. Here, the wavelength λ corresponds to the frequency $\sqrt{(f_1 f_2)} = f_1 \sqrt{2}$. Now the standing wave has virtually levelled out for all distances exceeding

$x > 0.5\lambda$, but there is still a pronounced increase of sound pressure if the wall is approached. This increase of $|p|^2$ to twice its far distance value is obviously caused by a certain relation between the phases of all impinging and reflected waves which is enforced by the wall. In any case we can conclude that in a diffuse sound field phase effects are limited to a relatively small range next to the walls which is of the order of half a wavelength.

Now we again consider a wall element with area dS. Its projection in the direction Φ, Θ is $dS \cos \Theta$ (*see* Fig. 2.9). Thus $I \cos \Theta\, dS\, d\Omega$ is the sound energy arriving per second on dS from an element $d\Omega$ of solid angle around the considered direction. By integrating this over all solid angle elements, assuming I independent of Φ and Θ, we obtain the total energy per second arriving at dS:

$$E_i = I\, dS \int_0^{2\pi} d\Phi \int_0^{\pi/2} \cos \Theta \sin \Theta\, d\Theta = \pi I\, dS \tag{2.39}$$

From the energy $I \cos \Theta\, dS\, d\Omega$ the fraction $\alpha(\Theta)$ is absorbed, thus the totally absorbed energy per second is

$$E_a = I\, dS \int_0^{2\pi} d\Phi \int_0^{\pi/2} \alpha(\Theta) \cos \Theta \sin \Theta\, d\Theta$$

$$= 2\pi I\, dS \int_0^{\pi/2} \alpha(\Theta) \cos \Theta \sin \Theta\, d\Theta \tag{2.40}$$

By dividing these two expressions we get the absorption coefficient for random or uniformly distributed incidence:

$$\alpha_{\text{uni}} = \frac{E_a}{E_i} = 2 \int_0^{\pi/2} \alpha(\Theta) \cos \Theta \sin \Theta\, d\Theta = \int_0^{\pi/2} \alpha(\Theta) \sin (2\Theta)\, d\Theta \tag{2.41}$$

This is occasionally referred to as the 'Paris' formula' in the literature.

For locally reacting surfaces we can express the angular dependence of the absorption coefficient by eqn (2.16). If this is done and the integration is performed, we obtain

$$\alpha_{\text{uni}} = \frac{8}{|\zeta|^2} \cos \mu \left[|\zeta| + \frac{\cos 2\mu}{\sin \mu} \arctan\left(\frac{|\zeta| \sin \mu}{1 + |\zeta| \cos \mu} \right) \right.$$

$$\left. - \cos \mu \ln(1 + 2|\zeta| \cos \mu + |\zeta|^2) \right] \tag{2.42}$$

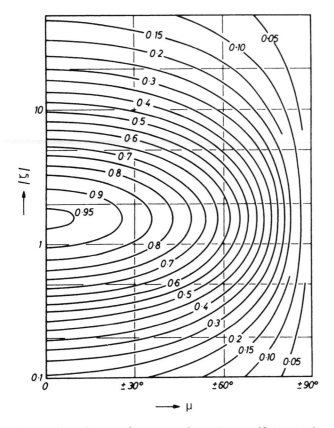

Figure 2.11 Curves of constant absorption coefficient in the impedance plane for random sound incidence. The ordinate is the absolute value. The abscissa is the phase angle of the specific impedance.

Here the wall impedance is characterised by the absolute value and the phase angle μ of the specific impedance

$$\mu = \arctan\left(\frac{\operatorname{Im}\zeta}{\operatorname{Re}\zeta}\right)$$

The content of this formula is represented in Fig. 2.11 in the form of curves of constant absorption coefficient α_{uni} in a coordinate system, the abscissa and the ordinate of which are the phase angle and the absolute value of the specific impedance, respectively. The absorption coefficient has its absolute maximum 0.951 for the real impedance $\zeta = 1.567$. Thus, in a diffuse sound field, a locally reacting wall can never be totally absorbent.

It should be mentioned that recently the validity of the Paris' formula has been called into question by Makita and Hidaka.[2] These authors recommend replacing the factor cos Θ in eqns (2.39) and (2.40) by a somewhat more complicated weighting function. This, of course, would also modify eqn (2.42).

2.6 Scattering, diffuse reflection

So far we have considered sound reflection from walls of infinite extension. If a reflecting wall is finite its boundary will become the origin of an additional sound wave when it is irradiated with sound. This additional wave is brought about by diffraction and hence may be referred to as a 'diffraction wave'. It spreads more or less in all directions.

The simplest example is diffraction by a semi-infinite wall, i.e. a rigid plane with one straight edge as depicted in Fig. 2.12. If this wall is exposed to a plane sound wave at normal incidence one might expect that it reflects some sound into a region A, while another region B, the 'shadow zone', would remain completely free of sound. This would indeed be true if the acoustical wavelength were vanishingly small. In reality, however, the diffraction wave originating from the edge of the wall modifies this picture as is shown in the diagram at the right side of the figure which plots the squared sound pressure at some distance d from the wall for $kd = 100$. Behind the wall, i.e. in region B, there is still some sound intruding into the shadow zone. And in region C ($x > 0$) the plane wave is disturbed by interferences with the diffraction wave. On the whole, the boundary between the shadow and the illuminated region is not sharp but blurred by the diffraction wave. A similar effect occurs at the upper boundary of region A.

If the 'wall' is a bounded reflector of limited extension, for example a freely suspended panel, the line source from which the diffraction wave originates is wound around the edge of the reflector, so to speak. As an

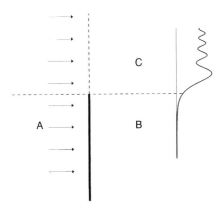

Figure 2.12 Diffraction of a plane wave from a rigid half-plane. The diagram shows the squared sound pressure amplitude at a distance d from the plane with $kd = 100$ (after Ref. 3).

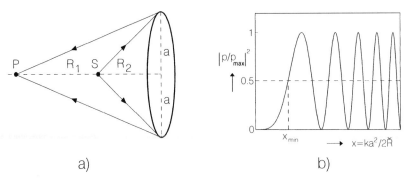

a)   b)

Figure 2.13 Sound reflection from a circular disc: (a) arrangement (S = sound source, P = observation point); (b) squared sound pressure amplitude of reflected wave, $\check{R} = 2(1/R_1 + 1/R_2)^{-1}$.

example, Fig. 2.13a shows a rigid circular disc with radius a, irradiated from a point source S. Consider the sound pressure at point P. Both P and S are situated on the middle axis of the disc at distances R_1 and R_2 from its centre, respectively. Figure 2.13b shows the squared sound pressure of the reflected wave in P as a function of the disc radius as calculated from the approximation

$$|p|^2 = p_{max}^2 \sin^2\left[\frac{\pi a^2}{2\lambda}\left(\frac{1}{R_1} + \frac{1}{R_2}\right)\right] \tag{2.43}$$

For very small disc radii, the reflected sound is negligibly weak since the primary sound wave is nearly completely diffracted around the disc, the obstacle is virtually not present. With increasing disc radius, the pressure in P grows considerably from a certain value on it shows strong fluctuations. The latter are caused by interference between the sound reflected specularly from the disc plane and the diffraction wave from its rim. We consider the reflection from the disc as fully developed if $|p|^2$ equals its average value which is half its maximum value. This is the case if the argument of the sine in eqn (2.43) is $\pi/4$. This condition leads to a minimum frequency f_{min} above which the reflector is effective:

$$f_{min} = \frac{c\check{R}}{4a^2} \approx 85\frac{\check{R}}{a^2} \text{ Hz} \tag{2.44}$$

where the abbreviation

$$\check{R} = 2\left(\frac{1}{R_1} + \frac{1}{R_2}\right)^{-1} \tag{2.44a}$$

has been used. (In the second version of eqn (2.44) all lengths are to be expressed in metres.) A circular panel with a diameter of 1 m, for instance, viewed from a distance of 5 m ($R_1 = R_2 = 5$ m) is an effective reflector for frequencies exceeding 1700 Hz. For frequencies below this limit it has a much lower effect.

Similar considerations applied to a rigid strip with the width h yield for the minimum frequency of geometrical reflections

$$f_{min} = 0.53 \frac{c\check{R}}{(h \cos \Theta)^2} \approx 180 \frac{\check{R}}{(h \cos \Theta)^2} \text{ Hz} \tag{2.45}$$

with the same meaning of $\check{R}$ as in eqn (2.44a). Here Θ is the angle of sound incidence. (In another estimate[5] the factor 0.53 is omitted.)

Generally, any body or surface of limited extension distorts a primary sound field by diffraction unless its dimensions are very small compared to the wavelength. Part of the diffracted sound is scattered more or less in all directions. For this reason this process is also referred to as 'sound scattering'. (The role of sound scattering by the human head in hearing has already been mentioned in Section 1.6.)

The scattering efficiency of a body is often characterised by its 'scattering cross-section', defined as the ratio of the total power scattered P_s and the intensity I_0 of the incident wave:

$$Q_s = \frac{P_s}{I_0} \tag{2.46}$$

If the dimensions of the scattering body are small compared to the wavelength, P_s and hence Q_s is very small. In the opposite case of short wavelengths, the scattering cross-section approaches twice its visual cross-section, i.e. $2\pi a^2$ for a sphere or a circular disc with radius a. Then one half of the scattered power is concentrated into a narrow beam behind the obstacle and forms its shadow by interference with the primary wave while the other half is deflected from its original direction.

Very often a wall is not completely plane but contains regular or irregular coffers, bumps or other projections. If these are very small compared to the wavelength, they do not disturb the wall's 'specular' reflection as treated in the preceding sections of this chapter. In the opposite case, i.e. if they are large compared with the wavelength, each of their faces may be treated as a plane or curved wall section, reflecting the incident sound specularly. There is an intermediate range of wavelengths, however, in which each projection adds a scattered wave to the specular reflection of the whole wall. If the wall has an irregular surface structure, a large fraction of the reflected sound energy will be scattered in all directions. In this case we speak of a

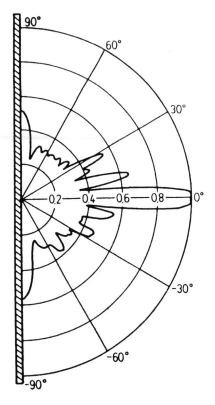

Figure 2.14 Directional distribution of sound, scattered from a highly irregular ceiling. Polar representation of the pressure amplitude.

'diffusely reflecting wall'. In Section 8.8 methods for measuring the scattering efficiency of acoustically rough surfaces will be described.

As an example of a sound scattering boundary, we consider the ceiling of a particular concert hall.[4] It is covered with many bodies made of gypsum such as pyramids, spherical segments, etc.; their depth is about 30 cm on the average. Figure 2.14 shows the directional distribution of the sound reflected from that ceiling, measured at a frequency of 1000 Hz at normal incidence of the primary sound wave; the plotted quantity is the sound pressure level. (This measurement has been carried out on a model ceiling). The pronounced maximum at 0° corresponds to the specular component which is still of considerable strength.

Diffuse or partially diffuse reflections occur not only at walls with a geometrically structured surface but also at walls which are smooth and have non-uniform impedance instead. To understand this we return to Fig. 2.12 and imagine that the rigid screen is continued upwards by a totally absorbing wall. This would not change the structure of the sound field left of the

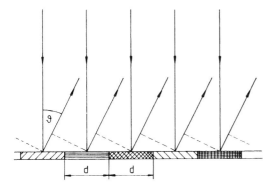

Figure 2.15 Sound reflection from an arrangement of parallel and equidistant strips with different reflection factors.

wall, i.e. the disturbance caused by the diffraction wave. Therefore we can conclude that any change of wall impedance creates a diffraction wave provided the range in which the change occurs is small compared with the wavelength.

A practical example of this kind are walls lined with relatively thin panels which are mounted on a rigid framework. At the points where the lining is fixed it is very stiff and cannot react to the incident sound field. Between these points, however, the lining will perform bending vibrations, particularly if the frequency of the exciting sound field is close to the resonance frequency of the lining (*see* eqn (2.28)). Scattering will be even more effective if adjacent partitions are tuned to different resonance frequencies due to variations of the panel masses or the depths of the air space behind them.

In Fig. 2.15 we consider a plane wall subdivided into strips with equal width d and with different reflection factors $R_n = |R_n| \exp(i\chi_n)$. We assume that d is noticeably smaller than the wavelength. If a plane wave arrives normally at the wall, it will excite all strips with equal amplitude and phase, and each of them will react to it by emitting a secondary wave or wavelet. We consider those wave portions which are re-emitted (i.e. reflected) from corresponding points of the strips at some angle ϑ. Their phases contain the phase shifts χ_n caused by the reflection and those due to the path differences $d \sin \vartheta$ between wavelets from adjacent strips. The sound pressure far from the wall is obtained by summation over all contributions:

$$p(\vartheta) \propto \sum_n |R_n| \exp[i(\chi_n - nkd \sin \vartheta)] \tag{2.47}$$

If all strips had the same reflection factor, all contributions would have the same phase angles for $\vartheta = 0$ and add to a particularly high pressure amplitude, corresponding to the specular reflection. It is evident that by varying

$|R_n|$ and χ_n the specular reflection can be destroyed more or less and its energy scattered into non-specular directions instead.

In the following we assume that the reflection factor of all partitions shown in Fig. 2.15 has the magnitude 1. Our goal is to achieve maximum diffusion of the reflected sound. In principle, this could be effected by distributing the phase angles χ_n randomly within the interval from 0 to 2π since randomising the phase angles is equivalent to randomising the directions in eqn (2.47). Complete randomness, however, would require a very large number of elements.

Approximately the same effect can be reached with so-called pseudo-random sequences of phase angles. If these sequences are periodic they lead to reflection phase gratings with the grating constant Nd if N denotes the number of elements within one period. As with optical gratings, constructive interference of the wavelets reflected from corresponding elements will occur if the condition

$$\sin \vartheta = m \frac{2\pi}{kNd} = m \frac{\lambda}{Nd} \tag{2.48}$$

is fulfilled. The integer m is the 'diffraction order'. Introducing this condition into eqn (2.47) yields the sound pressure in the mth diffraction order:

$$p_m \propto \sum_{n=0}^{N} \exp\left(i\chi_n\right) \exp\left(-2\pi i \frac{mn}{N}\right) \tag{2.49}$$

p_m is the discrete Fourier transform of the sequence $\exp(i\chi_n)$ as may be seen by comparing this expression with eqn (1.35c). Hence, a uniform distribution of the reflected energy over all diffraction orders can be achieved by finding phase shifts χ_n for which the power spectrum of $\exp(i\chi_n)$ is flat. Arrangements of this kind are often called 'Schroeder diffusers', after their inventor.[6] The required phase shifts can be realised by troughs in the wall surface which are separated by rigid walls: a sound wave intruding into a trough of depth h_n will have attained a phase shift of $\chi_n = 2kh_n$ when it reappears at the surface after reflection from the rear end. Accordingly the required depths are

$$h_n = \frac{\chi_n}{2k} = \frac{\lambda_d}{4\pi} \chi_n \tag{2.50}$$

$f_d = c/\lambda_d$ is the 'design frequency' of the diffuser.

One sequence which fulfils the condition of flat power spectrum is based on 'quadratic residues'[7]

$$\chi_n = 2\pi \frac{n^2 \bmod N}{N} \tag{2.51}$$

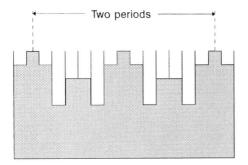

Figure 2.16 Quadratic residue diffuser (QRD) for $N = 7$.

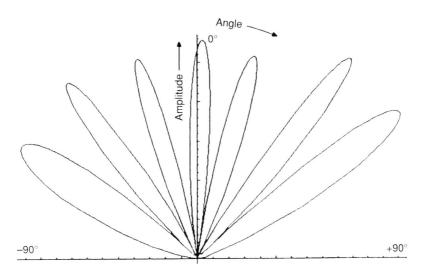

Figure 2.17 Scattering diagram of a QRD with $N = 7$ consisting of 14 elements with a uniform spacing of $\lambda/2$, calculated with a more exact theory (*see* Schroeder[7]).

with N being a selected prime number. The modulus function accounts for the fact that all relevant phase angles are in the range from 0 to 2π. Quadratic residue diffusers (QRD) are effective over a frequency range from f_s to $(N-1)f_s$. Figure 2.16 shows two periods of a QRD consisting of seven different elements. In Fig. 2.17 the directional pattern of sound diffused by it is presented. The fact that the lobes have finite widths and are not completely equal and symmetric is due to the finite extension of the diffuser.

Quadratic residue gratings which scatter sound in two dimensions can also be constructed. Furthermore, several other sequences are known upon which the design of Schroeder diffusers can be based, for instance primitive roots of prime numbers, or Legendre sequences. For an overview, *see*

Ref. 8 where more literature on this interesting matter may be found. Schroeder diffusers have an interesting side effect, namely significant sound absorption in a wide frequency range. More will be said on this subject in Section 6.8.

References

1 Mechel, F., *Schallabsorber*, S. Hirzel Verlag, Stuttgart, 1989/95/98.
2 Makita, Y. and Hidaka, T., *Acustica*, **63** (1987) 163; *ibid.*, **67** (1988) 214.
3 Morse, P.M. and Ingard, K.U., *Theoretical Acoustics*, McGraw-Hill, New York, 1968.
4 Meyer, E. and Kuttruff, H., *Acustica*, **9** (1959) 465.
5 Fasold, W., Kraak, W. and Schirmer, W., *Taschenbuch Akustik*, Part 2, 9.3.2.3, VEB Verlag Technik, Berlin, 1984.
6 Schroeder, M.R., *J. Acoust Soc. America*, **65** (1979) 958.
7 Schroeder, M.R., *Number Theory in Science and Communication*, 2nd edn, Springer-Verlag, Berlin, 1986.
8 Schroeder, M.R., *Acustica*, **81** (1995) 364.

3 The sound field in a closed space (wave theory)

In the preceding chapter we saw the laws which a plane sound wave obeys upon reflection from a single plane wall and how this reflected wave is superimposed on the incident one. Now we shall try to obtain some insight into the complicated distribution of sound pressure or sound energy in a room which is enclosed on all sides by walls which are at least partially reflecting.

We could try to describe the resulting sound field by means of a detailed calculation of all the reflected sound components and by finally adding them together; that is to say, by a manifold application of the reflection laws which we dealt with in the previous chapter. Since each wave which has been reflected from a wall A will be reflected from walls B, C, D, etc., and will arrive eventually once more at wall A, this procedure leads only asymptotically to a final result, not to mention the calculations which grow like an avalanche. Nevertheless, this method is highly descriptive and therefore it is frequently applied in a much simplified form in geometrical room acoustics. We shall return to it in the next chapter.

In this chapter we shall choose a different way of tackling our problem which will lead to a solution in closed form – at least a formal one. This advantage is paid for by a higher degree of abstraction, however. Characteristic of this approach are certain boundary conditions which have to be set up along the room boundaries and which describe mathematically the acoustical properties of the walls, the ceiling and the other surfaces. Then solutions of the wave equations are sought which satisfy these boundary conditions. This method is the basis of what is frequently called 'the wave theory of room acoustics'.

It will turn out that this method in its exact form too can only be applied to highly idealised cases with reasonable effort. The rooms with which we are concerned in our daily life, however, are more or less irregular in shape, partly because of the furniture, which forms part of the room boundary. Rooms such as concert halls, theatres or churches deviate from their basic shape because of the presence of balconies, galleries, pillars, columns and other wall irregularities. Then even the formulation of boundary conditions may turn out to be quite involved, and the solution of a given problem requires extensive numerical calculations. For this reason the immediate application of wave theory to practical problems in room acoustics is very limited. Nevertheless, wave theory is the most reliable and appropriate theory from a physical point of view, and therefore it is essential for a more than superficial understanding of sound propagation in enclosures. For the same reason we should keep in mind the results of wave theory when we are applying more simplified methods, in order to keep our ideas in perspective.

3.1 Formal solution of the wave equation

The starting point for a wave theory representation of the sound field in a room is again the wave equation (1.5), which will be used here in a time-independent form. That is to say, we assume, as earlier, a harmonic time law for the pressure, the particle velocity, etc., with an angular frequency ω. Then the equation, known as the Helmholtz equation, reads

$$\Delta p + k^2 p = 0 \quad k = \frac{\omega}{c} \tag{3.1}$$

Furthermore, we assume that the room under consideration has locally reacting walls and ceiling, the acoustical properties of which are completely characterised by a wall impedance depending on the coordinates and the frequency but not on the angle of sound incidence.

According to eqn (1.2), the velocity component normal to any wall or boundary is

$$v_n = -\frac{1}{i\omega\rho_0}(\text{grad } p)_n = \frac{i}{\omega\rho_0}\frac{\partial p}{\partial n} \tag{3.2}$$

The symbol $\partial/\partial n$ denotes partial differentiation in the direction of the outward normal to the wall. We replace v_n by p/Z (see eqn (2.2)) and obtain

$$Z\frac{\partial p}{\partial n} + i\omega\rho_0 p = 0 \tag{3.2a}$$

or, using the specific impedance ζ,

$$\zeta\frac{\partial p}{\partial n} + ikp = 0 \tag{3.2b}$$

Now it can be shown that the wave equation yields non-zero solutions fulfilling the boundary condition (3.2a) or (3.2b) only for particular discrete values of k, called 'eigenvalues'.[1,2] In the following material, we shall frequently distinguish these quantities from each other by an index number n or m, though it is often more convenient to use a trio of subscripts because of the three-dimensional nature of the problem.

Each eigenvalue k_n is associated with a solution $p_n(\mathbf{r})$, which is known as an 'eigenfunction' or 'characteristic function'. (Here $\mathbf{r}$ is used as an abbreviation for the three spatial coordinates.) It represents a three-dimensional standing wave, a so-called 'normal mode' of the room. As mentioned earlier, for a given enclosure the explicit evaluation of the eigenvalues and eigenfunctions is generally quite difficult and requires the application of numerical methods such as the Finite Element Method (FEM)[3]. There are only a few room shapes for which the eigenfunctions can be presented in closed form. An important example will be given in the next section.

At this point we need to comment on the quantity k in the boundary condition (3.2a) or (3.2b). Implicitly, it is also contained in ζ, since the specific wall impedance depends in general on the frequency $\omega = kc$. We can identify it with k_n, the eigenvalue to be evaluated, by solving our boundary problem. Then in general the boundary condition contains the parameters which we are looking for. Another possibility is to give k (and hence ω) in the boundary condition a fixed value, which may be given by the driving frequency of a sound source.

It is only the former case for which one can prove that the eigenfunctions are mutually orthogonal, which means that

$$\iiint_V p_n(\mathbf{r})p_m(\mathbf{r})\, dV = \begin{cases} K_n & \text{for } n = m \\ 0 & \text{for } n \neq m \end{cases} \qquad (3.3)$$

where the integration has to be extended over the whole volume V enclosed by the walls. Here K_n is a constant.

If all the eigenvalues and eigenfunctions, which in general are functions of the frequency, are known, we can in principle evaluate any desired acoustical property of the room; for instance, its steady state response to arbitrary sound sources. Suppose the sound sources are distributed continuously over the room according to a density function $q(\mathbf{r})$, where $q(\mathbf{r})\, dV$ is the volume velocity of a volume element dV at $\mathbf{r}$. Here $q(\mathbf{r})$ may be a complex function taking account of possible phase differences between the various infinitesimal sound sources. Furthermore, we assume a common driving frequency ω. By adding $\rho_0 q(\mathbf{r})$ to the right-hand side of eqn (1.3) it is easily seen that the Helmholtz equation (3.1) now has to be modified into

$$\Delta p + k^2 p = -i\omega\rho_0 q(\mathbf{r}) \qquad (3.4)$$

with the same boundary condition as above. Since the eigenfunctions form a complete and orthogonal set of functions, we can expand the source function in a series of p_n:

$$q(\mathbf{r}) = \sum_n C_n p_n(\mathbf{r}) \quad \text{with } C_n = \frac{1}{K_n} \iiint_V p_n(\mathbf{r}) q(\mathbf{r}) \, dV \qquad (3.5)$$

where the summation is extended over all possible combinations of subscripts. In the same way the solution $p_\omega(\mathbf{r})$, which we are looking for can be expanded in eigenfunctions:

$$p_\omega(\mathbf{r}) = \sum_n D_n p_n(\mathbf{r}) \qquad (3.6)$$

Our problem is solved if the unknown coefficients D_n are expressed by the known coefficients C_n. For this purpose we insert both series into eqn (3.4):

$$\sum D_n(\Delta p_n + k^2 p_n) = i\omega\rho_0 \sum C_n p_n$$

Now $\Delta p_n = -k_n^2 p_n$. Using this relation and equating term by term in the equation above, we obtain:

$$D_n = i\omega\rho_0 \frac{C_n}{k^2 - k_n^2} \qquad (3.7)$$

The final solution assumes a particularly simple form for the important case of a point source at the point $\mathbf{r}_0$ which has a volume velocity Q. The source function is represented mathematically by a delta function in this case:

$$q(\mathbf{r}) = Q\delta(\mathbf{r} - \mathbf{r}_0)$$

Because of eqn (1.42) the coefficients C_n in eqn (3.5) are then given by

$$C_n = \frac{1}{K_n} Q p_n(\mathbf{r}_0)$$

Using this relation and eqns (3.7) and (3.6), we finally find for the sound pressure in a room excited by a point source of angular frequency ω:

$$p_\omega(\mathbf{r}) = iQ\omega\rho_0 \sum \frac{p_n(\mathbf{r})p_n(\mathbf{r}_0)}{K_n(k^2 - k_n^2)} \qquad (3.8)$$

This is called 'Green's function' of the room under consideration. It is interesting to note that it is symmetric in the coordinates of the sound source and of the point of observation. If we put the sound source at $\mathbf{r}$, we observe at point $\mathbf{r}_0$ the same sound pressure as we did before at $\mathbf{r}$, when the sound source was at $\mathbf{r}_0$. Thus eqn (3.8) is the mathematical expression of the famous reciprocity theorem which can be applied sometimes with advantage to measurements in room acoustics.

Since the boundary conditions are usually complex equations containing k_n, the latter are in general complex quantities. Putting

$$k_n = \frac{\omega_n}{c} + i\frac{\delta_n}{c} \tag{3.9}$$

and assuming that $\delta_n \ll \omega_n$, we obtain from eqn (3.8)

$$p_\omega(\mathbf{r}) = iQc^2\omega\rho_0 \sum_n \frac{p_n(\mathbf{r})p_n(\mathbf{r}_0)}{(\omega^2 - \omega_n^2 - 2i\delta_n\omega_n)K_n} \tag{3.10}$$

Considered as a function of the frequency, this expression is the transfer function of the room between the two points $\mathbf{r}$ and $\mathbf{r}_0$. At the angular frequencies $\omega = \omega_n$, the associated term of this series assumes a particularly high absolute value. The corresponding frequencies $f_n = \omega_n/2\pi$ are called 'eigenfrequencies' of the room; sometimes they are referred to as 'resonance frequencies' because of some sort of resonance occurring in the vicinity of those frequencies. The δ_n will turn out later to be 'damping constants'.

If the sound source is not emitting a sinusoidal signal but instead a signal which is composed of several spectral components, then $Q = Q(\omega)$ can be considered as its spectral function and we can represent the source signal as a Fourier integral (*see* Section 1.4):

$$s(t) = \int_{-\infty}^{+\infty} Q(\omega) \exp(i\omega t)\, d\omega$$

where we have used $\omega = 2\pi f$ as a variable of integration instead of f. Since the response to any spectral component with angular frequency ω is just given by eqns (3.8) or (3.10), the sound pressure at the point $\mathbf{r}$ as a function of time is

$$p(\mathbf{r}, t) = \int_{-\infty}^{+\infty} p_\omega(\mathbf{r}) \exp(i\omega t)\, d\omega$$

where Q in the formulae for p_ω has to be replaced by $Q(\omega)$.

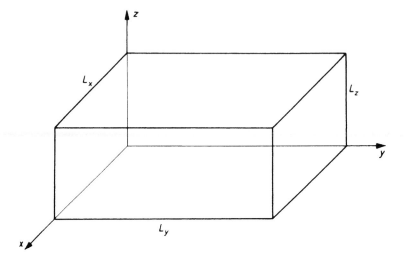

Figure 3.1 Rectangular room.

3.2 Normal modes in rectangular rooms with rigid boundaries

In order to put some life into the abstract formalism outlined in the preceding section, we consider a room with parallel pairs of walls, the pairs being perpendicular to each other. It will be referred to in the following as a 'rectangular room'. In practice rooms with exactly this shape do not exist. On the other hand, most concert halls or other halls, churches, lecture rooms and so on are much closer in shape to the rectangular room than to any other of simple geometry, and so the results obtained for strictly rectangular rooms can be applied at least qualitatively to many rooms encountered in practice. Therefore our example is not only intended for the elucidation of the theory discussed above but has some practical bearing as well.

Our room is assumed to extend from $x = 0$ to $x = L_x$ in the x-direction, and similarly from $y = 0$ to $y = L_y$ in the y-direction and from $z = 0$ to $z = L_z$ in the z-direction (*see* Fig. 3.1). As far as the properties of the wall are concerned, we start with the simplest case, namely that of all walls being rigid. That is to say, that at the surface of the walls the normal components of the particle velocity must vanish.

In cartesian coordinates the Helmholtz equation (3.1) may be written

$$\frac{\partial^2 p}{\partial x^2} + \frac{\partial^2 p}{\partial y^2} + \frac{\partial^2 p}{\partial z^2} + k^2 p = 0$$

The variables can be separated, which means that we can compose the solution of three factors:

$$p(x, y, z) = p_1(x)p_2(y)p_3(z)$$

which depend on x only, on y only and on z only, respectively. If this product is inserted into the Helmholtz equation, the latter splits up into three ordinary differential equations. The same is true for the boundary conditions. For instance, p_1 must satisfy the equation

$$\frac{d^2p_1}{dx^2} + k_x^2 p_1 = 0 \tag{3.11}$$

together with the boundary condition

$$\frac{dp_1}{dx} = 0 \quad \text{for } x = 0 \text{ and } x = L_x \tag{3.11a}$$

Analogous equations hold for $p_2(y)$ and $p_3(z)$; the newly introduced constants are related by

$$k_x^2 + k_y^2 + k_z^2 = k^2 \tag{3.12}$$

Equation (3.11) has the general solution

$$p_1(x) = A_1 \cos (k_x x) + B_1 \sin (k_x x) \tag{3.13}$$

The constants A_1 and B_1 are used for adapting this solution to the boundary conditions (3.11a). So it is seen immediately that we must put $B_1 = 0$, since only the cosine function possesses at $x = 0$ the horizontal tangent required by eqn (3.11a). For the occurrence of a horizontal tangent too at $x = L_x$, we must have $\cos (k_x L_x) = \pm 1$, thus $k_x L_x$ must be an integral multiple of π. The constant k_x must therefore assume one of the allowed values

$$k_x = \frac{n_x \pi}{L_x} \tag{3.14a}$$

as a consequence of the boundary conditions, n_x being a non-negative integer. Similarly, we obtain for the allowed values of k_y and k_z

$$k_y = \frac{n_y \pi}{L_y} \tag{3.14b}$$

$$k_z = \frac{n_z \pi}{L_z} \tag{3.14c}$$

Inserting these values into eqn (3.12) results in the following equation for the eigenvalues of the wave equation:

$$k_{n_x n_y n_z} = \pi \left[\left(\frac{n_x}{L_x} \right)^2 + \left(\frac{n_y}{L_y} \right)^2 + \left(\frac{n_z}{L_z} \right)^2 \right]^{1/2} \tag{3.15}$$

The eigenfunctions associated with these eigenvalues are simply obtained by multiplication of the three cosines, each of which describes the dependence of the pressure on one coordinate:

$$p_{n_x n_y n_z}(x, y, z) = C \cos \left(\frac{n_x \pi x}{L_x} \right) \cos \left(\frac{n_y \pi y}{L_y} \right) \cos \left(\frac{n_z \pi z}{L_z} \right) \tag{3.16}$$

where C is an arbitrary constant. This formula represents a three-dimensional standing wave; of course, it is incomplete without the factor $\exp(i\omega t)$ describing the time dependence of the sound pressure. The sound pressure is zero for all times at those points at which at least one of the cosines becomes zero. This occurs for all values of x which are odd integers of $L_x/2n_x$, and for the analogous values of y and z. So these points of vanishing sound pressure form three sets of equidistant planes, called 'nodal planes', which are mutually orthogonal. The numbers n_x, n_y and n_z indicate the numbers of nodal planes perpendicular to the x-axis, the y-axis and the z-axis, respectively. (For non-rectangular rooms the surfaces of vanishing sound pressure are generally no longer planes. They are referred to as 'nodal surfaces'.)

In Fig. 3.2 the sound pressure distribution in the plane $z = 0$ is depicted for $n_x = 3$ and $n_y = 2$. The loops are curves of constant pressure amplitude, namely for $|p/p_{max}| = 0.25, 0.5$ and 0.75. The intersections of vertical nodal planes with the plane $z = 0$ are indicated by dotted lines. On either side of such a line the sound pressures have opposite signs.

The eigenfrequencies corresponding to the eigenvalues of eqn (3.15), which are real because of the special boundary condition (3.11a), are given by

$$f_{n_x n_y n_z} = \frac{c}{2\pi} k_{n_x n_y n_z} \tag{3.17}$$

In Table 3.1 the lowest 20 eigenfrequencies (in Hz) of a rectangular room with dimensions $L_x = 4.7$ m, $L_y = 4.1$ m and $L_z = 3.1$ m are listed for $c = 340$ m/s, together with the corresponding combinations of subscripts, which indicate immediately the structure of the mode which belongs to the respective eigenfrequency.

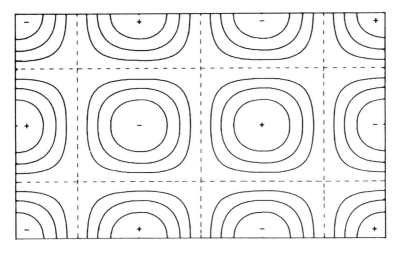

Figure 3.2 Sound pressure distribution in the plane $z = 0$ of a rectangular room for $n_x = 3$ and $n_y = 2$.

Table 3.1 Eigenfrequencies of a rectangular room with dimensions $4.7 \times 4.1 \times 3.1$ m^3 (in hertz)

f_n	n_x	n_y	n_z	f_n	n_x	n_y	n_z
36.17	1	0	0	90.47	1	2	0
41.46	0	1	0	90.78	2	0	1
54.84	0	0	1	99.42	0	2	1
55.02	1	1	0	99.80	2	1	1
65.69	1	0	1	105.79	1	2	1
68.55	0	1	1	108.51	3	0	0
72.34	2	0	0	109.68	0	0	2
77.68	1	1	1	110.05	2	2	0
82.93	0	2	0	115.49	1	0	2
83.38	2	1	0	116.16	3	1	0

By using the complex representation of vibrational quantities, i.e. by employing $\cos x = (e^{ix} + e^{-ix})/2$, eqn (3.16) can be written in the following form:

$$p_{n_x n_y n_z} = \frac{C}{8} \sum \exp\left[\pi i \left(\pm \frac{n_x}{L_x} x \pm \frac{n_y}{L_y} y \pm \frac{n_z}{L_z} z \right) \right] \qquad (3.18)$$

wherein the summation has to be extended over the eight possible combinations of signs in the exponent. Each of these eight terms – multiplied by the usual time factor $\exp(i\omega t)$ – represents a plane travelling wave, whose

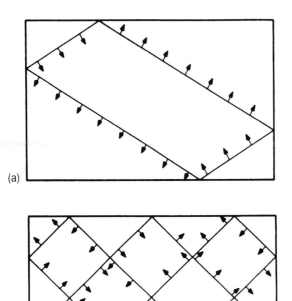

Figure 3.3 Plane wavefronts creating standing waves in a rectangular room:
(a) $n_x:n_y = 1:1$; (b) $n_x:n_y = 3:2$.

direction of propagation is defined by the angles β_x, β_y and β_z, which it
makes with the coordinate axes, where

$$\cos\beta_x : \cos\beta_y : \cos\beta_z = \left(\pm\frac{n_x}{L_x}\right) : \left(\pm\frac{n_y}{L_y}\right) : \left(\pm\frac{n_z}{L_z}\right) \tag{3.19}$$

If one of the three subscripts, for instance n_z, equals zero, then the corresponding angle (β_z in this example) is 90°; the propagation takes place
perpendicularly to the respective axis, i.e. parallel to all planes which are
perpendicular to that axis. The corresponding vibration pattern is frequently
referred to as a 'tangential mode'. If there is only one non-zero subscript,
the propagation is parallel to one of the coordinate axes, i.e. parallel to one
of the room edges. Then we are speaking of an 'axial mode'. In Fig. 3.3, for
the analogous two-dimensional case, two combinations of plane waves are
shown which correspond to two different eigenfunctions.

We can get an illustrative survey on the arrangement, the types and the
number of the eigenvalues by the following geometrical representation. We

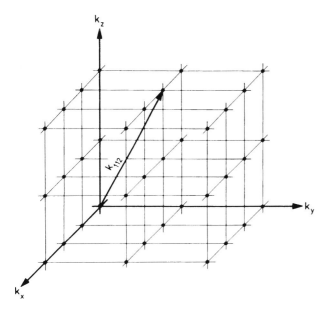

Figure 3.4 Eigenvalue lattice in the *k*-space for a rectangular room. The arrow pointing from the origin to an eigenvalue point indicates the direction of one of the eight plane waves which the corresponding mode consists of; its length is prortional to the eigenvalue.

interpret k_x, k_y and k_z as cartesian coordinates in a *k*-space. Each of the allowed values of k_x, given by eqn (3.14*a*), corresponds to a plane perpendicular to the k_x-axis. The same statement holds for the values of k_y and k_z, given by eqns (3.14*b*) and (3.14*c*). These three equations therefore represent three sets of equidistant, mutually orthogonal planes in the *k*-space. Since for one eigenvalue these equations have to be satisfied simultaneously, each intersection of three mutually orthogonal planes corresponds to a certain eigenvalue in our representation. These intersections in their totality form a rectangular point lattice in the first octant of our *k*-space (*see* Fig. 3.4). (Negative values obviously do not yield new eigenvalues, since eqn (3.15) is not sensitive to the signs of the subscripts!) The lattice points corresponding to tangential and to axial modes are situated on the coordinate planes and on the axes, respectively. The straight line connecting the origin of the coordinate system to a certain lattice point has – according to eqn (3.19) – the same direction as one of the plane waves of which the associated mode is made up (*see* eqn (3.18)).

This representation allows a simple estimation of the number of eigenfrequencies which are located between the frequency 0 and some other given frequency. Considered geometrically, eqn (3.12) represents a spherical surface in the *k*-space with radius *k*, enclosing a 'volume' $4\pi k^3/3$. Of this volume, however, only the portion situated in the first octant is of interest, i.e. the volume $\pi k^3/6$. On the other hand, the distances between one certain lattice point and its nearest neighbours in the three coordinate directions are π/L_x, π/L_y and π/L_z. The k-'volume' per lattice point is therefore $\pi^3/L_xL_yL_z = \pi^3/V$, where V is the real geometrical volume of the room under consideration. Now we are ready to write down the number of lattice points inside the first octant up to radius k, which is equivalent to the number of eigenfrequencies from 0 to an upper limit $f = kc/2\pi$:

$$N_f = \frac{\pi k^3/6}{\pi^3/V} = \frac{Vk^3}{6\pi^2} = \frac{4\pi}{3} V\left(\frac{f}{c}\right)^3 \tag{3.20}$$

The average density of eigenfrequencies on the frequency axis, i.e. the number of eigenfrequencies per Hz at the frequency f, is

$$\frac{\mathrm{d}N_f}{\mathrm{d}f} = 4\pi V\frac{f^2}{c^3} \tag{3.21}$$

Strictly speaking, in the course of the derivation of the above formulae, we have made an error inasmuch as we have regarded the lattice points on the coordinate planes only as halves and those on the axes only as quarters, since we have restricted our consideration strictly to the first octant, although the points on the coordinate planes and the axes represent full eigenvalues. Correcting this yields, instead of eqn (3.20), the more exact formula

$$N_f = \frac{4\pi}{3}V\left(\frac{f}{c}\right)^3 + \frac{\pi}{4}S\left(\frac{f}{c}\right)^2 + \frac{L}{8}\frac{f}{c} \tag{3.20a}$$

In this expression S is the area of all walls $2(L_xL_y + L_xL_z + L_yL_z)$ and $L = 4(L_x + L_y + L_z)$ the sum of all edge lengths occurring in the rectangular room.

It can be shown that in the limiting case $f \to \infty$ eqn (3.20) is valid not only for rectangular rooms but also for rooms of arbitrary shape. This is not too surprising since any enclosure can be conceived as being composed of many (or even infinitely many) rectangular rooms. For each of them eqn (3.20) yields the number N_i of eigenfrequencies. Since this equation is linear in V, the total number of eigenfrequencies is just the sum of all N_i.

We bring this section to a close by applying our approximate formulae (3.20) and (3.21) to two simple examples. The volume of the rectangular room for which we have calculated the first eigenfrequencies in Table 3.1 is 59.7 m³. For an upper frequency limit of 116 Hz, eqn (3.20) indicates a total number of eigenfrequencies of 10 as compared with the 20 we have listed in the table. Using the more accurate formula (3.20a) we obtain exactly 20 eigenfrequencies. That means that we must not neglect the corrections due to tangential and axial modes when dealing with such small rooms at low frequencies. Now we consider a rectangular room with dimensions $50 \text{ m} \times 24 \text{ m} \times 14 \text{ m}$ whose volume is $16\,800 \text{ m}^3$. (This might be a large concert hall, for instance.) In the frequency range from 0 to 10 000 Hz there are, according to eqn (3.20), about 1.8×10^9 eigenvalues. At 1000 Hz the number of eigenfrequencies per hertz is about 5400, thus the average distance of two eigenfrequencies on the frequency axis is less than 0.0002 Hz. These figures underline the enormous volume of numerical calculation which would be required to evaluate accurately the sound field in a room of even the simplest geometry.

3.3 Non-rigid walls

In this section we are still dealing with rectangular rooms. But now we assume that the walls are not completely rigid, but allow the normal components of particle velocity to have non-vanishing values. Therefore we have to replace the boundary condition (3.11a) by the more general conditions of eqn (3.2b). For the walls perpendicular to the x-axis of our coordinate system we therefore require

$$\zeta_x \frac{dp_1}{dx} = ikp_1 \quad \text{for } x = 0$$

$$\zeta_x \frac{dp_1}{dx} = -ikp_1 \quad \text{for } x = L_x \tag{3.22}$$

The specific impedance ζ_x of the x-walls is assumed to be constant; the same holds for the analogous boundary conditions concerning the walls perpendicular to the y-axis and the z-axis, respectively. Thus each pair of walls has uniform acoustical properties. The frequency contained in k and in ζ is considered as constant, and so we expect the resulting eigenfunctions to be mutually orthogonal.

We have tacitly assumed that the solution of the wave equation – as in the preceding section – can be split into three factors p_1, p_2 and p_3, each of which depends on one spatial coordinate only.

For the present purpose it is more useful to write the general solution for p_1 in the complex form:

$$p_1(x) = C_1 \exp(-ik_x x) + D_1 \exp(ik_x x) \tag{3.23}$$

which, however, is completely equivalent to eqn (3.13). By inserting p_1 into the boundary conditions (3.22) we obtain two linear and homogeneous equations for the constants C_1 and D_1:

$$C_1(k + k_x \zeta_x) + D_1(k - k_x \zeta_x) = 0$$

$$C_1(k - k_x \zeta_x) \exp(-ik_x L_x) + D_1(k + k_x \zeta_x) \exp(ik_x L_x) = 0 \tag{3.24}$$

which have a non-vanishing solution only if the determinant of their coefficient is zero. This leads to the following equation, from which the allowed values of k_x can be determined:

$$\exp(ik_x L_x) = \pm \frac{k - k_x \zeta_x}{k + k_x \zeta_x} \tag{3.25}$$

which is equivalent to

$$\tan u = i\frac{2u\zeta_x}{kL_x} \quad \text{and} \quad \tan u = i\frac{kL_x}{2u\zeta_x} \tag{3.25a}$$

with

$$u = \tfrac{1}{2}k_x L_x$$

Since the specific wall impedance is usually complex, $\zeta_x = \xi_x + i\eta_x$, we must also expect complex values for the solution k_x:

$$k_x = k'_x + ik''_x$$

which is to be compared with eqn (3.9).

Once the allowed values of k_x have been determined, the ratio of the two constants C_1 and D_1 can be evaluated from eqns (3.24); for instance, from the first of them

$$\frac{C_1}{D_1} = -\frac{k - k_x \zeta_x}{k + k_x \zeta_x} = \mp\exp(ik_x L_x)$$

the latter equality resulting from eqn (3.25). Thus the x-dependent factor of the eigenfunction reads

$$p_1(x) \sim \begin{cases} \cos[k_x(x - L_x/2)] & \text{(even)} \\ \sin[k_x(x - L_x/2)] & \text{(odd)} \end{cases} \tag{3.26}$$

The complete eigenfunction is made up of three such factors.

We do not pursue a thorough discussion of eqn (3.25) or (3.25a) and its solutions here, which can be found elsewhere. (In fact, graphical solutions to eqn (3.25a) obtained by conformal mapping are known as Morse's charts in the literature.[4]) Here we restrict ourselves to two special cases which make the contrast with a rigid wall sufficiently evident. In the following we suppose $|\zeta| \gg 1$.

First let the wall impedance be purely imaginary, i.e. $\xi_x = 0$. At the walls, therefore, no energy loss will occur, since the absolute value of the reflection coefficient is 1 (*see* eqn (2.7)). The right-hand terms of eqns (3.25a) are real in this case, and therefore the same is true for the allowed values of u and k_x, as was the case for rigid walls. A closer investigation of eqn (3.25a) shows that k_x is lower or higher than $n_x \pi / L_x$ (see eqn (3.14a)) depending on whether η_x is positive, indicating that the wall has mass character, or negative which means that the wall is compliant. The difference becomes smaller with increasing n_x. If the allowed values of k_x are denoted by k_{xn_x}, the eigenvalues of the original differential equation are given as earlier by

$$k_{n_x n_y n_z} = (k_{xn_x}^2 + k_{yn_y}^2 + k_{zn_z}^2)^{1/2} \tag{3.27}$$

From this relation it can be concluded that for missing energy losses at the wall, i.e. for purely imaginary wall impedances, all eigenvalues are only shifted by a certain amount.

As a second case we consider walls with very large real impedances. From eqns (3.25) we obtain

$$\exp(ik_x' L_x) \exp(-k_x'' L_x) = \pm \frac{k - k_x \xi_x}{k + k_x \xi_x} \approx \mp \left(1 - \frac{2k}{k_x \xi_x}\right) \tag{3.25b}$$

Since we have supposed $\xi_x \gg 1$, we conclude $k_x'' \ll k_x'$, and so we can safely replace k_x by k_x' on the right-hand side. Then $\exp(ik_x' L_x) \approx \mp 1$, the allowed values of k_x' are nearly the same as those of k_x from eqn (3.14a). Furthermore, it follows from eqn (3.25b) that

$$\exp(-k_x'' L_x) \approx 1 - k_x'' L_x \approx 1 - \frac{2k}{k_x' \xi_x}$$

hence

$$k_x'' \approx \frac{2k}{k_x' L_x \xi_x} \tag{3.28}$$

Analogous approximate formulae are obtained for the other coordinates. The quantities k' are, by the way, called 'phase constants'.

Now we put the calculated values of k_x, k_y and k_z into eqn (3.27) and obtain for the eigenvalues

$$k_{n_x n_y n_z} = [(k_{n_x}' + ik_{n_x}'')^2 + (k_{n_y}' + ik_{n_y}'')^2 + (k_{n_z}' + ik_{n_z}'')^2]^{1/2}$$

$$\approx k_{n_x n_y n_z}' + i \frac{k_{n_x}' k_{n_x}'' + k_{n_y}' k_{n_y}'' + k_{n_z}' k_{n_z}''}{k_{n_x n_y n_z}'}$$

where

$$k'^2_{n_x n_y n_z} \approx \pi^2 \left[\left(\frac{n_x}{L_x} \right)^2 + \left(\frac{n_y}{L_y} \right)^2 + \left(\frac{n_z}{L_z} \right)^2 \right]$$

If we finally insert the approximate values from eqn (3.28) into our expression for $k_{n_x n_y n_z}$, we get

$$k_{n_x n_y n_z} \approx k'_{n_x n_y n_z} + i \frac{2\omega}{ck'_{n_x n_y n_z}} \left(\frac{1}{L_x \xi_x} + \frac{1}{L_y \xi_y} + \frac{1}{L_z \xi_z} \right) \tag{3.29}$$

In Fig. 3.5 the absolute value of the x-dependent factor of a certain eigenfunction is represented for three cases: for rigid walls ($\zeta_x = \infty$), for mass-loaded walls with no energy loss ($\xi_x = 0$, $\eta_x > 0$), and for walls with purely real impedances. In the second case, the nodes are simply shifted

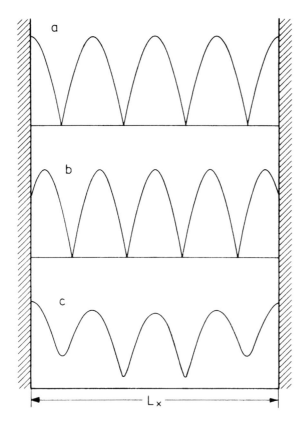

Figure 3.5 One-dimensional normal mode, pressure distribution for $n_x = 4$: (a) $\zeta = \infty$; (b) $\zeta = i$; (c) $\zeta = 2$.

together by a certain amount, but the shape of the standing wave remains unaltered. On the contrary, in the third case of lossy walls, there are no longer exact nodes and the pressure amplitude is different from zero at all points. This can easily be understood by keeping in mind that the walls dissipate energy, which must be supplied by waves travelling towards the walls, thus a pure standing wave is not possible. This situation is comparable to a standing wave in front of a single plane with a reflection factor less than unity as shown in Fig. 2.3.

3.4 Steady state sound field

In Section 3.1 we saw that the steady state acoustical behaviour of a room, when it is excited by a sinusoidal signal with angular frequency ω, is described by a series of the form

$$p_\omega = \sum_n \frac{A_n}{\omega^2 - \omega_n^2 - 2\mathrm{i}\delta_n\omega_n} \tag{3.30}$$

where we are assuming $\delta_n \ll \omega_n$ as before. By comparing this with our earlier eqn (3.10) we learn that the coefficients A_n are functions of the source position, of the receiving position, and of the angular frequency ω. If both points are considered as fixed, eqn (3.30) is the transfer function of the room between both points. (If p_ω is to represent a true transfer function, certain relationships between the eigenvalues must be met, which we shall not discuss here.)

Since we have supposed that the constants δ_n are small compared with the corresponding ω_n, the absolute value of one series term changes so rapidly in the vicinity of $\omega = \omega_n$ if the frequency is altered that we can safely neglect any frequency dependence except that of the denominator. Since it is the term $\omega^2 - \omega_n^2$ which is responsible for the strong frequency dependence, ω_n can be replaced by ω in the last term of the denominator without any serious error. The absolute value of the nth series term then becomes

$$\frac{|A_n|}{[(\omega^2 - \omega_n^2)^2 + 4\omega^2\delta_n^2]^{1/2}}$$

and thus agrees with the amplitude–frequency characteristics of a resonance system, according to eqn (2.29). Therefore the stationary sound pressure in a room and at one single exciting frequency proves to be the combined effect of numerous resonance systems with resonance (angular) frequencies ω_n and damping constants δ_n. The half-widths of the various resonance curves are according to eqn (2.31):

$$(\Delta f)_n = \frac{1}{2\pi}(\Delta\omega)_n = \frac{\delta_n}{\pi} \tag{3.31}$$

In the next section it will be seen that the damping constants in normal rooms lie mostly between 1 and 20 s^{-1}. Therefore our earlier assumption concerning the relative magnitude of the damping constants seems to be justified. Furthermore, we see from this that the corresponding half-widths, within which the various resonance terms assume their highest values, are of the order of magnitude of 1 Hz.

This figure is to be compared with the average spacing of eigenfrequencies on the frequency axis which is the reciprocal of dN_f/df after eqn (3.21). If the mean spacing of resonance frequencies is substantially larger than the average half-width $\langle\delta_n\rangle/\pi$ we expect that most of the room resonances are well separated, and each of them can be individually excited and detected. In a tiled bathroom, for example, the resonances are usually weakly damped, and thus one can often find one or several resonances by singing or humming. If, on the contrary, the average half-width of the resonances is much larger than the average spacing of the eigenfrequencies, there will be strong overlap of resonance peaks and the latter cannot be separated. Instead, at any frequency several or many terms of the sum in eqn (3.30) will have significant values, hence several or many normal modes will contribute to the total sound pressure. According to M. Schroeder[5,6] a limiting frequency separating both cases can be defined by the requirement that on average three eigenfrequencies fall into one resonance half-width, or, with eqn (3.21):

$$\langle\Delta f_n\rangle = 3\frac{c^3}{4\pi V f^2}$$

(The angle brackets indicate averages). Introducing the average damping constant by eqn (3.31), the sound speed $c = 340$ m/s and solving for the frequency yields the limiting frequency, the so-called 'Schroeder frequency':

$$f_S \approx \frac{5400}{\sqrt{(V\langle\delta_n\rangle)}}\,\text{Hz} \approx 2000\sqrt{\frac{T}{V}} \tag{3.32}$$

In this expression, the so-called 'reverberation time' $T = 6.91/\langle\delta\rangle$ has been introduced. The room volume V has to be expressed in cubic metres.

For large halls the Schroeder frequency is typically about 20 or 30 Hz, hence there is strong modal overlap in the whole frequency range of interest, and there is no point in evaluating any eigenfrequencies. It is only in small rooms that a part of the important frequency range lies below f_S, and in this range the acoustic properties are determined largely by the values of individual eigenfrequencies. To calculate the expected number N_{f_S} of eigenfrequencies in the range from zero to f_S, eqn (3.32) is inserted into eqn (3.20) with the result:

$$N_{f_S} \approx 900\sqrt{\frac{T^3}{V}} \tag{3.33}$$

Thus, in a classroom with a volume of 200 m³ and a reverberation time of 1 s, about 60–70 eigenfrequencies dominate the acoustical behaviour below the Schroeder frequency which is about 140 Hz. This example illustrates the somewhat surprising fact that the acoustics of small rooms are in a way more complicated than those of large ones.

It should be noted that eqn (3.32) separates not only two frequency ranges of different modal structure but also large rooms from small ones. By solving for V, one gets a criterion for 'acoustically large rooms':

$$V > V_S \quad \text{with} \quad V_S \approx \left(\frac{2000}{f}\right)^2 T \qquad (3.32a)$$

(f in Hz, T in seconds). After the previous discussion it is not surprising that this limit depends on frequency.

For the rest of this section we restrict our discussion to the frequency range above the Schroeder limit, $f > f_S$. Hence, if the room under consideration is excited with a pure tone its steady state response is made up by contributions of several or even many normal modes with randomly distributed phases. The situation may be elucidated by the vector diagram in Fig. 3.6. Each numbered vector or arrow represents the contribution of one term in eqn (3.30) (nine significant terms in this example). The resulting sound pressure is obtained as the vector sum of all components. For a different frequency or at a different point in the room, this diagram has the same general character, but it looks quite different in detail, provided that the change in frequency or location is sufficiently great.

Since the different components (the different series terms) can be considered as mutually independent, we can apply to the real part as well as to the imaginary part of the resulting sound pressure p_ω the central limit theorem of probability theory, according to which both quantities are random variables obeying nearly a Gaussian distribution. This statement implies that the squared absolute value of the sound pressure p, divided by its frequency

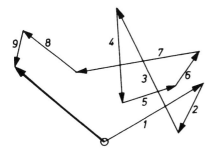

Figure 3.6 Vector diagram of the components of the steady state sound pressure in a room and their resultant for sinusoidal excitation (in most practical cases the number of components is much larger).

(or space) average, $y = |p|^2/\langle|p|^2\rangle$, which is proportional to the energy density, is distributed according to an exponential law or, more precisely, the probability of finding this quantity between y and $y + dy$ is given by

$$P(y)\,dy = e^{-y}\,dy \qquad (3.34)$$

Its mean value and also its variance $\langle y^2\rangle - \langle y\rangle^2$ is 1, as is easily checked.

The probability that a particular value of y exceeds a given limit y_0 is

$$P_i(y > y_0) = \int_{y_0}^{\infty} P(y)\,dy = e^{-y_0} \qquad (3.34a)$$

It is very remarkable that the distribution of the energy density is completely independent of the type of the room, i.e. on its volume, its shape or its acoustical qualities.

Figure 3.7a presents a typical 'space curve', i.e. the sound pressure level recorded with a microphone along a straight line in a room while the driving frequency is kept constant. Such curves express the space dependence of eqn (3.30). Their counterpart are 'frequency curves', i.e. representations of the sound pressure level observed at a fixed microphone position by slowly varying the excitation frequency. They are based upon the frequency dependence of eqn (3.30). A section of such a frequency curve is shown in Fig. 3.7b. Recorded at another microphone position or in another room it would look quite different in detail; its general appearance, however, would be similar to the shown one. A similar statement holds for space curves. (At this point it should be mentioned that for recording

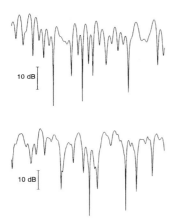

10 dB

10 dB

Figure 3.7 Steady state sound pressure: (a) measured along a straight line at constant frequency ('space curve'); (b) measured at a fixed position with slowly varying driving frequency ('frequency curve').

correct space or frequency curves the microphone must not be too close to the exciting loudspeaker.)

Both curves in Fig. 3.7 have a similar general appearance: they are highly irregular with deep valleys. A maximum of the pressure level occurs if in Fig. 3.6 many or all arrows happen to point in about the same direction, indicating similar phases of most contributions. Similarly, a minimum appears if these contributions more or less mutually cancel. Therefore, the maxima of frequency curves are not related to particular room resonances or eigenfrequencies but are the result of accidental phase coincidences. The general similarity of space and frequency curves is not too surprising: both sample the same distribution of squared sound pressure amplitudes, namely that given by eqn (3.34). But since they do it in a different way, there are indeed differences which can be demonstrated by their autocorrelation functions. As before, we consider $y = |p|^2/\langle|p|^2\rangle$ as the significant variable. Thus, in contrast to Section 1.4, the 'signals' to which the autocorrelation functions refer are $y(x)$ and $y(f)$, respectively, with x denoting the coordinate along the straight line where the pressure level is recorded. For space curves in rooms with uniform distribution of the directions of sound propagation, the autocorrelation function reads:

$$\Phi_{yy}(\Delta x) = 1 + \left(\frac{\sin(k\Delta x)}{k\Delta x}\right)^2 \tag{3.35a}$$

while the autocorrelation function of frequency curves is given by[7]

$$\Phi_{yy}(\Delta f) = 1 + \frac{1}{1 + (\pi\Delta f/\langle\delta\rangle)^2} \tag{3.35b}$$

These autocorrelation functions are also useful for deriving expressions for the average distance of maxima. According to a famous formula by S.O. Rice[8], the average number of maxima per second of a random signal $y(t)$ with normally distributed values of y is

$$\frac{1}{2\pi}[-\Phi^{(4)}(t)/\Phi^{(2)}(t)]^{1/2}$$

where the numbers in brackets indicate the order of differentiations. By replacing the time t with the variables Δx and Δf, respectively, and performing the required differentiations we obtain the average distance of adjacent maxima of space curves

$$\langle\Delta x_{max}\rangle \approx 0.79\,\lambda \tag{3.36a}$$

while the mean spacing of frequency curve maxima is

$$\langle \Delta f_{max} \rangle \approx \frac{\langle \delta_n \rangle}{\sqrt{3}} \approx \frac{4}{T} \tag{3.36b}$$

where again T denotes the reverberation time, as in eqn (3.32).

A quantity which is especially important to the performance of sound reinforcement systems in rooms is the absolute maximum of a frequency curve within a given frequency bandwidth B. In order to calculate this we represent the frequency curve by N equidistant samples provided they are sufficiently close. Then we define the absolute maximum y_{max} by requiring that this value be exceeded by just one sample, i.e.

$$P_i(y > y_{max}) = \frac{1}{N}$$

or, by employing eqn (3.34a):

$$y_{max} = \ln N$$

The corresponding level difference between the maximum and the average of the energetic frequency curve is

$$\Delta L_{max} = 10 \log_{10}(\ln N) = 4.34 \ln(\ln N) \text{ dB}$$

Because of the double logarithm ΔL_{max} depends only weakly on N, i.e. its value is not critical. A fair representation of the frequency curve is certainly achieved if we take four samples per $\langle \Delta f_{max} \rangle$. This leads to

$$N = 4 \frac{B}{\langle \Delta f_{max} \rangle} \approx BT$$

Hence, the final expression for the maximum level in a frequency curve reads

$$\Delta L_{max} = 4.34 \ln[\ln(BT)] \text{ dB} \tag{3.37}$$

This interesting formula is due to M. Schroeder[9] who derived it in a somewhat different manner. As an example, let us consider a room with a reverberation time of 2 s. According to eqn (3.37), the absolute maximum of its frequency curve in the range from 0 to 10 kHz is about 10 dB above its energetic average.

If the driving frequency is slowly varied not only does the amplitude of the sound pressure at a fixed point change in an irregular manner but so

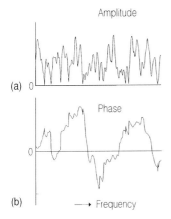

Figure 3.8 (a) Magnitude and (b) phase of a room transfer function.

does its phase. However, a monotonic change in phase with respect to the driving signal is superimposed on these quasi-statistical fluctuations. The corresponding average phase shift per hertz is given by[10]

$$\left\langle \frac{d\psi}{df} \right\rangle = \frac{\pi}{\langle \delta_n \rangle} \approx 0.455\, T \tag{3.38}$$

Figure 3.8 shows in its upper part an amplitude–frequency curve. It is similar to that shown in Fig. 3.7b with the difference that the plotted quantity is not the sound pressure level but the absolute value of the sound pressure. The lower part plots the corresponding phase variation obtained after subtracting the monotonic change according to eqn (3.38). Since this figure represents the transfer function between two points within a room, the phase spectrum of any signal which is transmitted in it will be randomized by transmission. This can be demonstrated in the following way. A loudspeaker placed in a reverberant room is alternatively fed with two signals which have equal amplitude spectra, but different phase spectra, e.g. a sequence of rectangular impulses, and by a maximum length sequence (*see* Section 8.2) made up of rectangular impulses of the same length as those in the first sequence (*see* Fig. 3.9). If the listener is close to the loudspeaker he can clearly hear that both signals sound quite different provided the repetition rate $1/T$ is not too high. However, when he slowly steps into the room the difference gradually fades out, and at a certain distance the signals have become indistinguishable.

   We close this section by emphasising again that the general properties of room transfer functions, especially the distribution of its absolute values

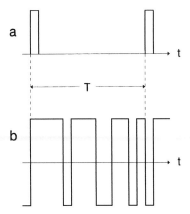

Figure 3.9 Two periodic signals with equal amplitude spectrum but different phase spectra.

and thus the depth of its irregularities, the sequence of maxima and the phase change associated with it, do not depend in a specific way on the room or on the point of observation. In particular, it is impossible to base a criterion of the acoustic quality on these quantities. This is in complete contrast to what has been expected in the past from an examination of frequency curves. From experience gained in the use of transmission lines, amplifiers and loudspeakers, etc., one had supposed originally that a room would be better acoustically if it had a smooth frequency curve. That this is not so is due to several reasons. First, speech and music exhibit such rapid variations in signal character that a large room does not reach steady state conditions when excited by them except perhaps during very slow musical passages. Furthermore, more recent investigations have shown that our hearing organ is unable to perceive fluctuations of the spectrum of a signal with respect to frequency if these irregularities are spaced closely enough on the frequency axis (*see* Section 7.3).

3.5 Decaying modes, reverberation

If a room is excited not by a stationary sinusoidal signal as in the preceding sections but instead by a very short sound impulse emitted at time $t = 0$, we obtain, in the limit of vanishing pulse duration, an impulse response $g(t)$ at some receiving point of the room. According to the discussion in Section 1.4, this is the Fourier transform of the transfer function. Hence

$$g(t) = \int_{-\infty}^{+\infty} p_\omega \exp{(i\omega t)} \, d\omega$$

Generally the evaluation of this Fourier integral, applied to p_ω after eqn (3.9) or (3.30), is rather complicated since both ω_n and δ_n depend on the driving frequency ω. At any rate the solution has the form

$$g(t) = \begin{cases} 0 & \text{for } t < 0 \\ \displaystyle\sum_n A_n' \exp(-\delta_n' t) \cos(\omega_n' t + \psi_n') & \text{for } t \geq 0 \end{cases} \tag{3.39}$$

It is composed of sinusoidal oscillations with different frequencies, each dying out with its own particular damping constant. This is quite plausible since each term of eqn (3.30) corresponds to a resonator whose reaction to an excitation impulse is a damped oscillation. If the wall losses in the room are not too large, the frequencies ω_n' and damping constants δ_n' differ only slightly from those occurring in eqn (3.30). As is seen from the more exact representation (3.10), the coefficients A_n' contain implicitly the location of both the source and the receiving point.

If the room is excited not by an impulse but by a stationary signal $s(t)$ which is switched off at $t = 0$, the resulting room response $h(t)$ is, according to eqn (1.44),

$$h(t) = \int_{-\infty}^{0} s(\tau) g(t - \tau) \, d\tau$$

$$= \sum_n A_n' \exp(-\delta_n' t)[a_n \cos(\omega_n' t + \psi_n') + b_n \sin(\omega_n' t + \psi_n')] \quad \text{for } t \geq 0$$

where

$$\left.\begin{matrix} a_n \\ b_n \end{matrix}\right\} = \int_{-\infty}^{0} s(x) \exp(\delta_n' x) \left\{\begin{matrix} \cos \\ \sin \end{matrix}\right\} (\omega_n' x) \, dx$$

The above expression for $h(t)$ can be written more simply as

$$h(t) = \sum_n c_n \exp(-\delta_n' t) \cos(\omega_n' t - \phi_n) \quad \text{for } t > 0 \tag{3.40}$$

with

$$c_n = A_n' \sqrt{(a_n^2 + b_n^2)}$$

It is evident that only such modes can contribute to the general decay process whose eigenfrequencies are not too remote from the frequencies which are contained in the spectrum of the driving signal. If the latter is a sinusoidal tone switched off at some time $t = 0$, then only such components contribute noticeably to $h(t)$, the frequencies ω'_n of which are separated from the driving frequency ω by not more than a half-width, i.e. by about δ'_n.

The decay process described by eqn (3.40) is called the 'reverberation' of the room. It is one of the most important and obvious acoustical phenomena of a room, familiar also to the layman.

An expression proportional to the energy density is obtained by squaring $h(t)$:

$$w(t) \sim [h(t)]^2 = \sum_n \sum_m c_n c_m \exp\left[-(\delta'_n + \delta'_m)t\right] \cos\left(\omega'_n t - \phi_n\right) \cos\left(\omega'_m t - \phi_m\right)$$

$$(3.41)$$

This expression can be considerably simplified by averaging it with respect to time. Since the damping constants are small compared with the eigenfrequencies, the exponential terms vary slowly and we are permitted to average the cosine products only. The products with $n \neq m$ will cancel on the average, whereas each term $n = m$ yields a value $\frac{1}{2}$. Thus we obtain

$$\overline{w(t)} = \sum c_n^2 \exp\left(-2\delta'_n t\right) \tag{3.41a}$$

where all constants of no importance have been omitted.

Now we imagine that the sum is rearranged according to increasing damping constants δ'_n. Additionally, the sum is supposed to consist of many significant terms. Then we can replace it by an integral by introducing a damping density $H(\delta)$. This is done by denoting the sum of all c_n^2 with damping constants between δ and $\delta + d\delta$ by $H(\delta)\, d\delta$, and by normalising $H(\delta)$ so as to have

$$\int_0^\infty H(\delta)\, d\delta = 1$$

Then the integral envisaged becomes simply

$$\overline{w(t)} = \int_0^\infty H(\delta) \exp\left(-2\delta t\right) d\delta \tag{3.42}$$

Just as with the coefficient c_n, the damping distribution $H(\delta)$ depends on the sound signal, on the location of the sound source, and on the point of observation. From this representation we can derive some interesting general properties of reverberation.

Usually reverberation measurements are based on the sound pressure level of the decaying sound field:

$$L_r = 10 \log_{10}\left(\frac{\overline{w}}{w_0}\right) = 4.34 \ln\left(\frac{\overline{w}}{w_0}\right) \mathrm{dB}$$

Its decay rate is

$$\dot{L}_r = 4.34\frac{\dot{\overline{w}}}{\overline{w}} \ \mathrm{dB/s} \tag{3.43a}$$

while the second derivative of the decay level is

$$\ddot{L}_r = 4.34\frac{\overline{w}\ddot{\overline{w}} - \dot{\overline{w}}^2}{\overline{w}^2} \ \mathrm{dB/s} \tag{3.43b}$$

(Each overdot in these formulae means one differentiation with respect to time.) By caculating the derivatives of $\overline{w}$ from eqn (3.42) it is easy to show that the second derivative of the decay level L_r is nowhere negative which means that the decay curves are curved upwards. As a limiting case, they can be a straight line. The latter occurs if all damping constants involved in the decay process are equal, i.e. if the distribution $H(\delta)$ is a Dirac function.

For $t = 0$ the curve has its steepest part, its initial slope as obtained from eqn (3.43a)

$$(\dot{L}_r)_{t=0} = -8.69\int_0^\infty H(\delta)\delta \ \mathrm{d}\delta = -8.69\langle\delta\rangle \tag{3.44a}$$

is determined by the mean value of the distribution $H(\delta)$. Furthermore, eqn (3.43b) leads to

$$(\ddot{L}_r)_{t=0} = 17.37(\langle\delta^2\rangle - \langle\delta\rangle^2) \tag{3.44b}$$

This means, the second derivative of the level which is roughly the initial curvature of the decay curve is proportional to the variance of the damping distribution $H(\delta)$.

In Fig. 3.10 are shown some examples of distributions of damping constants together with the corresponding logarithmic reverberation curves. The distributions are normalised so that their mean values (and hence the initial slopes of the corresponding reverberation curves) agree with each other. Only when all the damping constants are equal (case d) are straight curves are obtained.

Very often the damping constants of the modes are very close to each other, and accordingly the decay curves are straight lines apart from some random

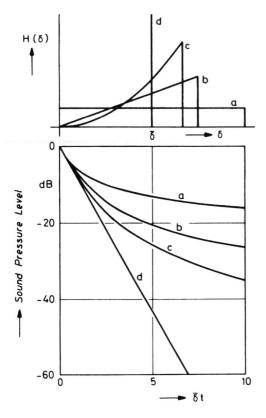

Figure 3.10 Various distributions of damping constants and corresponding reverberation curves.

or quasi-random fluctuations as shown in Fig. 3.11. (These irregularities are due to beats between the decaying modes.) Then all decay constants can be replaced without much error by their average $\langle\delta\rangle$.

It is usual in room acoustics to characterise the duration of sound decay not by damping constants but by the 'reverberation time' or 'decay time' T, introduced by W.C. Sabine. It is defined as the time interval in which the decay level drops down by 60 dB. From

$$-60 = 10 \log_{10}[\exp(-2\langle\delta\rangle T]$$

it follows that the reverberation time

$$T = \frac{6.91}{\langle\delta\rangle} \tag{3.45}$$

a relation which was already used in Section 3.4.

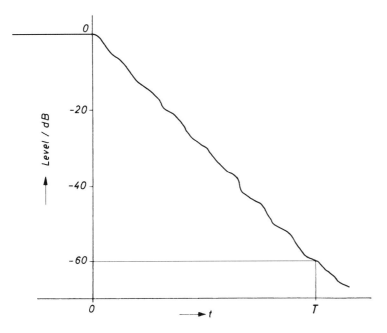

Figure 3.11 Definition of the reverberation time.

Typical values of reverberation times run from about 0.3 s (living rooms) up to 10 s (large churches, reverberation chambers). Most large halls have reverberation times between 0.7 and 2 s. Thus the average damping constants encountered in practice are in the range 1 to 20 s⁻¹.

The previous statements on the general shape of logarithmic decay curves, in particular on their curvature, are not valid for coupled rooms, i.e. for virtually separate rooms, connected by relatively small coupling apertures only or by partially transparent walls. That different conditions are to be expected can be understood in the following way.

Let us consider two partial rooms not too different from each other, which are coupled to each other and whose eigenfrequencies, if they were not coupled, would be $\omega_1, \omega_2, \ldots, \omega_n$ and $\omega'_1, \omega'_2, \ldots, \omega'_n, \ldots$, respectively. For each eigenfrequency of the one room, we can find an eigenfrequency of the other room, having nearly the same value. By introducing the coupling element these pairs of eigenfrequencies – as with any coupled system – are pushed apart by a small amount $\Delta\omega$, where $\Delta\omega$ is of the same order of magnitude for all pairs of eigenfrequencies and depends on the amount of coupling. In the decay process, according to eqn (3.40), beats will occur with a relatively low beat frequency $\Delta\omega/2$ which cannot be eliminated by short-time averaging as applied in the derivation of eqn (3.41a), and the shape of the reverberation curve may exhibit more complicated features than described above. Only if the coupling is so strong that the frequency shifts, and hence the beat frequencies become comparable with the eigenfrequencies themselves, will a short-time averaging process remove everything except the exponential factors, and we can apply eqn (3.41a). For that case, however, the coupling aperture has to be so large that we can speak of one single room and its splitting up into partial rooms would be artificial. In Chapter 5 we shall discuss the properties of coupled rooms from a statistical point of view. For the exact wave theoretical treatment of coupled rooms, the reader is referred to the literature.[10]

References

1 Morse, P.M. and Feshbach, H., *Methods of Theoretical Physics*, McGraw-Hill, New York, 1953, Chapter 11.
2 Morse, P.M. and Ingard, K.U., *Theoretical Acoustics*, McGraw-Hill, New York, 1968, Chapter 9.
3 Zienkiewicz, O.C. and Taylor, R.L., *The Finite Element Method*, McGraw-Hill, London, 1991.
4 Morse, P.M., *J. Acoust. Soc. America*, **11** (1939) 205.
5 Schröder, M., *Acustica*, **4** (1954) 594.
6 Kuttruff, K.H. and Schroeder, M.R., *J. Acoust. Soc. America*, **34** (1962) 76.
7 Schroeder, M.R., *J. Acoust. Soc. America*, **34** (1962) 1819.
8 Rice, S.O., Mathematical Analysis of Random Noise, in *Selected Papers on Noise and Stochastic Processes*, ed. N. Wax, Dover, New York, 1954, p. 211.
9 Schroeder, M.R., Proceedings of the Third International Congress on Acoustics, Stuttgart, 1959, ed. L. Cremer, Elsevier, Amsterdam, 1961, p. 771.
10 Schroeder, M.R., Proceedings of the Third International Congress on Acoustics, Stuttgart, 1959, ed. L. Cremer, Elsevier, Amsterdam, 1961, p. 897.
11 Morse, P.M. and Ingard, K.U., *Theoretical Acoustics*, McGraw-Hill, New York, 1968, Chapter 10.

4 Geometrical room acoustics

The discussions of the preceding chapter have clearly shown that it is not very promising to apply the methods of wave theory in order to find answers to questions of practical interest, especially if the room under consideration is large and somewhat irregular in shape. In such cases even the calculation of one single eigenvalue and the associated normal mode is quite difficult. Moreover, in order to obtain a survey of the sound fields which are to be expected for different types of excitation it would be necessary to calculate not one but a very large number of modes. On the other hand, such a computation, supposing it were at all practicable, would yield far more detailed information than would be required and meaningful for the judgement of the acoustical properties of the room.

We arrive at a greatly simplified way of description – just as in geometrical optics – by employing the limiting case of vanishingly small wavelengths, i.e. the limiting case of very high frequencies. This assumption is permitted if the dimensions of the room and its walls are large compared with the wavelength of sound. This condition is frequently met in room acoustics; at a medium frequency of 1000 Hz, corresponding to a wavelength of 34 cm, the linear dimensions of the walls and the ceiling, and also the distances covered by the sound waves, are usually larger than the wavelength by orders of magnitude. Even if the reflection of sound from a balcony face is to be discussed, for instance, a geometrical description is applicable, at least qualitatively.

In geometrical room acoustics, the concept of a wave is replaced by the concept of a sound ray. The latter is an idealisation just as much as the plane wave. As in geometrical optics, we mean by a sound ray a small portion of a spherical wave with vanishing aperture which originates from a certain point. It has a well-defined direction of propagation and is subject to the same laws of propagation as a light ray, apart from the different propagation velocity. Thus, according to the above definition, the total energy conveyed by a ray remains constant provided the medium itself does not cause any energy losses. However, the intensity within a diverging bundle of rays falls as $1/r^2$, as in every spherical wave, where r denotes the distance from its origin. Another fact of particular importance for room acoustics is the law of reflection. In contrast, the transition to another medium, and the refraction accompanying it, does not occur in room acoustics, neither does the curvature of rays in an inhomogeneous medium. But the finite velocity of propagation must be considered in many cases, since it is responsible for many important effects such as reverberation, echoes and so on.

Diffraction phenomena are neglected in geometrical room acoustics, since propagation in straight lines is its main postulate. Likewise, interference is not considered, i.e. if several sound field components are superimposed their mutual phase relations are not taken into account; instead, simply their energy densities or their intensities are added. This simplified procedure is permissible if the different components are 'incoherent' with respect to each other, which is usually the case if the components have wide frequency spectra. Criteria for characterising the coherence of sound signals will be discussed in Chapters 7 and 8.

It is self-evident that geometrical room acoustics can reflect only a partial aspect of the acoustical phenomena occurring in a room. This aspect is, however, of great importance – especially of practical importance – and therefore we must deal with it in some detail.

4.1 Enclosures with plane walls, image sources

If a sound ray strikes a solid surface it is usually reflected from it. This process takes place according to the reflection law well known in optics. It states that the ray during reflection remains in the plane defined by the incident ray and the normal to the surface, and that the angle between the incident ray and reflected ray is halved by the normal to the wall. In vector notation, this law which is illustrated in Fig. 4.1 reads:

$$\mathbf{u}' = \mathbf{u} - 2(\mathbf{un}) \cdot \mathbf{n} \tag{4.1}$$

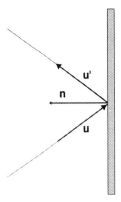

Figure 4.1 Illustration of vectors in eqn (4.1).

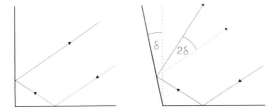

Figure 4.2 Reflection of a sound ray from a corner.

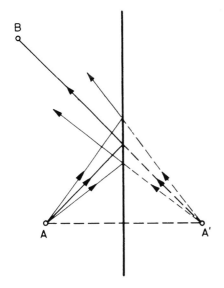

Figure 4.3 Construction of an image source.

Here **u** and **u'** are unit vectors pointing into the direction of the incident and the reflected sound ray, respectively, and **n** is the normal unit vector at the point where the arriving ray intersects the surface.

One simple consequence of this law is that any sound ray which undergoes a double reflection in an edge (corner) formed by two (three) perpendicular surfaces will travel back in the same direction as shown in Fig. 4.2a, no matter from which direction the incident ray arrives. If the angle of the edge deviates from a right angle by δ, the direction of the reflected ray will differ by 2δ from that of the incident ray (Fig. 4.2b).

In this and the next two sections the law of specular reflection will be applied to enclosures the boundaries of which are composed of plane and uniform walls. In this case one can benefit from the notion of image sources which greatly facilitates the construction of sound paths within the enclosure. This is explained in Fig. 4.3. Suppose there is a point source A in front of a plane wall or wall section. Then each ray reflected from this wall can be thought of as originating from a virtual sound source A′ which is located behind the wall, on the line perpendicular to the wall, and at the same distance from it as the original source A. Without the image source, the reflection path connecting the sound source A with a given point B could only be found by trial and error.

Once we have constructed the image source A′ associated with a given original source A, we can disregard the wall altogether, the effect of which is now replaced by that of the image source. Of course, we must assume that the image emits exactly the same sound signal as the original source and that its directional characteristics are symmetrical to those of A. If the extension of the reflecting wall is finite, then we must restrict the directions of emission of A′ accordingly or, put in a different way, for certain positions of the observation point B the image source may become 'invisible'. This is the case if the line connecting B with the image source does not intersect the actual wall.

Usually not all the energy striking a wall is reflected from it; part of the energy is absorbed by the wall (or it is transmitted to the other side, which amounts to the same thing as far as the reflected fraction is concerned). The fraction of sound energy (or intensity) which is not reflected is characterised by the absorption coefficient α of the wall, which has been defined in Section 2.2 as the ratio of the non-reflected to the incident intensity. It depends generally, as we have seen, on the angle of incidence and, of course, on the frequencies which are contained in the incident sound. Thus the reflected ray generally has a different power spectrum and a lower total intensity than the incident one. Using the picture of image sources, these circumstances can be taken into account by modifying the spectrum and the directional distribution of the sound emitted by A′. With such refinements, however, the usefulness of the concept of image sources is degraded considerably. So usually a mean value only of the absorption coefficient is accounted for by reducing the intensity of the reflected ray by a fraction $1 - \alpha$ of the primary intensity.

Suppose we follow a sound ray originating from a sound source on its way through a closed room. Then we find that it is reflected not once but many times from the walls, the ceiling and perhaps also from the floor. This succession of reflections continues until the ray arrives at a perfectly absorbent surface. But even if there is no perfectly absorbent area in our enclosure the energy carried by the ray will become vanishingly small after some time, because with each reflection a certain part of it is lost by absorption.

If the room is bounded by plane surfaces, a more complicated sound path can be constructed by extending the concept of image sources. This leads to images sources of higher order. They are obtained by applying the mirroring process to previously found images as is shown in Fig. 4.4. Suppose a sound ray emitted by the original source A hits a wall, from then on it will

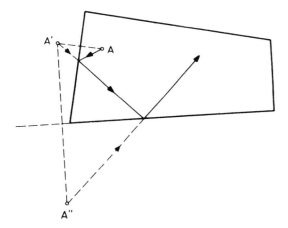

Figure 4.4 Image sources of first and second order.

proceed as if it were originating from the first-order image A′ until it reaches a second wall. The next section of the ray path is found by means of the second-order image A″ which is the mirror image of A′ with respect to that second wall. We continue in this way, obtaining more and more image sources as the total path length of the ray increases.

For a given enclosure and sound source position, the image sources can be constructed without referring to a particular sound path. Suppose the enclosure is made up of N-plane walls. Each wall is associated with one image of the original sound source. Now each of these image sources of first order is mirrored by each wall, which leads to $N(N-1)$ new images which are of second order. By repeating this procedure again and again a rapidly growing number of images is generated with increasing distances from the original source. The number of images of order i is $N(N-1)^{i-1}$ for $i \geq 1$; the total number of images of order up to i_0 is obtained by adding all these expressions:

$$N(i_0) = N\frac{(N-1)^{i_0} - 1}{N - 2} \tag{4.2}$$

It is obvious that the number of image sources grows rapidly with increasing i_0. For enclosures with high symmetry (*see* Fig. 4.6, for instance) many of the higher order images coincide. It shoud be noted, however, that each image source has its own directivity since it 'illuminates' only a limited solid angle, determined by the limited extension of the walls. Hence it may well happen that a particular image source is 'invisible' or rather 'inaudible' from a given receiving location. This problem has been carefully discussed by Borish.[1] More will be said about this subject in Section 9.6.

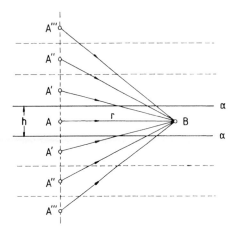

Figure 4.5 System of image sources of an infinite flat room: A is the original sound source; A', A'', etc., are image sources; B is the receiving point.

These complications are not encountered with enclosures of high regularity, which in turn produce regular patterns of image sources. As a simple example, which also may illustrate the usefulness of the image model, let us consider a very flat room, the height of which is small compared with its lateral dimensions. Since most points in this enclosure are far from the side walls, the effect of the latter may be totally neglected. Then we arrive at a space which is bounded by two parallel, infinite planes. We assume a sound source A and an observation point B in the middle between both planes, radiating constant power P uniformly in all directions. The corresponding image sources (and image spaces) are depicted in Fig. 4.5. The source images form a simple pattern of equidistant points situated on a straight line, and each of them is a valid one, i.e. it is 'visible' from any observation point B. Its distance from an image of nth order is $(r^2 + n^2 h^2)^{1/2}$, if r denotes the horizontal distance of B from the original source A and h is the 'height' of the room. If we furthermore assume, for the sake of simplicity, that both planes have the same absorption coefficient α independent of the angle of sound incidence, the total energy density in B is given by the following expression:

$$w = \frac{P}{4\pi c} \sum_{n=-\infty}^{\infty} \frac{(1-\alpha)^{|n|}}{r^2 + n^2 h^2} \tag{4.3}$$

which can easily be evaluated with a programmable pocket calculator. A graphical representation of this formula will be found in Section 9.4.

Another example is obtained by dropping the assumption of very large lateral dimensions. Then we have to take the side walls into account, which we assume to be perpendicular to the floor and the ceiling, and also to each

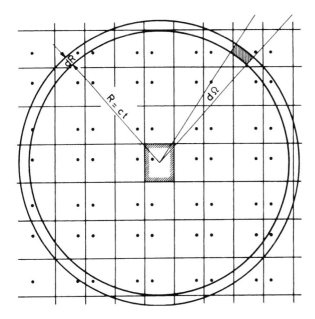

Figure 4.6 Image sound sources of a rectangular room. The pattern continues in an analogous manner in the direction perpendicular to the drawing plane.

other. The resulting enclosure is a rectangular room, as depicted in Fig. 3.1. For this room shape certain image sources of the same order are complementary with respect to their directivity and coincide. The result is the regular pattern of image rooms as shown in Fig. 4.6, each of them containing exactly one image source. So the four image rooms adjacent to the sides of the original rectangle contain one first-order image each, whereas those adjacent to its corners contain second-order images and so on. The lattice depicted in Fig. 4.6 has to be completed in the third dimension, i.e. we must imagine an infinite number of such patterns one upon the other at equal distances, one of them containing the original room.

In both examples, all image sources are valid ones. This is because the totality of image rooms, each of them containing one source image, fills the whole space without leaving uncovered regions and without any overlap. Enclosures of less regular shape would produce much more irregular patterns of image sources, and their image spaces would overlap each other in an almost unpredictable way. In these cases the validity or invalidity of each image source with respect to a given receiving point must be carefully examined.

When all image sources have been detected, the original room is no longer needed. The sound signal received in a given point is then obtained as the superposition of the contributions of all significant image sources

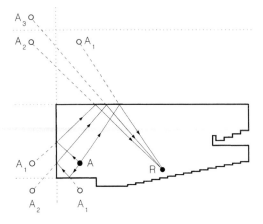

Figure 4.7 Longitudinal section of an auditorium with image sources: A = sound source; A_1 = first-order image sources; A_2 = second-order image sources etc.

under the assumption that all sources including the original one simultaneously emit the same sound signal. Because of the different travelling distances, the waves (or rays) originating from these sources arrive at the receiving point with different delays and strengths as illustrated in Fig. 4.7. To obtain the signal at the receiving point one has just to add the sound pressures of all contributions. The strength of a particular contribution must also include the absorptivity of the walls which are crossed by the straight line connecting the image source with the receiving point.

If the absorption coefficients of all walls are frequency independent, the received signal $s'(t)$ is the superposition of infinitely many replicas of the original signal, each of them with its particular strength A_n and delayed by its particular travelling time t_n:

$$s'(t) = \sum_n A_n s(t - t_n)$$

Accordingly, the impulse response of the room reads in our simplified picture:

$$g(t) = \sum_n A_n \delta(t - t_n) \tag{4.4}$$

In reality, an incident Dirac impulse is deformed when it is reflected from a wall, i.e. the reflected signal is not the exact replica of the original impulse but is transformed into a somewhat different signal $r(t)$. This signal is by definition the 'reflection response' of the surface, and its Fourier transform is the reflection factor R as introduced in Section 2.1.

Under certain conditions the addition of sound pressures can be replaced by the addition of intensities. Suppose we have to add two sinusoidal signals of equal angular frequency ω with amplitudes $\hat{p}_1$ and $\hat{p}_2$ and delays t_1 and t_2:

$$p(t) = \hat{p}_1 \cos\left[\omega(t - t_1)\right] + \hat{p}_2 \cos\left[\omega(t - t_2)\right]$$

To obtain the resulting the intensity or energy density one has to square this expression. This produces – apart from the squared first and second term – a mixed term which describes the interference between both signals:

$$2\hat{p}_1\hat{p}_2 \cos\left[\omega(t - t_1)\right] \cos\left[\omega(t - t_2)\right] = \hat{p}_1\hat{p}_2\{\cos\left[\omega(t_1 - t_2)\right]$$
$$+ \cos\left[\omega(2t - t_1 - t_2)\right]\}$$

For signals the spectrum of which covers the wide frequency band typical of many sounds the squared sound pressure can be averaged over ω. By means of this operation the mixed term in the above expression vanishes provided the frequency bandwidth of the signal is large compared with $|t_1 - t_2|^{-1}$ while averaging the $\cos^2$ terms results in $\hat{p}_1^2/2$ and $\hat{p}_2^2/2$. Since the energy density w is proportional to the squared sound pressure, the total energy density is just the sum of both contributions:

$$w = w_1 + w_2$$

Sound signals with this property are called 'incoherent' or 'mutually incoherent'. In deriving eqn (4.3) it was tacitly assumed that the contributions of all image sources are mutually incoherent.

4.2 The temporal distribution of reflections

For the present discussion it is sufficient to assume frequency-independent reflection factors for all walls. Hence the simplified impulse response as expressed by eqn (4.4) will be considered in the following.

If we mark the arrival times of the various reflections by perpendicular dashes over a horizontal time axis and choose the heights of the dashes proportional to the relative strengths of reflections, i.e. to the coefficients A_n, we obtain what is frequently called a 'reflection diagram' or 'echogram'. It contains all significant information on the temporal structure of the sound field at a certain room point. In Fig. 4.8 a schematical reflection diagram is plotted. After the direct sound, arriving at $t = 0$, the first strong reflections occur at first sporadically, later their temporal density increases rapidly, however; at the same time the reflections carry less and less energy. As we shall see later in more detail, the role of the first isolated reflections with respect to our subjective hearing impression is quite different from that of the very numerous weak reflections arriving at later times, which merge

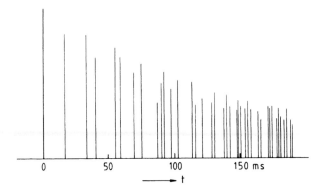

Figure 4.8 Schematic reflection diagram. The abscissa is the delay time of a reflection, and the ordinate is its level, both with respect to the direct sound arriving at $t = 0$.

into what we perceive subjectively as reverberation. Thus we can consider the reverberation of a room not only as the common effect of free decaying vibrational modes, as we did in Chapter 3, but also as the sum total of all reflections – except the very first ones.

A survey on the temporal structure of reflections and hence of the law of reverberation in a rectangular room can easily be obtained by using the system of image rooms and image sound sources (*see* Fig. 4.6). We suppose for this purpose that at some time $t = 0$ all mirror sources generate impulses of equal strengths. In the time interval from t to $t + \mathrm{d}t$, all those reflections will arrive in the centre of the original room which originate from image sources whose distances to the centre are between ct and $c(t + \mathrm{d}t)$. These sources are located in a spherical shell with radius ct. The thickness of this shell (which is supposed to be very small as compared with ct) is $c\,\mathrm{d}t$ and its volume is $4\pi c^3 t^2\,\mathrm{d}t$. In this shell volume, the volume V of an image room is contained $4\pi c^3 t^2\,\mathrm{d}t/V$ times; this figure is also the number of mirror sources contained in the shell volume. Therefore the average temporal density of the reflections arriving at time t is

$$\frac{\mathrm{d}N_r}{\mathrm{d}t} = 4\pi\frac{c^3 t^2}{V} \tag{4.5}$$

The mean density of sound reflections increases according to a quadratic law with respect to time.

It is interesting to note, by the way, that the above approach is the same as we applied to estimate the mean density of eigenfrequencies in a rectangular room (eqn (3.21)) with about the same result. In fact, the pattern of mirror sources and the eigenfrequency lattice are closely related to each other. Moreover, it can be shown that eqn (4.5) does not only apply to rectangular rooms but to rooms with arbitrary shape as well.

Each reflection – considered physically – corresponds to a narrow bundle of rays originating from the respective image source in which the sound intensity decreases proportionally as $(ct)^{-2}$, i.e. as the square of the reciprocal distance covered by the rays. Furthermore, the rays are attenuated by absorption in the medium and by incomplete reflections which correspond in the picture to the crossing of image walls. The former effect can be taken into account by the attenuation constant m as introduced in Section 1.2. According to eqn (1.16a) the factor $\exp(-mx/2)$ describes the decrement of the pressure amplitude when a plane wave travels a distance x in a lossy medium, hence its intensity is reduced by a factor $\exp(-mx) = \exp(-mct)$. Furthermore, the intensity of a ray bundle will be reduced by a factor $1 - \alpha$ whenever it crosses a wall of an image room; if this happens n-times per second, the energy or intensity of the ray bundle after some time t will have become smaller by $(1 - \alpha)^{nt} = \exp[nt\ln(1 - \alpha)]$. Therefore, the reflections arriving at time t at some observation point in the original room have an average intensity

$$\frac{A}{(ct)^2} \exp\{[-mc + n\ln(1 - \alpha)]t\}$$

A being a constant factor. Therefore the whole energy of all reflections at the point of observation (the exact location of which is of minor importance) as a function of time is

$$E(t) = E_0 \exp\{[-mc + n\ln(1 - \alpha)]t\} \quad \text{for } t \geq 0 \tag{4.6}$$

Now we must calculate the average number of wall reflections or wall crossings per second. For this purpose, as in Section 3.2, the dimensions of the rectangular room are denoted by L_x, L_y, L_z. A sound ray whose angle with respect to the x-axis is β_x will cross n_x mirror walls per second perpendicular to the x-axis where (*see* Fig. 4.9)

$$n_x(\beta_x) = \left| \frac{c}{L_x} \cos\beta_x \right| \tag{4.7}$$

Similar expressions hold for the average crossings of walls perpendicular to the y-axis and the z-axis. Hence, the total number of wall crossings, i.e. of reflections which a ray with given direction undergoes per second is

$$n(\beta_x, \beta_y, \beta_z) = n_x + n_y + n_z$$

with $\cos^2\beta_x + \cos^2\beta_y + \cos^2\beta_z = 1$. This would mean that each sound ray decays at its own decay rate.

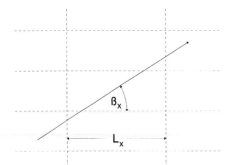

Figure 4.9 Wall crossings of a sound ray in a rectangular room and its mirror images.

One might be tempted to average $n(\beta_x, \beta_y, \beta_z)$ over all directions in order to arrive at a figure which is representative for the whole energy content of the room. This is only permissible, however, if the sound rays and the energy they transport change their direction once in a while.[2] This will never happen in a rectangular room with smooth walls. But enclosures of more irregular shape or with diffusely reflecting walls (*see* Section 2.6) do have the tendency to mix the directions of sound propagation. This tendency is supported by sound diffraction by obstacles within the enclosure. In the ideal case, such randomising effects could eventually result in what is called a 'diffuse sound field' in which the propagation of sound is completely isotropic.

Under this condition eqn (4.7) may be averaged over all directions:

$$\frac{c}{L_x}\langle|\cos \beta_x|\rangle = \frac{c}{L_x}\frac{1}{4\pi}2\pi 2\int_0^{\pi/2} \cos \beta_x \sin \beta_x \, d\beta_x = \frac{c}{2L_x}$$

The same average is found for n_y and n_z. Hence the total average of reflections per second is

$$\bar{n} = \frac{c}{2}\left(\frac{1}{L_x} + \frac{1}{L_y} + \frac{1}{L_z}\right) = \frac{cS}{4V} \tag{4.8}$$

Here S is the total wall area of the original room. By inserting this result into eqn (4.6) we arrive at a fairly general law of sound decay:

$$E(t) = E_0 \exp\left[-ct\frac{4mV - S\ln(1 - \alpha)}{4V}\right] \quad \text{for } t \geq 0 \tag{4.9}$$

The reverberation time, i.e. the time in which the total energy falls to one millionth of its initial value, is thus

$$T = \frac{1}{c} \frac{24V \ln 10}{4mV - S \ln(1 - \alpha)} \tag{4.10}$$

or, if we insert the numerical value of the sound velocity in air and express the volume V in m^3 and the wall area S in m^2,

$$T = 0.163 \frac{V}{4mV - S \ln(1 - \alpha)} \tag{4.11}$$

In the preceding, we have derived by rather simple geometric considerations the most important formula of room acoustics which relates the reverberation time, i.e. the most characteristic figure with respect to the acoustics of a room, to its geometrical data and to the absorption coefficient of its walls. We have assumed tacitly that the latter is the same for all wall portions and that it does not depend on the angle at which a wall is struck by the sound rays. In the next chapter we shall look more closely into the laws of reverberation by applying somewhat more refined methods, but the result will be essentially the same.

The exponential law of eqn (4.9) represents an approximate description of the temporal change of the energy carried by the reflections, neglecting many details which may be of great importance for the acoustics of a room. In practical cases the actual decrease of reflected energy succeeding an impulsive sound signal always exhibits greater or lesser pronounced deviations from this ideal law. Sometimes such deviations may be heard subjectively in a very unpleasant way and spoil the acoustical quality of a room. So it may happen, for instance, that a reflection arriving at a relatively large time delay carries far more energy than its contemporaries and stands out of the general reverberation. This can occur when the sound rays of which it is made up have undergone a reflection from a remote concave portion of wall. Such an outstanding component is perceived as a distinct echo and is particularly disturbing if the portion of wall which is responsible is irradiated by a loudspeaker. Another unfavourable condition is that of many reflections clustered together in a narrow time interval. Since our hearing has a limited time resolution and therefore performs some sort of short-time integration, this lack of uniformity may be audible and may exhibit undesirable effects which are similar to a single reflection of exceptional strength.

Particularly disturbing are reflections which form a periodic or a nearly periodic succession. This is true even if this periodicity is hidden in a great number of reflections distributed irregularly over the time axis, since our hearing is very sensitive to periodic repetitions of certain sound signals. For short periods, i.e. for repetition times of a few milliseconds, such periodic components are perceived as a 'colouration' of the reverberation; then the decay has a characteristic pitch and timbre. Hence speech or music in such a room will have its spectra changed. If the periods are longer, if they amount to 30, 50 or even 100 ms, the regular temporal structure itself becomes audible. This case, which is frequently referred to as 'flutter echo', occurs if sound is reflected repeatedly to and fro between parallel walls. Flutter echoes can be observed quite distinctly in corridors or other longish rooms where the end walls are rigid but the ceiling, floor and side walls are absorbent. They can also occur in rooms the shapes of which are less extreme, but then their audibility is mostly restricted to particular locations of source and observer.

4.3 The directional distribution of reflections, diffusion

We shall now take into consideration the third property which character-ises a reflection, namely the direction from which it reaches an observer. As before, we shall not attribute to each single reflection its proper direction, but we shall apply a summarising method, which commends itself not only because of the great number of reflections making up the resulting sound field in a room but also because we are usually not able to locate subject-ively the directions from which reflected and hence delayed components reach our ears. Nevertheless, whether the reflected components arrive uni-formly from all directions or whether they all come from one single direc-tion has considerable bearing on the acoustical properties of a room. The directional distribution of sound is also important for certain measuring techniques.

Consider a short time interval dt (in the vicinity of time t) on the time axis of a reflection diagram or echogram. As before, let the origin of the time axis be the moment at which the direct sound arrives. Furthermore, define some polar angle ϑ and azimuth angle φ as the quantities which characterise certain directions. Around a certain direction, imagine a 'direc-tional cone' with a small aperture, i.e. solid angle $d\Omega$. The total energy contributed by reflections arriving in dt from the solid angle element $d\Omega$ is denoted by

$$d^3E = E_t(\varphi, \vartheta) \, dt \, d\Omega \qquad (4.12)$$

$E_t(\varphi, \vartheta)$ is the time-dependent directional distribution of the reflection energy or reverberation energy.

If we integrate eqn (4.12) over all directions, we obtain the time distribu-tion of the reflected sound energy discussed in the preceding section:

$$E(t) = \iint E_t(\varphi, \vartheta) \, d\Omega \qquad (4.13)$$

If we integrate, however, eqn (4.12) over all times from zero to infinity, we obtain the steady state directional distribution:

$$I(\varphi, \vartheta) = \int_0^\infty E_t(\varphi, \vartheta)\, dt \qquad (4.14)$$

This can be determined experimentally by exciting the room with a stationary sound signal and by measuring the sound components arriving from the various directions by the use of a directional microphone. The result, however, is always modified to some extent by the limited directional resolution of the microphone.

The difference between the time-dependent and the steady state directional distribution can be illustrated by invoking the system of image sound sources shown in Fig 4.6. For the energy arriving at time t from the solid angle element $d\Omega$ those image sources are responsible which are located in the area common to the cone $d\Omega$ and to the circular belt (in the cross-section shown) of width $c\, dt$ and radius ct; the stationary energy incident from the same solid angle element is due to all image sources in the whole cone.

If the directional distribution does not depend in any way on the angles φ and ϑ, the stationary sound field is called 'diffuse'. If in addition to this condition $E_t(\varphi, \vartheta)$ is independent of the angles φ and ϑ for all t, the decaying sound field is also diffuse for all t.

In a certain sense the diffuse sound field is the counterpart of a plane wave. Just as certain properties can be attributed to plane waves, so relationships describing the properties of diffuse sound can be established. Some of these have already been encountered in Chapter 2. They are of particular interest to the whole of room acoustics, since, although the sound field in a concert hall or theatre is not completely diffuse, its directional structure resembles much more that of a diffuse field than that of a plane wave. Or, put in another way, the sound field in an actual room, which always contains some irregularities in shape, can be approximated fairly well by a sound field with uniform directional distribution on account of its great complexity. In contrast to this, a single plane wave is hardly ever encountered in a real situation.

The directional distribution in a rectangular room can be discussed again – at least qualitatively – by the use of Fig. 4.6. The cross-hatched region, which of course must be imagined as continued into the third dimension, has the volume $c^3t^2\, dt\, d\Omega$. If V again denotes the volume of the original room, the region referred to contains on the average $c^3t^2\, dt\, d\Omega/V$ image sources, their number thus being independent of the direction. If there is no absorption by the walls, the sound components reaching the centre of the original room are not subject to any directionally dependent attenuation; the time-dependent as well as the stationary directional distribution is therefore uniform.

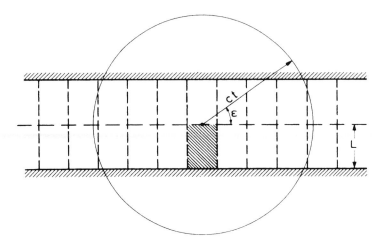

Figure 4.10 System of image rooms for a rectangular room, one side of which is perfectly sound absorbing. The original room is cross-hatched.

Matters are not the same if the walls have an absorption coefficient different from zero. In this case there are directions from which the strength of arriving reflections is particularly reduced, since the mirror sources in these directions are predominantly of higher order. It is only in the directions of the axes that the image sources of first order are received, i.e. components which have undergone one reflection only from a wall. The resulting sound field is therefore by no means diffuse. This means that the averaging which we have performed to obtain eqn (4.8) is not, strictly speaking, permissible in this form and ought to be replaced by some weighted average which would yield a result different from eqn (4.9).

A somewhat extreme example of a room with non-diffuse conditions is presented by a strictly rectangular room, whose walls are perfectly rigid except for one which absorbs the incident sound energy completely. Its behaviour with respect to the formation and distribution of reflections is elucidated by the image room system depicted in Fig. 4.10, consisting of only two 'stores' since the absorbing wall generates no images of the room and the sound source. In the lateral directions, however (and perpendicular to the plane of the figure), the system is extended infinitely.

We denote the distance between the absorbing wall and the wall opposite to it by L and the elevation angle by ε, measured from the point of observation which may be located in the centre of the reflecting ceiling for the sake of simplicity. The time-dependent directional distribution is then given by

$$E_t(\varphi, \varepsilon) = \begin{cases} \text{const} & \text{for } |\varepsilon| \le \varepsilon_0 \\ 0 & \text{for } |\varepsilon| > \varepsilon_0 \end{cases} \qquad (4.15)$$

where

$$\varepsilon_0(t) = \arcsin\left(\frac{L}{ct}\right) \quad \text{for } t \geq \frac{L}{c}$$

The range of elevation angle subtended by the image sources contracts more and more with increasing time. With the presently used meaning of the angle ε, the element of solid angle becomes $\cos \varepsilon \, d\varepsilon \, d\varphi$; hence the integration indicated by eqn (4.13) yields the following expression for the sound decay:

$$E(t) \approx 2 \int_0^{2\pi} d\varphi \int_0^{\varepsilon_0} E_t(\varphi, \varepsilon) \cos \varepsilon \, d\varepsilon = \text{const } \frac{4\pi L}{ct} \quad \text{for } t \geq \frac{L}{c} \qquad (4.16)$$

As a consequence of the non-uniform distribution of the wall absorption the decay of the reverberant energy does not follow an exponential law but is inversely proportional to the time. The steady state directional distribution is given by

$$I(\varepsilon) \approx \frac{\text{const}}{|\sin \varepsilon|} \qquad (4.17)$$

4.4 Enclosures with curved walls

In this section we consider enclosures the boundaries of which contain curved walls or wall sections. Practical examples are domed ceilings as are encountered in many theatres or other performance halls, or the curved rear walls of many lecture theatres. Concavely curved surfaces in rooms are generally considered as critical or even dangerous in that they have the tendency to impede the uniform distribution of sound energy in a room or to concentrate it to certain spots.

Formally, the law of specular reflection as expressed by eqn (4.1) is valid for curved surfaces as well as for plane ones, since each curved surface can be approximated by many small plane sections. Keeping in mind the wave nature of sound, however, one should not apply this law to a surface the radius of curvature of which is not very large compared to the acoustical wavelength. Whenever the radius of curvature is comparable or even smaller than the wavelength the surface will scatter an impinging sound wave rather than reflect it specularly, as described in Section 2.6.

Very often, curved walls in rooms or halls are spherical or cylindrical segments, or they can be approximated by such surfaces. Then we can apply the laws of rays reflected at a concave or convex mirror, known from optics. It should be kept in mind that the direction of the ray paths can be inverted.

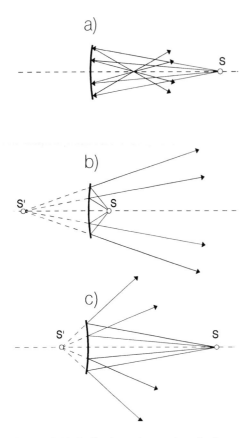

Figure 4.11 Reflection of a ray bundle from concave and convex mirrors.

In Fig. 4.11a the section of a concave, spherical or cylindrical mirror with radius R is depicted. A bundle of rays originating from a point S is reflected at the mirror and is focused into the point P from which it diverges. Focusing of this kind occurs when the distance of the source from the mirror is larger than $R/2$; if the incident bundle is parallel the focus is at distance $R/2$. The source distance a, the distance of the focus b and the radius of the mirror are approximately related by

$$\frac{1}{a} + \frac{1}{b} = \frac{2}{R}$$

(4.18)

If the source is closer to the mirror than $R/2$ (*see* Fig. 4.11b), the reflected ray bundle is divergent (although less divergent than the incident one) and seems to originate from a point beyond the mirror. Equation (4.18) is still valid and leads to a negative value of b.

Finally, we consider the reflection at a convex mirror as depicted in Fig. 4.11c. In this case the divergence of any incident ray bundle is increased by the mirror. Again, eqn (4.18) can be applied to find the position of the 'virtual' focus after replacing R with $-R$. As before, the distance b is negative.

The effect of curved surfaces can be studied more quantitatively comparing the intensity of the reflected ray bundle with that of a bundle reflected at a plane mirror. The latter is given by

$$I_0 = \frac{A}{|a + x|^n}$$

while the intensity of the bundle reflected at a curved mirror is

$$I_r = \frac{B}{|b - x|^n}$$

In both formulae A and B are constants; x is the distance from the centre of the mirror, and the exponent n is 1 for a cylindrical mirror and equals 2 for a spherical one. (It should be kept in mind that the distance b has a negative sign for concave mirrors with $a < R/2$ and for convex mirrors.) At $x = 0$ both intensities must be equal which yields $A/B = |a/b|^n$. Thus the ratio of both intensities is

$$\frac{I_r}{I_0} = \left| \frac{1 + x/a}{1 - x/b} \right|^n \tag{4.19}$$

Figure 4.12 plots the level $L_r = 10 \log_{10}(I_r/I_0)$ derived from this ratio for the cases depicted in Fig. 4.11 with $n = 2$ (spherical mirror). The concentration

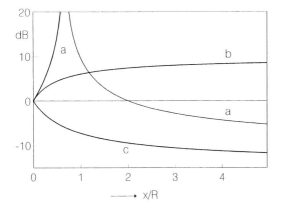

Figure 4.12 Level difference in ray bundles reflected from a curved and a plane reflector, at distance x from the reflector: (a) concave mirror, $a = 2R$; (b) concave mirror, $a = R/3$; (c) convex mirror, $a = 2R$.

occurring for $a > R/2$ (curve a) is clearly seen as a pole. Apart from this, there is a range of increased intensity in which $L_r > 0$. From eqns (4.18) and (4.19) it can be concluded that this range is given by

$$x < 2\left(\frac{1}{b} - \frac{1}{a}\right)^{-1} = \left(\frac{1}{R} - \frac{1}{a}\right)^{-1} \tag{4.20}$$

Outside that range, the level L_r is negative indicating that the reflected bundle is more divergent than it would be when reflected from a plane mirror. If $a < R/2$ (curve b), the intensity is increased at all distances x. Finally, the convex mirror (curve c) reduces the intensity of the bundle everywhere. According to eqn (4.19) the limit of L_r for very large distances is

$$L_r \rightarrow 10 \log_{10}\left|\frac{b}{a}\right|^n \quad \text{for} \quad x \rightarrow \infty \tag{4.21}$$

From these findings a few practical conclusions may be drawn. A concave mirror may concentrate the impinging sound energy in certain regions, but it may also be an effective scatterer which distributes the energy over a wide angular range. Whether the one or the other effect dominates depends on the positions of the source and the observer. Generally, the following rule[3] can be derived from eqn (4.20). Suppose the mirror in Fig. 4.11 is completed to a full circle with radius R. Then, if both the sound source and the receiver are outside this volume, the undesirable effects mentioned at the beginning of this section are not to be expected.

The laws outlined above are valid only for narrow ray bundles, i.e. as long as the inclination of the rays against the axis is sufficiently small, or, what amounts to the same thing, as long as the aperture of the mirror is not too large. Whenever this condition is not met, the construction of reflected rays becomes more difficult. Either the surface has to be approximated piecemeal by circular or spherical sections, or the reflected bundle must be constructed ray by ray. As an example, the reflection of a parallel bundle of rays from a concave mirror of large aperture is shown in Fig. 4.13. Obviously, the reflected rays are not collected within one point, instead, they form an envelope which is known as a caustic. Next to the axis, the caustic reaches the focal point in the distance $b = R/2$ in accordance with eqn (4.18) with $a \rightarrow \infty$. A concave surface in which sound concentration in exactly one point can occur even if the aperture is large is the ellipse or the ellisoid, which, by definition, has two foci as shown in Fig. 4.14. If a sound source S is placed in one of them, all the rays emitted by it are collected in the other one. For this reason, enclosures with elliptical floor plan are plagued by quite unequal sound distribution even if neither the sound source nor the listener are in a geometrical focus. The same holds, of course, for halls with circular floor plan since the circle is a limiting case of the ellipse.

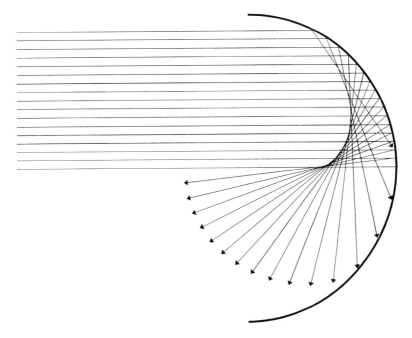

Figure 4.13 Reflection of a parallel ray bundle from a spherical concave mirror of large aperture.

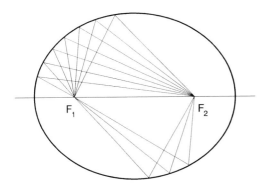

Figure 4.14 Collection of sound rays in an elliptical enclosure.

A striking experience can be made in halls of this shape if a speaker is close to its wall. A listener who is also next to the wall although distant from the sound source (*see* Fig. 4.15) can hear the speaker quite clearly even if the latter speaks in a very low voice or whispers. The enclosure is said to form a 'whispering gallery' in this case. The explanation for this phenomenon is simple. If the speaker's head is more or less parallel to the wall,

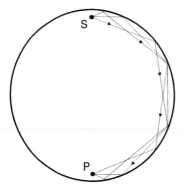

Figure 4.15 Whispering gallery.

most of the sound rays hit the wall at grazing incidence and are repeatedly reflected from it. If the wall is smooth and uninterrupted by pillars, niches, etc., the rays remain confined within an annular region; in other words: the wall conducts the sound along its perimeter. One of the most famous examples of a whispering gallery is in St. Paul's Cathedral in London which has a narrow annular platform above the floor which is open to visitors. Generally, a whispering gallery is an interesting curiosity, but if the hall is used for performances, the acoustical effects caused by it are rather disturbing.

4.5 Enclosures with diffusely reflecting walls

In Section 2.6 walls with diffuse reflection brought about by surface irregularities, rapidly changing wall impedence, etc., have been discussed. Enclosures the boundaries of which have this property at least in parts are quite different in their acoustical behaviour from those with specularly reflecting walls. Generally, diffuse wall reflections result in a more uniform distribution of the sound energy throughout the room.

The reflection from a surface is said to take place in a totally diffuse manner if the directional distribution of the reflected or the scattered energy does not depend in any way on the direction of the incident sound. This case can be realised physically quite well in optics. In contrast, in acoustics and particularly in room acoustics, only partially diffuse reflections can be achieved. But nevertheless the assumption of totally diffuse reflections comes often closer to the actual reflecting properties of real walls than that of specular reflection, particularly if we are concerned not only with one but instead with many successive ray reflections from different walls or portions of walls. This is the case with reverberation processes and in reverberant enclosures.

Totally diffuse reflections from a wall take place according to Lambert's cosine law: suppose an area element dS is 'illuminated' by a bundle of

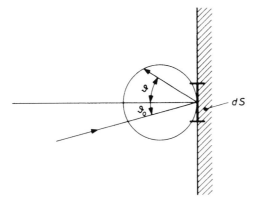

Figure 4.16 Ideally diffuse sound reflection from an acoustically rough surface.

parallel or nearly parallel rays which make an angle ϑ_0 to the wall normal, whose intensity is I_0. Then the intensity of the sound which is scattered in a direction characterised by an angle ϑ, measured at a distance r from dS, is given by

$$I(r) = I_0 \, dS \frac{\cos \vartheta \cos \vartheta_0}{\pi r^2} = B_0 \, dS \frac{\cos \vartheta}{\pi r^2} \tag{4.22}$$

B_0 being the so-called 'irradiation strength', i.e. the energy incident on unit area of the wall per second. This formula holds provided that there is no absorption, i.e. the incident energy is re-emitted completely. If this is not the case, $I(r, \vartheta)$ has to be multiplied by an appropriate factor $1 - \alpha(\vartheta)$. Figure 4.16 shows the wall element dS and a circle representing the directional distribution of the scattered sound; the length of the arrow pointing to its periphery is proportional to $\cos \vartheta$.

According to eqn (4.22), each surface element has to be considered as a secondary sound source, which is expressed by the fact that the distance r, which determines the intensity reduction due to propagation, must be measured from the reflecting area element dS. This is not so with specular reflection: here the geometrical intensity decrease of a sound ray originating from a certain point is determined by the total length of the path between the sound source and the point of observation with no regard as to whether this path is bent or straight.

In the following we assume that the whole boundary of the considered enclosure reflects the impinging sound in a completely diffuse manner. This assumption enables us to describe the sound field within the room in a closed form, namely by an integral equation. To derive it, we start by considering two wall elements, dS and dS', of a room of arbitrary shape

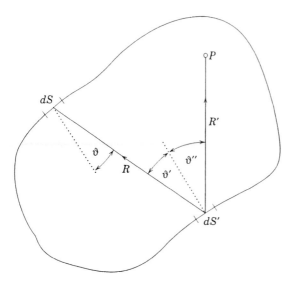

Figure 4.17 Illustration of eqn (4.24).

(*see* Fig. 4.17). Their locations are characterised by the vectors **r** and **r'**, respectively, each of them standing for a trio of suitable coordinates. The straight line connecting them has the length R, and the angles between this line and the wall normals in dS and dS' are denoted by ϑ and ϑ'.

Suppose the element dS' is irradiated by the energy $B(\mathbf{r'})$ dS' per second, where B is the 'irradiation strength'. The fraction ρ of it will be re-radiated from dS' into the space, where the 'reflection coefficient'

$$\rho = 1 - \alpha$$

To avoid unnecessary complication we assume that the absorption coefficient α and hence ρ is independent of the angles ϑ and ϑ'.

According to Lambert's law of diffuse reflection as formulated in eqn (4.22), the intensity of the energy re-radiated by dS' and received at dS is

$$dI = B(\mathbf{r'})\rho(\mathbf{r'}) \frac{\cos \vartheta'}{\pi R^2} \, dS' \tag{4.23}$$

The total energy per second and unit area received at **r** from the whole boundary is obtained by multiplying this equation by $\cos \vartheta$ and integrating it over all wall elements dS'. If the direct contribution B_d from some sound source is added, the following relation is obtained:[4,5]

$$B(\mathbf{r}, t) = \frac{1}{\pi} \iint_S \rho(\mathbf{r'}) B\left(\mathbf{r'}, t - \frac{R}{c}\right) \frac{\cos \vartheta \cos \vartheta'}{R^2} \, dS' + B_d(\mathbf{r}, t) \tag{4.24}$$

It takes regard of the finite travelling time of sound energy from the transmitting wall element dS' to the receiving one dS by replacing the argument t with $t - R/c$.

Equation (4.24) is an inhomogeneous integral equation for the irradiation strength B of the wall. It is fairly general in that it contains both the steady state case (for B_d and B independent of time t) and that of a decaying sound field (for $B_d = 0$). Once it is solved, the energy density at any point P inside the room can be obtained from

$$w(\mathbf{r}, t) = \frac{1}{\pi c} \iint_S \rho(\mathbf{r}')B\left(\mathbf{r}', t - \frac{R'}{c}\right) \frac{\cos \vartheta''}{R'^2} \, dS' + w_d(\mathbf{r}, t) \tag{4.25}$$

R' is the distance of the inner point from the element dS' while ϑ'' – as before – denotes the angle between the wall normal in dS' and the line connecting dS' with the receiving point.

Generally, the integral equation (4.24) must be numerically solved. Closed solutions are available for a few simple room shapes only. One of them is the spherical enclosure, for which

$$\frac{\cos \vartheta \cos \vartheta'}{\pi R^2} = \frac{1}{S}$$

with S denoting the surface of the sphere. Then the above integral equation reads simply

$$B = \langle \rho B \rangle + B_d$$

where the brackets indicate averaging over the whole surface. From this the following steady state solution is easily obtained

$$B = \frac{\langle \rho B_d \rangle}{1 - \langle \rho \rangle} + B_d \tag{4.26}$$

Of more practical interest is the flat room as already mentioned in Section 4.1. It consists of two parallel walls (ceiling and floor); in lateral directions it is unbounded. Many shallow factory halls or open plan bureaus may be treated as such a flat room as long as neither the sound source nor the observation point are close to one its side walls. As in Section 4.1 (*see* Fig. 4.5) we assume that both walls have the same, constant absorption coefficient α or 'reflection coefficient' $\rho = 1 - \alpha$ and that the sound source is in the middle between both planes. The steady state solution of eqn (4.26) for this situation is[6]

$$w(r) = \frac{P}{4\pi c} \left(\frac{1}{r^2} + \frac{4\rho}{h^2} \int_0^\infty \frac{e^{-z} J_0(rz/h)z \, dz}{1 - \rho z K_1(z)} \right) \tag{4.27}$$

In this expression, J_0 is the Bessel function of order zero, and K_1 is a modified Bessel function of first order (*see* Ref. 7). Here r is the horizontal distance from a point source with the power output P.

This equation is certainly too complicated for practical applications. However, it can be approximated by a simpler formula which will be presented in Section 9.4 along with a diagram explaining its content.

References

1 Borish, S., *J. Acoust. Soc. America*, **75** (1985) 1827.
2 Cremer, H. and Cremer, L., *Akust. Zeitschr.*, **2** (1937) 225.
3 Cremer, L. and Müller, H.A., *Principles and Applications of Room Acoustics*, Vol. 1. Applied Science, London, 1982.
4 Kuttruff, H., *Acustica*, **25** (1971) 333; *ibid.*, **35** (1976) 141.
5 Joyce, W.B., *J. Acoust. Soc. America*, **64** (1978) 1429; *ibid.*, **65** (1979) 51(A).
6 Kuttruff, H., *Acustica*, **57** (1985) 62.
7 Abramowitz, M. and Stegun, I.A., *Handbook of Mathematical Functions*, Dover, New York, 1965.

5 Reverberation and steady state energy density

Reverberation is a phenomenon which plays a major role in every aspect of room acoustics and which as yet yields the least controversial criterion for the judgement of the acoustical qualities of every kind of room. It is this fact which justifies devoting the major part of a chapter to reverberation and to the laws which govern it. Another important subject to be dealt with in this chapter is the diffuse sound field. Both reverberation and diffusion are closely related to each other: the laws of reverberation can be formulated in a simple way only for sound fields where all directions of sound propagation contribute equal sound intensities, not only in steady state conditions but at each moment in decaying sound fields, at least in the average over time intervals which are short compared with the duration of the whole decaying process. Likewise, simple relationships for the steady state energy density in a room as will be derived in Section 5.5 are also based on the assumption of a diffuse field. It is clear that in practical situations these stringent conditions are met only approximately. A completely diffuse sound field can be realised fairly well in certain types of measuring rooms, such as reverberation chambers. But in other rooms, too, the approximation of the actual sound fields by diffuse ones is not too crude an approach. In most instances in this chapter we shall therefore assume complete uniformity of sound field with respect to directional distribution.

In Chapter 3 we regarded reverberation as the common decaying of free vibrational modes. In Chapter 4, however, reverberation was understood to be the sum total of all sound reflections arriving at a certain point in the room after the room was excited by an impulsive sound signal. The present chapter presents a more thorough discussion of sound field diffusion since this is the basic condition for the validity of the common reverberation laws. Furthermore some extensions and generalisations will be described including sound decay in enclosures with imperfect sound field diffusion, and in systems consisting of several coupled rooms. As in the preceding chapter, we shall consider the case of relatively high frequencies, i.e. we shall neglect interference and diffraction effects which are typical wave phenomena and which only appear in the immediate vicinity of reflecting walls or when obstacle dimensions are comparable with the wavelength.

We therefore suppose that the applied sound signals are of such a kind that the direct sound and all reflections from the walls are mutually incoherent, i.e. that they cannot interfere with each other (*see* Section 4.1). Consequently, their energies or intensities can simply be added together regardless of mutual phase relations. Under these assumptions sound behaves in much the same way as white light. We shall, however, not so much consider sound rays but instead we shall stress the notion of, 'sound particles' i.e. of small energy packets which travel with a constant velocity c along straight lines – except for wall reflections – and are supposed to be present in very large numbers. If they strike a wall with absorption coefficient α, only the fraction $1 - \alpha$ is reflected from the wall. Thus the absorption coefficient will be interpreted as an 'absorption probability'.

Of course, the sound particles considered in room acoustics are purely hypothetical and have nothing to do with the sound quanta or phonons known from solid state physics. To bestow some physical reality upon them we can consider the sound particles to be short sound pulses with a broad spectrum propagating along sound ray paths. Their shape is not important; in principle they are not even required to have uniform shapes, but they must all have the same power spectrum. The most important condition is their mutual incoherence.

5.1 Basic properties and realisation of diffuse sound fields

As mentioned before, the uniform distribution of sound energy in a room is the crucial condition for the validity of most common expressions describing either the decay of sound fields or the steady state energy contained in them. Therefore it is appropriate to deal first with some properties of diffuse sound fields and, furthermore, to discuss the circumstances under which we can expect them in enclosures.

Suppose we select from all sound rays crossing an arbitrary point P in a room a bundle within a vanishingly small solid angle $d\Omega$. Since the rays of the bundle are nearly parallel, an intensity $I(\varphi, \vartheta)\, d\Omega$ can be attributed to them with φ and ϑ characterising their direction (*see* Fig. 5.1). Furthermore, we can apply eqn (1.29) to these rays, according to which the energy density

Figure 5.1 Bundle of nearly parallel sound waves.

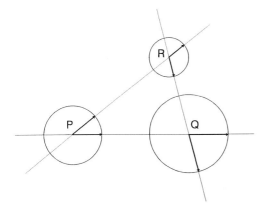

Figure 5.2 Constancy of energy density in a diffuse sound field.

$$dw = \frac{I(\varphi, \vartheta)}{c} \, d\Omega \qquad (5.1)$$

is associated with them.

Now the condition of a diffuse sound field requires that the quantity I does not depend on the angles φ and ϑ, hence integrating over all directions is achieved by multiplication by 4π, and the total energy density is

$$w = \frac{4\pi I}{c} \qquad (5.2)$$

To prove the spatial constancy of the energy density in Fig. 5.2 the directional distributions in three points of a diffuse sound field, P, Q, and R are shown as polar diagrams. These diagrams are circles because we assumed sound field isotropy. Each pair of points has exactly one sound ray in common. Since the energy propagated along a sound ray does not change with distance (*see* Chapter 4) it follows that they contribute the same amount of energy in both points. Therefore the circles must have equal diameters. Of course, this argument applies to all points of the space. Thus we can conclude that in a diffuse sound field the energy density is everywhere the same, at least under stationary conditons.

Another important property of a diffuse sound field has already been derived in Section 2.5. According to eqn (2.39), the energy incident on a wall element dS per second is $\pi I dS$ if I does not depend on the angle of incidence or, if we introduce the 'irradiation strength' B obtained by dividing that energy by dS (*see* Section 4.5):

$$B = \pi I \qquad (5.3)$$

With the same argument as above we can conclude that the irradiation strength B is also constant over the whole wall if the sound field is diffuse. Combining eqns (5.2) and (5.3) leads to the important relation

$$B = \frac{c}{4}w \qquad (5.4)$$

which is to be compared with the corresponding eqn (1.29) for a plane wave. As we shall see it is this relation which enables us to derive simple formulae for the sound decay and the energy density under steady state conditions.

We are now in a position to set up an energy balance from which a simple law for the sound decay in a room can be derived. Suppose a sound source feeds the acoustical power $P(t)$ into a room. It is balanced by an increase of the energy content Vw of the room and by the losses due to the absorptivity of its boundary which has the absorption coefficient α:

$$P(t) = V\frac{dw}{dt} + B\alpha S$$

or, by using eqn (5.4) and replacing αS with A, the so-called 'equivalent absorption area' of the room:

$$P(t) = V\frac{dw}{dt} + \frac{cA}{4}w \qquad (5.5)$$

For steady state conditions P is constant and the differential quotient is zero and we obtain the energy density:

$$w = \frac{4P}{cA} \qquad (5.6)$$

If, on the other hand, the sound source is switched off at $t = 0$, i.e. for $P(t) = 0$ for $t \geq 0$, the differential equation (5.5) becomes homogeneous and has the solution

$$w(t) = w_0 e^{-2\delta t} \quad \text{for } t \geq 0 \qquad (5.7)$$

with the damping constant

$$\delta = \frac{cA}{8V} \qquad (5.7a)$$

The damping constant is related to the reverberation time T according to eqn (3.45). After inserting the numerical value of the sound speed in air one obtains:

$$T = 0.163\frac{V}{A} \text{ seconds} \tag{5.8}$$

(all lengths expressed in metres). This is probably the best-known formula in room acoustics. It is due to to W.C. Sabine[1], who derived it first from the results of numerous ingenious experiments, later on also from considerations similar to the present ones. Nowadays, it is still the standard formula for predicting the reverberation time of a room, although it is obvious that it fails for high absorptivities. In fact, even for $\alpha = 1$ it predicts a finite reverberation time although an enclosure without of any sound reflections from walls cannot reverberate. The reason for the limited validity of eqn (5.8) is that the room is not – as assumed – in steady state conditions during sound decay, and is less the faster the sound energy decays. In the following sections more exact decay formulae will be derived which can also be applied to relatively 'dead' enclosures. Furthermore, eqn (5.8) and its more precise versions will be extended to the case of non-uniform absorptivity of its boundary.

In the rest of this section the circumstances will be discussed on which the diffusity of the sound field depends.

It is obvious that a diffuse sound field cannot exist in enclosures whose walls have the tendency to concentrate the reflected sound energy in certain regions or directions. Likewise, a very non-uniform distribution of wall absorption will continuously extinguish potential ray paths and hence impede the formation of a diffuse sound field. In contrast, highly irregular room shapes help to establish a diffuse sound field by continuously redistributing the energy in all possible directions. Particularly efficient in this respect are rooms with acoustically rough walls, the irregularities of which scatter the incident sound energy in a wide range of directions, as has been already described in Section 2.6. Such walls are referred to as 'diffusely reflecting', either partially or completely. The latter case is characterised by Lambert's law as expressed in eqn (4.22). Although this ideal behaviour is frequently assumed as a model of diffuse reflection, it will hardly ever be encountered in reality. Any wall or ceiling will, although it may be structured by numerous columns, niches, cofferings and other 'irregular' decorations, diffuse only a certain fraction of the incident sound whereas the remaining part of it is reflected into specular directions. The reader will be reminded of Fig. 2.14 which presented the scattering characteristics of an irregularly shaped ceiling.

But even if the boundary of an enclosure produces only partially diffuse reflections its contribution to sound field diffusion is considerable since in each reflection some 'specular sound energy' is converted into non-specular energy, whereas the reverse process, the conversion of diffuse energy into specular energy, never occurs.

This may be illustrated by the following consideration: We split the reflected energy fraction $(1 - \alpha)$ into two parts, namely into the portion $s(1 - \alpha)$, which is reflected specularly, and the portion $(1 - s)(1 - \alpha)$, which is scattered in non-specular directions. Under steady state conditions the regularly reflected components add up to the energy density

$$w_g \propto \sum_{n=1}^{\infty} s^n (1 - \alpha)^n = \frac{s(1 - \alpha)}{1 - s(1 - \alpha)}$$

whereas the total energy density except for the contribution due to direct sound is given by

$$w \propto \sum_{n=1}^{\infty} (1 - \alpha)^n = \frac{1 - \alpha}{\alpha}$$

Hence the fraction of non-specularly reflected energy in the stationary sound field is

$$\frac{w - w_g}{w} = 1 - \frac{\alpha s}{1 - s(1 - \alpha)} \tag{5.9}$$

This relation is represented graphically in Fig. 5.3. The contribution of diffuse sound components to the total energy density is actually higher than indicated by these curves, since the specularly reflected components travel across the room in quite different directions and thus themselves contribute to the increase in diffusion. Nevertheless, the diagram makes it evident that complete diffusion of a sound field is never reached in real enclosures.

Quite a different method of achieving a diffuse sound field is not to provide for rough or corrugated walls, and thus to destroy specular reflections, but instead to disturb the free propagation of sound in the space. This is effected by suitable objects – rigid bodies or shells – which are suspended freely in the room at random positions and orientations, and which scatter the arriving sound waves or sound particles in all directions. This method is quite efficient even when applied only to parts of the room, or in enclosures with partially absorbing walls. Of course, no architect would agree to fill the free space of a concert hall or a theatre completely with such 'volume diffusors', therefore a uniform distribution of them can only be installed in certain measuring rooms, so-called reverberation chambers (*see* Section 8.7), for which achieving a diffuse sound field is of particular importance.

To estimate the efficiency of volume scatterers we assume N of them to be randomly distributed in a room with volume V, but with constant mean density $\langle n_s \rangle = N/V$. The scattering efficiency of a single obstacle or diffusor is characterised by its 'scattering cross-section' Q_s, which is defined as the

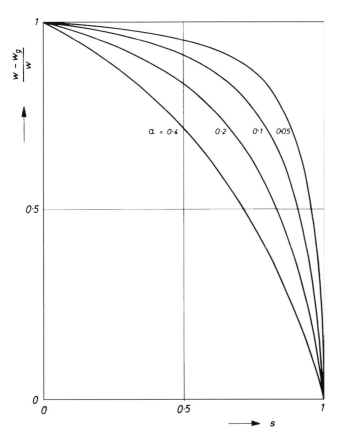

Figure 5.3 Fraction of diffuse sound components in a steady state sound field for partially diffuse wall reflections.

sound energy it scatters per second divided by the intensity of an incident plane sound wave. If we again stress the notion of sound particles, the probability that a particle will travel a distance r or more without being scattered by a diffusor is $\exp(-\langle n_s \rangle Q_s r)$ or $\exp(-r/\bar{r})$, where we have introduced the mean free path $\bar{r}$ between two collisions of sound particles with diffusors. In Section 5.2 we shall introduce the mean free path of sound particles between successive wall reflections $\bar{l} = 4V/S$, with S denoting the wall surface of a room. Obviously the efficiency of volume diffusors depends on the ratio $\bar{r}/\bar{l}$. The probability that a sound particle will undergo no collision between two successive wall reflections and hence the fraction of unscattered sound energy is

$$s = \exp(-\bar{l}/\bar{r}) \approx 1 - \bar{l}/\bar{r}$$

The latter approximation is permitted since in most cases $\bar{r} \gg \bar{l}$.

This expression is inserted into eqn (5.9) assuming small wall absorption ($\alpha \ll 1$). Then the fraction of diffused sound energy in a stationary sound field is obtained as

$$\frac{w - w_g}{w} \approx \frac{1}{1 + \alpha \bar{r}/\bar{l}} \tag{5.9a}$$

If a diffusor is not small compared with the acoustical wavelength, its scattering cross-section Q_s is roughly twice its visual cross-section. However, only half of this value represents scattering of energy in different directions; the other half corresponds to the energy needed to form the 'shadow' behind the obstacle by interfering with the sound wave (*see* Section 2.6). For non-spherical diffusors, the cross-section has to be averaged over all directions of incidence.

We conclude this section by emphasising that sound field diffusion must strictly be distinguished from diffuse wall reflections. The diffuse sound field in a room is an ideal condition which can only be approached by any kind of diffusor. Even if the latter diffuse the incident sound perfectly, the result – namely the diffusion of the sound field – may be much less than ideal.

5.2 Mean free path and average rate of reflections

In the following material we shall make use of the concept of 'sound particles', already introduced at the beginning of this chapter. We imagine that the sound field is composed of a very great number of sound particles. Our goal is the evaluation of the laws according to which the sound energy decreases with time in a decaying sound field. For this purpose we have firstly to follow the 'fate' of one sound particle and subsequently to average over many of these fates.

In this connection the notion of the 'mean free path' of a sound particle is frequently encountered in literature on room acoustics. The notion itself appears at first glance to be quite clear, but its use is sometimes misleading, partly because it is not always evident whether it refers to the time average or the particle (ensemble) average.

We shall start here from the simplest concept: a sound particle is observed during a very long time interval t; the total path length ct covered by it during this time is divided by N, the number of wall reflections which have occurred in the time t:

$$\bar{l} = \frac{ct}{N} = \frac{c}{\bar{n}} \tag{5.10}$$

where $\bar{n} = N/t$ is the average reflection frequency, i.e. the average number of wall reflections per second.

Here $\bar{l}$ and $\bar{n}$ are clearly defined as time averages for a single sound particle; they may differ from one particle to another. In order to obtain averages which are representative of all sound particles, we should average $\bar{l}$ and $\bar{n}$ once more, namely over all possible particle fates. In general, the result of such a procedure would depend on the shape of the room as well as on the chosen directional distribution of sound paths.

Fortunately we can avoid such cumbersome methods and arrive at simple and general relations between room geometry and the required averages by assuming the sound field to be diffuse. Then no additional specification of the directional distribution is required. Furthermore, no other averaging is necessary. This is so because – according to our earlier discussions – a diffuse sound field is established by non-predictable changes in the particle directions either by diffuse wall reflections or by particles being scattered by obstacles during their free propagation. In any case the sound particles change their roles and their direction again and again, and during this process they completely lose their individuality. Thus the distinction between time averages and particle or ensemble averages is no longer meaningful; it does not matter whether the mean free path and all other averages are evaluated by averaging over many free paths traversed by one particle or by averaging for one instant over a great number of different particles. Or in short:

time average = ensemble average

Now we shall calculate the mean free path of sound particles in rooms of arbitrary shape with walls which reflect the incident sound in an ideally diffuse fashion, i.e. according to Lambert's cosine law of eqn (4.22). For the present purpose we shall formulate that law in a slightly different way: the probability of a sound particle being reflected or re-emitted into a solid angle element $d\Omega$, which includes an angle ϑ with the wall normal under consideration, is

$$P(\vartheta)\,d\Omega = \frac{1}{\pi}\cos\vartheta\,d\Omega \tag{5.11}$$

It is thus entirely independent of the particle's previous history.

We consider all possible free paths, i.e. all possible chords in the enclosure (*see also* Fig. 4.17) and intend to carry out an averaging of their lengths R over all wall elements dS as well as over its directions.

These paths are, however, not traversed with equal probabilities. When averaging over all directions we have to concede a greater chance to the small angles ϑ according to eqn (5.11) by using a proper weighting function. Therefore we obtain

$$\bar{l} = \frac{1}{S}\iint_S dS \frac{1}{\pi}\iint_{2\pi} R_{dS}(\vartheta)\cos\vartheta\,d\Omega'$$

$R_{dS}(\vartheta)$ is the length of the chord originating from dS under an angle ϑ with respect to the wall normal and S is the total wall area of the room. Now we interchange the order of integrations, keeping in mind, however, that ϑ is not measured against a fixed direction but against the wall normal, which changes its direction from one wall point to another. Thus we obtain

$$\bar{l} = \frac{1}{\pi S} \iint_{2\pi} d\Omega' \iint_S R_{dS}(\vartheta) \cos \vartheta \, dS$$

The second integrant is the volume of an infinitesimal cylinder with axis R_{dS} and base dS; the second integral is thus the double volume $2V$ of the room. The remaining integral simply yields 2π and therefore our final result is

$$\bar{l} = \frac{4V}{S} \qquad (5.12)$$

We should remember that this formula, which has been derived by Kosten[2] in a somewhat similar way, is valid only for rooms with diffusely reflecting walls.

The direct calculation of the mean reflection frequency $\bar{n}$ is even simpler. Let us suppose that a single sound particle carries the energy e_0. Its contribution to the energy density of the room is

$$w = \frac{e_0}{V} \qquad (5.13)$$

On the other hand, if the sound particle strikes the wall $\bar{n}$ times per second, it transports on average the energy per second and unit area

$$B = \bar{n} \frac{e_0}{S} \qquad (5.14)$$

to the wall. By inserting these expressions into eqn (5.4) one arrives at the important relation

$$\bar{n} = \frac{cS}{4V} \qquad (5.15)$$

This expression, which is the time average as well as the particle average, has already been derived in Section 4.2 for rectangular rooms with specularly reflecting walls. It is evident, that the present derivation is more general and, in a way, more satisfying than the previous one. By inserting it into eqn (5.10) it again leads to the famous expression for the mean free path length, eqn (5.12).

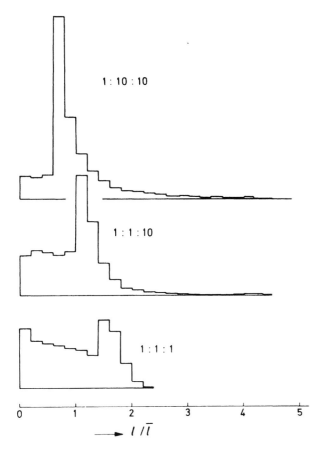

Figure 5.4 Distribution of free path lengths for rectangular rooms with diffusely reflecting walls.

The mean free path is the mean value of the probability density governing the occurrence of a free path l between two subsequent wall reflections. The probability density itself depends on the shape of the room, and the same is true for other characteristic values such as the variance. As an illustration Fig. 5.4 shows the distributions of free path lengths for three different shapes of rectangular rooms with diffusely reflecting walls; abscissa is the path length divided by its mean value $\bar{l}$. These distributions have been calculated by application of a Monte-Carlo method, i.e. by simulating the sound propagation.[3]

Typical parameters of path length distributions, evaluated in the same way for different rectangular rooms, are listed in Table 5.1. The first column contains the relative dimensions of the various rooms and the second lists the corresponding results of the Monte-Carlo computation for the

Table 5.1 Some Monte-Carlo results of mean free paths and of γ^2 for rectangular rooms with diffusely reflecting walls

Relative dimensions	$\bar{l}_{MC}/\bar{l}$	γ^2
1:1:1	1.0090	0.342
1:1:2	1.0050	0.356
1:1:5	1.0066	0.412
1:1:10	1.0042	0.415
1:2:2	1.0020	0.363
1:2:5	1.0085	0.403
1:2:10	0.9928	0.465
1:5:5	1.0035	0.464
1:5:10	0.9993	0.510
1:10:10	1.0024	0.613

mean free path divided by the 'classical' value of eqn (5.12). These numbers are very close to unity and can be looked upon as an 'experimental' confirmation of eqn (5.12), since the Monte-Carlo method could be characterised as 'computer experiments'. The remaining insignificant deviations from 1 are due to random errors which are inherent in the method. It may be added that a similar investigation of rooms with specularly reflecting walls, which are equipped with scattering elements in the interior, yields essentially the same result. Finally, the third column of Table 5.1 contains the 'relative variance' of the path length distributions:

$$\gamma^2 = \frac{\overline{l^2} - \bar{l}^2}{\bar{l}^2} \tag{5.16}$$

Its significance will be discussed in Section 5.4.

5.3 Sound decay and reverberation time

As far back as Chapter 4, formulae have been derived for the time dependence of decaying sound energy and for the reverberation time of rectangular rooms (eqns (4.9) to (4.11)). In the preceding section it has been shown that the value $cS/4V$ of the mean reflection frequency, which we have used in Chapter 4, is valid not only for rectangular rooms but for rooms of arbitrary shape provided that the sound field in their interior is diffuse. Thus the general validity of those reverberation formulae has been proven.

If the sound absorption coefficient of the walls depends on the direction of sound incidence, which will usually be the case, we must use the average value α_{uni} of eqn (2.41) instead of α.

Further consideration is necessary if the absorption coefficient is not constant along the walls but depends on the location of a certain wall element.

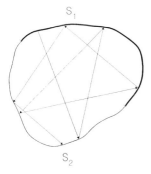

Figure 5.5 Enclosure with two different types of boundary.

For the sake of simplicity we assume that there are only two different absorption coefficients in the room under consideration. The subsequent generalisation of the results for more than two different types of wall will be obvious.

We therefore attribute an absorption coefficient α_1 to the wall portion with area S_1 and α_2 to the portion with area S_2, where $S_1 + S_2 = S$. The situation is depicted in Fig. 5.5. We follow the life of a particular sound particle over N wall reflections, among which there are N_1 reflections from S_1 and $N_2 = N - N_1$ reflections from S_2. These numbers can be assumed to be distributed in some way about their mean values

$$\overline{N}_1 = N\frac{S_1}{S} \quad \text{and} \quad \overline{N}_2 = N\frac{S_2}{S} \tag{5.17}$$

S_1/S and S_2/S are the *a priori* probabilities for the arrival of a sound particle at wall portion S_1 and S_2, respectively.

In a diffuse sound field subsequent wall reflections are stochastically independent from each other, i.e. the probability of hitting one or other portion of the wall does not depend on the past history of the particle. In this case the probability of N_1 collisions with wall portion S_1 among a total number of reflections N is given by the binomial distribution

$$P_N(N_1) = \binom{N}{N_1}\left(\frac{S_1}{S}\right)^{N_1}\left(\frac{S_2}{S}\right)^{N-N_1} \tag{5.18}$$

After N_1 collisions with S_1 and $N_2 = N - N_1$ collisions with S_2, a sound particle has the remaining energy

$$E_N(N_1) = E_0(1 - \alpha_1)^{N_1}(1 - \alpha_2)^{N-N_1} \tag{5.19}$$

The expectation value of this expression with respect to the distribution (5.18) is

$$\langle E_N \rangle = \sum_{N_1=0}^{N} E_N(N_1)P_N(N_1) = E_0 \left[\frac{S_1}{S}(1 - \alpha_1) + \frac{S_2}{S}(1 - \alpha_2) \right]^N$$

where we have applied the binomial theorem. Since $S_1 + S_2 = S$, this can be written as

$$\langle E_N \rangle = E_0(1 - \bar{\alpha})^N = E_0 \exp [N \ln(1 - \bar{\alpha})] \tag{5.20}$$

with

$$\bar{\alpha} = \frac{1}{S}(S_1\alpha_1 + S_2\alpha_2) \tag{5.20a}$$

This latter formula is the most important result of the foregoing derivation. It indicates that the absorption coefficients of the various portions of wall have to be averaged arithmetically using the respective areas as weighting factors. Finally, we replace the total number N of wall reflections in time t by its expectation value or mean value $\bar{n}t$ with $\bar{n} = cS/4V$ and obtain for the energy of the 'average' sound particle and hence for the total energy in the room

$$E(t) = E_0 \exp \left[\frac{cS}{4V} t \ln(1 - \bar{\alpha}) \right] \quad \text{for } t \geq 0 \tag{5.21}$$

From this we can evaluate the reverberation time, i.e. the time interval T in which the reverberating sound energy reaches one millionth of its initial value

$$T = -\frac{24V \ln 10}{cS \ln(1 - \bar{\alpha})} \tag{5.22}$$

As in eqns (4.6) to (4.11), the effect of air attenuation may be taken into account by an additional factor $\exp(-mct)$ in eqn (5.21). This leads, after inserting the numerical value for the sound velocity, to the final expression

$$T = -0.163 \frac{V}{S \ln(1 - \bar{\alpha}) - 4mV} \tag{5.23}$$

with

$$\bar{\alpha} = \frac{1}{S}\sum S_i \alpha_i \qquad (5.23a)$$

where we have already generalised eqn (5.20a) for any number of different portions of the wall. In this formula all lengths have to be expressed in metres; T is measured in seconds.

Equations (5.22) or (5.23) together with (5.23a) are known as Eyring's reverberation formula, although they have been derived independently by Norris as well as by Schuster and Waetzmann.

For many practical purposes it is safe to assume that the average absorption coefficient $\bar{\alpha}$ is small compared with unity. Then the logarithm in eqn (5.23) can be expanded into a series

$$-\ln(1 - \bar{\alpha}) = \bar{\alpha} + \frac{\bar{\alpha}^2}{2} + \frac{\bar{\alpha}^3}{3} + \dots$$

and all terms of higher than the first order in $\bar{\alpha}$ may be neglected. This results in Sabine's reverberation formula:

$$T = 0.163 \frac{V}{S\bar{\alpha} + 4mV} \qquad (5.24)$$

This has already been derived in the preceding section (*see* eqn (5.8)), however in a different way and without the term $4mV$ which can be neglected for small rooms.

In deriving eqn (5.20) the quantities NS_1/S and NS_2/S have been considered as mean values or expectation values of the probability distribution (5.18). If they are considered instead as the *exact* collision rates with the wall portions S_1 and S_2, i.e. if they are inserted for N_1 and N_2 in eqn (5.19), we get instead of eqn (5.21)

$$E(t) = E_0 \exp\left(-\frac{cS}{4V}\bar{\alpha}t\right) \qquad (5.25)$$

with the average 'absorption exponent'

$$\bar{a}' = -\frac{1}{S}\sum_i S_i \ln(1 - \alpha_i) \qquad (5.25a)$$

The resulting equation

$$T = 0.163 \frac{V}{S\bar{a}'} \tag{5.26}$$

which could again be completed by taking into account the air attenuation by adding a term $4mV$ to the denominator, is known as Millington–Sette's formula. It differs from eqn (5.23) only in the manner in which the absorption coefficients of the various portions of wall are averaged; here the average absorption coefficient is replaced by the average absorption exponent.

The averaging according to eqn (5.25a) has a strange consequence: let us suppose that a room has a portion of wall, however small, with the absorption coefficient $\alpha_i = 1$. It would make the average (5.25a) infinitely large and hence the reverberation time evaluated by eqn (5.26) would be zero. This is obviously an unreasonable result.

5.4 The influence of unequal path lengths

The incorrect averaging rule of eqn (5.25a) was the result of replacing a probability distribution by its mean value. However, in the derivation of eqn (5.21) we have practised a similar simplification in that we have replaced the actual number of reflections in the time t by its average $\bar{n}t$. For a more correct treatment we ought to introduce the probability $P_t(N)$ of exactly N wall reflections occurring in a time t and to calculate $E(t)$ as the expectation value of eqn (5.20) with respect to this probability distribution:

$$E(t) = E_0 \sum_{N=0}^{\infty} P_t(N) \exp \left[N \ln(1 - \bar{\alpha}) \right] \tag{5.27}$$

As an abbreviation we introduce, in a similar way as in eqn (5.25), the 'absorption exponent'

$$a = -\ln(1 - \bar{\alpha}) \tag{5.28}$$

If, for the moment, N is considered as a continuous variable, the function $\exp(-Na)$ in eqn (5.27) can be expanded in a Taylor series around $\bar{n}t$ by setting $N = \bar{n}t + (N - \bar{n}t)$. Truncating this series after its third term yields

$$\exp(-Na) \approx \exp(-\bar{n}ta) \left[1 - \frac{N - \bar{n}t}{1!}a + \frac{(N - \bar{n}t)^2}{2!}a^2 \right]$$

Before inserting this expression into eqn (5.27) it should be kept in mind that

$$\sum P_t(N) = 1 \quad \text{and} \quad \sum (N - \bar{n}t)P_t(N) = 0$$

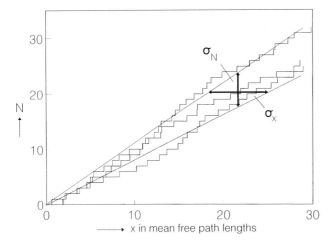

Figure 5.6 Time histories of three sound particles – relation between σ_x and σ_N.

whereas

$$\sum (N - \bar{n}t)^2 P_t(N) = \sigma_N^2$$

is the variance of the distribution $P_t(N)$. Hence

$$E(t) \approx E_0 \exp(-\bar{n}ta)(1 + \tfrac{1}{2}\sigma_N^2 a^2) \approx E_0 \exp(-\bar{n}ta + \tfrac{1}{2}\sigma_N^2 a^2) \qquad (5.29)$$

The latter approximation is permissible if the second term in the bracket is small compared with unity. On the other hand, σ_N^2 is closely related to the relative variance γ^2 of the path length distribution as defined in eqn (5.16). To illustrate this Fig. 5.6 plots the individual 'fates' of three particles, i.e. the number N of their wall collisions as a function of the distance x they travelled. It is obvious that

$$\frac{\sigma_N}{\sigma_x} = \frac{\bar{n}t}{x} = \frac{\bar{n}t}{ct}$$

Now suppose a particle travels N successive and independent free paths l_1, $l_2, \ldots, l_N$. According to basic laws of probability (*see* Ref. 4, for instance), their sum x has the variance $\sigma_x^2 = N\bar{l}^2\gamma^2$ since $\bar{l}^2\gamma^2$ is the relative variance of the free path lengths. After inserting σ_x into the relation above one arrives at

$$\left(\frac{\bar{n}}{c}\right)^2 N\bar{l}^2\gamma^2 = N\gamma^2$$

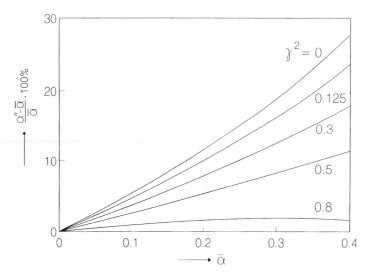

Figure 5.7 Relative difference between a'' and $\bar{\alpha}$ in per cent after eqn (5.33).

or, if we finally replace N by its mean value $\bar{n}t$,

$$\sigma_N^2 \approx \bar{n}t\gamma^2 \tag{5.30}$$

This expression, inserted into eqn (5.29), yields the final result

$$E(t) \approx E_0 \exp\left[-\bar{n}ta\left(1 - \frac{\gamma^2}{2}a\right)\right] \tag{5.31}$$

Accordingly, the reverberation time is

$$T = 0.163\frac{V}{Sa''} \tag{5.32}$$

with the modified absorption exponent

$$a'' = -\ln(1 - \bar{\alpha})\left[1 + \frac{\gamma^2}{2}\ln(1 - \bar{\alpha})\right] \tag{5.33}$$

In Fig. 5.7 the corrected absorption exponent a'' is compared with the absorption coefficient α as is used in Sabine's formula (eqn (5.24) with $m = 0$ and uniform absorption). It plots the relative difference between both quantities for various parameters γ^2. The curve $\gamma^2 = 0$ corresponds to Eyring's formula (5.22 and 5.23). Accordingly, the latter is strictly valid for one-dimensional enclosures only where all paths have exactly the same length. For $\gamma^2 \neq 0$, a'' is smaller than $-\ln(1-\alpha)$. Hence the reverberation time is longer than that evaluated by the Eyring formula.

With eqn (5.32) we have for the first time arrived at a reverberation formula in which the shape of the room is accounted for by the quantity γ^2. Unfortunately the latter can be calculated directly only for a limited number of room shapes with high symmetry. For a sphere, for instance, it turns out to be 1/8. For other shapes γ^2 can be determined by computer simulation. Results obtained in this way for rectangular rooms have already been presented in Table 5.1. It is seen that for most shapes γ^2 is close to 0.4 and it is likely that this value can also be applied to other enclosures provided that their shapes do not deviate too much from that of a rectangular room. It should be noted that for higher values of γ^2 eqn (5.33) is not very accurate because of the approximations we have made in its derivation. Suppose, for instance, the free path lengths are exponentially distributed, i.e. according to

$$P(l)\,dl \propto \exp\left(-\frac{l}{\bar{l}}\right)dl$$

It has the relative variance $\gamma^2 = 1$. On the other hand, the exponential distribution of path lengths is associated with the Poisson distribution of collision number,[4] i.e.

$$P_t(N) = e^{-\bar{n}t}\frac{(\bar{n}t)^N}{N!}$$

If this expression is inserted into eqn (5.27) we get

$$E(t) = E_0\, e^{-\bar{n}t}\sum_{N=0}^{\infty}\frac{[\bar{n}t(1-\bar{\alpha})]^N}{N!} = E_0 \exp(-\bar{n}t\bar{\alpha})$$

This corresponds with Sabine's formula[5] (5.24) (with $m = 0$). It means that the correct curve for $\gamma^2 = 0$ in Fig. 5.7 coincides with the horizontal axis.

For rooms with suspended 'volume diffusors' (*see* Section 5.1), the distribution of free path lengths is greatly modified by the scattering obstacles. The same applies to γ^2 but not to the mean free path length.[3]

5.5 Enclosure driven by a sound source

In Section 5.1 a differential equation (5.5) was derived for the energy density w in a room in which a sound source with time-dependent power output $P(t)$ is operated. This equation has the general solution:

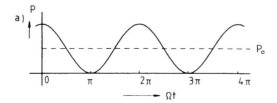

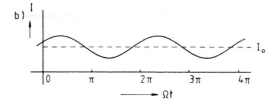

Figure 5.8 Flattening effect of transmission in a room on the modulation of sound signals: (a) power of original sound signal; (b) received intensity.

$$w(t) = \frac{1}{V} \int_{-\infty}^{t} P(\tau) \exp\left[-2\delta(t - \tau)\right] d\tau = \frac{1}{V} \int_{0}^{\infty} P(t - \tau) \exp\left(-2\delta\tau\right) d\tau$$

(5.34)

with $\delta = cA/8V$. Accordingly, the energy density is calculated by convolving the power output $P(t)$ with the 'energetic impulse response' of the enclosure:

$$w(t) = P(t) * \frac{1}{V} e^{-2\delta t}$$

(5.34a)

As a first application we consider, as shown in Fig. 5.8, a sound source the power output of which varies sinusoidally with the angular frequency Ω:

$$P(t) = P_0(1 + \cos \Omega t)$$

(5.35)

Inserting this into eqn (5.34) and carrying out the integration leads after some obvious manipulations to

$$w(t) = \frac{P_0}{2\delta V}[1 + m \cos \Omega(t - t_0)]$$

(5.36)

with

$$m(\Omega) = \frac{2\delta}{\sqrt{(4\delta^2 + \Omega^2)}}$$

(5.36a)

and

$$t_0 = \arctan\left(\frac{\Omega}{2\delta}\right) = \frac{1}{\Omega}\arccos m(\Omega) \qquad (5.36b)$$

Since m is always smaller than unity the reverberation of the room has a flattening effect on the modulation imposed by the energy input to the room and – at the same time – a typical delay by t_0 as shown in Fig. 5.8b.

The function $m(\Omega)$ is often referred to as the 'modulation transfer function' (MTF) since it expresses the way in which the modulation index m is changed by the transient behaviour of the room. Its magnitude may be combined with the phase shift Ωt_0 to the complex MTF which in the present case reads:

$$\overline{m}(\Omega) = \left(1 + \frac{i\Omega}{2\delta}\right)^{-1} \qquad (5.36c)$$

An even more important – and simpler – example is that of a source with constant power output P. Here eqn (5.34) yields immediately:

$$w_r = \frac{P}{2\delta V} = \frac{4P}{cA} \qquad (5.37)$$

This formula agrees with eqn (5.6) which was obtained directly from eqn (5.5) by setting the time derivative zero. The subscript r is to indicate that w_r is the energy density of the 'reverberant field' excluding the contribution of the direct sound.

The application of eqn (5.37) to practical problems becomes questionable for average absorption coefficients $\bar{\alpha} = A/S$ which are not small compared with unity. This is because the contribution of the very first reflections, which are not randomly distributed, to the total energy density is relatively high then. Therefore the range of validity of the above formulae with respect to $\bar{\alpha}$ is substantially smaller than that of the reverberation formulae developed in the preceding sections.

This is one of the reasons why the absorption of a room and its reverberation time is determined by decay measurements and not usually by measuring the steady state energy density and application of eqn (5.37) which would be possible in principle.

On the other hand, however, steady state measurements are quite useful for the evaluation of the total power P of a sound source using eqn (5.37) if $\bar{\alpha}$ is known or determined by a reverberation measurement. This procedure is free from objection as long as the room utilised for this purpose is a 'reverberation chamber' with a long reverberation time and hence with low absorption. We should bear in mind that in the measurement of acoustic

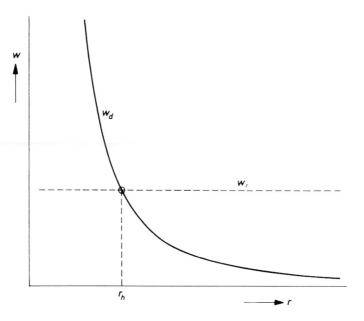

Figure 5.9 Space dependence of direct and reverberant energy density w_d and w_r.

power an error of 10% (corresponding to 0.4 dB) can usually be tolerated, but not so in the determination of absorption or reverberation time.

The above formulae for the stationary energy density are only valid with some degree of accuracy as long as the point of observation is not too close to the sound source, otherwise direct sound would prevail. Assuming omni-directional sound radiation, the direct sound energy density is given by (compare eqns (1.28a) and (1.32))

$$w_d = \frac{P}{4\pi c r^2}$$

In Fig. 5.9 w_r and w_d are presented schematically as a function of distance r from the sound source. For a certain distance $r = r_h$ both energy densities are equal. This quantity r_h is called the 'reverberation distance' and is given by

$$r_h = \frac{1}{4}\left(\frac{A}{\pi}\right)^{1/2} = 0.1\left(\frac{V}{\pi T}\right)^{1/2} \tag{5.38}$$

In the latter expression we have introduced the reverberation time T from Sabine's formula (with $m \approx 0$); V is to be measured in m³.

Many sound sources have a certain directivity which can be characterised by their 'gain' or 'directivity factor' γ. The latter is defined as the ratio of the maximum intensity (or energy density) and the intensity averaged over all directions:

$$\gamma = \frac{I_{max}}{P/4\pi r^2} = \frac{w_{max}}{P/4\pi c r^2} \tag{5.39}$$

Then the maximum reverberation distance is

$$r_h = \sqrt{\left(\frac{\gamma A}{16\pi}\right)} \approx 0.1\sqrt{\left(\frac{\gamma V}{\pi T}\right)} \tag{5.40}$$

In any case, the total energy density can be expressed as

$$w = w_d + w_r = \frac{4P}{cA}\left(1 + \frac{r_h^2}{r^2}\right) \tag{5.41}$$

5.6 Enclosures with diffusely reflecting walls

So far we have dealt with enclosures in which the sound field is perfectly diffuse – a condition which, as we know – can only be approximately realised. In this section we do not need to know anything about the structure of the sound field which may not in fact be diffuse. Instead it is assumed that the boundary reflects the sound energy in a perfectly diffuse manner. This is a somewhat less stringent but nevertheless also an ideal condition which can only be approached by real walls. On the other hand it has been shown by Hodgson[6] that in all practical situations a part of the sound energy is diffusely reflected by the boundary, and since the decaying sound field is made up mainly of higher order reflections, and since the conversion of 'specular sound' into 'diffuse sound' is irreversible, one can safely assume that after a few reflections nearly all sound energy has undergone at least one diffuse reflection.

In this case the propagation of sound energy within the enclosure can be described by the integral equation (4.24) for the 'irradiation strength' B of the boundary, as discussed in Section 4.5. Since we are interested only in sound decay we can omit the term due to direct irradiation by a sound source. Then the integral equation reads:

$$B(\mathbf{r}, t) = \frac{1}{\pi}\iint_S \frac{\cos \vartheta \cos \vartheta'}{R^2} B\left(\mathbf{r}', t - \frac{R}{c}\right)\rho(\mathbf{r}')\,dS' \tag{5.42}$$

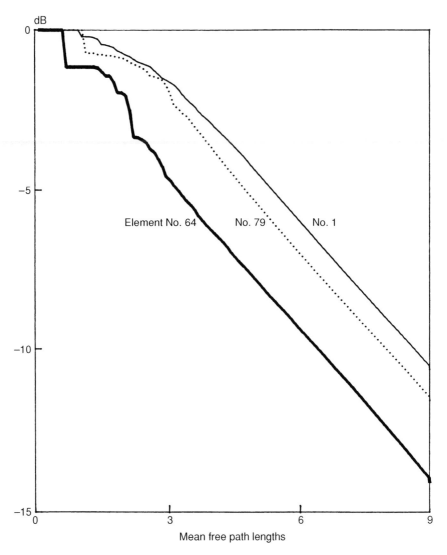

Figure 5.10 Logarithmic decay curves in a rectangular room with relative dimensions 1:2:3, calculated from eqn (5.42) for three different receiver positions. Floor (2:3) is totally absorbing, the remaining walls are free of absorption. The abscissa unit is the mean free path length.

Figure 5.10 presents a few decay curves obtained by numerically solving this equation for a rectangular room with relative dimensions 1:2:3. The 'floor' (i.e. one of the walls with dimensions 2:3) was assumed to be totally absorbent ($\rho = 0$), whereas the remaining walls are free of absorption ($\rho = 1$). The curves show the decay of the irradiation strengths at three different

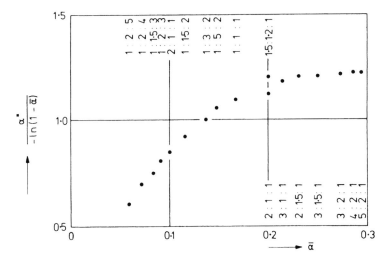

Figure 5.11 Effective absorption exponents α^*, divided by $-\ln(1 - \bar{\alpha})$, as obtained from Monte-Carlo computations for rectangular rooms with $\alpha = 1$ for one wall and $\alpha = 0$ for the others. Numbers in the figure indicate the relative room dimensions; the first two numbers refer to the absorbing wall.

locations. At the beginning there are some fluctuations which, however, gradually fade out leaving a straight line according to an exponential decay of the sound energy. It should be noted that the final slope is the same for all three curves. (Generally, the independence of the final slope has been proven by R.N. Miles[7]). However, it differs from that predicted by Eyrings's or Sabine's reverberation formulae, eqns (5.23) and (5.23a). In the example of Fig. 5.10, the slope is about -1.55 dB/MFP (mean free path), whereas after Eyring's formula (5.23) it is only $10 \log_{10}(1 - 3/11) = -1.38$ dB/MFP.

Deviations from Eyring's predictions are typical for enclosures with imperfect sound field diffusion. To illustrate this Fig. 5.11 presents the results of some computer simulations carried out for rectangular rooms of various shapes. In these examples one of the six walls is assumed to be totally absorbent ($\alpha = 1$), while the remaining ones are supposed to be free of absorption ($\alpha = 0$). Each room is characterised by its relative dimensions; the first two numbers refer to the absorbing wall. The plotted quantity is the effective absorption exponent divided by its Eyring value $-\ln \bar{\rho}$; the abscissa is the mean absorption coefficient $\bar{\alpha}$. It is seen that the results deviate from the ordinate 1 in both directions; in particular, for relatively flat rooms with a highly absorbing floor (see right side of the figure) the absorption exponent is higher, hence the reverberation time is shorter than predicted by the Eyring formulae. This is of practical interest since virtually all auditoria are of this general type because of the high audience absorption.

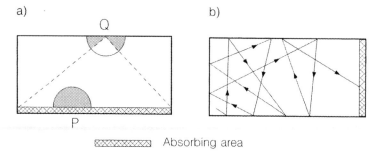

Figure 5.12 Sound absorption in a long room: (a) with an absorbing 'floor';
(b) with absorbing 'side wall'.

How can we understand such deviations? Let us have a look at Fig. 5.12 in which a section through a rectangular room is depicted. In Fig. 5.12a it is assumed that the 'floor' of it is highly absorbing while the remaining walls are rigid or nearly rigid. As indicated, a floor point P is 'irradiated' from all directions while a ceiling (or wall) point Q does not receive energy from the floor because of its high absorption. Hence the floor receives and absorbs more energy than it would under diffuse conditions. In Fig. 5.12b the absorbing surface is a side wall. In this case it is obvious that sound particles in the left part of the enclosure are not much affected by the absorbing wall. Therefore we expect that in the right half of the enclosure there is less energy than in the left one, and hence the absorbing wall is hit by less sound particles than it would be in a diffuse field.

To predict the slope of the final decay and hence the reverberation time, several numerical iteration schemes have been developed[7,8] which do not require a complete solution of eqn (5.42). For the practical design of a hall, such methods are too complicated. In the following, a relatively simple correction to the Eyring absorption exponent is described which is more useful. We introduce in eqn (5.42)

$$B(\mathbf{r}, t) = B(\mathbf{r}) \exp(-\bar{n}a^*t) \tag{5.43}$$

where $\bar{n} = cS/4V$ is the average number of a sound particle's collisions with a wall per second and a^* is the absorption exponent to be determined. Furthermore, the distance R in the exponential of eqn (5.42) is replaced with the mean free path $\bar{l} = c/\bar{n}$. These substitutions leave

$$B(\mathbf{r}) = \frac{\exp(a^*)}{\pi} \iint_S \frac{\cos \vartheta \cos \vartheta'}{R^2} B(\mathbf{r}')\rho(\mathbf{r}')\,dS' \tag{5.44}$$

This equation is integrated over the whole boundary. By interchanging the order of integrations on the right-hand side and observing that

$$\frac{1}{\pi} \int\int_S \frac{\cos \vartheta \cos \vartheta'}{R^2} \, dS = 1$$

one obtains

$$a^* = \ln\left(\frac{\int\int B \, dS}{\int\int \rho B \, dS} \right) \tag{5.45}$$

In the following, we restrict ourselves to enclosures of polyhedral shape, i.e. to rooms bounded by N plane walls with areas S_n. Furthermore, we assume the reflection coefficient and the irradiation strength to be constant over each wall. Then the double integrals in eqn (5.45) become sums over the wall index. Now we replace the missing knowledge of the exact irradiation strengths by a reasonable guess. Obviously the irradiation strength of one particular wall with index n consists of the contributions from the $N - 1$ remaining walls, and each of them is proportional to the reflection coefficient and to the area of the wall which produces it:

$$B_n \sim \sum_{m=1}^{N} \rho_m S_m - \rho_n S_n = \bar{\rho} S - \rho_n S_n \tag{5.46}$$

Inserting the latter expression into the modified eqn (5.45) yields, after some easy manipulation,

$$a^* \approx \ln\left(\frac{1}{\bar{\rho}} \right) + \ln\left(1 + \frac{\sum \rho_n (\rho_n - \bar{\rho}) S_n^2}{\bar{\rho}^2 S^2 - \sum \rho_n^2 S_n^2} \right) \tag{5.47}$$

In most cases the second term in the denominator is much smaller than the first and hence can be neglected. Finally, we can expand the second logarithm into a power series and neglect all terms of higher than first order:

$$a^* \approx a_{ey} + \frac{\sum \rho_n (\rho_n - \bar{\rho}) S_n^2}{(\bar{\rho} S)^2} \tag{5.48}$$

The second term of this expression is always positive – a consequence of our somewhat crude approach. Therefore this correction formula applies only to situations in which the effective absorption exponent is expected to exceed the Eyring value (right side of Fig. 5.11). According to the previous discussion, however, these are the practically important cases, and it is easily verified that eqn (5.48) accounts quite well for the deviations.

5.7 Coupled rooms

Sometimes a room is shaped in such a way that it can barely be considered as a single enclosure but rather as a collection composed of partial rooms separated by virtually non-transparent walls. The only communication is by relatively small apertures in these walls. The same situation is encountered if the partition walls are totally closed but are not completely rigid, and have some slight sound transparency. A particular aspect of such 'coupled rooms' has been discussed in Chapter 3. Now their acoustical properties will be dealt with from a geometrical and statistical point of view.

Let us suppose that the sound field in every partial room is a diffuse one and that reverberation would follow an exponential law if there were no interaction between them. Then for the ith partial room we have after eqn (5.5) (with $P_i = 0$):

$$\frac{\mathrm{d}w_i}{\mathrm{d}t} = -2\delta_i w_i$$

δ_i being the damping constant of that room without coupling.

The coupling elements permit an energy exchange between the partial rooms. If there are wall apertures with areas S_{ij} between rooms i and j, the energy loss in room i per second due to coupling is $\sum'_j B_i S_{ij} = cS'_i w_i/4$ with $S'_i = \sum'_j S_{ij}$. On the other hand, the energy increase contributed by room j per second is $cS_{ij} w_j/4$. Hence the energy balance yields for the ith room

$$\frac{\mathrm{d}w_i}{\mathrm{d}t} + \left(2\delta_i + \frac{cS'_i}{4V_i}\right)w_i = \sum_j{}' \frac{cS_{ij}}{4V_i} w_j \qquad (5.49)$$

The apostrophe indicates that the summation index must be extended over all integers from 1 to m except i, where m is the total number of partial rooms. This system of linear differential equations can be further simplified to read

$$\frac{\mathrm{d}w_i}{\mathrm{d}t} = \sum_{j=1}^{m} k_{ij} w_j \quad (i = 1, 2, \ldots, m) \qquad (5.50)$$

where

$$k_{ii} = -\left(2\delta_i + \frac{cS'_i}{4V_i}\right) \quad k_{ij} = \frac{cS_{ij}}{4V_i} \quad \text{for } i \neq j$$

First we look for the conditions under which the decay process obeys an exponential law with one common damping constant δ'. In this case we would obtain $dw_i/dt = -2\delta'w_i$. Inserting this into eqns (5.50) yields m homogeneous linear equations. For the energy densities w_i:

$$k_{i1}w_1 + k_{i2}w_2 + \ldots + (k_{ii} + 2\delta')w_i + \ldots + k_{im}w_m = 0 \quad (i = 1, 2, \ldots, m)$$

(5.51)

which have non-vanishing solutions only if their coefficient determinant is zero. This condition is an equation of degree m (secular equation) for δ' with m roots $\delta_1', \delta_2', \ldots, \delta_m'$. If they are inserted one after the other into eqns (5.51), the energy densities associated with a certain root can be determined except for a common factor

$$w_1^{(r)}, w_2^{(r)}, \ldots, w_m^{(r)} \quad (r = 1, 2, \ldots, m)$$

For a certain root δ_r' the mutual ratios of the $w_i^{(r)}$ remain constant during the whole decay process. Hence they also represent the ratios of the initial values $w_{i0}^{(r)}$. This result can be summarised as follows. There are at most (since in principle several roots δ' can happen to coincide) m possibilities for the reverberation to follow the same exponential law throughout the whole room system. A particular set of initial energy densities is required for each of these possibilities.

The general solution is obtained as a linear superposition of the special solutions evaluated above:

$$w_i(t) = \sum_{r=1}^{m} c_r w_{i0}^{(r)} \exp(-2\delta_r' t) \quad (i = 1, 2, \ldots, m)$$

(5.52)

If the energy densities $w_i(0)$ of all partial rooms at the beginning of the decay process are given, the constants c_r can be determined unambiguously from eqn (5.52) by setting $t = 0$. The decay of sound energy in the ith partial room is then represented by

$$w_i(t) = \sum_{j=1}^{m} a_{ij} \exp(-2\delta_j' t)$$

(5.52a)

which is similar to eqn (3.41a). In contrast to the coefficients c_n^2 of the latter, however, the a_{ij} are not necessarily all positive and so we cannot draw the conclusion (as we did in Section 3.5) that the logarithmic decay curves are either straight lines or curved upwards.

If the system of coupled rooms is driven by sound sources, a term P_i/V_i must be added on the right-hand side of each of the equations (5.50) with P_i denoting the power output of the source in the partial room i. For constant power P_i the steady state energy densities are obtained by setting the time derivatives to zero. This yields the equations:

$$-\frac{P_i}{V_i} = \sum_{j=1}^{m} k_{ij} w_j \quad (i = 1, 2, \ldots, m)$$

(5.53)

They can be used to determine the initial values $w_i(0)$ for the energy decay which starts after all sound sources have been stopped at $t = 0$, according to eqn (5.52).

If the subroom i is not driven by a sound source ($P_i = 0$), the sum on the right-hand side of eqn (5.53) is zero, and the same is true for the time derivative in eqn (5.50) immediately after switching off all sources:

$$\left(\frac{dw_i}{dt}\right)_{t=0} = 0$$

i.e. the decay curve starts with zero slope. In the same way it may be inferred that not only the initial slope of the decay curve but also its initial curvature vanishes if neither the considered room nor one of its adjacent neighbours are driven by an own sound source.

These findings may be illustrated by an example depicted in Fig. 5.13. It refers to three coupled rooms of equal volumes in a line, but only one of them is driven directly by a sound source. Accordingly the steady state level from which the decay process starts is highest in room 1, and only in this room the decay curve begins with a negative slope. The decay rate in this

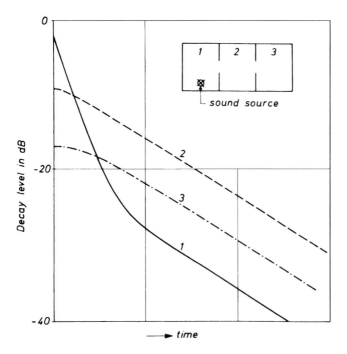

Figure 5.13 Example for sound decay in three coupled rooms: $\delta_2 = k_{12} = \delta_1/10$, $\delta_3 = \delta_1/2$, $k_{13} = 0$, $k_{23} = \delta_1/5$.

room becomes gradually less steep since the adjacent rooms feed some of the energy stored in them back to room 1. The decay curves in the rooms 2 and 3 have horizontal tangents at $t = 0$; moreover, the initial curvature of decay curve 3 is zero.

On the whole we can see that in coupled rooms the variety of possible decay curves is considerably greater than it is in a single uncoupled room.

The occurrence of typical coupling effects as outlined above is not restricted to room systems of a special geometrical structure. They can also be observed in apparently normal rooms if the exciting conditions are such that they excite one or several normal modes whose eigenfrequencies are close to those of other modes but whose energy exchange is only slight. Convexly curved decay curves (viewed from the positive ordinate direction) are a safe indication of the presence of several energy stores which are only weakly coupled to each other.

The transition from coupled systems to normal rooms is, of course, a gradual one. The simple theory of coupled rooms applies to all cases where the energy per second being exchanged by coupling is not substantially larger than the energy being lost by absorption. If it is assumed that the latter is small compared with the energy $cS_i w_i / 4V_i$ striking the walls per second, and if coupling is effected by apertures, the condition for the occurrence of coupling effects reads simply

$$S_i' \ll S_i$$

or, more generally,

$$|k_{ii}| \ll \frac{cS_i}{4V_i} \tag{5.54}$$

This means that typical coupling phenomena are to be expected if the probability of a sound particle being absorbed or of escaping to a neighbouring partial room is small compared with the probability of it being reflected from any wall of the room under consideration.

Sometimes, when calculating the reverberation time of a room, it is advisable to take coupling effects into account. This aspect will be discussed in Chapter 9.

References

1 Sabine, W.C., *The American Architect* 1900, see also *Collected Papers on Acoustics No. 1*, Harvard University Press, Cambridge, 1923.
2 Kosten, C.W., *Acustica*, **10** (1960) 245.
3 Kuttruff, H., *Acustica*, **23** (1970) 238; *ibid.*, **24** (1971) 356.
4 Papoulis, A., *Probability, Random Variables, and Stochastic Processes*, 2nd edn, Intern Student Edition, McGraw-Hill, 1985.

5 Schroeder, M.R., Proceedings of the Fifth International Congress on Acoustics, Liege, 1965, paper G31.
6 Hodgson, M., *J. Acoust. Soc. America*, **89** (1991) 765.
7 Miles, R.N., *J. Sound Vibr.*, **92**(2) (1984) 203.
8 Gilbert, E.N., *J. Acoust. Soc. America*, **69** (1981) 178.
9 Kuttruff, H., *J. Acoust. Soc. America*, **98** (1995) 288.

6 Sound absorption and sound absorbers

Of considerable importance to the acoustics of a room are the loss mechanisms which reduce the energy of sound waves when they are reflected from walls as well as during their free propagation in the air. They influence the strengths of the direct sound and of all reflected components and therefore all acoustical properties of the room.

The attenuation of sound waves in the free medium becomes significant only in large rooms and at relatively high frequencies; for scale model experiments, however, it causes serious limitations. We have to consider it inevitable and something which cannot be influenced by the efforts of the acoustician. Nevertheless, in reverberation calculations it has to be taken into account. Therefore it is sufficient in this context to give a brief description of the causes of air attenuation and to present the important numerical values.

The situation is different in the case of the absorption to which sound waves are subjected when they are reflected. The magnitude of wall absorption and its frequency dependence varies considerably from one material to another. With the proper choice of materials used in construction and finish or by applying special arrangements, the absorption and hence the sound transmission in a room can be substantially influenced in a desired way; furthermore, a particular frequency dependence can be given to it. There is also an unavoidable contribution to the wall absorption which depends on certain physical properties of the medium, but it is so small that in most cases it is not significant.

Since it is one of the most common tasks of an acoustic consultant to achieve a desired reverberation time in a room with a prescribed frequency dependence and since this is done by selecting the proper wall materials and absorbers, this chapter will discuss in some detail the principles and mechanisms of the most important types of sound absorbers. For a comprehensive account the reader is referred to F. Mechel's book on sound absorption.[1]

6.1 The attenuation of sound in air

In the derivation of the wave equation (1.5) it was tacitly assumed that the changes in the state of the air, caused by the sound waves, occurred without loss. This is not quite true, however. We shall refrain here from a proper amendment of the basic equations and from a quantitative treatment of attenuation. Instead the most prominent loss mechanisms are briefly described in the following. As earlier, the propagation losses will be characterised by the decrease of the intensity in a plane sound wave, which is, according to eqn (1.16*a*):

$$I(x) = I_0 \exp(-mx)$$

(*a*) Equation (1.4) is based on the assumption that the changes in the state of a volume of gas take place adiabatically, i.e. there is no heat exchange between neighbouring volume elements. The equation states that a compressed volume element has a slightly higher temperature than an element which is rarefied by the action of the sound wave. Although the temperature differences occurring at normal sound intensities amount to small fractions of a degree centigrade only, they cause a heat flow because of the finite thermal conductivity of the air. This flow is directed from the warmer to the cooler volume elements. The changes of state are therefore not taking place entirely adiabatically. According to basic principles of physics, the energy transported by these thermal currents cannot be reconverted completely into mechanical, i.e. into acoustical energy; some energy is lost to the sound wave. The corresponding portion of the attenuation constant *m* increases with the square of the frequency.

(*b*) In a plane sound wave each volume element becomes periodically longer or shorter in the direction of sound propagation. This distortion of the original element can be considered as a superposition of an omnidirectional compression or rarefaction and of a shear deformation, i.e. of a pure change of shape. The medium offers an elastic reaction to the omnidirectional compression proportional to the amount of compression, whereas the shear is controlled by viscous forces which are proportional to the shear velocity. Hence – as with every frictional process – mechanical energy is irreversibly converted into heat. This 'viscous portion' of the attenuation constant *m* also increases proportionally with the square of the frequency.

(*c*) Under normal conditions the above-mentioned causes of attenuation in air are negligibly small compared with the attenuation caused by what is called 'thermal relaxation'. It can be described briefly as follows. Under equilibrium conditions the total thermal energy contained in a certain quantity of a uniform polyatomic gas is distributed among several energy stores (degrees of freedom) of the gas molecules, namely as translational, vibrational and rotational energy of the molecules. If the gas is suddenly compressed, i.e. if its energy is suddenly increased, the whole additional energy will be stored at first in the form of translational energy. Afterwards a gradual redistribution among the other stores will take place. Or in other words: the establishment of a new equilibrium requires a finite time. If

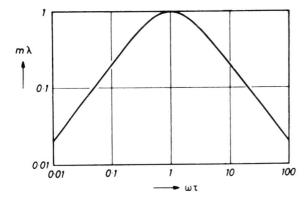

Figure 6.1 Intensity attenuation constant ($m\lambda$) for a relaxation process. The abscissa is the product of angular frequency ω and relaxation time τ.

compressions and rarefactions change periodically as in a sound wave, a thermal equilibrium can be maintained – if at all – only at very low frequencies; with increasing frequency the actual energy content of certain molecular stores will lag behind the external changes and will accept or deliver energy at the wrong moments.

This is a sort of 'internal heat conduction' which weakens the sound wave just like the normal heat conduction with which we are more familiar. The relative amount of energy being dissipated along one wavelength has a maximum when the duration of one sound period is comparable with a specific time interval, the so-called 'relaxation time' being characteristic of the time lag in internal energy distribution.

In Fig. 6.1 the attenuation constant m multiplied by the wavelength for a single relaxation process is plotted in arbitrary units as a function of the product of frequency and relaxation time. The very broad frequency range in which it appears is characteristic of a relaxation process. (For comparison we refer to the resonance curve in Fig. 2.8*b*.) Moreover, the relaxation of a medium causes not only a substantial increase in absorption but also a slight change in sound velocity, but this is not of importance in this connection.

For mixtures of polyatomic gases such as air, which consists mainly of nitrogen and oxygen, matters are much more complicated because there are many more possibilities of internal energy exchange which we shall not discuss here.

Because of their importance in room acoustics and, in particular for the calculation of reverberation time, a few numerical values of the intensity related absorption constant m are listed in Table 6.1.

Table 6.1 Attenuation constant of air at 20°C and normal atmospheric pressure, in 10^{-3} m^{-1} (after Bass *et al.*[2])

Relative humidity (%)	Frequency (kHz)						
	0.5	1	2	3	4	6	8
40	0.60	1.07	2.58	5.03	8.40	17.71	30.00
50	0.63	1.08	2.28	4.20	6.84	14.26	24.29
60	0.64	1.11	2.14	3.72	5.91	12.08	20.52
70	0.64	1.15	2.08	3.45	5.32	10.62	17.91

6.2 Unavoidable wall absorption

Even if the walls, the ceiling and the floor of a room are completely rigid and free from pores, they cause a sound absorption which is small but different from zero. It only becomes noticeable, however, when there are no other absorbents or absorbent portions of wall in the room, no people, no porous or vibrating walls. This is the case for measuring rooms which have been specially built to obtain a high reverberation time (reverberation chambers; *see* Section 8.7). Physically this kind of absorption is again caused by the heat conductivity and viscosity of the air.

According to eqn (1.4), the periodic temperature changes caused by a sound wave are in phase with the corresponding pressure changes – apart from the slight deviations discussed in the preceding section. Therefore the maximum sound pressure amplitude which is observed immediately in front of a rigid wall should be associated with a maximum of 'temperature amplitude', which in turn is possible only if the wall temperature can completely follow the temperature fluctuations produced by the sound field. In reality the contrary is true: because of its high thermal capacity the wall surface remains virtually at a constant temperature. Therefore, in some boundary layer adjacent to the wall, strong temperature gradients will develop and hence a periodically alternating heat flow will be directed to and from the wall. This energy transport occurs at the expense of the sound energy, since the heat which was produced by the wave in a compression phase can only be partly reconverted into mechanical energy during the rarefaction phase.

As we saw earlier, the component of the particle velocity which is normal to the wall vanishes in front of a perfectly rigid wall. The parallel component, i.e. the y-component of the particle velocity, can be calculated from eqn (2.15) by applying

$$v_y = -\frac{1}{i\omega\rho_0}\frac{\partial p}{\partial y} \tag{6.1}$$

which follows from eqn (1.2). The result (for $x = 0$ and $R = 1$) is

$$v_y = \frac{2\hat{p}_0}{\rho_0 c} \sin \theta \exp (-iky \sin \theta) \tag{6.2}$$

It indicates that the parallel component does not vanish for oblique sound incidence ($\theta \neq 0$). This, however, cannot be true, since in a real medium the molecular layer immediately on the wall is fixed to the latter, which means $v_y = 0$ for $x = 0$. For this reason our assumption of a perfectly reflecting wall is not correct, in spite of its rigidity. In reality a boundary layer is again formed between the region of unhindered parallel motion in the air and the wall; at oblique incidence particularly high viscous forces and hence a substantial conversion of mechanical energy into heat takes place in the boundary layer.

Although the energy dissipation occurs due to both loss processes in a certain layer of air, its effect is commonly described by an absorption coefficient ascribed to the wall. It can be shown that the thicknesses of the boundary layers are inversely proportional to the square root of the frequency. Since, on the other hand, the gradients of the temperature and of the parallel velocity component increase proportionally with frequency, both contributions to the absorption coefficient are proportional to the square root of the frequency. Their dependence on the angle of incidence, however, is different. The viscous portion is zero for normal sound incidence, as can easily be seen from eqn (6.1), whereas the heat flow to and from the wall does not vanish at normal incidence.

Both effects are very small even at the highest frequencies relevant in room acoustics. For practical design purposes they can be safely neglected.

6.3 Sound absorption by vibrating or perforated boundaries

For the acoustics of a room it does not make any difference whether the apparent absorption of a wall is physically brought about by dissipative processes, i.e. by conversion of sound energy into heat, or by parts of the energy penetrating through the wall into the outer space. In this respect an open window is a very effective absorber, since it acts as a sink for all the arriving sound energy.

A less trivial case is that of a wall or some part of a wall forced by a sound field into vibration with a substantial amplitude. (Strictly speaking, this happens more or less with any wall, since completely rigid walls cannot be constructed.) Then a part of the wall's vibrational energy is re-radiated into the outer space. This part is withdrawn from the incident sound energy, viewed from the interior of the room. Thus the effect is the same as if it were really absorbed. It can therefore also be described by an absorption coefficient. In practice this sort of 'absorption' occurs with doors, windows, light partition walls, suspended ceilings, circus tents and similar 'walls'.

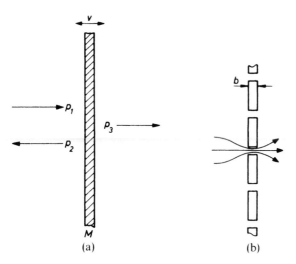

Figure 6.2 (a) Pressures acting on a layer with mass M per unit area.
(b) Perforated panel.

This process, which may be quite involved especially for oblique sound incidence, is very important in all problems of sound insulation. From the viewpoint of room acoustics, it is sufficient, however, to restrict discussions to the simplest case of a plane sound wave impinging perpendicularly onto the wall, whose dynamic properties are completely characterised by its mass inertia. Then we need not consider the propagation of bending waves on the wall.

Let us denote the sound pressures of the incident and of the reflected waves on the surface of a wall (*see* Fig. 6.2a) by p_1 and p_2, and the sound pressure of the transmitted wave by p_3. The total pressure acting on the wall is then $p_1 + p_2 - p_3$. It is balanced by the inertial force $i\omega M v$, where M denotes the mass per unit area of the wall and v the velocity of the wall vibrations. This velocity is equal to the particle velocity of the wave radiated from the rear side, for which $p_3 = \rho_0 c v$ holds. Therefore we have $p_1 + p_2 - \rho_0 c v = i\omega M v$, from which we obtain

$$Z = i\omega M + \rho_0 c \qquad (6.3)$$

for the wall impedance. Inserting this into eqn (2.8) yields

$$\alpha = \left[1 + \left(\frac{\omega M}{2\rho_0 c} \right)^2 \right]^{-1} \approx \left(\frac{2\rho_0 c}{\omega M} \right)^2 \qquad (6.4)$$

This simplification is permissible for the case frequently encountered in practice in which the characteristic impedance of air is small compared with the mass reactance of the wall. Thus the 'absorption' becomes noticeable only at low frequencies.

At a frequency of 100 Hz the absorption coefficient of a glass pane with 4 mm thickness is – according to eqn (6.4) – as low as 0.02 approximately. For oblique or random incidence this value is a bit higher due to the better matching between the air and the glass pane, but it is still very low. Nevertheless, the increase in absorption with decreasing frequency has the effect that rooms with many windows sometimes sound 'crisp' since the reverberation at low frequency is not as long as it would be in the same room without windows.

The absorption caused by vibrations of normal and single walls and ceilings is thus very low. Matters are different for double or multiple walls, provided that the partition on the side of the room under consideration is mounted in such a way that vibrations are not hindered and provided that it is not too heavy. Because of the interaction between the leaves and the enclosed volume of air such a system behaves as a resonance system. This will be discussed in the next section.

It is a fact of great practical interest that a rigid perforated plate or panel has essentially the same properties as a mass-loaded wall or foil. Let us look at Fig. 6.2b. Each hole in a plate may be considered as a short tube or channel with length b; the mass of air contained in it, divided by the cross-section, is $\rho_0 b$. Because of the contraction of the air stream passing through the hole, the air vibrates with a greater velocity than that in the sound wave remote from the wall, and hence the inertial forces of the air included in the hole are increased. The increase is given by the ratio S_2/S_1, where S_1 is the area of the hole and S_2 is the plate area per hole. Hence the equivalent mass of the perforated panel per unit area is

$$M = \frac{\rho_0 b'}{\sigma} \tag{6.5}$$

with

$$\sigma = \frac{S_1}{S_2} \tag{6.6}$$

The latter quantity is the perforation ratio of the plate; sometimes it is also called 'porosity' (generally in a different context).

In eqn (6.5) the geometrical tube length (or plate thickness) b has been replaced by an 'effective length' b', which is somewhat larger than b:

$$b' = b + 2\delta b \tag{6.7}$$

The correction term $2\delta b$, known as the 'end correction', accounts for the fact that the streamlines cannot contract or diverge abruptly but only gradually when entering or leaving a hole (*see* Fig. 6.2b). For circular apertures with radius a and with relatively large lateral distances it is given by

$$\delta b = 0.8a \tag{6.8}$$

Finally, the absorption coefficient of a perforated panel is obtained from eqn (6.4) by substituting M from eqn (6.5). Very often perforated plates are so light that they will vibrate as a whole when a sound waves strikes them. In this case M in eqn (6.5) must be replaced by

$$M' = \left(\frac{1}{M} + \frac{1}{M_s} \right)^{-1} \tag{6.9}$$

M_s is the mass of the panel per square metre. (The frictional forces within the holes are disregarded in this formula.)

The absorption coefficient given by eqn (6.4) is also the fraction of sound energy which is transmitted by a wall or a perforated panel (in the latter case it is necessary to use the first form of eqn (6.4)). It thus characterises the sound transparency of the wall. Let us illustrate this by an example: to yield a transparency of 90%, $\omega M/2\rho_0 c$ must have the value $\frac{1}{3}$. At 1000 Hz this is the case with a foil or perforated panel with an (equivalent) mass per unit area of about 45 g/m^2, which can be realised for instance by a 1-mm thick sheet with 7.5% perforation with holes having a diameter of 2 mm.

6.4 Extended resonance absorbers

In this section we take up again the earlier discussion of extended resonance absorbers (*see* Section 2.4). As shown in Fig. 6.3a, such an absorber consists basically of a layer with mass M per unit area, for instance a panel of wood, chipboard, or gypsum board, which is mounted in front of a rigid wall at a certain distance d. Under the influence of an impinging sound wave it will perform vibrations, the amplitude of which depends strongly on the sound frequency. The wall impedance of this system is given by eqn (2.27). Its real part r_s represents all vibrational losses of this system which may have several physical reasons. One of them has to do with the fact that any kind of panel must be fixed at certain points or along certain lines to a supporting construction which forces the panel to be bent when it vibrates. Now all elastic deformations of a solid, including those by bending, are associated with internal losses depending on the material and other circumstances. In metals, for instance, the intrinsic losses of the material

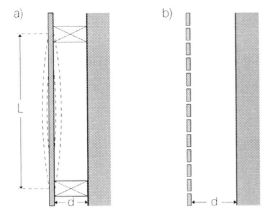

Figure 6.3 Resonance absorbers: (a) with vibrating panel; (b) with perforated panel.

are relatively small, but they may be substantial for plates made of wood or of plastic. If necessary the losses may be increased by certain surface layers.

According to the discussion of the preceding section, the mass layer can also be realised as a perforated plate (*see* Fig. 6.3b). If the holes are very narrow the intrinsic frictional losses occurring in them may be sufficient to ensure the low Q-factors which are needed for high efficiency of the absorber. Principally, this is a way to manufacture transparent resonance absorbers although it may prove difficult in practice to keep apertures with diameters below 1 mm free of dust particles and other obstructions.

For wider holes it is usually necessary to provide for additional losses. This can be achieved, for instance, by covering the holes by a porous fabric. Another method of adapting the magnitude of r_s for either kind of resonance absorber to a desired value is to fill the air space behind the panel partially or completely with porous material.

In the following discussion we assume the real part r_s of the wall impedance to be constant. Then all the eqns (2.27)–(2.34) can be applied to these structures. The absorption coefficient in particular reaches a maximum caused by resonance at the angular frequency ω_0 given by eqn (2.28). In Fig. 6.4 calculated absorption coefficients of panel resonators are plotted as a function of the ratio ω/ω_0 under the additional assumption $M\omega_0 = 10\rho_0 c$. The parameter of the curves is the quantity $r_s/\rho_0 c$. A maximum absorption coefficient of 1 is reached only for exact matching, i.e. for $r_s = \rho_0 c$. For $r_s > \rho_0 c$ the maximum absorption is less than unity and the curves are broadening. This is qualitatively the same behaviour as that of a porous layer which is arranged at some distance and in front of a rigid wall (compare Fig. 2.6). The resonance frequency of a panel absorber at normal sound

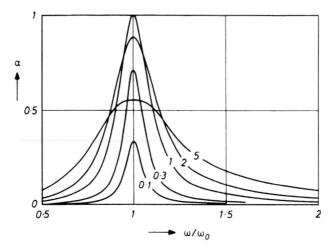

Figure 6.4 Absorption coefficient α (calculated) of resonance absorbers, similar to Fig. 6.3, as a function of frequency for normal sound incidence and for $M\omega_0 = 10\rho_0 c$. Parameter is the ratio $r_s/\rho_0 c$.

incidence can be expressed equally well in the following form as this is more useful for its practical application:

$$f_0 = \frac{600}{(Md)^{1/2}} \text{ Hz} \tag{6.10}$$

where M is in kg/m^2 and d in cm.

This formula is relatively reliable if the mass layer is a perforated panel, as in Fig. 6.3b, or a flexible membrane. Then the way in which the mass layer is fixed has no influence on its acoustical effect, at least as long as the sound waves arrive frontally. Matters are different for unperforated wall linings made of thick panels with noticeable bending stiffness. As mentioned before, such panels will perform bending vibrations since they must be fixed in some way, for instance by a lath construction mounted on the wall (Fig. 6.3a). Hence their vibrations are controlled not only by the air cushion behind them but also by their bending stiffness which adds to the restoring force of the air cushion. Accordingly, the resonance frequency will be higher than that given by eqn (6.10) namely

$$f_0' = \sqrt{(f_0^2 + f_1^2)} \tag{6.11}$$

with f_1 denoting the lowest bending resonance frequency of a panel supported (not clamped) at two opposite sides. The typical range of f_1 is about 10–30 Hz whereas f_0 is typically 50–100 Hz. This shows that the influence of the bending stiffness may be neglected in most practical cases, and eqn (6.10) may be applied to give at least a clue to the actual resonance frequency.

The practical importance of resonance absorbers stems from the possibility of choosing their significant data (dimensions, materials) from a wide range so as to give them the desired absorption characteristics. By a suitable combination of several types of resonance absorbers the acoustic consultant is able to achieve a prescribed frequency dependence of the reverberation time. The most common application of vibrating panels is to effect a low frequency balance for the strong absorption of the audience at medium and high frequencies, and thus to equalise the reverberation time. This is the reason for the generally favourable acoustical conditions which are frequently met in halls whose walls are lined with wooden panels or are equipped with similar components, i.e. walls or suspended decoration ceilings made of thin plaster. Thus it is not, as is sometimes believed by laymen, a sort of 'amplification' caused by 'resonance' which is responsible for the good acoustics of many concert halls lined with wooden panels. Likewise, audible decay processes of the wall linings, which are sometimes also believed to be responsible for good acoustics, do not occur in practical situations although they might be possible in principle. If a resonance system with the relative half-width (reciprocal of the Q-factor) $\Delta\omega/\omega_0$ is excited by an impulsive signal, its amplitude will decay with a damping constant $\delta = \Delta\omega/2$ according to eqn (2.31); thus the reverberation time of the resonator is

$$T' = \frac{13.8}{\Delta\omega} = \frac{2.2}{\Delta f} \tag{6.12}$$

To be comparable with the reverberation time of a room which is of the order of magnitude of 1 s, the frequency half-width Δf should be about 2 Hz. Such resonators can indeed be constructed. However, wall linings with vibrating or perforated panels in front of rigid walls usually have half-widths larger by several orders of magnitude.

Since neighbouring area elements of unperforated panels are strongly coupled one to the other by bending forces, they cannot be considered as 'locally reacting wall surfaces'. Therefore the simple angle dependence of the reflection factor or of the absorption coefficient expressed by eqns (2.14b) and (2.16) is not valid for them. On the contrary, at oblique incidence a forced bending wave is excited in the panel. The propagation of this wave is strongly affected by the sort of mounting, the arrangement of timber battening which carries the panels, also by the elastic properties of the plate material and by interaction with the air volume behind the panels. It is the structure of these bending waves which strongly affects the absorption coefficient of the whole arrangement at oblique incidence. Since general statements in this respect cannot be made, we shall not discuss this point in any further detail.

For resonators with perforated panels, the coupling of neighbouring holes is effected by the air space behind the panels. The coupling can be destroyed by hindering the lateral sound propagation in that air space. This is done by lateral partitions made of rigid material, or by filling the air space with porous and hence sound-absorbent materials like glass or mineral wool. Neighbouring elements of the plate can then be regarded as independent; the wall impedance and similarly the resonance frequency is independent of the direction of sound incidence. To achieve this it is sufficient to reduce the range of lateral coupling to about half a wavelength, since smaller regions at oblique incidence are excited at almost equal phases. In any case it is difficult to predict the exact resonance frequency of a resonance absorber and assess correctly its losses which determine its absorption. Therefore, the acoustical consultant must rely on his experience or on a good collection of typical absorption data. In cases of doubt it may be advisable to measure the absorption coefficient of a wall lining by putting a sufficiently large sample of it into a reverberation chamber (*see* Section 8.7).

In Fig. 6.5 the absorption coefficients of a wooden wall lining and of a resonance absorber with perforated panels are plotted as functions of the frequency, measured at omnidirectional sound incidence.

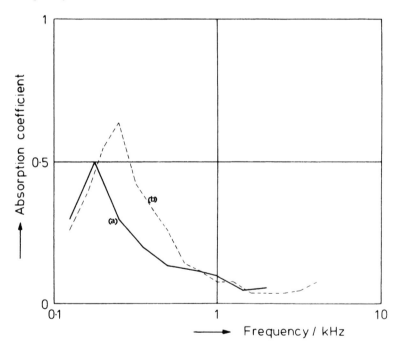

Figure 6.5 Measured absorption coefficient of resonance absorbers at random sound incidence: (a) wooden panels, 8 mm thick, 5 kg/m², 30 mm distant from rigid wall, with 20 mm thick rock wool plate behind (33.2 Rayl/cm); (b) panels, 9.5 mm thick, perforated at 1.6% (diameter of holes 6 mm), 5 cm distant from wall, air space filled with glass wool.

6.5 Helmholtz resonators

Sometimes sound absorbent elements are not distributed so as to cover the wall or the ceiling of a room but instead they are single or separate objects or things arranged either on a wall or in free space. Examples of this are chairs, small wall openings or lamps; musical instruments too can absorb sound. To sound absorbers of this sort we cannot attribute an absorption coefficient, since the latter always refers to a uniform surface. Instead their absorbing power is characterised by their 'absorption cross-section' or their absorption area, which is defined as the ratio of sound energy being absorbed per second by them and the intensity which the incident sound wave would have at the place of the absorbent object if it were not present:

$$A = \frac{P_{abs}}{I_0} \tag{6.13}$$

When calculating the reverberation time of a room, absorption of this type of absorbers is taken into account by adding their absorption areas A_i to the sum $\sum \alpha_i S_i$ (*see* eqn (5.23a)). The analogue holds for all other formulae and calculations in which the total absorption or the mean absorption coefficient $\bar{\alpha}$ of a room appears, as for instance in the calculation of the steady state energy density in a sound field according to eqn (5.37).

In this section we are discussing single sound absorbers with pronounced resonant behaviour. Their characteristic feature is an air volume which is enclosed by rigid boundaries and which is coupled to the surrounding space by an aperture as shown in Fig. 6.6a. The latter may equally well be a channel or a 'neck'. The whole structure is assumed to be small compared with the wavelength of sound and thus it has one single resonance only in the interesting frequency range. It is brought about by interaction of the air contained in the neck or in the aperture which is moved to and fro by the sound and acts essentially as a mass load while the air cushion in the enclosure is periodically compressed and rarefied, and opposes these changes of state with the stiffness of a spring. Arrangements of this type are called 'Helmholtz resonators'; examples of these are all kinds of bottles, vases and similar vessels. In ancient times, as 'Vitruv's sound vessels', they played an unknown, possibly only a surmised, acoustical role in antique theatres and other spaces.

Figure 6.6 depicts a Helmholtz resonator along with its schematic presentation. The neck has a length l and a cross-sectional area S; its opening is flush with the surface of a rigid wall of infinite extension. The basic parameters of the resonator are the mass $M = \rho_0 l S$ of the air enclosed in the neck, and the volume V_0 of the attached cavity. The shape of the latter is of no relevance. Furthermore, there are some internal losses represented by a resistance R_0, the opening is loaded by its radiation impedance R_r defined by

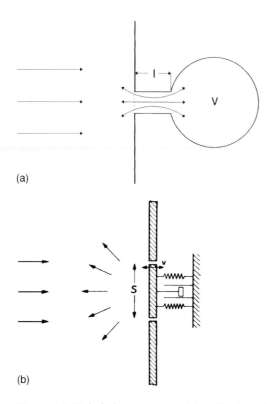

(a)

(b)

Figure 6.6 Helmholtz resonator: (a) realisation; (b) schematic.

$$P_r = R_r \overline{v^2}$$

(P_r = radiated power, v = air velocity in the neck). Since the lateral dimensions of the opening are small compared with the wavelength, P_r can be substituted from eqn (1.31) using $\hat{Q}^2 = (S\hat{v})^2 = 2S^2v^2$. However, we must keep in mind that the re-radiation of sound from the aperture is restricted to the half space only and hence is a factor of 2 higher than in eqn (1.31). Thus the radiation resistance is

$$R_r = \frac{\rho_0 \omega^2 S^2}{2\pi c} = 2\pi \rho_0 c \left(\frac{S}{\lambda}\right)^2 \tag{6.14}$$

Now we assume that the resonator is working at its resonance frequency. In this case all the reactive parts of the mechanical load will mutually cancel each other. The remainder of the impedance, the ratio of the force F acting on the piston and its velocity v is

$$\frac{F}{v} = R_0 + R_r$$

The energy converted to heat per second by the internal friction is

$$P_{abs} = R_0 \overline{v^2} = \frac{R_0}{(R_0 + R_r)^2} \overline{F^2} \tag{6.15}$$

where – as usual – the bars indicate time averaging. For a given radiation resistance, P_{abs} is maximum if R_0 is about equal to R_r. The force exerted externally on the piston arises from the sound field. If p denotes the sound pressure, the force is $F = 2pS$. The factor 2 takes into account the reflection from the rigid wall surrounding the piston. By application of eqn (1.28) we can express the sound pressure and hence the force in terms of the intensity I of the incident sound wave:

$$\overline{F^2} = 4S^2\overline{p^2} = 4\rho_0 cS^2 I \tag{6.16}$$

Now we are ready to evaluate eqns (6.13) and (6.15) with $R_0 = R_r$ by substituting from eqns (6.14) and (6.16), and we obtain as a final result

$$P_{abs} = \frac{\lambda_0^2}{2\pi} I \quad \text{and} \quad A_{max} = \frac{\lambda_0^2}{2\pi} \tag{6.17}$$

where λ_0 is the wavelength corresponding to the resonance frequency.

For the frequency dependence of the absorption area, we can essentially adopt eqn (2.32):

$$A(\omega) = \frac{A_{max}}{1 + Q_A^2[(\omega/\omega_0) - (\omega_0/\omega)]^2} \tag{6.18}$$

with

$$Q_A = \frac{M\omega_0}{2R_r} \tag{6.18a}$$

As for any resonance system, the angular resonance frequency is given by

$$\omega_0^2 = \frac{s}{M}$$

Here s is the elastic stiffness of the air enclosed in the resonator volume. To calculate it we suppose the air in the neck to be displaced by δx; the corresponding change in air pressure is p_i. According to the usual definition of the stiffness,

$$s = \frac{\text{force}}{\text{displacement}} = -\frac{p_i S}{\delta x}$$

On the other hand, the pressure change is associated with a change $\delta\rho$ in air density, which in turn is due to the volume change $S\delta x$. These quantities are related to each other by (*see* eqns (1.4) and (1.5a))

$$p_i = c^2 \delta\rho = -\rho_0 c^2 \frac{S\delta x}{V_0}$$

where V_0 denotes the resonator volume. Thus we obtain

$$s = \frac{\rho_0 c^2 S^2}{V_0}$$

Now we can insert $M = s/\omega_0^2 = \rho_0 c^2 S^2/\omega_0^2 V_0$ into eqn (6.18a) and express R_r by eqn (6.14) with the result

$$Q_A = \frac{\pi}{V_0}\left(\frac{c}{\omega_0}\right)^3 = \frac{\pi}{V_0}\left(\frac{\lambda_0}{2\pi}\right)^3 \tag{6.19}$$

We observe that the maximum absorption area of a resonator matched to the sound field is fairly large, according to eqn (6.17). On the other hand, the Q-factor given by eqn (6.19) is very large too, which means that the relative frequency half-width which is the reciprocal of the Q-factor is very small, i.e. large absorption will occur only in a very narrow frequency range. This is clearly illustrated by the following numerical example: suppose a resonator is tuned to a frequency of 100 Hz corresponding to an angular frequency of 628 s^{-1}. This can be achieved conveniently by a resonator volume of 1 litre. If it is matched, the resonator has a maximum absorption area which is as large as 1.87 m^2. Its Q-factor is – according to eqn (6.19) – about 500, the relative half-width is thus 0.002. This means, it is only in the range from 99.9 to 100.1 Hz that the absorption area of the resonator exceeds half its maximum value. Therefore the very high absorption in the resonance is paid for by the exceedingly narrow frequency bandwidth. This is why the application of such weakly damped resonators does not seem too useful. It is more promising to increase the losses and hence the bandwidth at the expense of maximum absorption.

Finally, we investigate the problem of audible decay processes, which we have already touched on in the preceding section. The reverberation time of the resonator can again be calculated by the relation (6.12)

$$T' = \frac{13.8}{\Delta\omega} = 13.8\frac{Q_A}{\omega_0}$$

In many cases this time cannot be ignored when considering the reverberation time of a room. What about the perceptibility of the decay process?

It is evident from the derivation of the absorption area, eqn (6.17), that the same amount of energy per second which is converted to heat in the interior of the resonator is being re-emitted by it, since we have assumed $R_0 = R_r$. Its maximum radiation power is thus $I(\lambda_0^2/2\pi)$, I being the intensity of the incident sound waves. Thus the intensity of the re-radiated sound at distance r is

$$I_s = \left(\frac{\lambda_0}{2\pi r}\right)^2 I = \left(\frac{c}{r\omega_0}\right)^2 I \tag{6.20}$$

Both intensities are equal at a distance

$$r = \frac{c}{\omega_0} = \frac{54}{f_0} \text{ metres} \tag{6.21}$$

The decay process of the resonator is therefore only audible in its immediate vicinity. In the example mentioned above this critical distance would be 0.54 m; at substantially larger distances the decay cannot be heard.

6.6 Sound absorption by porous materials

In Section 6.2 inevitable reflection losses of sound waves impinging on smooth surfaces were discussed which are caused by viscous and thermal processes. They occur within a boundary layer next to the surface, produced by the sound field. The thickness of this layer is typically in the range of 0.01 to 0.2 millimetres, depending on the frequency.

The absorption due to these effects is negligibly small if the surface is smooth (*see* Fig. 6.7a). It is larger, however, at rough surfaces since the roughness increases the volume of the zone in which the losses occur (Fig. 6.7b). And it is even more pronounced if the material contains pores, channels and voids connected with the air outside. A material of this kind is drawn schematically in Fig. 6.7c. Then the pressure fluctuations associated

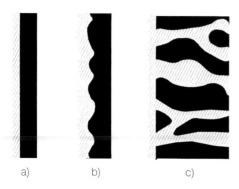

Figure 6.7 Lossy boundary layer: (a) in front of a smooth surface; (b) in front of a rough surface; (c) in front of and in a porous material.

with the external sound field give rise to alternating air flows in the pores and channels, the walls of which will be filled more or less by the lossy layer, so to speak. The consequence is that a significant amount of mechanical energy is withdrawn from the external sound field and is converted into heat.

This mechanism of sound absorption concerns all porous materials with pores accessible from the outside. Examples are the 'porous layers' which the reader encountered in Section 2.4 and which can be thought of as woven fabrics or thin carpets. More compact materials as used for reverberation control in rooms are mostly manufactured from incombustible fibres ('glass wool' or 'rock wool') or granules by pressing them together, often with the addition of suitable binding agents. Further common materials are foams of certain polymers, or porous bricks.

Of course it is not possible to describe exactly and in every detail the acoustical properties of such complicated structures; one usually has to resort to simplifying assumptions. In this presentation we do not attempt to give a description which pretends to be quantitative; instead we shall restrict our discussions to a highly idealised model of a porous material, the so-called Rayleigh model, which qualitatively exhibits the essential features.

It consists of a great number of similar equally spaced parallel channels which traverse a skeleton material considered to be completely rigid (*see* Fig. 6.8). It is assumed that the surface of that system, being located at $x = 0$, is perpendicular to the axes of the channels; in the positive x-direction it is assumed that the model is unbounded.

First we consider the sound propagation in a single channel. We suppose that it is so narrow that the profile of the air stream is determined almost completely by the viscosity of the air and not by any inertial forces. This is always the case at sufficiently low frequencies (compare also eqn (6.26)). Then the same lateral distribution of flow velocities prevails in the interior

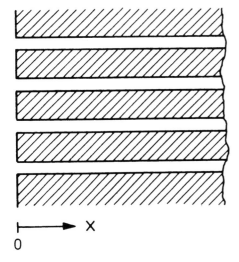

Figure 6.8 Rayleigh model, schematic representation.

of the channel as for constant (i.e. for non-alternating) flows; and likewise the flow resistance of the channel per unit length, which is defined by

$$\Xi' = -\frac{1}{\bar{v}}\frac{\partial p}{\partial x} \qquad (6.22)$$

has virtually the same value as for constant flow velocity. (In this formula $\bar{v}$ is the flow velocity averaged over the cross-section of the channel.) It is known from flow dynamics that for a flow between parallel planes at distance b, Ξ' is given by

$$\Xi' = \frac{12\eta}{b^2} \qquad (6.23)$$

whereas for narrow channels with circular cross-section (radius a)

$$\Xi' = \frac{8\eta}{a^2} \qquad (6.24)$$

In these formulae η denotes the viscosity of the streaming medium. For air under normal conditions $\eta = 1.8 \times 10^{-5}$ kg m^{-1} s^{-1}. In some texts on acoustics specific flow resistances are measured in units of 'Rayl/cm'. The conversion into the SI system is effected by the formula

$$1 \text{ Rayl/cm} = 1000 \text{ kg m}^{-3} \text{ s}^{-1}$$

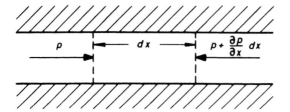

Figure 6.9 Forces acting on a length element in a rigid channel.

In order to study the sound propagation within one channel, consider a length element dx of it (*see* Fig. 6.9). The net force acting in positive x-direction on the air in it is $-(\partial p/\partial x)\,\mathrm{d}x\,\mathrm{d}S$, with d$S$ denoting the cross-sectional area of the channel. It is kept at equilibrium by an inertial force $\rho_0(\partial \bar{v}/\partial t)\,\mathrm{d}x\,\mathrm{d}S$ and a frictional force $\Xi'\bar{v}\,\mathrm{d}x\,\mathrm{d}S$, according to eqn (6.22). Thus the force equation which is analogous to eqn (1.2) reads

$$-\frac{\partial p}{\partial x} = \rho_0\frac{\partial \bar{v}}{\partial t} + \Xi'\bar{v} \tag{6.25}$$

This relation assumes that the flow velocity (or the particle velocity) is constant over the whole cross-section and equal to $\bar{v}$. This is of course not true. In reality a certain velocity distribution develops across and in the channel. However, a more thorough investigation shows that the representation (6.25) can be applied with sufficient accuracy so long as

$$\frac{\rho_0\omega}{\Xi'} \leq 4 \tag{6.26}$$

The equation of continuity (1.3) is not affected by the viscosity, thus

$$\rho_0\frac{\partial \bar{v}}{\partial x} = -\frac{\partial \rho}{\partial t} = -\frac{1}{c^2}\frac{\partial p}{\partial t} \tag{6.27}$$

Into eqns (6.25) and (6.27) we insert the following plane wave relations:

$$p = \hat{p}\exp\left[i(\omega t - k'x)\right], \quad \bar{v} = \hat{v}\exp\left[i(\omega t - k'x)\right]$$

and obtain two homogeneous equations for p and $\bar{v}$:

$$k'p - (\omega\rho_0 - i\Xi')\bar{v} = 0, \quad \omega p - \rho_0 c^2 k'\bar{v} = 0 \tag{6.28}$$

Setting the determinant, formed of the coefficients of p and $\bar{v}$, equal to zero yields the complex propagation constant

$$k' = \beta' - i\gamma' = \frac{\omega}{c}\left(1 - \frac{i\Xi'}{\rho_0\omega}\right)^{1/2} \tag{6.29}$$

with the phase constant $\beta' = 2\pi/\lambda'$ and the attenuation constant $\gamma' = m'/2$ (compare eqn (1.17)).

If we insert this result into one of eqns (6.28), we obtain the ratio of sound pressure to velocity, i.e. the characteristic impedance in the channel:

$$Z_0' = \frac{p}{\bar{v}} = \rho_0 c\left(1 - \frac{i\Xi'}{\rho_0\omega}\right)^{1/2} \tag{6.30}$$

For very high frequencies – or for very wide channels – these expressions approach the values ω/c and $\rho_0 c$, valid for free sound propagation, because then the viscous boundary layer occupies only a very small fraction of the cross-section. In contrast to this, at very low frequencies eqn (6.29) yields

$$\beta' = \gamma' \approx \left(\frac{\omega\Xi'}{2\rho_0 c^2}\right)^{1/2} \tag{6.31}$$

since $\sqrt{i} = (1 + i)/\sqrt{2}$. The attenuation in this range is thus considerable: a wave is reduced in its amplitude by 54.6 dB per wavelength.

From the characteristic impedance Z_0' inside the channels we pass to the 'average characteristic impedance' Z_0 of a porous material by use of the porosity σ as already introduced in eqn (6.6), which is the ratio of the cross-sectional area of one channel and the surface area per channel:

$$Z_0 = \frac{Z_0'}{\sigma} \tag{6.32}$$

Likewise, the 'outer flow resistance' Ξ, which can be measured directly by forcing air through a test sample of the material, is related to Ξ' by

$$\Xi = \frac{\Xi'}{\sigma} \tag{6.33}$$

For highly porous materials such as rock wool or mineral wool the porosity is close to unity, the specific flow resistance Ξ' is mostly in the range from 5000 to 10^5 kg m^{-3} s^{-1}.

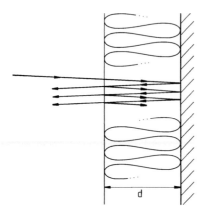

Figure 6.10 Porous layer in front of a rigid wall.

Now we apply the above relations to a typical arrangement consisting of a homogeneous layer of porous material in front of a rigid wall. The thickness of the layer is d (*see* Fig. 6.10). A sound wave arriving at the surface of the layer will be partially reflected from it; the remaining part of the sound energy will penetrate into the material and again reach the surface after its reflection from the rigid rear wall. Then it will again split up into one portion penetrating the surface and another one returning to the rear wall, and so on. This qualitative consideration shows that the reflected sound wave can be thought of as being made up of an infinite number of successive contributions, each of them weaker than the preceding one because of the considerable attenuation of the interior wave. Furthermore, it shows that the reflection factor and hence the absorption coefficient may show maxima and minima, depending on whether the various components interfere constructively or destructively at a given frequency.

For a quantitative treatment which will be restricted, however, to normal sound incidence we refer to eqn (2.20), according to which the 'wall impedance' of an air layer of thickness d in front of a rigid wall is $-i\rho_0 c \cot(kd)$. By replacing $\rho_0 c$ with Z_0 and k with k' we obtain for the wall impedance of the porous layer

$$Z = -iZ_0 \cot(k'd) \tag{6.34}$$

From this expression the reflection factor and the absorption coefficient can be calculated using eqns (2.7) and (2.8).

For the following discussion it is useful to separate the real and the imaginary part of the cotangent:

$$\cot(k'd) = \frac{\sin(2\beta'd) + i \sinh(2\gamma'd)}{\cosh(2\gamma'd) - \cos(2\beta'd)} \tag{6.35}$$

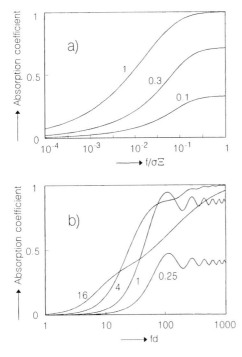

Figure 6.11 Absorption coefficient of a porous layer (Rayleigh model) in front of a rigid wall, normal sound incidence: (a) infinite thickness (frequency in Hz, Ξ' in kg m^{-3} s^{-1}; (b) finite thickness (fd in Hz m), $\sigma = 0.95$. The parameter is $\Xi'd/\rho_0c$. (When $\Xi'd/\rho_0c = 0.25$, the condition eqn (6.26) is only partially fulfilled.)

Then one can draw the following qualitative conclusions:

(a) For a layer which is thin compared with the sound wavelength, i.e. for $k'd \ll 1$, cot $(k'd)$ can be replaced with $1/k'd$. Hence the porous layer has a very large impedance and accordingly low absorption. In other words: substantial sound absorption cannot be achieved by just applying some kind of paint to a wall.

(b) If the sound waves inside the porous material undergo strong attenuation during one round trip, i.e. for $\gamma'd \gg 1$, the cotangent becomes i, according to eqn (6.35), and the wall impedance is

$$Z = \frac{Z_0'}{\sigma} = \frac{\rho_0 c}{\sigma}\left(1 - \frac{i\sigma\Xi}{\rho_0\omega}\right)^{1/2} \tag{6.36}$$

Figure 6.11a shows the absorption coefficient of the layer calculated from eqn (6.36). For high frequencies it approaches asymptotically the value

$$\alpha_\infty = \frac{4\sigma}{(1 + \sigma)^2} \tag{6.37}$$

(c) If, however, $\gamma'd \ll 1$, i.e. for small attenuation inside the material, the periodicity of the trigonometric functions in eqn (6.35) will dominate in the frequency dependence of the cotangent, and the same holds for that of the absorption coefficient represented in Fig. 6.11b. The latter has a maximum whenever $\beta'd$ equals $\pi/2$ or an odd multiple of it, i.e. at all frequencies for which the thickness d of the layer is an odd integer of $\lambda'/4$, with $\lambda' = 2\pi/\beta'$ denoting the wavelength inside the material. For higher values of $\Xi'd$ the fluctuations fade out. As a figure-of-merit we can consider $(fd)_{0.5}$, i.e. the value of the product fd for which the absorption coefficient exceeds 0.5. Its minimum value is $(fd)_{0.5} = 24$ which is achieved for $\Xi'd/\rho_0 c = 6$.

If we want a high absorption coefficient at low frequencies, we do not necessarily need a thick porous layer. The only essential thing is that there is a porous sheet with a sufficiently high flow resistance at a distance in front of a rigid wall which, at the interesting frequencies, amounts to about a quarter wavelength; between the porous layer and the wall there may simply be air. If we only have thin sheets of absorbent material at our disposal, it is better to mount them at a certain distance from the wall (Fig. 6.12b) than directly onto the wall (Fig. 6.12a). This saving in material is offset by an absorption coefficient which decreases at higher frequencies. In the limiting case of vanishingly thin absorbent sheets we ultimately arrive at the stretched fabric which we have already dealt with in Section 2.4.

In the ideal Rayleigh model with rigid channel walls, which we have been discussing, there is no lateral coupling. A surface perpendicular to the channel axes therefore has a wall impedance which is independent of the angle

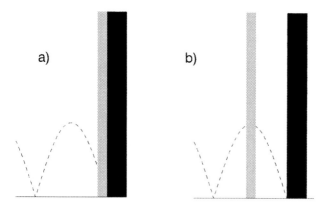

Figure 6.12 Porous layer in front of a rigid wall (dotted line: distribution of particle velocity without layer: (a) layer immediately on the wall; (b) layer at some distance from the wall.

of sound incidence. Its absorption coefficient at oblique incidence can be calculated from its impedance by eqn (2.16). Real absorbent materials behave differently in this respect, at least in principle, since their internal channels run in all directions and are interconnected by a great many side branches, thus effecting lateral coupling at oblique incidence. Only at low frequencies this coupling is negligible because of the high attenuation per wavelength γ'/β' in this range according to eqn (6.31).

We want to emphasise here that the Rayleigh model, even at normal sound incidence, is only useful for a qualitative understanding of the effects in a porous material but not for a quantitative calculation of the acoustical properties of real absorbent materials. The assumed rigidity of its skeleton is a simplification which is not entirely justified in practice. Furthermore, these materials do not contain well separated and distinguishable channels but rather irregularly shaped cavities which are mutually connected. The pores or channels are often so narrow that there must surely be some heat exchange between the air contained in the channels and the walls. Therefore the changes of state of the air occur neither adiabatically nor according to an isothermal law but somehow in between these limiting cases which causes an additional complication. In the past attempts have been made to take these effects, which are not covered by the simple Rayleigh model, into account by introducing a 'structure factor' which can, however, only be evaluated experimentally. From a practical point of view it therefore seems more advantageous to omit such a sophisticated treatment and to determine the absorption coefficient by measurement. This procedure is recommended all the more because the performance of porous absorbers depends only partially on the properties of the material and to a greater extent on its arrangement, on the covering and on other constructional details, which vary substantially from one situation to another.

When porous absorbent materials are used for reducing the reverberation time of a room, it will usually be necessary to cover these materials in some way on the side exposed to the room. Many of these materials will in the course of time shed small particles which must be prevented from polluting the air in the room. If the absorbent portions of wall are within the reach of people, a suitable covering is desirable too as a protection against unintentional thoughtless damage of the materials which are not usually very hard wearing. And, finally, the architect usually wishes to hide the rock wool layer which is not aesthetically pleasing behind a surface which can be treated according to his wishes. Very often, thin and highly perforated or slotted panels of wood, metal or gypsum board are employed for this purpose. Their surfaces can be painted and cleaned from time to time; however, care must be taken that the openings are not blocked.

To prevent purling (or to keep water away from the pores, as for instance in swimming baths) it is sufficient to bag the absorbent materials in very thin plastic foils. Furthermore, purling can be avoided by a somewhat denser porous front layer on the bulk of the material.

According to Section 6.3, foils, as well as perforated or slotted panels, have a certain sound transmissibility which may be close to unity at low frequencies and which is identical to the absorption coefficient in eqn (6.4). It would be wrong, however, to calculate the absorption of the combination of porous material plus covering by multiplying the absorption coefficient of the uncovered layer by the transmissibility of the covering. Instead one has to add the wall impedance $i\omega M$ of the perforated panel or of the foil to the impedance of the porous layer. The resulting impedance can be better matched in certain frequency ranges to the characteristic impedance of the air, in which case the absorption is increased by the covering. This will occur if the wall impedance of the uncovered arrangement has a negative imaginary part, i.e. if the distance between the surface of the porous layer and the rigid wall behind it is less than a quarter wavelength. The added mass reduces this imaginary part and this results in a higher absorption coefficient according to Fig. 2.2, the absorbent layer having been changed into a resonance absorber as discussed in Section 6.4.

We close this section by presenting a few typical results as measured in the reverberation chamber, i.e. at random sound incidence. This method will be described in more detail in Section 8.8. Although being very useful, it has the peculiarity that the results it yields for highly absorptive test samples are occasionally in excess of unity, although absorption coefficients beyond 1 are physically meaningless.

In Fig. 6.13 the absorption coefficient of two homogeneous rock wool layers, which are 50 mm thick, is shown as a function of the frequency. Both materials differ in their densities and hence in their flow resistances. Obviously the denser material exhibits an absorption coefficient close to 1 even at lower frequencies.

Figure 6.14 shows the absorption coefficient of a porous sheet with 30 mm thickness and a density of 46.5 kg/m³ which is mounted directly in front of a rigid wall in the first case; in the other case there is an air space of 50 mm between the sheet and the wall. The latter is partitioned off by wooden lattices with a pattern of 50 cm × 50 cm. Evidently, the air space achieves a significant shift of the steep absorption increase towards lower frequencies. Thus an air space behind the absorbent material considerably improves its effectiveness or helps to save material and costs.

The influence of a covering is demonstrated in Fig. 6.15. In both cases the porous layer has a thickness of 50 mm and is mounted directly onto the wall. The fraction of hole areas, i.e. the perforation, is 14%. The mass load corresponding to it is responsible for an absorption maximum at 800 Hz which is not present for the bare material. This shift of the absorption to lower frequencies can sometimes be very desirable. It must be paid for, however, by a loss of absorption at higher frequencies. At a higher degree of perforation this influence is much less pronounced, and with a perforation of 25% or more the effect of the covering plate can virtually be neglected.

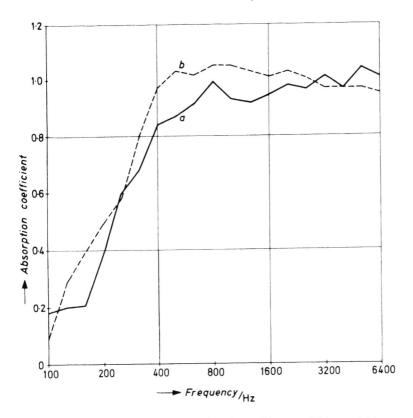

Figure 6.13 Absorption coefficient of rock wool layers of 50 mm thickness, mounted immediately on concrete (random incidence): (a) density 40 kg/m³, 12.7 Rayl/cm; (b) density 100 kg/m³, 22 Rayl/cm.

6.7 Audience and seat absorption

The purpose of most medium to large size halls is to accommodate a large number of spectators or listeners and thus enable them to watch events or functions of common interest. This is true for concert halls and lecture rooms, for theatres and opera houses, for churches and sports halls, cinemas, council chambers and entertainment halls of every kind. The important acoustical properties are therefore those which are present when the rooms are occupied or at least partially occupied. These properties are largely determined by the audience itself, especially by the sound absorption effected by the people or, strictly speaking, by their clothing. The only exceptions are broadcasting and television studios, which are not intended to be used with an audience present, and certain acoustical measuring rooms.

The absorption effected by an audience is due mainly to people's clothing and its porosity. Since clothing is not usually very thick, the absorption is

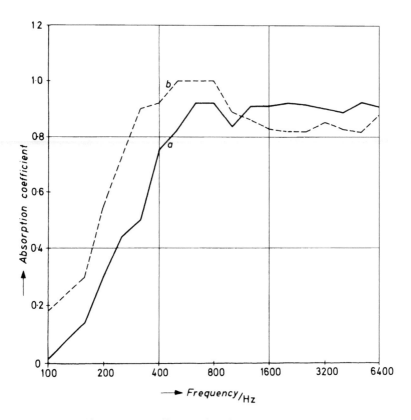

Figure 6.14 Absorption coefficient of rock wool layer of 30 mm thickness and density 46.5 kg/m³ (12 Rayl/cm), random incidence: (a) mounted immediately on concrete; (b) mounted 50 mm distant from concrete rear wall, air space laterally partitioned.

considerable only at medium and high frequencies; in the range of low frequencies it is relatively small. Since people's clothing differs from individual to individual, only average values of the audience absorption are available and it is quite possible that these values are changing with the passage of time according to changing fashion or season. Furthermore, audience absorption depends on the kind of seats and their arrangement, on the occupancy density, on the way in which the audience is exposed to the incident sound, on the interruption of 'blocks' by aisles, stairs, etc., and not least on the structure of the sound field. It is quite evident that a person seated at the rear of a box with a small opening, as was typical in 18th- to 19th-century theatres, absorbs much less sound energy than a person sitting among steeply raked rows of seats and who is thus well exposed to the sound. Therefore it is not surprising that there are considerable differences in the data on audience absorption which have been given by different authors.

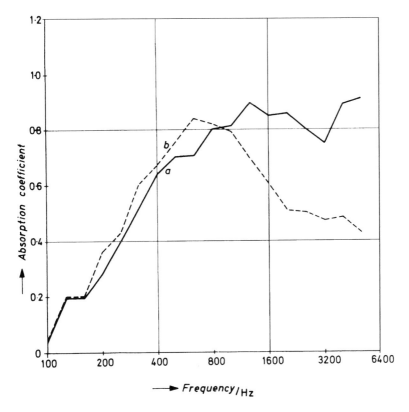

Figure 6.15 Absorption coefficient of 50 mm glass wool, mounted immediatley on concrete (random incidence): (a) uncovered; (b) covered by a panel of 5 mm thickness, perforated at 14%.

There are two ways to determine experimentally the sound absorption of audience and seats. One is to place seats and/or persons into a reverberation chamber and evaluate their absorption from the change in reverberation time they cause. This has the advantage that sound field diffusion which is a prerequisite for the applicability of the common reverberation formulae can be established by adequate means. On the other hand, it may be doubtful whether a 'block' consisting 20 or 25 seats is representative for an extended area covered with occupied or unoccupied seats. In the second method, completed concert halls are used as reverberation chambers, so to speak: the absorption data are derived from reverberation times measured in them. The structure of the sound field is unknown in the second method, but – provided the shape of the hall is not too unusual – it can at least be considered as typical for such halls.

The absorption of persons standing singly or seated is characterised most appropriately by their absorption cross-section or absorption area A,

Table 6.2 Absorption areas of single persons (in m²)

Type of person	Frequency (Hz)					
	125	250	500	1000	2000	4000
Male standing in heavy coat	0.17	0.41	0.91	1.30	1.43	1.47
Male standing without coat	0.12	0.24	0.59	0.98	1.13	1.12
Musician sitting with instrument (after Kath and Kuhl[3])	0.60	0.95	1.06	1.08	1.08	1.08

already defined in eqn (6.13) in Section 6.5. The absorption area of each person is added to the sum of eqn (5.23a), which in this case reads

$$\bar{\alpha} = \frac{1}{S}\left(\sum_i S_i \alpha_i + N_p A \right) \tag{6.38}$$

N_p being the number of persons.

Table 6.2 lists some absorption areas as a function of the frequency measured by Kath and Kuhl[3] in the reverberation chamber.

When people are seated close together (which is usual in occupied rooms) it seems to be more correct[4] to relate the absorption of audience and areas covered with equal chairs, not to the number of 'objects' but to their area, i.e. to characterise it by an apparent absorption coefficient, since this figure seems to be less dependent on the density of chairs or listeners. In Table 6.3 absorption coefficients of seated audience and of unoccupied seats as measured in a reverberation chamber are listed. Although the absorption of an audience in a particular hall may be different from the data shown, the latter demonstrate at least the general features of audience absorption: at increasing frequencies the absorption coefficients increase at first. For frequencies higher than 2000 Hz, however, they decrease. This decrease is presumably due to mutual shadowing of absorbent surface areas; this shadowing becomes more prominent at high frequencies because at higher frequencies it is not overcome by diffraction around the heads, arms and other parts of the listeners' bodies.

The effect of upholstered chairs essentially consists of an increase in absorption at low frequencies, whereas at frequencies of about 1000 Hz and above there is no significant difference between the absorption of audiences seated on upholstered or on unupholstered chairs.

Large collections of data on seat and audience absorption have been published by Beranek[6] and by Beranek and Hidaka,[7] the latter being obviously an update of the former. These authors determined absorption coefficients from the reverberation times of completed concert halls using the Sabine formula, eqn (5.24) with (5.23a). It should be emphasised that their calculations are based upon the 'effective seating area' S_a which includes

Table 6.3 Absorption coefficients of audience and chairs
(reverberation chamber data)

Type of seats	Frequency (Hz)						
	125	250	500	1000	2000	4000	6000
Audience seated on wooden chairs, two persons per m² (Ref. 5)	0.24	0.40	0.78	0.98	0.96	0.87	0.80
Audience seated on wooden chairs, one person per m² (Ref. 5)	0.16	0.24	0.56	0.69	0.81	0.78	0.75
Audience seated on moderately upholstered chairs, 0.85 m × 0.63 m	0.72	0.82	0.91	0.93	0.94	0.87	0.77
Audience seated on moderately upholstered chairs, 0.90 m × 0.55 m	0.55	0.86	0.83	0.87	0.90	0.87	0.80
Moderately upholstered chairs, unoccupied, 0.90 m × 0.55 m	0.44	0.56	0.67	0.74	0.83	0.87	0.80

not only the floor area covered by chairs but also a strip of 0.5 m around the actual area of a block of seating except for the edge of a block when it is adjacent to a wall or a balcony face. This correction is to account for the so-called 'edge effect', i.e. diffraction of sound which generally occurs at the edges of an absorbent area (*see* Section 8.7). Absorption coefficients for closed blocks of seats – unoccupied as well as occupied – are listed in Table 6.4. The data shown are averages over three groups of halls with different types of seat upholstery. They show the same general frequency dependency as the absorption coefficients listed in Table 6.3 apart from the slight decrease towards very high frequencies for occupied seats which is missing in Table 6.4. Evidently, the influence of seat upholstery is particularly pronounced in the low frequency range.

Beranek and Hidaka had the opportunity of assembling reverberation data from several halls before the chairs were installed. From these values they evaluated what they called the 'residual absorption coefficients', α_r, i.e. the total absorption for all walls, the ceiling, balcony faces, etc., except the floor, divided by their area S_r. Since these data are interesting in their own right we present their averages in Table 6.5. The residual absorption coefficients include the absorption of chandeliers, ventilation openings and other typical installations, and they show remarkably small variances.

It has been known for a long time that an audience does not only absorb the impinging sound waves, thus reducing the reverberation time of the

Table 6.4 Absorption coefficients of unoccupied and occupied seating areas in concert halls (after Beranek and Hidaka[7])

Type of seats		Frequency (Hz)					
		125	250	500	1000	2000	4000
Heavily upholstered	Unoccupied (seven halls)	0.70	0.76	0.81	0.84	0.84	0.81
	Occupied (seven halls)	0.72	0.80	0.86	0.89	0.90	0.90
Medium upholstered	Unoccupied (eight halls)	0.54	0.62	0.68	0.70	0.68	0.66
	Occupied (eight halls)	0.62	0.72	0.80	0.83	0.84	0.85
Lightly upholstered	Unoccupied (four halls)	0.36	0.47	0.57	0.62	0.62	0.60
	Occupied (six halls)	0.51	0.64	0.75	0.80	0.82	0.83

First group: 7.5 cm upholstery on front side of seat back, 10 cm on top of seat bottom, arm rests upholstered. Second group: 2.5 cm upholstery on front side of seat back, 2.5 cm on top of seat bottom, solid arm rests. Third group: 1.5 cm upholstery on front side of seat back, 2.5 cm on top of seat bottom, solid arm rests.

Table 6.5 Residual absorption coefficients α_r from concert halls (after Beranek and Hidaka[7])

Type of hall	Frequency (Hz)					
	125	250	500	1000	2000	4000
Group A: Halls lined with wood, less than 3 cm thick, or with other thin materials (six halls)	0.16	0.13	0.10	0.09	0.08	0.08
Group B: Halls lined with heavy material i.e. with concrete, plaster more than 2.5 cm thick etc. (three halls)	0.12	0.10	0.08	0.08	0.08	0.08

room, but it also attenuates the sound waves propagating parallel to the audience. About the same holds for unoccupied seats. Attenuation in excess of the $1/r$-law of eqn (1.19) or (1.21) is actually observed whenever a wave propagates along an absorbent surface and may be attributed to some sort of refraction which partially directs the sound wave into the absorbent material.

A characteristic phenomenon which has been observed by many researchers[8,9] at grazing sound incidence on empty chairs in large halls is the 'seat dip effect', i.e. a maximum of the excess attenuation occurring in the

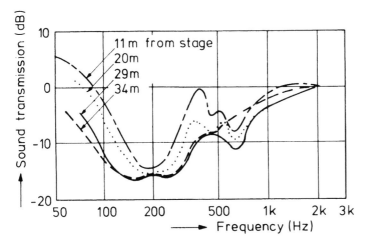

Figure 6.16 Transmission characteristics of the direct sound, measured at various seats of the main floor in the Boston Symphony Hall.[8] The numbers in the figure indicate the distance from the stage.

range of 80 to 200 Hz, depending on the angle of sound incidence and other parameters. An example is shown in Fig. 6.16, for which the attenuation due to spherical divergence has been subtracted from the data. The minimum in these curves is usually attributed to a vertical $\lambda/4$-resonance of the space between seating rows. Some authors have found a seat dip also with occupied seats, others have not. Figure 6.17 presents the excess sound pressure levels over occupied seats as a function of the frequency as measured by E. Mommertz[10] in a large hall with horizontal floor by employing maximum length sequence techniques (*see* Section 8.2). The figures indicate the number of the row where the microphone was located. An evaluation of these data shows that there is a linear level decrease from front to rear seats, indicating an excess attenuation of the audience of roughly 1 dB/metre in the range 500–2000 Hz. It should be noted that not only the direct sound but also reflections from vertical side walls are subject to this kind of excess attenuation.

The selective attenuation cannot be considered as an acoustical fault since it takes place in good concert halls as well as in poorer ones (except, of course, in the very first seating rows of main floors and balconies). Obviously it is not the spectral composition of the direct sound and of the side wall reflections which is responsible for the tonal balance but rather that of all contributions to the intensity at the listeners' ears.

Listening conditions will be impaired, however, if the sight lines from the listeners to the sound source are obscured by the heads of other listeners sitting in front of them or by other obstacles. Therefore it is important that the seats are arranged in such a way that the listeners are freely exposed to

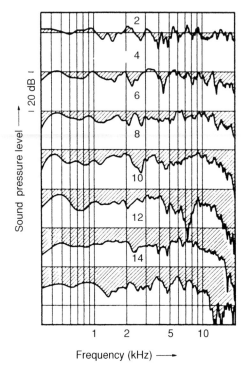

Figure 6.17 Sound pressure level over audience, relative to level at free propagation (horizontal lines). The figures denote the number of the seating row. The source is 2.5 m from the first row and 1.4 m high (after Mommertz[10]).

the direct sound and to the reflections arriving from the side walls (*see* also Sections 9.1 and 9.2).

6.8 Miscellaneous objects (freely hanging fabrics, pseudostochastic diffusers, etc.)

The first 'sound absorber' to be discussed in this section is a plane curtain of flexible and porous material in a room, well away from all its walls. Its acoustical properties are characterised by its flow resistance r_s and its mass M_s per unit area. These quantities are combined in Z_r which is defined as

$$Z_r = \frac{p - p'}{v_s} \tag{6.39}$$

similar to the definition of flow resistance in eqn (2.17). $p - p'$ is the difference of sound pressures on both sides of the layer, and v_s denotes the particle velocity on its surface and perpendicular to it.

These quantities are easily obtained from eqns (2.12*a*) and (2.13*b*) with $x = y = 0$. They yield $p = \hat{p}_0(1 + R)$ and $p' = \hat{p}_0 T$. The latter expression defines the 'transmission factor' T, $\hat{p}_0$ denotes the sound pressure amplitude of the incident wave. The normal component of the particle velocity is $v_s = \hat{p}_0(1 - R) \cos \Theta / \rho_0 c$ and, at the same time, $v_s = \hat{p}_0 T \cos \Theta / \rho_0 c$, where Θ denotes the angle of sound incidence. Equating both expressions leads to

$$T = 1 - R$$

while introducing v_s and $p - p'$ into eqn (6.39) yields

$$Z_r = \rho_0 c \frac{1 + R - T}{T \cos \Theta}$$

From both these relations the reflection factor R and the transmission factor T can be evaluated ($\zeta_r = Z_r / \rho_0 c$):

$$R(\Theta) = \frac{\dfrac{\zeta_r}{2} \cos \Theta}{1 + \dfrac{\zeta_r}{2} \cos \Theta} \tag{6.40}$$

and

$$T(\Theta) = \frac{1}{1 + \dfrac{\zeta_r}{2} \cos \Theta} \tag{6.41}$$

In contrast to the situation considered in Section 6.3, the curtain is not a boundary of the room. Therefore, the sound energy transmitted through it cannot be considered as lost or as 'absorbed'. Hence, to obtain the energy absorbed within the curtain one has to subtract both the reflected and the transmitted energy from the incident one. Therefore we arrive at

$$\alpha = 1 - |R|^2 - |T|^2$$

instead of eqn (2.1) This yields, after inserting eqns (6.40) and (6.41)

$$\alpha(\Theta) = \frac{\mathrm{Re}(\zeta_r) \cos \Theta}{|1 + (\zeta_r/2) \cos \Theta|^2} = \frac{\mathrm{Re}(\zeta_r) \cos \Theta}{(|\zeta_r|/2)^2 \cos^2 \Theta + \mathrm{Re}(\zeta_r) \cos \Theta + 1} \tag{6.42}$$

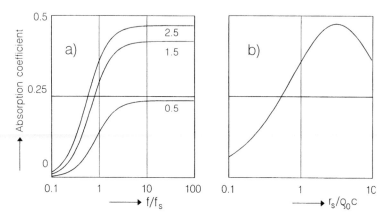

Figure 6.18 Absorption coefficient of freely hanging curtain, random sound incidence: (a) as a function of the frequency, parameter is $r_s/\rho_0 c$; (b) high frequency limit as a function of $r_s/\rho_0 c$.

Next we have to average eqn (6.42) over all incidence angles θ according to eqn (2.41). Since the last expression in eqn (6.42) is similar to eqn (2.16) we can immediately adopt eqn (2.42) as the result of this averaging by replacing the factor 8 with a factor 4, $\mathrm{Re}(\zeta)$ with $\mathrm{Re}(\zeta_r)/2$, and $|\zeta|$ with $|\zeta_r|/2$. The angle μ remains unaltered. Therefore the absorption coefficient of the curtain for random sound incidence reads:

$$\alpha_{uni} = \frac{16}{|\zeta_r|^2} \cos\mu \left[\frac{|\zeta_r|}{2} + \frac{\cos 2\mu}{\sin\mu} \arctan\left(\frac{|\zeta_r|\sin\mu}{2 + |\zeta_r|\cos\mu} \right) \right.$$

$$\left. - \cos\mu \ln\left(1 + |\zeta_r|\cos\mu + \frac{|\zeta_r|^2}{4} \right) \right] \tag{6.43}$$

In Figure 6.18a, α_{uni} of the curtain is plotted as a function of the frequency parameter F/F_s for various values of the flow resistance r_s. Far below the characteristic frequency $F_s = r_s/2\pi M_s$ (see eqn 2.17a) the absorption of the layer is very small since at these frequencies the layer follows nearly completely the vibrations imposed by the sound field. With increasing frequency, the inertia of the layer becomes more relevant, leading to an increasing motion of the air relative to the curtain. For high frequencies the layer stays practically at rest, and the absorption coefficient becomes frequency independent. This limiting value is plotted in Fig. 6.18b as a function of the the flow resistance r_s. It has a maximum of $\alpha_{uni} = 0.446$ occurring at $r_s = 3.136\rho_0 c$. This discussion shows that freely hanging curtains or large flags, etc. freely hanging in the room may considerably add to the absorption in it and may be used to control its reverberation.

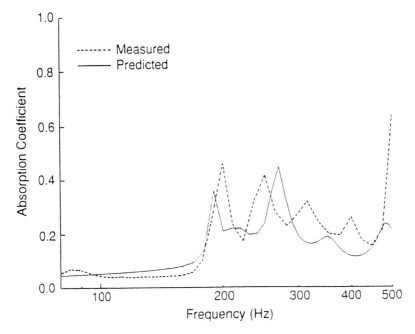

Figure 6.19 Absorption of a quadratic residue diffuser (QRD) with $N = 7$ (*see* Fig. 2.17), made of aluminium (after Fujiwara[12]).

The second object considered in this section is pseudostochastic diffusers. As mentioned by the end of Section 2.6, such devices show noticeable sound absorption even if they are manufactured from virtually loss-free materials. Recently such diffusers have been installed in several halls – mostly in form of QRD diffusers – and since possibly more halls will be equipped with them, the physical reasons for this absorption will be briefly discussed in this section.

The absorption of Schroeder diffusers was observed in 1992 by Fujiwara and Miyajima.[11] These authors found that the absorption of such diffusers could be reduced but not removed by careful surface treatment. In Fig. 6.19 the absorption coefficient of a QRD diffuser with a design frequency of 285 Hz is plotted. Being negligible at low frequencies, it shows a marked rise well below the design frequency and remains at a relatively high level although its value has several distinct maxima.

This effect can be explained by the fact[13,14] that, according to the simplified theory presented above, the waves reflected at the inner end of the troughs would cause abrupt phase jumps between adjacent openings. Such jumps are physically impossible; instead, any pressure differences will produce local air flows between the channel entrances which tend to equalise the pressure differences. These equalising flows may reach relatively high velocities which are not associated with far field radiation but which lead to additional viscous and thermal losses in the channels. As pointed out by Mechel,[15] additional losses are due to the fact that the local flows are forced to go around the sharp edges of adjacent troughs.

As was shown both by Fujiwara[12] and by Mechel,[15] surprisingly high absorptivities are not a peculiarity of pseudostochastic structures as discussed above but occur for any collection of wells or tubes with different lengths the openings of which are close to each other.

This leads us to the last 'absorbing' devices to be mentioned in this section namely to pipe organs which show remarkable sound absorption although no porous materials whatsoever are used in their construction. According to J. Meyer (see Ref. 6 of Chapter 1) the absorption coefficient of an organ, related to the area of its prospect, is as high as about 0.55 to 0.60 in the frequency range from 125 to 4000 Hz and has at least some influence on the reverberation time of a concert hall or a church.

6.9 Anechoic rooms

In the acoustical design of rooms, sound absorbers mounted on walls and ceilings are usually employed to meet one of the following objectives:

- to adapt the reverberation of the room, for instance of a concert hall, to the type of performances which are to be staged in it;
- to suppress sound reflections from remote walls which might be heard as echoes;
- to reduce the acoustical energy density and hence the sound pressure level in noisy rooms such as factories, for instance.

All these goals can be reached by sound absorbers of the kind described so far, although the elimination of echoes may require particular care, especially when the echo-producing wall shows a concave curvature. Matters are different for spaces which are intended for certain acoustical free field measurements such as the calibration of microphones or the determination of directional patterns of sound sources, etc. The same holds for psychoacoustic experiments. In all these cases the accuracy and the reliability of results would be impaired by the interference of the direct sound with sound components reflected from the boundaries.

One way to avoid reflections – except that from the ground – would be to perform such measurements or experiments in the open air. It has the disadvantage, however, that the experimenter depends on favourable weather conditions, which implies not only the absence of rain but of wind too. Furthermore, acoustic measurements in the open air can be affected by ambient noise.

A more convenient way is to use a so-called anechoic room or chamber, all boundaries of which are treated in such a way that virtually no sound reflections are produced by them, at least in the frequency range of interest. How stringent the conditions are which have to be met by the acoustical treatment may be illustrated by a simple example. If all boundaries of an enclosure have an absorption coefficient of 0.90, everybody would agree that the acoustics of this room is extremely 'dry' on account of its very low reverberation time. Nevertheless, the sound pressure level of a wave reflected from a wall would be only 10 dB lower than that of the incident wave! Therefore the usual requirement for the walls of an anechoic room is that the absorption coefficient is at least 0.99 for all angles of incidence. This requirement cannot be fulfilled with plane homogeneous layers of absorbent material; it can only be satisfied with a wall covering which achieves a stepwise or continuous transition of the characteristic impedance from that of the air to that of a highly lossy material.

In principle, this transition can be accomplished by a porous wall coating whose flow resistance increases in a well-defined way from the surface to the wall. It must be expected, however, that, at grazing sound incidence, the absorption of such a plane layer would be zero on account of total reflection. According to eqn (2.14b), the reflection factor becomes −1 when θ approaches 90°. Therefore it is more useful to achieve the desired transition by choosing a proper geometrical structure of the acoustical treatment than by varying the properties of the material. This can be achieved by pyramids or wedges of absorbent material which are mounted onto the walls. An incident sound wave then runs into channels with absorbent walls whose cross-sections steadily decrease in size, i.e. into reversed horns. The apertures at the front of these channels are very well matched to the characteristic impedance of the air and thus no significant reflection will occur.

This is only true, however, as long as the length of the channels, i.e. the thickness of the lining, is at least about one-third of the acoustical wavelength. This condition can easily be fulfilled at high frequencies, but only with great expense at frequencies of 100 Hz or below. For this reason every anechoic room has a certain lower limiting frequency, usually defined as the frequency at which the absorption coefficient of its walls becomes less than 0.99.

As to the production of such a lining, it is easier to utilise wedges instead of pyramids. The wedges must be made of a material with suitable flow resistance and sufficient mechanical solidity, and the front edges of neighbouring wedges or packets of wedges must be arranged at right angles to each other.

Since the floor, as well as the other walls, must be treated in the way just described, a net of steel cables or plastic wires must be installed in order to give access above the floor of the room. The reflections from this net can be safely neglected at audio frequencies.

The lower limiting frequency of an anechoic room can be further reduced by combining the pyramids or wedges with cavity resonators which are located between the latter and the rigid wall.[16] By choosing the apertures and

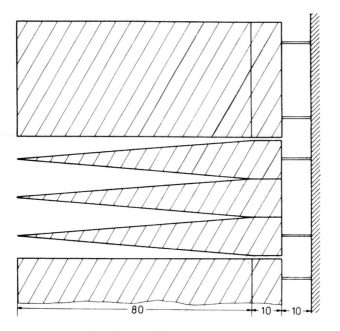

Figure 6.20 Absorbing wall lining of an anechoic room (dimensions in cm).

the depths of the resonators carefully, the reflection can be suppressed at frequencies at which substantial reflection would occur without the resonators.

In this way, for a particular anechoic room,[17] a lower limiting frequency of
80 Hz was achieved by lining to a total depth of 1 m. The absorber material has a density of 150 kg/m³ and a flow resistance of about 10⁵ kg/m³ s. It
is fabricated in wedges of 13 cm × 40 cm base area and 80 cm length, which
terminate in rectangular blocks of the same base area and 10 cm length.
Between these blocks there are narrow gaps of 1 cm width which run into
an air cushion of 10 cm depth between the absorber material and the concrete wall (*see* Fig. 6.20). The latter acts as a resonator volume, the necks of
which are the gaps between the wedges. Three wedges with parallel edge
are joined together in a packet; neighbouring packets are rotated by 90°
with respect to each other. A view of the interior of this anechoic room is
presented in Fig. 6.21.

Another way of achieving a continuous transition towards the wall is to
string dense rock wool cubes of increasing size onto wires – like strings of
pearls. These wires are stretched in parallel planes in front of the wall.[18]
Next to the wall, the cubes merge to form closed layers of rock wool. At
the ceiling the absorbent cubes are strung onto wires suspended from the
ceiling and, similarly, at floor level they are pushed onto steel rods in
a specific way and at prefixed distances. This arrangement seems to be

Figure 6.21 Anechoic room fitted with 65 loudspeakers for synthesising complex sound fields.

advantageous especially for sound at grazing incidence, since the fraction which is not absorbed is scattered uniformly rather than reflected in certain directions.

Anechoic rooms are usually checked by observing the way in which the sound amplitude decreases when the distance from a sound source is increased. This decrease should take place according to a $1/r$ law to simulate perfect outdoor conditions. In practice, with increasing distance, deviations from this simple law become more and more apparent in the form of random fluctuations. Since these fluctuations are caused by wall reflections, they can be used to evaluate the average absorption coefficient of the walls. Several methods have been worked out to perform these measurements and to determine the wall absorption from their results.[19,20]

References

1 Mechel, F., *Schallabsorber*, S. Hirzel Verlag, Stuttgart, 1989/95/98.
2 Bass, H.F., Sutherland, L.C., Zuckerwar, A.J., Blackstock, D.T. and Hester, D.M., *J. Acoust. Soc. America*, **97** (1995) 680.
3 Kath, U. and Kuhl, W., *Acustica*, **15** (1965) 127.
4 Beranek, L.L., *J. Acoust. Soc. America*, **32** (1960) 661.
5 Meyer, E., Kunstmann, D. and Kuttruff, H., *Acustica*, **14** (1964) 119.

6 Beranek, L.L., *Concert and Opera Halls: How They Sound*, Acoustical Society of America, Woodbury, New York, 1996.

7 Beranek, L.L. and Hidaka, T., *J. Acoust. Soc. America*, **104** (1998) 3169.

8 Schultz, T.J., and Watters, B.G., *J. Acoust. Soc. America*, **36** (1964) 885.

9 Sessler, G.M., and West, J.E., *J. Acoust. Soc. America*, **36** (1964) 1725.

10 Mommertz, E., *Acustica*, **79** (1993) 42.

11 Fujiwara, K. and Miyajima, T., *Appl. Acoustics*, **35** (1992) 149.

12 Fujiwara, K., *Acustica*, **81** (1995) 370.

13 Takahashi, D., Proceedings of the Sabine Centennial Symposium, Cambridge, Mass., (Acoustical Society of America, Woodbury, New York, 1994), p. 149.

14 Kuttruff, H., *Appl. Acoustics*, **42** (1994) 215.

15 Mechel, F.P., *Acustica*, **81** (1995) 379.

16 Kurtze, G., *Acustica*, **2** (Akust. Beihefte) (1951/52) 104.

17 Meyer, E., Kurtze, G., Severin, H. and Tamm, K., *Acustica*, **3** (1953) 409.

18 Rother, P. and Nutsch, J., Proceedings of the Fourth International Congress on Acoustics, Copenhagen, 1962, Paper M44.

19 Diestel, H.G., *Acustica*, **12** (1962) 113.

20 Delany, M.E. and Bazley, E.N., Proceedings of the Fourth International Congress on Acoustics, Budapest, 1971, Paper 24A6.

7 Characterisation of subjective effects

The preceding chapters were devoted exclusively to the physical side of room acoustics, i.e. the objectively measurable properties of sound fields in a room and to the circumstances which are responsible for their origin. We could be satisfied with this aspect if the only problems at stake were those of noise abatement by reverberation reduction and hence by reduction of the energy density, or if we only had to deal with problems of measuring techniques, which will be discussed in more detail in Chapter 8.

In most cases, however, the 'final consumer' of acoustics is the listener who wants to enjoy a concert, for example, or who attends a lecture or a theatre performance. This listener does not by any means require the reverberation time, at the various frequencies, to have certain values; neither does he insist that the sound energy at his seat should exhibit a certain directional distribution. Instead he expects the room with its 'acoustics' to support the music being performed or to render speech easily intelligible (as far as this depends on acoustic properties). This is true not only in the case of listeners who are personally present in the room under consideration but also when the sounds are transferred to another room, as for instance in broadcasting. Similarly, it does not matter whether the perceived sounds originate from the lips of an orator or from the membrane of a loudspeaker as long as the latter does not attract the listener's attention because of poor tonal quality or other undesirable effects.

Hence we must now focus our attention on the question as to which properties of the sound field are related to certain hearing impressions: whether and how a particular reflection will be perceived, which values of reverberation times at various frequencies are preferable for a particular kind of performance, and which other physical parameters may influence the listener's impression of the acoustics of a room in one way or another. With these considerations we leave the region of purely physical fact and enter the realm of psychoacoustics.

The previously mentioned questions and similar problems have in the past been the subject of numerous investigations – experimental investigations – since answers to these problems, which are not affected by the stigma of pure speculation, can only be obtained by experiments. Unfortunately their results do not form an unequivocal picture, in contrast to what we are accustomed to in the purely physical branch of acoustics. This is ascribed to the very involved physiological properties of our hearing organ but perhaps even more to the manner in which hearing sensations are processed by our brain; it can also be attributed to our hearing habits and, last but not least, to the personal aesthetic sensitivity of the listener – at least as far as musical productions are concerned. Another reason for our incomplete knowledge in this field is the great number of sound field components, which all may influence the subjective hearing impression. The experimental results which are available to date must therefore be considered in spite of the fact that many are unrelated or sometimes even inconsistent, and that every day new and surprising insights into psychoacoustic effects and their significance in room acoustics can be found.

There are basically two methods which are employed for investigating the subjective effects of complex sound fields, namely to synthesise sound fields with well-defined properties and to have them judged by test subjects, and to judge directly the acoustical qualities of completed halls, the objective properties of which are known from previous measurement. Each of these methods has its own merits and limitations, and each of them has contributed to understanding. The synthesis or laboratory simulation of sound fields permits easy and rapid variations of sound field parameters and the immediate comparison of different field configurations. It is not free, however, from a somewhat artificial character in that it is impossible to simulate sound fields of real halls in their full complexity. Instead certain simplifications have to be made which restrict the application of this method to the investigation of particular aspects.

As with any psychoacoustic experiments, systematic listening tests with synthetic sound fields are very time-consuming, and the quality of their results depends a good deal on the experience and goodwill of the test subjects and on the instructions given to them prior to the tests.

The direct judgement of real halls leads to relatively reliable results if speech intelligibility is the only property in question since the latter can be determined by special objective tests (*see* Section 7.4). The subjective assessment of the acoustics of concert halls or opera theatres, however, is affected by great uncertainties, one of which is the limited memory which impedes the direct comparison of different halls. Furthermore, two halls differ invariably in more than one respect which makes it difficult to correlate subjective opinions with one particular property such as, for instance, reverberation time. Nevertheless, many important facts have become known in the course of time just by interviewing many concert or opera goers.

Moreover, the immediate comparison of aural impressions from different halls has been greatly improved by progress in sound reproduction and signal processing techniques. They allow music samples played and recorded in different places to be reproduced with high fidelity. For this purpose it is not sufficient that all electro-acoustic components, such as microphones, recorders and loudspeakers, are of excellent quality. Of equal importance is that the system is capable of transmitting and reproducing all effects brought about by the complex structure of the original sound field. This is achieved by a system which exactly transplants the signals, which the original sound field would produce at both ears of a listener, to the ears of a remote listener.

As a first step, the signals in the original room must be recorded by a dummy head, i.e. by an artificial head with microphones built into the artifical ear channels. It is important that the dummy head which usually includes body and shoulders diffracts the arriving sound waves in a way which is representative for the majority of human listeners.[1] Nowadays, several types of dummy heads are available which meet this requirement. An example is shown in Fig. 7.1. The signals recorded in this way are stored using a digital tape recorder or another storage medium.

Equally important is the correct reproduction of the recorded and stored ear signals. In principle, high quality headphones could be used for this purpose. Unfortunately, this kind of reproduction is often plagued by 'in-head-localisation', i.e. for some reason the listener has the impression that the sound source is located within the rear part of his head. The problem with loudspeaker reproduction, on the other hand, is that without particular preventive measures the right-hand loudspeaker will inevitably send a cross-talk signal to the left ear and vice versa. This can be avoided by a filter which 'foresees' this effect and adds proper cancellation signals to the input signals. This technique, nowadays referred to as 'cross talk cancellation' (CTC), was invented and first demonstrated by Atal and Schroeder.[2] Fig. 7.2 depicts the principle of CTC. A more detailed description of it may be found in Ref. 3.

In this way, a listener can immediately compare music motifs which have been recorded in different halls or at different places in one hall. Moreover, these techniques can be used to create realistic listening impressions from models of auditoria which are still under design. And finally, by using such a system the acoustics of completely hypothetical enclosures can be judged and compared with those of existing environments. As will be described in Section 9.7, the sound propagation in a room with given or assumed geometrical and acoustical data can be simulated and represented by binaural impulse responses. Once the impulse response for a particular listening position has been evaluated, a digital filter with exactly that response can be established and used to modify applied sound signals in the same way as the assumed room would modify them. Hence, these techniques are useful not only to learn more about the subjective effects of constructional features (reverberation, volume, ceiling height, etc.) but also as a valuable tool in the acoustical design of auditoria.

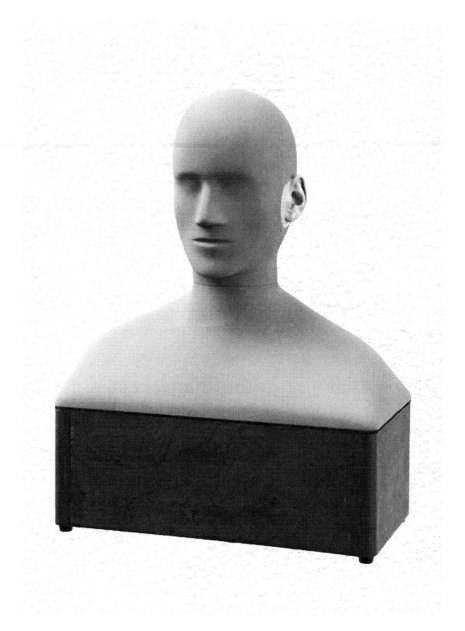

Figure 7.1 Dummy head (Institute of Technical Acoustics, Aachen, Germany).

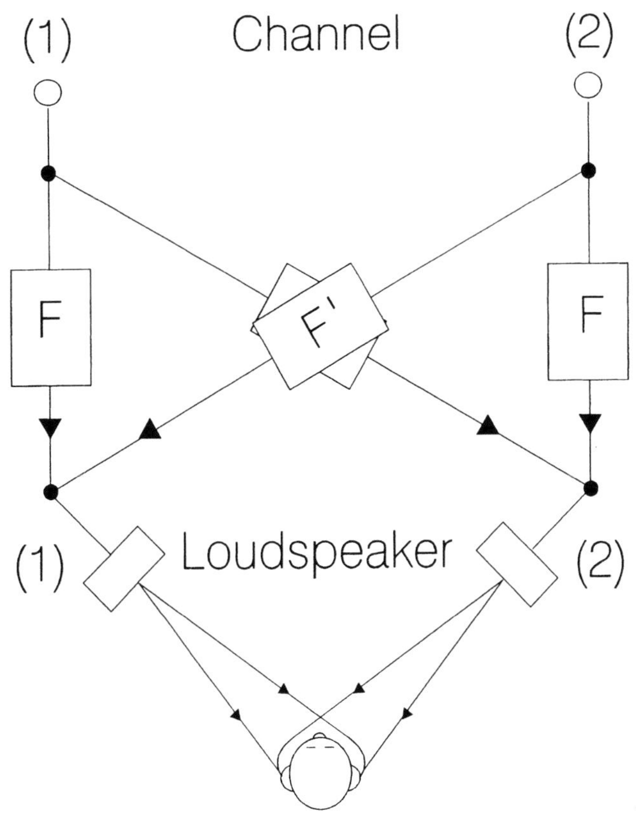

Figure 7.2 Principle of cross-talk cancellation in loudspeaker reproduction of binaural signals. F and F′ are digital filters.

7.1 Some general remarks on reflections and echoes

In the following discussion we shall regard the sound transmission between two points of a room as formally represented by the impulse response of the transmission path. According to eqn (4.4), this impulse response is composed of numerous repetitions of the original sound impulse as it is generated by the sound source. Since our hearing is sensitive to the direction of sound incidence, this description has to be completed by indicating the direction from which each repetition will arrive at the receiving point. As already mentioned in Section 4.1, the various components of the impulse response are not exact replicas of the original sound signal, strictly speaking, because of the frequency dependence of the wall reflectivities.

In the following two sections this fact will be disregarded, as has been done in eqn (4.4).

There are two experiences of the subjective effect of reflected portions of sound which are familiar to everyone: under certain conditions such a reflection can become a distinct 'echo'. In that case it is heard consciously as a repetition of the original signal. This can frequently be observed outdoors with sound reflections from the walls of houses or from the edge of forests. In closed rooms such experiences are less familiar, since the echoes in them are fortunately usually masked by the general reverberation of the room. Whether a reflection will become an echo or not depends on its delay with respect to the direct sound, on its relative strength, on the nature of the sound signal, and on the presence of other reflections which eventually mask the reflection under consideration.

The second common experience concerns our ability to localise sound sources in closed rooms. Although in a room which is not too heavily damped the sum of all reflected sound energies is mostly a multiple of the directly received energy, our hearing can usually localise the direction of the sound source without any difficulty. Obviously it is the sound signal to reach the listener first which subjectively determines the direction from which the sound comes. This fact is called – according to L. Cremer – the 'law of the first wave front'. In Section 7.3 we shall discuss the conditions under which it is valid.

In the following sections the subjective effects of sound fields with increasing complexity will be discussed. It is quite natural that the criteria of judgement become less and less detailed: in a sound field consisting of 1000 reflections we cannot investigate the effects of each reflection separately.

Many of the experimental results to be reported on have been obtained with the use of synthetic sound fields, as mentioned earlier: in an anechoic chamber the reflections, as well as the direct sound, are 'simulated' by loudspeakers which have certain positions *vis-à-vis* the test subject; these positions correspond to the desired directional distribution. The differences in the strengths of the various reflections are achieved by attenuators in the electrical lines feeding the loudspeakers, whereas their mutual delay differences are produced by electrical delay units. When necessary or desired, reverberation with prescribed properties can be added to the signals. For this purpose signals are passed through a so-called reverberator, which is also most conveniently realised with digital methods nowadays. (Other methods of reverberating signals will be mentioned in Section 10.5.) A typical setup for psychoacoustic experiments related to room acoustics is sketched in Fig. 7.3; it allows simulation of the direct sound, two side wall reflections and one ceiling reflection. The reverberated signal is reproduced by four additional loudspeakers. A more complete and flexible loudspeaker arrangement for similar purposes was shown in Fig. 6.21.

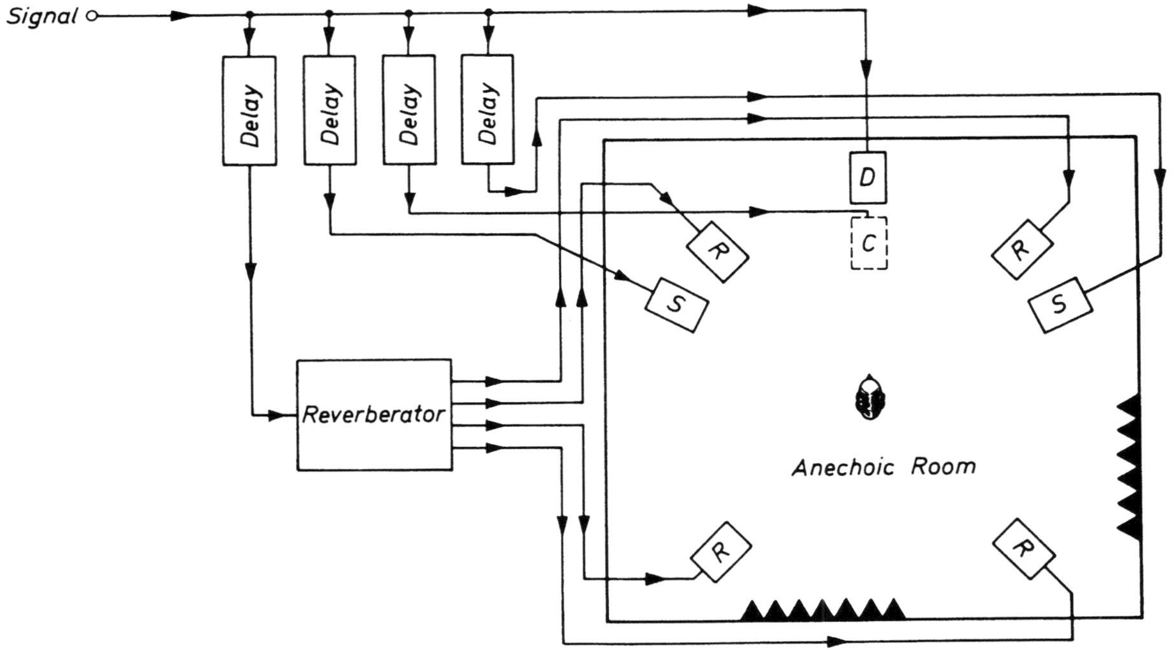

Figure 7.3 Schematic representation of simulation of sound fields in an anechoic room. The loudspeakers are denoted D = direct sound, S = side wall reflections, C = ceiling reflections (elevated), R = reverberation (after Reichardt and Schmidt[4]).

7.2 The perceptibility of reflections

In this and the next section we consider impulse responses with a very simple structure: they consist of the direct sound component and only a few or even one repetition of it. There are two questions which can be raised in this case, namely:

(1) Under what condition is a reflection perceivable at all, without regard to the way in which its presence is manifested, and under what condition is it masked by the direct sound?
(2) Under what condition does the presence of a reflection rate as a disturbance of the listening impression?

In the present section we deal with the first question, postponing the discussion of the second one to the next section. We start with the hypothesis that there is a threshold level separating the levels at which a reflection is audible from those at which it is completely masked. This 'threshold of absolute perceptibility' is a function not only of the time delay with respect to the direct sound but also of the direction of its incidence (and probably of other parameters). Through all the further discussions we assume the listener looking into the direction of direct sound incidence.

To find this threshold two alternate sound field configurations which differ in the presence or absence of a specified reflection are presented to test persons who have to decide whether they notice a difference or not. (One has to make sure, of course, that the test subjects do not know beforehand to which configuration they are listening at a given moment.) The answers of the subjects are evaluated statistically; the level at which 50% of the answers are positive is regarded as the threshold of absolute perceptibility.

For speech with a level of 70 dB, and for frontal incidence of the direct sound as well as of the reflected component, this threshold is

$$\Delta L \approx -0.6t_0 - 8 \text{ decibels} \tag{7.1}$$

where ΔL is the pressure level of the reflected sound signal relative to the sound pressure of the direct sound and t_0 is the time delay in milliseconds. For an example take a reflection delayed by 60 ms with respect to the direct sound. According to eqn (7.1) it is audible even when its level is lower by 40 dB than that of the direct signal.

Figure 7.4 plots for three different signals (continuous speech, a short syllable and a white noise pulse with a duration of 50 ms) the thresholds of absolute perceptibility of a reflection delayed by 50 ms as a function of the angle under which the reflections arrive. (The investigated directions have been restricted to the horizontal plane.) It is evident to which extent the thresholds depend on the type of sound signal. In any case, however, the masking effect of the direct sound is most pronounced at equal directions of

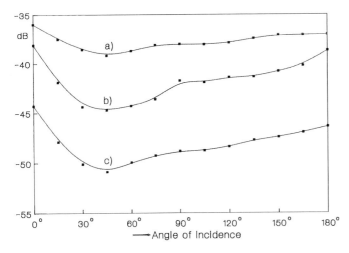

Figure 7.4 Threshold of absolute perceptibility of a reflection with 50 ms delay, obtained with (a) continuous speech, (b) a short syllable, (c) noise pulses of 50 ms duration. Abscissa is the horizontal angle at which the reflection arrives. The direct signal arrives from the front at a level of 75 dB (after Burgtorf and Oehlschlägel[5]).

both components or, in other words, our hearing is more sensitive to reflections arriving from lateral directions than to those arriving from the front or the rear. It should be added that reflections arriving from above are also masked more effectively by the direct sound than are lateral reflections.

If the sound signal is not speech but music, our hearing is generally much less sensitive to reflections. This is the general result of investigations carried out by Schubert,[6] who measured the threshold with various music motifs. One of his typical results is presented in Fig. 7.5, which plots the average threshold taken over six different music samples. With increasing delay time it falls much less rapidly than according to eqn (7.1); its maximum slope is about −0.13 dB/ms. As with speech, the threshold is noticeably lower for reflections arriving from lateral directions than with frontal incidence. Furthermore, added reverberation renders the detection of a reflection more difficult. Obviously reverberated sound components cause additional masking, at least with continuous sound signals.

For more than one reflection the number of parameters to be varied increases rapidly. Fortunately each additional reflection does not create a completely new situation for our hearing. This is demonstrated in Fig. 7.6, which shows the absolute threshold for a variable reflection which is added to a masking sound field consisting of the direct sound plus one, two, three or four reflections at fixed delay times.[7] In this case all the reflections arrive from the same direction as the direct sound. The fixed reflections are indicated as vertical lines over the delay times belonging to them; their heights are a measure of the strength of the reflections. If all the reflections – the

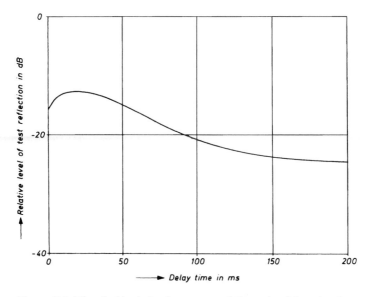

Figure 7.5 Threshold of absolute perceptibility of a delayed reflection as a function of delay time. The threshold is an average taken over six different music samples (frontal incidence of reflection) (after Schubert[6]).

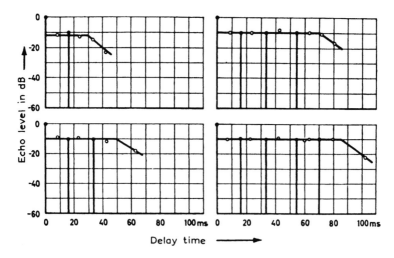

Figure 7.6 Threshold of absolute perceptibility of a delayed signal (reflection) being added to a sound field consisting of direct sound plus one, two, three or four reflections at fixed delay times and relative levels, which are denoted by vertical lines. The original sound signal is speech. All sound components arriving from the front (after Seraphim[7]).

fixed ones as well as the variable one – and the direct sound arrive from different directions, the thresholds are different from those of Fig. 7.6 in that they immediately begin to fall and then jump back to the initial value at the delay time of one of the fixed reflections.

Apart from the thresholds of perceptibility, the differential thresholds for reflections are also of great interest. They have been measured by Reichardt and Schmidt[4] employing test equipment similar to that shown in Fig. 7.3. According to these authors level variations as small as about ±1.5 dB in the level of reflections can be detected if music is used as a test signal. In contrast, the auditive detection of differences in delay times is afflicted with great uncertainty.

7.3 Echoes and colouration

A reflection which is perceived at all does not necessarily reach the consciousness of a listener. At low levels it manifests itself only by an increase of loudness of the total sound signal, by a change in timbre, or by an increase of the apparent size of the sound source. But at higher levels a reflection can be heard as a separate event, i.e. as a repetition of the original sound signal. This effect is commonly known as an 'echo', as already mentioned in Section 7.1. But what outdoors usually appears as an interesting experience may be rather unpleasant in a concert hall or in a lecture room in that it distracts the listeners' attention. In severe cases an echo may severely reduce our enjoyment of music or impair the intelligibility of speech, since subsequent speech sounds or syllables are mixed up and the text is confused.

In the following the term 'echo' will be used for any sound reflection which is subjectively noticeable as a temporal or spatially separated repetition of the original sound signal, and we are discussing the conditions under which a reflection will become an echo. Thus we are taking up again the second question raised at the outset of the foregoing section.

From his outdoor experience the reader may know that the echo produced by sound reflection from a house front, etc., disappears when he approaches the reflecting wall and when his distance from it becomes less than about 10 m, although the wall still reflects the sound. Obviously it is the reduction of the delay time between the primary sound and its repetition which makes the echo vanish. This shows that our hearing has only a restricted ability to resolve succeeding acoustical events, a fact which is sometimes attributed to some kind of 'inertia' of hearing. Like the absolute threshold of perceptibility, however, the echo disturbance depends not only on the delay of the repetition but also on its relative strength, its direction, on the type of sound signal, on the presence of additional components in the impulse response and other circumstances.

Systematic experiments to find the critical echo level of reflections are performed in much the same way as those for investigating the threshold of

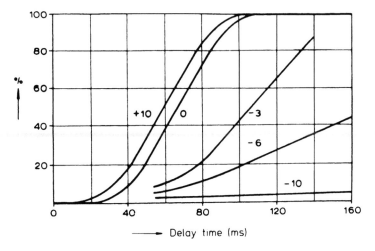

Figure 7.7 Percentage of listeners disturbed by a delayed speech signal. Speaking rate is 5.3 syllables per second. The relative echo levels (in dB) are indicated by numbers next to the curves (after Haas[8]).

absolute perceptibility, but with a different instruction given to the test subjects. It is clear that there is more ambiguity in fixing the critical echo levels than in establishing the absolute perception threshold since an event which is considered as disturbing by one person may be found quite tolerable by others.

Classical experiments of this kind were carried out as early as 1950 by Haas[8] using continuous speech as a primary sound signal. This signal was presented by two loudspeakers: the input signal of one of them could be attenuated (or amplified) and delayed with respect to the other.

Figure 7.7 shows one of Haas' typical results. It plots the percentage of subjects who felt disturbed by an echo of given relative level as a function of the time delay between the undelayed signal (or primary sound) and the delayed one (reflection). The numbers next to the curves indicate the level of the artificial reflection in dB relative to that of the primary sound. The rate of speech was 5.3 syllables per second; the listening room had a reverberation time of 0.8 s. At a delay time of 80 ms, for instance, only about 20% of the observers felt irritated by the presence of a reflection with a relative level of −3 dB, but the percentage was more than 80% when the level was +10 dB.

Analogue results have been obtained for different speaking rates or reverberation times of the listening room. They are summarised in Table 7.1. The numbers in the last column denote the median values of the delay time distributions, i.e. the delay times in milliseconds at which the curves analogous to those of Fig. 7.7 cross the 50% line.

Muncey *et al.*[9] have performed similar experiments for speech as well as for various kinds of music. As could be expected, these investigations clearly

Table 7.1 Critical echo delays at equal levels of direct sound and reflection
(after Haas[8])

Reverberation time of listening room (s)	Speaking rate (syllables/s)	Critical delay time (ms)
0	5.3	43
0.8	5.3	68
1.6	5.3	78
0.8	3.5	93
0.8	5.3	68
0.8	7.4	41

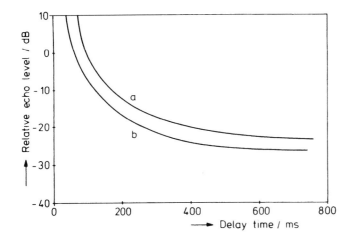

Figure 7.8 Critical echo level (re-direct sound pressure) as a function of delay time for (a) organ music and (b) string music (after Muncey *et al.*[9]).

showed that our hearing is less sensitive to echoes in music than in speech. The reason for this is obviously the fact that music does not have to be 'understood' in the same sense as speech. The annoyance of echoes in very slow music, as for example organ music, is particularly low. In Fig. 7.8 the critical echo level (50% level) for fast string music and organ music is plotted as a function of time delay.

The most striking result of all these experiments can be seen most clearly from Fig. 7.7: if the relative echo level is raised from 0 to +10 dB, there is only a small change in the percentage of observers feeling disturbed by the reflected sound signal. Hence no disturbance is expected to occur for a reflection with time delay of, say, 20 ms even if its energy is ten times the energy of the direct sound. This finding is frequently referred to as 'Haas effect' and has important applications in the design of public address systems.

Careful investigations into the above-mentioned Haas effect and of related phenomena have been performed by Meyer and Schodder.[10] In order

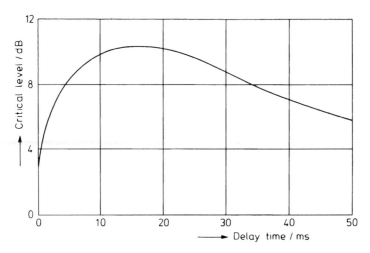

Figure 7.9 Critical level difference between echo and undelayed signal, resulting in apparently equal loudness of both signals (speech). Abscissa is the delay time (after Meyer and Schodder[10]).

to restrict the range of possible judgements, the test subjects were not asked to indicate the level at which they were disturbed by an echo; instead they had to indicate the level at which they heard both the delayed signal and the undelayed one equally loudly. Since in these tests the undelayed signal reached the test subject from the front, the delayed one from a lateral angle of 90°, the test subjects could also be asked to indicate the echo level at which the sound seemed to arrive from halfway between both directions. Both criteria of judgement led to the same results. One of them is shown in Fig. 7.9, where the critical level difference between primary sound and reflection is plotted as a function of the delay time. It virtually agrees with the test results obtained by Haas and renders them somewhat more precise. For our hearing sensation the primary sound determines the impression of direction even when the reflection – provided it has a suitable delay time – is stronger by up to 10.5 dB. If the reflection is split up into several small reflections of equal strengths and with successive mutual delay times of 2.5 ms, leaving constant the total reflection energy, the curve shown in Fig. 7.9 is shifted upwards by another 2.5 dB at maximum.

This result shows that many small reflections separated by short time intervals of the order of milliseconds cause about the same disturbance as one single reflection provided the total reflected energy and the (centre) delay time are the same for both configurations.

These results can be summarised in the following statement: in room acoustics the law of the first wave front can be considered to be valid in general. Exceptions, i.e. erroneous localisations and reflections which are audible as echoes, will occur only in special situations, as for example when most of the room boundaries, except for a few remote portions of wall, are lined with an absorbent material or when certain portions of wall are concavely curved and hence produce reflections of more than average intensity by focusing the sound.

The superposition of a strong isolated reflection onto the direct sound can cause another undesirable effect, especially with music, namely a 'colouration', i.e. a characteristic change of timbre. The same is true for a regular, i.e. equidistant, succession of reflections.

If the impulse response $g_1(t)$ of a room were to consist only of the direct sound and one reflection which is weaker by a factor of q,

$$g_1(t) = \delta(t) + q\delta(t - t_0) \tag{7.2}$$

the corresponding squared absolute value of its Fourier transform is given according to eqn (1.46a) by

$$|G_1(f)|^2 = |1 + q\exp(2\pi i f t_0)|^2 = 1 + q^2 + 2q\cos(2\pi f t_0) \tag{7.3}$$

This is the squared transfer function of a comb filter with a ratio of maximum to minimum of $(1 + q)^2/(1 - q)^2$; the separation of adjacent maxima is $1/t_0$. An infinite and regular succession of reflections would be given by

$$g_2(t) = \sum_{n=0}^{\infty} q^n \delta(t - nt_0) \tag{7.4}$$

and its squared absolute spectrum reads

$$|G_2(f)|^2 = [1 + q^2 - 2q\cos(2\pi f t_0)]^{-1} \tag{7.5}$$

with the same distance of the maxima and the same relative 'roughness' as before. However, the peaks are much sharper here than with a single reflection, except for $q \ll 1$ (*see* Fig. 7.10).

Whether such a comb filter – and likewise a room with similar impulse response – will produce audible colourations or not depends on the delay time t_0 and on the relative heights of the maxima.[11] The absolute threshold for audible colourations rises as the delay time or distance t_0 increases, i.e. when the distance $1/t_0$ between subsequent maxima on the frequency axis is smaller (*see* Fig. 7.11). This finding makes understandable why the very high but closely spaced irregularities of room frequency curves do not cause audible colourations.

If t_0 exceeds a certain value, say 25 ms or so, the regularity of impulse responses does not appear subjectively as colouration, i.e. of changes of the timbre of sound, but rather the sounds have a rough character, which means that we become aware of the regular repetitions of the signal as a phenomenon occurring in the time domain (echo or flutter echo). This is

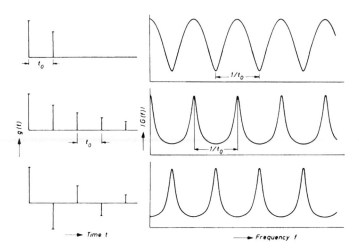

Figure 7.10 Impulse responses and absolute values of transfer functions of various comb filters ($q = 0.7$).

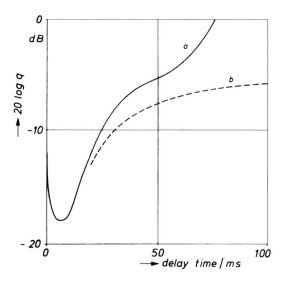

Figure 7.11 Critical values of q resulting in just audible colouration of white noise passed through (a) comb filter according to eqn (7.3) and (b) comb filter according to eqn (7.5) (after Atal *et al.*[11]).

because our ear is not just a sort of frequency analyser but is also sensitive to the temporal structure of the sound signals. Or more correctly expressed: our hearing performs a short-time spectral analysis.

In Section 8.4 we shall discuss an objective criterion for the perceptibility of sound colouration or of a flutter echo which is based on thresholds of the kind shown in Fig. 7.11.

So far this discussion has been restricted to the somewhat artificial case that the sound field consists of the primary or direct sound followed by just one single repetition or a regular succession of repetitions of the sound signal. As we know from Chapter 4, however, impulse responses of most real rooms have a much more complicated structure, and it is clear that the presence of numerous reflections must influence the way we perceive one of them in particular. On the other hand, from a practical point of view it would be desirable to have a criterion to indicate whether a certain peak in a measured impulse response or 'reflectogram' hints at an audible echo and should be removed by suitable constructive measures.

The first criterion of this kind was developed by Niese.[12] This author compared the energy E_F contained within the first 30 ms of a measured impulse response $g(t)$ with the energy E_{NF} of all portions of $[g(t)]^2$ for $t > 30$ ms which are in excess of an idealised decay curve. From both quantities he calculated the fraction

$$\varepsilon = \frac{E_{NF}}{E_F + E_{NF}} \tag{7.6}$$

which was called the 'echo coefficient' (originally 'Echograd'). The idea behind this definition is that reverberation itself is not an acoustical fault in a room.

Another echo criterion was proposed by Dietsch and Kraak[13] in 1986. It is based on the ratio

$$t_S(\tau) = \frac{\displaystyle\int_0^\tau |g(t)|^n t\, dt}{\displaystyle\int_0^\tau |g(t)|^n\, dt} \tag{7.7}$$

with $g(t)$ denoting as before the impulse response under consideration. Here $t_S(\tau)$ is a monotonous function of τ approaching a certain limiting value $t_S = t_S(\infty)$ for $\tau \to \infty$. This latter value is the first moment of $[g(t)]^n$, and the function $t_S(\tau)$ indicates its temporal build-up (Fig. 7.12). The quantity used for rating the strength of an echo is based upon the difference quotient of $t_S(\tau)$:

$$EC = \text{maximum of } \frac{\Delta t_S(\tau)}{\Delta \tau} \tag{7.8}$$

where $\Delta \tau$ can be adapted to the character of the sound signal. The dependence of the echo criterion EC on the directional distribution of the various reflections is accounted for by recording two impulse responses with a dummy head and adding the energies of both responses.

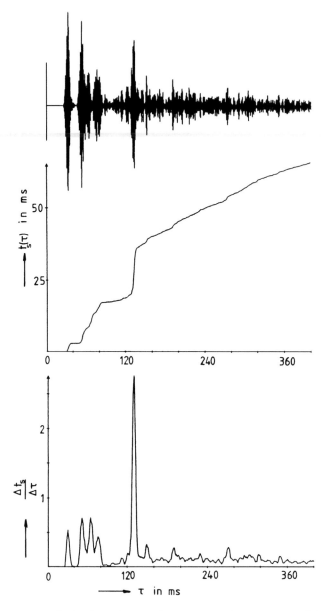

Figure 7.12 First 400 ms of a room impulse response, of the associated build-up function $t_s(\tau)$ and of the difference quotient $\Delta t_s(\tau)/\Delta \tau$ (with $\Delta \tau = 5$ ms). *EC* is 2.75 in this example.

Table 7.2 Characteristic data for the echo criterion of Dietsch and Kraak[13]

Sound signal	n	$\Delta\tau$ *(ms)*	EC_{crit}	Bandwidth of test signal (Hz)
Speech	2/3	9	1.0	700–1400
Music	1	14	1.8	700–2800

By numerous subjective tests, both with synthetic sound fields and in real halls, the authors referred to determined not only suitable values for the exponent n and for $\Delta\tau$ but also the critical values EC_{crit}, which must not be exceeded to ensure that not more than 50% of the listeners will hear an echo (Table 7.2). (The 10% thresholds are slightly lower.) It should be noted that particularly high frequency spectral components may cause echo disturbances. For practical purposes, however, it seems sufficient to employ test signals with a bandwidth of 1 or 2 octaves.

7.4 Early energy: definition, clarity index, speech transmission index

The occurrence of echoes is not the only factor which can impair speech intelligibility; another one is too long a sound decay which is brought about by the great number of sound reflections with relatively long delay times following each other in closer and closer succession. Of course, it would be hopeless to consider each of them separately in order to assess its effect on the listening conditions. Instead several authors have proposed somewhat coarser criteria which compare different parts of the impulse response with each other in order to arrive at objective measures for the intelligibility of speech, for the 'clarity' or 'transparency' of the perceived sounds and similar categories. Such a procedure is not just an expedient dictated by the limitations of time and facilities but is justified by the limited ability of our hearing to distinguish all the countless repeated sound signals.

In the preceding sections it was shown that a reflection is not perceived subjectively as something separate from the direct sound as long as its delay and its relative strength do not exceed certain limits. Their only effect is to make the sound source appear somewhat more extended and to increase the apparent loudness of the direct sound. Since such reflections give support to the sound source they are considered useful.

Reflections which arrive at the listener with longer delays are noticed as echoes in unfavourable cases; in favourable cases they contribute to the reverberation of the room. In principle, any reverberation impairs the intelligibility of speech because it blurs its time structure and mixes up the spectral characteristics of successive phonemes or syllables. More delayed reflections are considered to be detrimental from the viewpoint of speech transmission. From our everyday experience with outdoor echoes, but even more precisely from Haas' results (*see* Fig. 7.7) and similar findings, it can be concluded that the critical delay time separating useful from detrimental reflections is somewhere in the range from 50 to 100 ms.

Most of the following criteria compare the energy conveyed in useful reflections, including that of the direct sound, with the energy contained in the remaining ones. To validate them it is necessary to determine the speech intelligibility directly. This can be done in the following way. A sequence of meaningless syllables (so-called 'logatoms') is read aloud in the environment under test. To obtain representative results it is advisable to use phonetically balanced material (from so-called PB lists) for this purpose, i.e. sets of syllables in which initial consonants, vowels and final consonants are properly distributed. Listeners placed at various positions are asked to write down what they have heard. The percentage of syllables which have been correctly understood is considered to be a relatively reliable measure of speech intelligibility, called 'syllable intelligibility'.

The earliest attempt to define an objective criterion of what may be called the distinctness of sound, derived from the impulse response, is due to Thiele,[14] who named it 'definition' (originally 'Deutlichkeit'):

$$D = \frac{\int_0^{50\,\text{ms}} [g(t)]^2\,\mathrm{d}t}{\int_0^\infty [g(t)]^2\,\mathrm{d}t} \, 100\% \qquad (7.9)$$

Both integrals must include the direct sound. Obviously, D will be 100% if the impulse response does not contain any components with delays in excess of 50 ms, for instance for outdoor sound transmission.

The relation between D and the syllable intelligibility has been established by Boré,[15] who performed subjective tests in different rooms, both with and without a public address system in operation. As test signals for the impulse response he used tone impulses with a duration of 20 ms; the final value of the 'definition' was obtained by a somewhat involved averaging process over the frequency range 340–3500 Hz. The results are shown in Fig. 7.13; they indicate that there is indeed a good correlation between the intelligibility and the 'definition' D.

A quantity which is formally similar to 'definition' but intended to characterise the transparency of music in a concert hall is the 'clarity index' C (originally 'Klarheitsmaß') as introduced by Reichardt *et al.*[16] It is defined by

$$C = 10 \log_{10} \left\{ \frac{\int_0^{80\,\text{ms}} [g(t)]^2\,\mathrm{d}t}{\int_{80\,\text{ms}}^\infty [g(t)]^2\,\mathrm{d}t} \right\} \, \text{dB} \qquad (7.10)$$

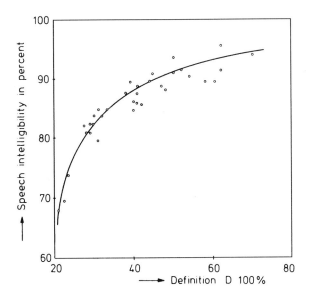

Figure 7.13 Relation between syllable intelligibility and 'definition' (after Boré[15]).

The higher limit of delay time (80 ms compared with 50 ms in eqn (7.9)) makes allowance for the fact that with music a reflection is less detectable than it is with speech signals. By subjective tests with synthetic sound fields these authors have determined the values of C preferred for the presentation of various styles of orchestral music. They found that $C = 0$ dB indicates that the subjective clarity is sufficient even for fast musical passages, whereas a value of $C = -3$ dB seems to be still tolerable. Nowadays, C (mainly referred to as C80 or C_{80}) is widely accepted as a useful criterion for the clarity and transparency of musical sounds in concert halls. According to a recent investigation on concert halls in Europe and the USA carried out by Gade[17] its typical range is from about -5 to $+3$ dB.

The assumption of a sharp delay limit separating useful from non-useful reflections is certainly a crude approximation to the way in which repetitions of sound signals are processed by our hearing. From a practical point of view it has the unfavourable effect that in critical cases a small change in the arrival time of a strong reflection may result in a significant change in D or C. Therefore several authors have proposed a gradual transition from useful to detrimental reflections by calculating the useful energy with a continuous weighting function $a(t)$:

$$E_{\text{F}} = \int_0^\infty a(t)[g(t)]^2 \, dt \qquad (7.11)$$

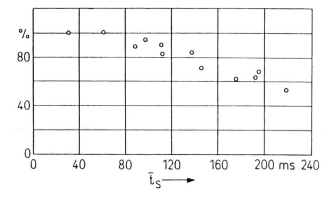

Figure 7.14 Relation between speech intelligibility and centre time t_s (after Kürer[18]).

For a linear transition $a(t)$ is given by

$$
a(t) = \begin{cases} 1 & \text{for } 0 \le t < t_1 \\[2mm] \dfrac{t_2 - t}{t_2 - t_1} & \text{for } t_1 \le t \le t_2 \\[2mm] 0 & \text{for } t > t_2 \end{cases} \tag{7.11a}
$$

No delay limit whatsoever is involved in the 'centre time' ('Schwerpunktszeit') which was proposed and investigated by Kürer[18] and which is defined as the first moment of the squared impulse response:

$$
t_S = \frac{\displaystyle\int_0^\infty [g(t)]^2 t \, dt}{\displaystyle\int_0^\infty [g(t)]^2 \, dt} \tag{7.12}
$$

Obviously a reflection with given strength contributes more to t_S the longer it is delayed with respect to the direct sound. High transparency or speech intelligibility is indicated by low values of the centre time t_S. The high (negative) correlation between measured values of t_S and intelligibility scores is demonstrated in Fig. 7.14.

Quite a different approach to quantify the speech intelligibility from objective sound field data is based on the modulation transfer function (MTF) already introduced in Section 5.5. It quantifies the levelling effect of reverberation on the envelope of speech signals as mentioned before. For

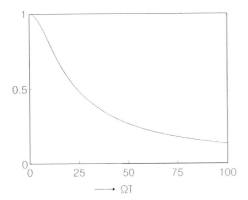

Figure 7.15 Modulation transfer function for exponential sound decay.
T = reverberation time, Ω = angular modulation frequency.

strictly exponential sound decay with a reverberation time $T = 6.91/\delta$ the
complex MTF reads (see eqn (5.36c))

$$\bar{m}(\Omega) = \frac{1}{1 + i\Omega/2\delta} \qquad (7.13)$$

where Ω is the angular frequency of the modulation. The modulus of $\bar{m}(\Omega)$

$$m(\Omega) = |\bar{m}(\Omega)| = \left[1 + \left(\frac{\Omega T}{13.8}\right)^2\right]^{-1/2} \qquad (7.14)$$

(with $T = 6.91/\delta$) is plotted in Fig. 7.15. It shows that very slow variations
of a signal's envelope are not levelled out to any noticeable extent, but very
rapid fluctuations are almost completely eliminated by the reverberant trail.
Usually, however, the sound decay does not follow a simple exponential
law, hence real modulation transfer functions deviate more or less from
that in Fig. 7.15. Furthermore, the MTF depends on the spectral composition of the sound signal, for instance on its frequency, if a modulated
sine signal is applied.

Houtgast and Steeneken[19] have developed a procedure to convert MTF
data measured in seven octave bands and at several modulation frequencies
into one single figure of merit, which they called the 'speech transmission
index' (STI). This conversion involves averaging over a certain range of
modulation frequencies; furthermore, it makes allowance for the different
contributions of the various frequency bands to speech quality and also for
the mutual masking between adjacent frequency bands occurring in our
hearing organ. Finally, they have shown in numerous experiments that the

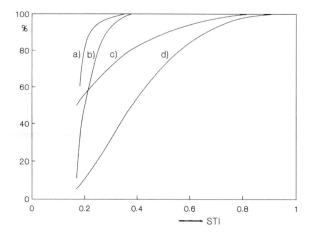

Figure 7.16 Relation between STI and the scores of intelligibility, obtained with: (a) numbers and spell alphabet; (b) short sentences; (c) diagnostic rhyme test; (d) logatoms (after Houtgast and Steeneken[19]).

STI is very closely related to the speech intelligibility determined with various types of speech signals (Fig. 7.16).

We conclude this section with a few observations which apply more or less to all the above criteria. Firstly, it is evident that they are highly correlated among each other. If, for example, a particular impulse response is associated with a short 'centre time' t_s, its evaluation according to eqn (7.9) will yield a high value of 'definition' D and vice versa. Therefore there is no point in measuring many or all of them in order to collect as much information as possible.

Secondly, if the sound decay in the room under consideration would strictly obey an exponential law according to eqn (4.9) or (5.21), all the parameters defined above could be directly expressed by the reverberation time, as has already been done in eqn (7.14). Hence they would not yield any information beyond the reverberation time. In real situations, however, the exponential law is a useful but nevertheless crude approximation to a much more complicated process. Especially in its early portions an impulse response is far from being a smooth function of time; furthermore, the pattern of reflections (*see*, for example, the uppermost part of Fig. 7.12) usually varies from one observation point to the other, accordingly these parameters too may vary over a wide range within one hall and are quite sensitive to geometrical and acoustical details of a room. Therefore they are well suited to describe differences of listening conditions at different seats in a hall whereas the reverberation time does not significantly depend on the place where it has been measured.

7.5 Reverberation and reverberance

If we disregard all details of the impulse response of a room, we finally arrive at the general decay the sound energy undergoes after an impulse excitation or after a sound source has been stopped. As discussed in earlier chapters of this book, the duration of this decay is characterised by the reverberation time or decay time, at least if the energy decay obeys an exponential law in its gross appearance.

Historically, the reverberation time was the first quantity which could be measured objectively and could be expected to reflect the acoustical merits of a room. It was introduced into room acoustics by W.C. Sabine[20] during the last years of the 19th century. Sabine has also developed several methods to measure reverberation times with ever increasing accuracy, and he was the first to formulate the laws of reverberation. Furthermore, he investigated the sound absorbing power of numerous materials. So he was not just an outstanding pioneer but rather the inventor and founder of the science of room acoustics. The measuring techniques and the general understanding of sound propagation in rooms have been improved since then, but Sabine's ideas continue to be the basis of modern room acoustics.

In particular, the reverberation time (or decay time) is still considered as the most important objective quantity in room acoustics, although it has been evident for some time that it characterises only one special aspect of sound propagation in rooms and needs to be supplemented by additional parameters if a full description of the prevailing listening conditions is to be obtained. This predominance of reverberation time has at least three reasons. Firstly, it can be measured and predicted with reasonable accuracy and moderate expenditure. Secondly, the reverberation time of a room does not usually depend significantly on the observer's position in a room, a fact which is also underlined by the simple structure of the formulae by which it can be calculated from room data (*see* Sections 5.3 and 5.4). Hence it is well suited to characterise the overall acoustic properties of a hall, neglecting details which may vary from one place to another. And, finally, abundant data on reverberation times of existing halls are available nowadays, including their frequency dependence. They can be used as a yardstick, so to speak, namely to get an idea of how the result of a particular reverberation measurement or calculation is to be judged.

Before discussing the important question which reverberation times are desirable or optimal for the various types of rooms and halls a remark on the just audible differences in reverberation time, i.e. on the difference threshold of reverberation time, may be in order. By presenting exponentially decaying noise impulses with variable decay times, bandwidths and centre frequencies to a large number of test subjects, Seraphim[21] was able to show that the relative difference threshold of the decay time is about 4% of its actual value, at least in the most important range of decay times. Although these results were obtained under somewhat unrealistic conditions, they show at least that there is no point in stating reverberation times with a greater accuracy than about 0.05 or 0.1 s.

In principle, preferred ranges of the reverberation time can be obtained by subjective tests, for instance by intelligibility scores of speech, or by judging music samples of various types. To lead to meaningful results such tests should be performed, strictly speaking, in environments (real enclosures or synthetic sound fields) which allow suitable variations of the reverberation time under otherwise unchanged conditions. This cannot be achieved just by comparing sound recordings from different halls unless the answers of test persons are subject to a more involved procedure of evaluation (*see* Section 7.8).

A more empirical approach consists in collecting the reverberation times of halls which are generally considered as acoustically satisfactory or even excellent for the purpose they have to serve (lectures, drama theatre, operatic performances, orchestra or chamber music, etc.). Sometimes the acoustical acceptance of a hall or of several of them is assessed by systematic enquiries.[22,23] In any case it should be noted that the collection of subjective opinions on acoustical qualities and hence the conclusions drawn from them are afflicted with several factors of uncertainty. This holds especially for music. One of them is the question of who is able to utter meaningful acoustical criticism. Certainly musicians have the best opportunity of comparison, since many of them perform in different concert halls. On the other hand, musicians have a very special standpoint (meant literally as well as metaphorically) which does not necessarily agree with that of a listener. The same is true for acousticians and sound recording engineers, who have a professional attitude towards acoustical matters and may frequently concentrate their attention on special properties which are insignificant to the average concert listeners. The latter, however, as for example the concert subscribers, often lack the opportunity or the desire to compare several concert halls or else they are not very critically minded in acoustical matters, or their opinion is influenced from the point of view of local patriotism. Furthermore, there are – and again this applies particularly to musical events and their appropriate surroundings – individual differences in taste which cannot be discussed in scientific terms. And, finally, it is quite possible that there are certain trends of 'fashion' towards longer or shorter reverberation times. All these uncertainties make it understandable that it is impossible to specify one single optimum value of reverberation time for each room type or type of presentation, instead only ranges of favourable values can be set up.

We start with rooms used only for speech, such as lecture rooms, congress halls, parliament, theatres for dramatic performances and so on. As mentioned earlier, no reverberation whatsoever is required for such rooms in principle, since any noticeable sound decay has the tendency to blur the syllables and thus to reduce speech intelligibility. On the other hand, a highly absorbing treatment of all walls and of the ceiling of a room would certainly remove virtually all the reverberation, but at the same time it would prevent the formation of useful reflections which increase the loudness of the perceived sounds and which are responsible for the relative ease with which communication is possible in enclosures as compared to outdoor communication. Furthermore, the lack of any audible reverberation in a closed space creates an unnatural and uncomfortable feeling, as can be observed when entering an anechoic room, for instance. Obviously one subconsciously expects to encounter some reverberation which bears a certain relation to the size of the room. Therefore the reverberation time in rooms of this kind should not fall short of 0.5 s approximately (except for very small rooms such as living rooms), and values of about 1.2 s are still tolerable especially for larger rooms.

As is well known, low frequencies contribute very little to speech intelligibility. Therefore it is an advantage to apply suitably designed sound absorbers to the walls of rooms used for speech in order to reduce the reverberation time and hence the stationary sound level at low frequencies.

Now we shall turn to the reverberation times which can be considered to be optimum for concert halls. In order to discover these values, we are completely dependent on subjective opinions concerning existing halls, at least so long as there are no results available of systematic investigations with synthetic or simulated sound fields. As has been pointed out before, there is always some divergence of opinion about a certain concert hall; furthermore, they are not always constant in time. Old concert halls particularly are often commented on enthusiastically, probably more than is justified by their real acoustical merits. (This is true especially for some halls which were destroyed by war or other catastrophes.)

In spite of all these reservations, it is a matter of fact that certain concert halls enjoy a high reputation for acoustical reasons. This means, among other things, that at least their reverberation time does not give cause for complaint. On the whole it seems that the optimum values for occupied concert halls are in the range from about 1.6 to 2.1 s at mid-frequencies. Table 7.3 lists the reverberation times of several old and new concert halls, both for low frequencies (125 Hz) and for the medium frequency range (500–1000 Hz).

At first glance it may seem curious that that which is good for speech, namely a relatively short reverberation time, should be bad for music. This discrepancy can be resolved by bearing in mind that, when listening to speech, we are interested in perceiving each element of the sound signal, since this increases the ease with which we can understand what the speaker is saying. When listening to music, it would be rather disturbing to hear every detail including the bowing noise of the string instruments or the air flow noise of flutes, or minor shortcomings of the synchronism among the instruments of an orchestra. These and similar imperfections are hidden or masked by reverberation. What is even more important, reverberation of

Table 7.3 Reverberation time of occupied concert halls

Hall	Volume (m³)	Number of seats	Year of completion (reconstruction)	T_{125}	$T_{500-1000}$	Source
Großer Musikvereinssaal, Vienna	14 600	2000	1870	2.3	2.05	Beranek[23]
St Andrew's Hall, Glasgow	16 100	2130	1877	2.1	2.2	Parkin *et al.*
Chiang Kai Shek Memorial, Taipei	16 700	2077	1987	1.95	2.0	Kuttruff
Symphony Hall, Boston	18 800	2630	1900	2.2	1.8	Beranek[23]
Concergebouw, Amsterdam	19 000	2200	1887	2.3	2.2	Geluk
Neues Gewandhaus, Leipzig	21 000	1900	1884 (1981)	2.0	2.0	Fasold
Neue Philharmonie, Berlin	24 500	2230	1963	2.4	1.95	Cremer
Concert Hall 'De Doelen', Rotterdam	27 000	2220	1979	2.3	2.2	De Lange

sufficient strength affects the blending of musical sounds and increases their loudness and richness as well as the continuity of musical line. The importance of all these effects for musical enjoyment becomes obvious if one listens to music in an environment virtually free of reverberation, as for example to a military band or a light orchestra playing outdoors: the sounds are brittle and harsh, and it is obvious that it is of no advantage to be able to hear every detail. Furthermore, the loudness of music heard outdoors is reduced rapidly as the distance increases from the sound source.

But perhaps the most important reason why relatively long reverberation times are adequate for music is simply the fact that listeners are accustomed to hearing music in environments which happen to have reverberation times of the order of magnitude mentioned. This applies equally well to composers who unconsciously take into account the blending of sounds which is produced in concert halls of normal size.

As regards the frequency dependence of the reverberation time, it is generally considered tolerable, if not as favourable, to have an increase of the reverberation time towards lower frequencies, beginning at about 500 Hz (*see* Table 7.3). From the physical point of view, such an increase is quite natural since the sound absorption from the audience is generally lower at low frequencies than it is at medium and high frequencies (*see*, for instance, Tables 6.3 and 6.4). Concerning the subjective sensation, it is often believed that increasing the reverberation time towards low frequencies is responsible for what is called the 'warmth' of musical sounds. On the other hand, there are quite a number of concert halls with reverberation times which do not increase towards the low frequencies or which even have a slightly decreasing reverberation time and which are nevertheless considered to be excellent acoustically.

The optimum range of reverberation time as indicated above refers to the performance of orchestral and choral music. For smaller ensembles, starting with soloists and including all kinds of chamber music, a reverberation time of 1.4 to 1.6 s is certainly more adequate.

Apart from this dependence of the reverberation time on the ensemble size, there is another one on the style of music to be performed. It has been investigated by Kuhl[24] in a remarkable round robin experiment. In this experiment three different pieces of music were recorded in many concert halls and broadcasting studios with widely varying reverberation times. These recordings were later replayed to a great number of listeners – musicians as well as acousticians, music historians, recording engineers and other engineers, i.e. individuals who were competent in that field in one way or another. They were asked to indicate whether the reverberation times in the different recordings, whose origin they did not know, appeared too short or too long. The pieces of music played back were the first movement of Mozart's Jupiter Symphony (KV551), the fourth movement of Brahms' 4th Symphony (E minor) and the 'Danse Sacrale' of Stravinsky's 'Le Sacre du Printemps'.

The final result was that a reverberation time of 1.5 s was considered to be most appropriate for the Mozart symphony as well as for the Stravinsky piece, whereas 2.1 s was felt to be most suitable for the Brahms symphony. In the first two pieces there was almost complete agreement in the listeners' opinions; in the Brahms symphony, however, there was considerable divergence of opinion.

These results should certainly not be overvalued since the conditions under which they have been obtained were far from ideal in that they were based on monophonic recordings, replayed in rooms with some reverberation. But they show clearly that no hall can offer optimum conditions for all types of music and explain the large range of 'optimum' reverberation times for concert halls.

In opera houses the listener should be able to enjoy the full sound of music as well as to understand the text, at least partially. Therefore one would expect that these somewhat contradictory requirements can be reconciled by a compromise as far as the reverberation time is concerned, and that consequently the optimum of the latter would be somewhere about 1.5 s. As a matter of fact, however, the reverberation times of well-renowned opera theatres scatter over a wide range (*see* Table 7.4). Traditional theatres have reverberation times close to 1 s only, whereas more modern ones show a definite trend towards longer values. One is tempted to explain these differences by a changed attitude of the listeners, who nowadays seem to give more preference to a full and smooth sound of music than to the intelligibility of the text, whereas earlier opera goers presumably just wanted to be entertained by the plot. The truth, however, is probably much simpler. Old theatres were designed in such a way as to seat as many spectators as possible, while the architects of more modern ones (including the Festspielhaus in Bayreuth, which was specially designed to stage Wagner's operas) tried to follow more or less elaborate acoustical concepts.

The question of optimum reverberation times is even more difficult to answer if we turn to churches and other places of worship which cannot be considered merely under the heading of acoustics. It depends on the character of the service whether more emphasis is given to organ music and liturgical chants or to the sermon. In the first case longer reverberation times are to be preferred, but in the latter case the reverberation time should certainly not exceed 2 s. Frequently, however, churches with still shorter reverberation times are not well accepted by the congregation for reasons which have nothing to do with acoustics. This shows that the churchgoers' acoustical expectations are not only influenced by rational arguments such as that of speech intelligibility but also by hearing habits.

As mentioned above, the reverberation time is a meaningful measure for the duration of the decay process only if the latter is exponential, i.e. if the decay level decreases linearly with time. If, on the contrary, a logarithmic decay curve is bent and consequently each section of it has its own decay

Table 7.4 Reverberation time of occupied opera theatres

Opera house	Volume (m³)	Number of seats/standing	Year of completion (reconstruction)	T_{125}	$T_{500-1000}$	Source
La Scala, Milano	10 000	2290/400	1778 (1946)	1.2	0.95	Furrer
Covent Garden, London	10 100	2180/60	1858	1.2	1.1	Parkin et al.
Festspielhaus, Bayreuth	11 000	1800	1876	1.7	1.5	Reichardt
National Theatre, Taipei	11 200	1522	1987	1.6	1.4	Kuttruff
Staatsoper, Wien	11 600	1658/560	1869 (1955)	1.5	1.3	Reichardt
Staatsoper, Dresden	12 500	1290	1878 (1985)	2.3	1.7	Kraak
Neues Festspielhaus, Salzburg	14 000	2158	1960	1.7	1.5	Schwaiger
Metropolitan Opera House, New York	30 500	3800	1966	2.25[a]	1.8[a]	Jordan

[a] with 80% occupancy only.

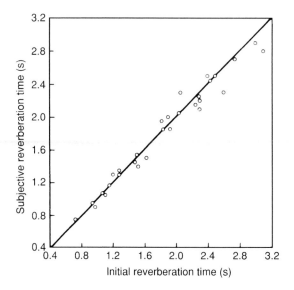

Figure 7.17 Subjective reverberation time as a function of the initial reverberation time T_{160} (after Atal *et al.*[25]).

rate, the question arises which of these sections is most significant for the subjectively perceived 'reverberance' of a room.

To answer this question Atal *et al.*[25] added non-exponential artificial reverberation produced by a number of computer-simulated comb filters (*see* Section 10.5) to speech and music samples. The signals modified in this way were presented over earphones to test subjects, who were asked to compare them with exponentially reverberated signals in order to find the subjectively relevant decay rate of the non-exponential decays. The results are plotted in Fig. 7.17. The abscissa represents the reverberation time corresponding to the initial slope (first 160 ms) of the non-exponential decay; the ordinate is the reverberation time of an exponential decay giving the same impression of reverberance, i.e. the subjective or effective reverberation time. Similar results were obtained with sound signals reverberated in concert halls.

These findings can be explained by the fact that the smoothing effect of reverberation on the irregular level fluctuations of continuous speech or music is mainly achieved by the initial portion of the decay process, while its later portions add up to a general 'background' which is not felt subjectively as a typical effect of reverberation but rather as some sort of noise. Only final or other isolated chords present the listener with the opportunity of hearing the complete decay process; but these chords occur too rarely for them to influence to any great degree the overall impression which a listener gains of the hall's reverberance.

Nowadays it has become common to characterise the rate of sound decay in its initial portion by the 'early decay time' (EDT) following a proposal of V. Jordan.[26] This is the time in which the first 10 dB fall of a decay process occurs, multiplied by a factor 6. It may be longer or shorter than the Sabine reverberation time. Recent listening tests based on binaural impulse responses recorded in different concert halls confirmed that the perceived reverberance is closely related to EDT.[17]

The overall reverberation time does not show substantial variations with room shape. This is so because the decay process as a whole is made up of numerous reflections with different delays, strengths and wall portions where they originated. On the contrary, the 'early decay time' is strongly influenced by early reflections, and therefore depends noticeably on the measuring position; furthermore, it is sensitive to details of the room geometry. In this respect it resembles to some extent the parameters discussed in the preceding sections.

7.6 Sound pressure level, strength factor

For a long time the stationary sound pressure level or energy density a sound source produces in a hall was not considered as an acoustical quality criterion because it depends mostly on the power output of the source and the absorption area (or the reverberation time) of the room. In recent times, however, the general attitude towards the overall level has changed since high definition or clarity is of little use if the sound is too weak to be heard at a comfortable loudness. Moreover, the simple eqn (5.6) which relates the energy density to the absorption area and the source power P is valid for diffuse sound fields only, and the field within a real hall deviates more or less from this ideal condition.

If the sound pressure level (SPL) in an enclosure is to merely reflect properties of the enclosure and not of the source, it must be measured by using a non-directional sound source and its power output must be accounted for by some suitable normalization. This can be done by subtracting the level SPL_Λ which the sound source would produce in an anechoic room at a distance $r_\Lambda = 10$ m from the SPL, i.e. the level observed in the enclosure. As will be shown in Section 8.3, this difference is equivalent to what is known as the 'strength factor' nowadays:

$$G = 10 \log_{10} \left\{ \frac{\int_0^\infty [g(t)]^2 \, dt}{\int_0^\infty [g_\Lambda(t)]^2 \, dt} \right\} \tag{7.15}$$

g_Λ is the impulse response measured with the same sound source in an anechoic room at 10 m distance.

By inserting $A = 0.163 \, V/T$ into eqn (5.6) and setting $w_\Lambda = P/4\pi r_{\Lambda C}^2 c$ the strength factor in a diffuse sound field would be

$$G_d = 10 \log_{10}\left(\frac{w}{w_\Lambda}\right) = 10 \log_{10}\left(\frac{T}{V}\right) + 45 \text{ dB} \qquad (7.16)$$

On the other hand, Gade and Rindel[27] found from their measurements in 21 Danish concert halls that the strength factor shows a linear decrease from the front to the rear of any hall which corresponds to 1.2–3.3 per distance doubling, and that its average in each hall falls short of the value predicted by eqn (7.16) by 2–3 dB. Furthermore, the steady state level does not depend in a simple way on the reverberation time or on geometrical data of the hall. From these results it may be concluded that the sound fields in real concert halls are not perfectly diffuse, and that the strength factor is indeed a useful figure of merit.

7.7 Spaciousness of sound fields

The preceding discussions of this chapter predominantly referred to the temporal structure of the impulse response of a room and to the auditive sensations associated with them. A subjective effect not mentioned so far, which is nevertheless of utmost importance, at least for concert halls, is the acoustical 'sensation of space' which a listener usually experiences in a room. It is caused by the fact that the sound in a closed room reaches the listener from quite different directions and that our hearing although not able to locate these directions separately processes them into an overall impression, namely the mentioned sensation or feeling of space.

It is quite evident that this sensation is not achieved just by reverberation itself; if music with reverberation is replayed through a single loudspeaker in a relatively 'dry' environment, it never suggests acoustically the illusion of being in a room of some size, no matter if the reverberation time is long or short. Likewise, if the music is replayed through several loudspeakers which are placed at equal distance but in different directions seen from the listener, and which are fed by identical signals, the listener will not feel more enveloped by the sound. Instead, all the sound seems to arrive from a single imaginary sound source, a so-called 'phantom source' which can easily be located and which seems, at best, somewhat more extended than a single loudspeaker. The same effect occurs if a great number of loudspeakers in an anechoic room are arranged in a hemisphere (*see* Fig. 6.21) and are connected to the same signal source. A listener in the centre of the hemisphere does not perceive a 'spacious' or 'subjectively diffuse' sound field but instead he perceives a phantom sound source immediately overhead. Even the usual two-channel stereophony employing two similar loudspeaker signals, which differ in a certain way from each other, cannot provide a full acoustical impression of space since the apparent directions of sound incidence remain restricted to the region between both loudspeakers.

The 'sensation of space' has attracted the interest of acoustic researchers for many years, but only since the late 1960s has real progress been made in finding the cause of this subjective property of sound fields. The different authors used expressions like 'spatial responsiveness', 'spatial impression', 'ambience', 'apparent source width', 'subjective diffusion', 'Räumlichkeit', 'spaciousness' 'listener envelopment' and others to circumscribe this sensation. Assuming that all these verbal descriptions are to signify the same thing, we shall prefer the term 'spaciousness' or 'spatial impression' in the following.

For a long time it was common belief among acousticians that spaciousness was a direct function of the uniformity of the directional distribution (*see* Section 4.3) in a sound field: the more uniform this distribution, the higher the degree of spaciousness. This belief originated from the fact that the ceiling and walls of many famous concert halls are highly structured by cofferings, niches, pillars, statuettes and other projections which supposedly reflect the sound in a diffuse manner rather than specularly.

It was the introduction of synthetic sound fields as a research tool which led to the insight that the uniformity of the stationary directional distribution is not the primary cause of spaciousness. According to Damaske[29], spatial impression can be created with quite a few synthetic reflections provided they reach the listener from lateral directions, and the signals they carry are mutually incoherent although derived from the same original signal (*see* Section 4.1).

Mathematically, the degree of coherence can be expressed by the correlation coefficient or correlation factor Ψ: let $p_1(t)$ and $p_2(t)$ denote the sound pressures of two acoustic signals, then

$$\Psi = \frac{\overline{p_1 p_2}}{(\overline{p_1^2 p_2^2})^{1/2}} \tag{7.17}$$

(The horizontal overbars indicate averaging with respect to time.) For complete coherence this quantity assumes the value +1 or −1 (the second value occurs when both signals are equal but of opposite sign). $\Psi = 0$ is the condition for complete incoherence. (Strictly speaking, $\Psi = 0$ is only a necessary but not a sufficient condition for incoherence. This may be seen by applying eqn (7.17) to the two cosine signals considered at the end of Section 4.1 for which the correlation factor is $\cos \omega(t_2 - t_1)$, i.e. it assumes all values between −1 and +1. If pure tones are excluded, however, the magnitude of Ψ can be taken as a good measure the degree of coherence.)

If p_2 in eqn (7.17) is the replica of p_1 apart from a delay τ, the correlation factor becomes proportional to the autocorrelation function of the sound signal, $\phi_{pp}(\tau)$. From measured data of music samples (*see* Fig. 1.10), we learn that their autocorrelation functions have fallen well below their maximum value if the delay τ exceeds a few milliseconds. Hence it can be concluded that in a large hall the usual delays of lateral reflections are sufficient to destroy their coherence.

That only the lateral reflections (i.e. not reflections from the front, from overhead or from the rear) contribute to spaciousness has been emphasised especially by Marshall,[29] although it had been observed by earlier authors.[30] Virtually all the later publications have confirmed this hypothesis. A very extensive investigation on the spaciousness caused by early lateral reflections is due to Barron.[31] He found the contribution of a reflection to spaciousness to be proportional to its energy and to cos θ, θ being the angle between the axis through a listener's ears and the direction of sound incidence, provided the delay is in the range from 5 to 80 ms. Furthermore, this contribution is independent of other reflections and of the presence or absence of reverberation. Based on these results the 'early lateral energy fraction'[32] was proposed as an objective measure for the spatial impression:

$$LEF = \frac{\int_{5\ ms}^{80\ ms} [g(t)\cos\theta]^2\ dt}{\int_{0}^{80\ ms} [g(t)]^2\ dt} \tag{7.18}$$

(The replacement of cos θ with $\cos^2\theta$ in the numerator of this expression is a concession to the experimental feasibility.) In large halls, the LEF may vary from 0 to about 0.5.

Another way of characterising the laterality of reflected sounds is based upon the fact that sound impinging on a listener's head from its vertical symmetry plane will produce equal sound pressures at both his ears whereas sound, i.e. reflections, from outside the symmetry plane will produce different ear signals. Generally, the similarity or dissimilarity of two signals is measured by their cross correlation function as defined in eqn (1.40). Applied to the impulse responses g_r and g_l measured at the right and the left ear, and suitably normalised this function reads:

$$\varphi_{rl} = \frac{\int_{0}^{t_0} g_r(t)g_l(t+\tau)\ dt}{\left\{\int_{0}^{t_0} [g_r(t)]^2\ dt \int_{0}^{t_0} [g_l(t)]^2\ dt\right\}^{1/2}} \tag{7.19}$$

The upper limit t_0 (= 100 ms, for instance) is to restrict the integration on the range of 'early reflections', hence φ_{rl} is some 'short time' correlation function. The maximum of its absolute value within the range $|\tau| < 1$ ms is called the 'interaural cross correlation' (IACC)[33,34]. Of course, this quantity is negatively correlated with the spatial impression. High values of the IACC mark a low degree of spaciousness. It should be mentioned that several versions of the IACC are in use which differ in the upper limit t_0 in eqn (7.19), or in the type of filtering exerted on impulse responses prior to inserting them into eqn (7.19). Beranek[47] prefers the use of an IACC which comprises three octave bands with mid-frequencies 0.5, 1 and 2 kHz, and reports that the values of this quantity are as low as 0.3 in excellent concert halls.

But laterality of the early reflections is not the only factor on which the impression of spaciousness depends. As early as 1967 Reichardt and Schmidt[4] found that the spatial impression, for which they established a subjective scale, increases monotonically with the reverberant energy E_r relative to that of the energy E_0 of the direct sound:

$$H = 10 \log_{10}(E_r/E_0) \text{ dB} \tag{7.20}$$

Furthermore, Keets[35] observed that the spatial impression depends strongly on the listening level. There seems to be some agreement nowadays that spatial impression is not a 'one-dimensional' sensation, but consists of at least two components which are more or less independent. The most prominent of these components are the 'apparent source width' (ASW) and 'listener envelopment'.[36] If this view is adopted it seems reasonable to attribute Damaske's and Barron's results to the apparent source width ASW and to consider the objective quantities LEF and IACC as predictors of this particular sensation.

This leaves us with the question which objective parameters of the sound field are responsible for the remaining component, namely the sense of 'listener envelopment'.

This question was the subject of careful experiments performed by Bradley and Soulodre[36] who created a synthetic sound field with five loudspeakers, namely a frontal one and four more loudspeakers at lateral angles of ±35° and ±90°. These loudspeakers simulated the direct sound and isolated early reflections delayed by 15, 40, 50 and 70 ms as well as reverberation with onset times exceeding 80 ms. This system enabled the experimenters to vary independently the reverberation time, the relative energy of the late reflections expressed by the clarity index C_{80} (*see* eqn (7.10), the A-weighted sound pressure level, and the angular distribution of the reverberated signals, whereas the IACC and the LEF were kept constant through all combinations.

It turned out that the angular distribution had the largest effect. The wider it was, the higher is the listener envelopment. Another strong influence was that of the overall sound level, while the relative strength of the early energy (C_{80}) and the reverberation time was found to be less significant. A correlation analysis revealed that the best objective predictor for the perceived listener envelopment is the strength factor (*see* eqn (7.15)) restricted to the late lateral reflections:

$$LG_{80}^{\infty} = 10 \log_{10} \left\{ \frac{\left| \int_{80 \text{ ms}}^{\infty} [g(t) \cos \theta]^2 \, dt \right|}{\int_0^{\infty} [g_\Lambda(t)]^2 \, dt} \right\} \text{dB} \qquad (7.21)$$

and to a frequency range covering the octave bands with mid-frequencies 125, 250, 500 and 1000 Hz, thus accounting for the fact that high frequency components do not contribute much to the sense of listener envelopment. The range from missing to maximum envelopment corresponds to a range in LG_{80}^{∞} from −20 to 2 dB.

Thus the present state of the art can be summarised in the statement that 'spatial impression' is caused by reflections impinging on the listener from lateral directions. If their delays with respect to the direct sound are below about 80 ms they increase the 'apparent source width' while those with longer delays contribute to the sensation of 'listener envelopment'. This insight has immediate implications for the acoustical design of concert halls.

7.8 Assessment of concert hall acoustics

Although nowadays quite a number of parameters are at the acousticians' disposal to quantify the listening conditions in a concert hall (or particular aspects of them), the situation is still unsatisfactory in that important questions remain unanswered. Do these parameters yield a complete description of the acoustics of a hall? Are they independent from each other? Which relative weight is to be given to each of them? Is it possible, for instance, to compensate insufficient reverberation by a large amount of early lateral energy?

Conventional attempts to correlate the acoustical quality of a concert hall with an objective measure or a set of them have not been very satisfactory because they concentrated on one particular aspect only or, as for instance Beranek's elaborate rating system,[23] relied on plausible but unproven assumptions. Since about 1970, however, researchers have tried to get a complete picture of the factors which contribute to good acoustics, including their relative significance, by employing modern psychometric methods.

The basic idea of this approach is first to detect the number and significance of independent scales of auditive perception and then, as a second step, to find out the physical parameters which show the highest correlation to these scales.

To collect the material for this analysis, music samples are recorded in different concert halls or at different places in one hall, using a dummy

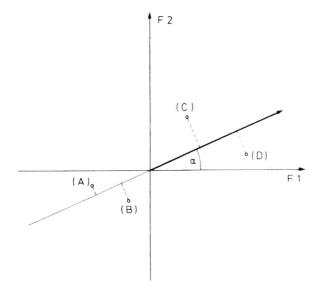

Figure 7.18 Two-dimesional perceptual space with factors F_1 and F_2. The vector represents the preference scale of one subject. The points A, B, C, etc. denote different concert halls or seats.

head. These samples are presented to test subjects, either by headphones or by loudspeakers in an anechoic room. In the latter case it is advantageous to employ the cross-talk cancellation (CTC) techniques described at the end of the introduction to this chapter. The subjects are asked either to assess in some way the differences between subsequent listening impressions[37,38] or to give scores to the presented signals using a number of bipolar rating scales with verbally labelled extremes such as 'dull–brilliant', 'cold–warm', etc.,[39,40] or simply to say which of two presentations they prefer.[41,42] Such data are collected from many listeners and then are subjected to a mathematical procedure called factor analysis. It results in r of independent perceptual scales, called 'factors', and the relative significance of each of these factors.

The meaning of these factors or scales is principally unknown, but sometimes they can be circumscribed vaguely by verbal labels such as 'resonance' or 'proximity'.

These factors can be thought of as coordinate axes of an r-dimensional 'perceptual space' in which each listening situation (concert hall, or seat in a hall) is represented by a point. Suppose $r = 2$; accordingly, the perceptual space is a plane with rectangular coordinates F_1 and F_2 as shown in Fig. 7.18. If the preceding factor analysis was based on preference tests, the individual preference scale of each subject can be represented by a vector in this plane. Fig. 7.18 shows just one of them. According to the angle α which it includes with the axis F_1, this particular listener gives in his preference judgement a weight of $\cos \alpha$ to the factor F_1 and of $\sin \alpha$ to the factor F_2. The projections of the 'concert hall points' A, B, C, etc. on this vector indicate this listener's personal preference rating of these halls. Similarly, if bipolar rating scales have been used, these scales can be presented as directions in such a diagram.

Wilkens and Plenge[40,43] collected their test samples by following an orchestra on its tour playing the same programme (Mozart, Bartok, Brahms) in six different halls. They used headphones for the reproduction and found three factors to be relevant, which they labelled as follows:

F_1: strength factor (47%)
F_2: distinctness factor (28%)
F_3: timbre factor (14%)

The numbers in the brackets denote the relative significance of the three factors. They add up to 89% only, which means that there are further, however insignificant, factors. It is interesting to note that there seem to be two groups of listeners: one group which prefers loud sounds (high values of F_1) and one giving more preference to distinct sounds (high values of F_2). (A similar division of the subjects into two groups with different preferences has been found by Barron.[22])

In the course of this research project, physical sound field parameters have been measured at the same positions in which the sound recordings have been made. Lehmann[44] has analysed them in order to select those which show highest correlation with the factors F_1 to F_3. He found that F_1 is highly correlated with the strength factor G from eqn (7.15), whereas F_2 shows high (negative) correlation with Kürer's 'centre time' t_s (*see* Section 7.4). Finally, the factor F_3 seems to be related to the frequency dependence of the 'early decay time'.

In contrast to the aforementioned authors, Siebrasse[42] collected his test samples by replaying 'dry', i.e. reverberation-free music, namely a motif of Mozart's Jupiter Symphony, stereophonically from the stages of 25 European concert halls and by re-recording them with an artificial head. The samples prepared in this way were presented to the test subjects in the free field at constant level employing a CTC system mentioned in the introduction to this chapter. The subjects were asked to judge preference between pairs of presentations. Application of factor analysis indicated four factors F_1 to F_4 with relative significances of 45%, 16%, 12% and 7%. In Fig. 7.19, which is analogous to Fig. 7.18, part of his results are plotted in the plane of factors F_1 and F_2. The vectors representing the individual preference scales have different lengths since they have non-vanishing components also in F_3- and F_4-directions. The fact that they all are directed towards the right side leads to the conclusion that F_1 is a 'consensus factor', whereas the components in F_2-direction reflect differences in the listeners' personal taste.

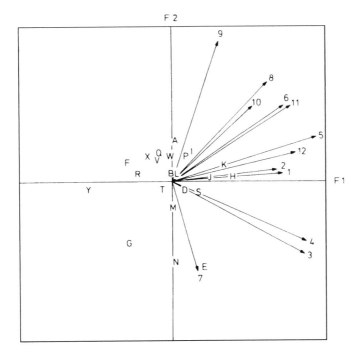

Figure 7.19 Individual preference scales of 12 test subjects (arrows) and 22 concert hall points (A, B, ..., Y) represented in the F_1–F_2 plane of a four-dimensional perceptual space.

This holds as well with regard to the factors F_3 and F_4. In order to find out the objective sound field parameter with the highest correlation to the consensus factor F_1, Gottlob[34] analysed the impulse responses observed at the same places where the music samples had been recorded. The reverberation time proved to be important only when it deviated substantially from an optimum range centred on 2 s. If halls with unfavourable reverberation times are excluded, F_1 shows high correlation with several parameters, of which the interaural cross-correlation (IACC) (*see* Section 7.7) seems to be of particular interest, since it is virtually independent of the reverberation time. Another highly correlated quantity is the width of a concert hall. Both the IACC and the width of a hall are negatively correlated to F_1, i.e. narrow concert halls are generally preferred. This again proves the importance of early lateral reflections which are particularly strong in narrow halls and, on the other hand, lead to a low value of the IACC. In a more recent publication[45] an even higher correlation to F_1 has been reported for the sum of the early lateral energy and the reverberant energy, where the latter is obtained by integrating the squared impulse response from 80 ms to infinity. This may be considered as an early indication that the spatial impression in a room is made up of two components, namely 'apparent source width' and 'listener envelopment', and that both contribute to the quality of a concert hall.

The fact that both investigations reported above show such poor agreement may have several explanations: the differences in the way the test samples were collected and presented to the subjects, different choice of halls, and different judging schemes. It is not surprising, however, that in the second study the strength or loudness of the sound signal does not show up since here all test samples were presented to the subjects at equal loudness.

A somewhat different approach to arrive at a consistent rating system for concert halls is due to Ando[46], who simulated sound fields consisting of a direct sound, two distinct reflections and subsequent, electronically generated reverberation (*see* Section 10.5). The latter was radiated by four loudspeakers which were distributed along a circle and fed with mutually delayed signals. The electrical signals were computer controlled in such a way that four independent parameters could be varied, namely the overall listening level, the 'initial time delay gap' Δt_1 (i.e. the delay of the first reflection), the subsequent reverberation time T, and the interaural cross-correlation IACC. Ando summarised the results of his extended preference tests in a figure-of-merit which he called the 'total subjective preference':

$$S_a = -\sum_{i=1}^{4} \alpha_i \, | \, X_i \, |^{3/2} \qquad (7.22)$$

with

$$X_1 = 20 \log_{10}\left(\frac{p}{p_p}\right), \quad \alpha_1 = \begin{cases} 0.07 \text{ for } X_1 \geq 0 \\ 0.04 \text{ for } X_1 < 0 \end{cases}$$

(p = rms sound pressure in arbitrary units)

$$X_2 = \log_{10}\left[\frac{\Delta t_1}{(\Delta t_1)_p}\right], \quad \alpha_2 = \begin{cases} 1.42 \text{ for } X_2 \geq 0 \\ 1.11 \text{ for } X_2 < 0 \end{cases}$$

$$X_3 = \log_{10}\left(\frac{T}{T_p}\right), \quad \alpha_3 = \begin{cases} 0.45 + 0.74A \text{ for } X_3 \geq 0 \\ 2.36 - 0.42A \text{ for } X_3 < 0 \end{cases}$$

$$X_4 = \text{IACC}, \quad \alpha_4 = 1.45$$

The quantities X_1, X_2 and X_3 are the deviations of the A-weighted sound pressure level, of Δt_1 and of T from certain standard values, the so-called 'most preferred values' denoted with the index p. The weight factors α_i depend on the sign of the deviation. Here p_p corresponds to a level of 79 dB(A), whereas $(\Delta t_1)_p = (1 - \log_{10}A)\tau_e$ and $T_p = 23\tau_e$. A is the square root of the energy contained in all reflections relative to the energy of the direct sound, and τ_e is the effective duration of the autocorrelation function of the sound signal (*see* Section 1.7). The most preferred value of the IACC is zero. Ando's 'total subjective preference' S_a vanishes if all the parameters assume their most preferred values, negative values of S_a indicate certain acoustical deficiencies.

Beranek[47] has modified this rating scheme by adding two further components to it, namely 'warmth' (equal to low frequency divided by mid-frequency reverberation time) and an index for the surface diffusivity of a concert hall to be determined by visual inspection. He applied it to his famous collection of data on concert halls and opera theatres. On the other hand he assigned each of these concert halls into one of six categories of acoustical quality, ranging from 'fair' (category C) to 'superior' (category A_+) by evaluating numerous interviews with musicians and music critics. Comparing the category of a particular hall with the rating number it earned demonstrated satisfactory agreement with its subjectively assessed quality.

In a way, Ando's approach seems to answer the questions raised at the beginning of this section. However, it does not fully agree with the reported results of factor analysis from which the initial time delay gap did not emerge as a significant acoustical criterion. Furthermore, it states that there is an optimum acoustical environment regardless of obvious differences in listeners' taste. If all designers of concert halls consequently decided to follow the guidelines of this system, the result would be halls not only equally good but of equal acoustics. We doubt whether this is a desirable goal of room acoustical effort, since variations in acoustical impressions are just as enjoyable as different architectural solutions or different musical interpretations.

We have to admit that the insights which have been reported in this chapter do not combine to form a well-rounded picture of concert hall acoustics; they are not free of inconsistencies and even contradictions, and hence are to be considered as preliminary only. Nevertheless, it is obvious that major progress has been made during the past few decades; there is at least some agreement on likely important issues for concert hall design.

References

1 Schmitz, A., *Acustica*, **81** (1995) 416.
2 Atal, B.S. and Schroeder, M.R., *Gravesaner Blätter*, **27/28** (1966) 124.
3 Neu, G., Mommertz, E. and Schmitz, A., *Acustica*, **76** (1992) 183; Urbach, G., Mommertz, E. and Schmitz, A., *Acustica*, **77** (1992) 153.
4 Reichardt, W. and Schmidt, W., *Acustica*, **17** (1966) 75; *ibid.*, **18** (1967) 274.
5 Burgtorf, W. and Oehlschlägel, H.K., *Acustica*, **14** (1964) 254.
6 Schubert, P., *Zeitschr. Hochfrequenztechn. u. Elektroakust.*, **78** (1969) 230.
7 Seraphim, H.P., *Acustica*, **11** (1961) 80.
8 Haas, H., *Acustica*, **1** (1951) 49.
9 Muncey, R.W., Nickson, A.F.B. and Dubout, P., *Acustica*, **3** (1953) 168.
10 Meyer, E. and Schodder, G.R., *Nachr. Akad, Wissensch. Göttingen, Math.-Phys. Kl.*, No. 6 (1952) 31.

11 Atal, B.S., Schroeder, M.R. and Kuttruff, H., Proceedings of the Fourth International Congress on Acoustics, Copenhagen, 1962, Paper H31.

12 Niese, H., *Zeitschr. Hochfrequenztechn. u. Elektroakust.*, **65** (1956) 4: ibid. **66** (1957) 70; *Acustica*, **11** (1961) 199.

13 Dietsch, L. and Kraak, W., *Acustica*, **60** (1986) 205.

14 Thiele, R., *Acustica*, **3** (1953) 291.

15 Boré, G., Kurzton-Meßverfahren zur punktweisen Ermittlung der Sprachverständlichkeit in lautsprecherbeschallten Räumen. Dissertation, Technische Hochschule, Aachen, 1956.

16 Reichardt, W., Abdel Alim, O. and Schmidt, W., *Appl. Acoustics*, **7** (1974) 243; *Acustica*, **32** (1975) 126.

17 Gade, A.C., Proceedings of the Sabine Centennial Syposium, Cambridge, Mass., (Acoustical Society of America, Woodbury, New York, 1994), p. 191.

18 Kürer, R., *Acustica*, **21** (1969) 370; Proceedings of the Seventh International Congress on Acoustics, Budapest, 1971, Paper 23 A5.

19 Houtgast, T. and Steeneken, H.J.M., *Acustica*, **28** (1973) 66; Steeneken, H.J.M. and Houtgast, T., *J. Acoust. Soc. America*, **67** (1980) 318; Houtgast, T., Proceedings of the 12th International Congress on Acoustics, Toronto, 1986, Paper E4-13.

20 Sabine, W.C., *Collected Papers on Acoustics*, Dover, New York, 1964 (first published 1922).

21 Seraphim, H.-P., *Acustica*, **8** (1958) 280.

22 Barron, M., *Acustica*, **66** (1988) 1.

23 Beranek, L.L., *Music, Acoustics and Architecture*, John Wiley, New York/London, 1962.

24 Kuhl, W., *Acustica*, **4** (1954) 618.

25 Atal, B.S., Schroeder, M.R. and Sessler, G.M., Proceedings of the Fifth International Congress on Acoustics, Liege, 1965, Paper G32.

26 Jordan, V.L., *J. Acoust. Soc. America*, **47** (1970) 408.

27 Gade, A.C. and Rindel, J.H., in *Fortschr. d. Akustik – DAGA '85*, Bad Honnef, DPG-GmbH, 1985.

28 Damaske, P., *Acustica*, **19** (1967/68) 199.

29 Marshall, A.H., Proceedings of the Sixth International Congress on Acoustics, Tokyo, 1968, Paper E-2-3.

30 Meyer, E. and Kuhl, W., *Acustica*, **2** (1952) 77.

31 Barron, M., *J. Sound Vibr.*, **15** (1971) 475.

32 Barron, M. and Marshall, A.H., *J. Sound Vibr.*, **77** (2) (1981) 211.

33 Damaske, P. and Ando, Y., *Acustica*, **27** (1972) 232.

34 Gottlob, D., Vergleich objektiver Parameter mit Ergebnissen subjektiver Untersuchungen an Konzertsälen. Dissertation, University of Göttingen, 1973.

35 Keets, W. de Villiers, Proceedings of the Sixth International Congress on Acoustics, Tokyo, 1968, Paper E-2-4.

36 Bradley, J.S. and Soulodre, G.A., *J. Acoust. Soc. America*, **98** (1995) 2590.

37 Yamaguchi, K., *J. Acoust. Soc. America*, **52** (1972) 1271.

38 Edwards, R.M., *Acustica*, **30** (1974) 183.

39 Hawkes, R.J. and Douglas, H., *Acustica*, **24** (1971) 235.

40 Wilkens, H. and Plenge, G., The correlation between subjective and objective data of concert halls, in *Auditorium Acoustics*, ed. R. Mackenzie, Applied Science, London, 1974.

41 Schroeder, M.R., Gottlob, D. and Siebrasse, K.F., *J. Acoust. Soc. America*, **56** (1974) 1195.

42 Siebrasse, K.F., Vergleichende subjektive Untersuchungen zur Akustik von Konzertsälen. Dissertation, University of Göttingen, 1973.

43 Wilkens, H., *Acustica*, **38** (1977) 10.

44 Lehmann, P., Über die Ermittlung raumakustischer Kriterien und deren Zusammenhang mit subjektiven Beurteilungen der Hörsamkeit. Dissertation, Technical University of Berlin, 1976.

45 Gottlob, D., Siebrasse, K.F. and Schroeder, M.R., in *Fortschr. d. Akustik – DAGA '75*. Physik-Verlag GmbH, Weinheim, 1975.

46 Ando, Y., *J. Acoust. Soc. America*, **74** (1983) 873.

47 Beranek, L.L., *Concert and Opera Halls: How They Sound*, Acoustical Society of America, Woodbury, New York, 1996.

8 Measuring techniques in room acoustics

The starting point of modern room acoustics is marked by attempts to find and to define objective parameters which have a mediatory function, in that they are related in a known way with geometrical and other room data on the one hand and with certain listening impressions on the other. As we have seen in the preceding chapter, quite a number of such parameters have been introduced in room acoustics since then with varied justification and significance, and it is the object of the present chapter to describe how such quantities can be measured and which kind of equipment is required for this purpose.

Measurements in room acoustics are not only necessary to increase our knowledge of the factors which govern the subjectively perceivable acoustical qualities of a room but they are also a valuable diagnostic tool and can give useful supporting information in the design of large halls. If, for instance, an existing hall is to be refurbished or to be used for other purposes than was originally intended, or if there are certain acoustical deficiencies to be eliminated by constructive modifications, measurements of at least the reverberation time are indispensable. When a new hall is being designed, it may be very advantageous to perform measurements on a model of this hall in order to predict its acoustical behaviour and to detect possible acoustical faults and their causes as early as possible. Furthermore, it is advisable to carry out measurements during the various phases of the construction of a hall in order to check the acoustical concepts upon which the designs are based and, if necessary, to propose modifications in the inner finish, for instance in the choice of wall materials, seat upholstery and so on, at a time when this can be realised without much additional costs.

Other acoustical measurements which are not directly related to subjective impressions concern the investigation of the acoustic properties of materials, especially of the absorption of materials for walls and ceiling, of seats, etc. Knowledge of such data is absolutely essential for any planning in room acoustics. Many of them can be found in published collections, but often the acoustical consultant is faced with new products or with specially designed wall linings, for instance, for which no absorption data are available. This holds even more with regard to the scattering efficiency of acoustically 'rough' surfaces, for which almost no data have been published so far.

During the past decade, the conventional measuring equipment which consisted of electronic 'hardware' has been widely replaced with digital components (digital computers in connection with analogue-to-digital converters, transient recorders, printers and plotters, etc.). Nevertheless, some of the traditional measuring procedures still keep their place nowadays. Since the sound waves are basically 'analogue', i.e. not digital, at least the transducers (sound sources, microphones) continue to be of the analogue type. In the following we are going to describe both kinds of measuring procedures and equipment.

8.1 General remarks on instrumentation

Viewed from our present state of the art, the equipment which W.C. Sabine[1] had at his disposal for his famous investigation of reverberation appears quite modest: he excited the room under test with a few organ pipes and used his ear as a measuring instrument in conjunction with a simple stop watch. With the development and introduction of the electrical amplifier in the 1920s, almost all measuring techniques became electrical. In acoustics, the ear was replaced with a microphone and the fall in sound level was observed with electromechanical level recorders. Furthermore, electrical filters became available, and the mechanical sound source was often replaced with a loudspeaker. More recently, the introduction of the digital computer has triggered off a second revolution in measuring techniques: all kinds of signal processing (filtering, storing and evaluation of measured signals as well as the presentation of results) can now be made with digital means which are generally more powerful, precise and flexible – and less expensive – than with the more traditional equipment.

For field measurement of the reverberation time, the most convenient way to excite the room is still by using a pistol since it is easy to operate and sufficiently powerful even if there is some background noise. (In his own interest, the user should wear ear protectors.) The same holds for wooden hand clappers or bursting air balloons which yield high excitation especially at low frequencies. However, the use of electrical loudspeakers in combination with a signal generator and a power amplifier opens the possibility to produce any kind of excitation signal (frequency modulated tones, filtered random noise, specially shaped impulses, etc.) by which the signal-to-noise ratio may be greatly improved. For reverberation measurements, no particular requirements concerning the uniformity of the radiation must be met by the loudspeaker since the various sound components will anyway be mixed during the decay process.

This is different if the impulse response of the room or the directional distribution of sound energy is to be observed. Then any directionality of the sound source should be avoided, otherwise the result of the measurement

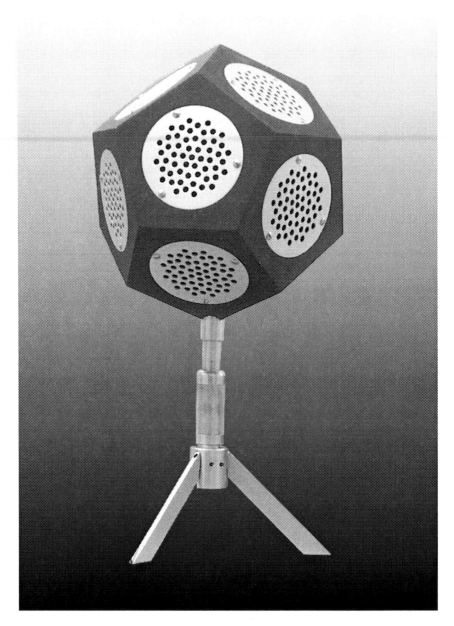

Figure 8.1 Dodecahedron loudspeaker for acoustical measurements.

would depend not only on the position of the source but also on its orientation. One way to obtain uniform sound radiation is to employ 12 or 20 equal and equally fed loudspeaker systems mounted on the faces of a regular polyhedron (dodecaeder or icosaeder). A dodecaeder loudpeaker is shown in Fig. 8.1.

It should be noted that even this kind of source is omnidirectional only at low frequencies. A different approach is to employ the driver of a powerful horn loudspeaker and to replace the horn by a tube, the open end of which radiates the sound uniformly provided its diameter is small compared with the wavelength. The resonances of the tube can be suppressed by inserting some damping material into it. Almost omnidirectional radiation of powerful acoustical wide-band impulses can also be achieved by specially designed electrical spark gaps.[2]

To pick up the sound in the enclosure, pressure-sensitive microphones with omnidirectional characteristics are usually employed. For certain measurements, however, gradient receivers, i.e. figure-of-eight microphones, must be used. Receivers with still higher directivity are needed to determine the directional distribution of sound energy at a certain position. They consist of arrays of microphones, or of a standard microphone fitted out with a special device such as a concave mirror or a slotted tube. Although the experimenter should have a certain idea of the sensitivity of his microphone, absolute calibration is not required since virtually all measurements in room acoustics are relative sound measurements. The only exception is field measurements of the 'strength factor' (*see* Section 7.6), or when several microphones are to be used.

Usually, the output signal of the microphone needs some pre-amplification. Then the signal can be stored for further evaluation in the laboratory with a magnetic tape recorder or with a digital recorder. A more convenient alternative is to feed the received signal immediately into a portable digital computer where it is stored in the computer's memory or is directly processed to yield the parameters which one is interested in. This requires, of course, that the computer is fitted out with an analogue-to-digital converter with sufficient dynamic range.

8.2 Measurement of the impulse response

According to system theory all properties of a linear transmission system are contained in its impulse response or, alternatively, in its transfer function, which is the Fourier transform of the impulse response. Since a room can be considered as an acoustical transmission system, the impulse response yields a complete description of the changes a sound signal undergoes when it travels from one point in a room to another, and almost all of the parameters we discussed in the preceding chapter can be derived from it, at least in principle. Parameters related to spatial or directional effects can be based upon the 'binaural impulse response' determined for both ears of a listener (or of an artificial head). From these remarks it is clear that the experimental determination of impulse responses is one of the most fundamental tasks in room acoustics. It requires high quality standards for all measuring components, which must be free not only of linear amplitude distortions but also of phase shifts.

By its very definition the impulse response of a system is the signal obtained at the system's output after its excitation by a vanishingly short impulse (yet with non-vanishing energy), i.e. by a Dirac or delta impulse (*see* Section 1.4). Since we are interested only in frequencies below, say, 10 kHz, this signal can be approximated by a short impulse of arbitrary shape, the duration of which is smaller than about 50 ms. However, it should be kept in mind that all loudspeakers show linear distortions. If a Dirac impulse $\delta(t)$ is applied to a loudspeaker's input, the impulse response is not another Dirac impulse but a different signal $g_{LS}(t)$, and accordingly the response $g'(t)$ of the room is its own impulse response $g(t)$ convolved with $g_{LS}(t)$, or after eqn (1.44) or (1.44a):

$$g'(t) = \int_{-\infty}^{\infty} g(t')g_{LS}(t - t') \, dt' \tag{8.1}$$

To remove the influence of the loudspeaker both sides of eqn (8.1) can be subjected to a Fourier transform which results in

$$G'(f) = G(f)G_{LS}(f) \tag{8.2}$$

from which the correct room impulse response $g(t)$ can be recovered by inverse Fourier transformation of $G(f) = G'(f)/G_{LS}$ (*see* eqn (1.33a)). This requires, of course, the use of a digital computer which is capable of performing Fourier transforms on a sufficiently large number of samples. If f_m denotes the maximum frequency component in $G(f)$ the measured function should be sampled with a rate of at least $2f_m$ samples per second to comply with Nyquist's sampling theorem. Since the duration of an impulse response is roughly the reverberation time T of the enclosure,

$$N = 2f_m T \tag{8.3}$$

Equidistant samples (typically 2^{12} to 2^{16}) are needed to represent $g(t)$ or $g'(t)$.

In field measurements there is always some background noise, and it may turn out that it is difficult to overcome this noise by producing sufficiently powerful excitation impulses. This difficulty can be circumvented by spreading the energy of the excitation signal over a wider time interval. Suppose the system under test, i.e. the room, is excited by an arbitrary signal $s(t)$.

Principally, the influence of that signal can be eliminated from the resulting output signal (*see* eqn (1.44))

$$s'(t) = \int_{-\infty}^{\infty} s(t')g(t-t')\,dt' = \int_{-\infty}^{\infty} g(t')s(t-t')\,dt' \qquad (8.4)$$

by applying the same recipe as before, namely by 'deconvolution' which is equivalent to a division in the frequency domain. The Fourier transform of eqn (8.4) reads

$$S'(f) = S(f)G(f) \qquad (8.5)$$

Then $G(f)$ is obtained as S'/S provided the magnitude of S is non-zero within the whole frequency range of interest. Particularly well-suited for this techniques, known as 'two-channel FFT', are broadband excitation signals with flat power spectra as for instance white noise, sine signals with linearly increasing frequency, or 'maximum length sequences' as discussed below.

An alternative to this method is to form the cross-correlation function of the input signal s and the output signal s'. This is achieved by inserting the second version of eqn (8.4) into eqn (1.40):

$$\phi_{ss'}(\tau) = \lim_{T_0 \to \infty} \frac{1}{T_0} \int_{-T_0/2}^{+T_0/2} s(t)\,dt \int_{-\infty}^{+\infty} g(t')s(t+\tau-t')\,dt'$$

or, after interchanging the order of integrations,

$$\phi_{ss'}(\tau) = \int_{-\infty}^{+\infty} g(t') \left[\lim_{T_0 \to \infty} \frac{1}{T_0} \int_{-T_0/2}^{+T_0/2} s(t)s(t+\tau-t')\,dt \right] dt'$$

$$= \int g(t')\phi_{ss}(\tau-t')\,dt' \qquad (8.6)$$

according to eqn (1.38). Comparing the latter expression with eqn (1.42) shows that this measuring procedure (*see* Fig. 8.2) yields the impulse response g if the autocorrelation function of the exciting sound signal is the delta function or at least approximates it.

One 'signal' with an autocorrelation function concentrated at $\tau = 0$, which therefore could be used for this measurement, is random noise. To obtain a reasonable signal-to-noise ratio, however, the averaging time T_0 for each choice of the delay τ must not be too short (typically of the order 0.1 s). On the other hand, quite a number of delays are needed to resolve all details of

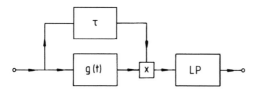

Figure 8.2 Measurement of the impulse response by cross-correlation (LP = lowpass filter).

an impulse response of some length. Therefore the measurement of impulse responses using white noise is a relatively time-consuming procedure.

More useful than random noise are 'pseudo-random' test signals, which have similar properties to random noise in a way although they are deterministic. Among these signals, binary impulse sequences are especially well suited for digital generation and processing. These are sequences of delta impulses or rectangular impulses with equal amplitudes, but with polarities changing according to a particular pattern.

An example of transient signals of this type are Barker coded impulse sequences. Since the length of these sequences does not exceed 13 elements, the achieved improvement of the signal-to-noise ratio is limited.[3] Another extremely powerful measuring scheme is based on 'maximum length sequences', which are stationary and have a period comprising

$$l = 2^n - 1$$

elements s_k, where n is a positive integer. They can be generated by a digital n-step shift register with the outputs of certain stages fed back to the input.[4] Their main advantage, however, is that the required correlation process can be performed in a very efficient way by employing fast Hadamard transform. This method, which was introduced into room acoustics by Schroeder and Alrutz,[5] will be described in more detail in the following.

Let s_k (with $k = 0, 1, \ldots, l$) be a maximum length sequence with the length l, for instance for $n = 3$:

$$-1, +1, +1, -1, +1, -1, -1$$

Because of its periodicity we have $s_{k+l} = s_k$, and it has the general property

$$\sum_{k=0}^{l-1} s_k = -1 \tag{8.7}$$

Since s_k is a discrete function, its autocorrelation function is defined by analogy with eqn (1.38) by

a)

b)

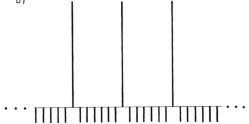

Figure 8.3 Maximum length sequence with $n = 3$ and its autocorrelation function.

$$(\phi_{ss})_m = \sum_{k=0}^{l-1} s_{k+m} \qquad (8.8)$$

and has the values l for $m = 0, l, 2l, \ldots$ and -1 for all other values of m (Fig. 8.3).

Now we excite the room under consideration with a close succession of equally high impulses which have the duration Δt and the signs of which correspond to the sequence s_k. The received signal $s'(t)$ is sampled at the rate $1/\Delta t$. Its samples are given by

$$s'_k = \sum_{j=0}^{l-1} s_j g_{k-j} \qquad (8.9)$$

As mentioned before, the sampling interval Δt should be shorter that half the period of the highest frequency f_m encountered in $g(t)$, i.e. $\Delta t < 1/2f_m$.

Equation (8.9) is the discrete version of eqn (8.4). It can equally well be formulated by means of a matrix $\mathbf{S}$ which consists of a cyclic arrangement of the elements s_k and one additional row and column of ones:

$$
\begin{bmatrix} \bar{s} \\ s'_0 \\ s'_1 \\ s'_2 \\ \vdots \\ s'_{l-1} \end{bmatrix}
=
\begin{bmatrix}
1 & 1 & 1 & 1 & \cdots & 1 \\
1 & s_0 & s_1 & s_2 & \cdots & s_{l-1} \\
1 & s_1 & s_2 & s_3 & \cdots & s_0 \\
1 & s_2 & s_3 & s_4 & \cdots & s_1 \\
\vdots & \vdots & \vdots & \vdots & \vdots & \vdots \\
1 & s_{l-1} & s_0 & s_1 & \cdots & s_{l-2}
\end{bmatrix}
\begin{bmatrix} 0 \\ g_l \\ g_{l-1} \\ g_{l-2} \\ \vdots \\ g_1 \end{bmatrix}
\qquad (8.9a)
$$

or in short-hand notation:

$$s' = S \cdot g \tag{8.9b}$$

In eqn (8.9a) we introduced $\bar{s}$ as the negative sum of all values of s'_k:

$$\bar{s} = -\sum_{k=0}^{l-1} s'_k = \sum_{k=0}^{l-1} g_k$$

It is easy to prove that the symmetrical matrix S has the property

$$S \cdot S = (l+1)\begin{pmatrix} 1 & 0 & \cdots & 0 \\ 0 & 1 & \cdots & 0 \\ & & \cdots & \\ 0 & 0 & \cdots & 1 \end{pmatrix}$$

Hence, if both sides of eqn (8.9b) are multiplied from the left side with S one obtains

$$S \cdot s' = S \cdot S \cdot g = (l+1)g$$

or

$$g = \frac{1}{l+1} S \cdot s' \tag{8.10}$$

which is the formal solution of our problem, namely to recover the impulse response $g(t)$ (or the g_k) from the measured function $s'(t)$ or the samples s'_k taken from it, provided the duration of $g(t)$ is shorter than the period l of the maximum length sequence.

At first glance the introduction of the matrix S may appear as an unnecessary complication of eqn (8.9). The great advantage of this formalism, however, is that by interchanging rows and columns according to a certain scheme this matrix can be transformed into a Hadamard matrix H_n which contains $(l+1)(l+1) = 2^{2n}$ elements $+1$ or -1 in a highly regular pattern and which can be obtained by a simple recursion:

$$H_{n+1} = \begin{bmatrix} H_n & H_n \\ H_n & -H_n \end{bmatrix} \quad \text{with } H_0 = (1) \tag{8.11}$$

For our previous example with $n = 3$ the matrix S reads

$$\begin{bmatrix}
1 & 1 & 1 & 1 & 1 & 1 & 1 & 1 \\
1 & -1 & 1 & 1 & -1 & 1 & -1 & -1 \\
1 & 1 & 1 & -1 & 1 & -1 & -1 & -1 \\
1 & 1 & -1 & 1 & -1 & -1 & -1 & 1 \\
1 & -1 & 1 & -1 & -1 & -1 & 1 & 1 \\
1 & 1 & -1 & -1 & -1 & 1 & 1 & -1 \\
1 & -1 & -1 & -1 & 1 & 1 & -1 & 1 \\
1 & -1 & -1 & 1 & 1 & -1 & 1 & -1
\end{bmatrix}$$

After interchanging its rows as well as its columns according to the following scheme:

old number: 1 2 3 4 5 6 7 8
new number: 1 8 7 4 2 6 3 5

the re-ordered matrix is

$$\begin{bmatrix}
1 & 1 & 1 & 1 & 1 & 1 & 1 & 1 \\
1 & -1 & 1 & -1 & 1 & -1 & 1 & -1 \\
1 & 1 & -1 & -1 & 1 & 1 & -1 & -1 \\
1 & -1 & -1 & 1 & 1 & -1 & -1 & 1 \\
1 & 1 & 1 & 1 & -1 & -1 & -1 & -1 \\
1 & -1 & 1 & -1 & -1 & 1 & -1 & 1 \\
1 & 1 & -1 & -1 & -1 & -1 & 1 & 1 \\
1 & -1 & -1 & 1 & -1 & 1 & 1 & -1
\end{bmatrix}$$

which is the Hadamard matrix H_3.

To obtain the same result as with the matrix S, the Hadamard matrix must not be applied to the sequence or one-column matrix s' but to a modified version s'' of it, which is obtained by interchanging its elements according to the above scheme, and after execution of the matrix multiplication $H_n \cdot s''$ the elements of the resulting one-column matrix have to be rearranged into the original order to yield g.

The important point is that, on account of the regular structure of H_n, the multiplication $H_n \cdot s'$ can be carried out with a very time-efficient algorithm, a so-called 'butterfly' algorithm.

The necessary length l of the maximum length sequence s_k depends, of course, on the desired length of the impulse response. If the latter has significant components in the time interval from 0 to t_m, the inequality

$$l \geq 2f_m t_m \qquad\qquad (8.12)$$

has to be fulfilled. It is of crucial importance, of course, that the sampling rate of the received signal $s'(t)$ agrees exactly with the rate at which the excitatory impulses $s(t)$ are generated and emitted.

It is beyond the scope of this representation to describe the algorithm of fast Hadamard transform, i.e. for the multiplication $\mathbf{H}_n \cdot \mathbf{s}'$; the same holds for the general rule according to which the elements of $\mathbf{s}'$ have to be permutated. For these details the reader is referred to the literature.[5,6]

8.3 Correlation measurement

Besides the impulse responses, various types of correlation functions have several useful applications in room acoustics. One of them was mentioned in the preceding section, where the cross-correlation of two signals was used to determine the impulse response of a linear system, in particular of a room. Another example is the interaural cross-correlation function (IACC) defined in Section 7.7. Further applications will be described in subsequent sections. In this section a few procedures to measure correlation functions will be described.

Generally correlation functions can be used to detect or to characterise the causal relationship between two different time functions (cross-correlation function), or the degree of randomness of one function (autocorrelation function). They are especially useful in such cases where the functions to be compared are stochastic functions or have at least such a complicated structure that a mutual relationship cannot be recognised by simple inspection. It is just this aspect which frequently applies to room acoustics, as for instance in the impulse response of the transmission path between two points of a room.

Let $s_1(t)$ and $s_2(t)$ be two stationary time functions. Their cross-correlation function $\phi_{12}(\tau)$ is formed according to eqn (1.40). Its evaluation or experimental determination is meaningful only in such cases where no analytical representation of both functions is possible or available. A special case of it with $s_1 = s_2$ is the autocorrelation function ϕ_{11}, already defined in eqn (1.38). It compares different sections of the same function and thus is a measure of how far functional relationship extends. Obviously ϕ_{11} is an even function in τ.

The function to be investigated most frequently in room acoustics is the impulse response $g(t)$ for the transmission between two points. In contrast to s_1 and s_2 it is, however, not a stationary function of time; instead it begins at a certain time and vanishes for $t \to \infty$. If the room under investigation (*see* Fig. 8.4) is excited by white noise $r(t)$, the response to this sound signal at two different points in the room is given according to eqn (1.44) by

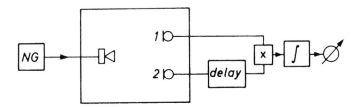

Figure 8.4 Measurement of cross-correlation functions in a room employing steady state excitation.

$$s_{1,2}(t) = \int_{-\infty}^{t} r(x)g_{1,2}(t-x)\, dx = \int_{0}^{\infty} g_{1,2}(x)\, r(t-x)\, dx \qquad (8.13)$$

These functions are stationary and can be inserted into eqn (1.40), which, after interchanging the order of integration, yields

$$\Phi_{12}(\tau) = \int_{0}^{\infty} g_1(x)\, dx \int_{0}^{\infty} g_2(y)\, dy \left[\lim \frac{1}{T_0} \int_{0}^{T_0} r(t-x)r(t-y+\tau)\, dt \right] \qquad (8.14)$$

The expression in the brackets is the autocorrelation function of the random noise signal $r(t)$, taken at the argument $\tau + x - y$, which has virtually the character of a delta function because of the flat frequency spectrum of $r(t)$. Thus we obtain

$$\Phi_{12}(\tau) = \int_{-\infty}^{\infty} g_1(x)g_2(x+\tau)\, dx \qquad (8.15)$$

This means the cross-correlation function may be directly obtained from both impulse responses by replacing the noise generator NG in Fig. 8.4 with an impulse generator. The same holds for the measurement of the autocorrelation function of one impulse response, say of g_1; in this case the input of the delaying device is connected to microphone 1 too, with the result

$$\Phi_{11}(\tau) = \int_{-\infty}^{\infty} g_1(x)g_1(x+\tau)\, dx \qquad (8.16)$$

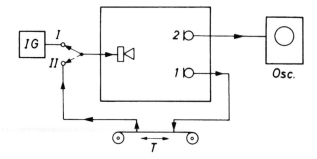

Figure 8.5 Measurement of cross-correlation functions in a room by play-back.

Another useful method for performing correlation measurement is the play-back method depicted schematically in Fig. 8.5. Again the room is excited by a short impulse at switch position I; the output of microphone 1 yields the impulse response $g_1(t)$, which is stored in some way. Then the signal is replayed in reverse time order, and the reversed impulse response $g_1(-t)$ thus obtained is applied once more to the room as an exciting signal (switch position II). As a result the output voltage of the microphone will be proportional to the function

$$\int_{-\infty}^{+\infty} g_1(-x)g_2(t-x)\,\mathrm{d}x = \int_{-\infty}^{+\infty} g_1(x)g_2(x+t)\,\mathrm{d}x$$

which agrees with eqn (8.15) and is thus the cross-correlation function $\Phi_{12}(t)$ which is obtained as a function of real time and can hence be observed directly on the screen of an oscilloscope. During the same phase of the measurement, the microphone 1 yields the autocorrelation function of the impulse response g_1 according to eqn (8.16). No delaying unit and no multiplicator is needed in this method. Sometimes it may be desirable or necessary to restrict the frequency range of a correlation measurement. This can be achieved by inserting a suitable filter into the electrical signal path or – if the measurement is carried out with impulse excitation – to employ test signals with the desired frequency spectrum. Then the autocorrelation function modified by the filter is

$$\Phi_{11}^{\mathrm{mod}}(\tau) = \Phi_{11}(\tau) * \Phi_{\mathrm{FF}}(\tau) \tag{8.17}$$

with Φ_{FF} denoting the autocorrelation function of the filtered test signal.

As an example of both the play-back method and the effect of filtering Fig. 8.6 shows an autocorrelogram obtained with the play-back method in a reverberation chamber which was excited by an impulse with Gaussian envelope having a centre frequency of 2000 Hz and a duration of about

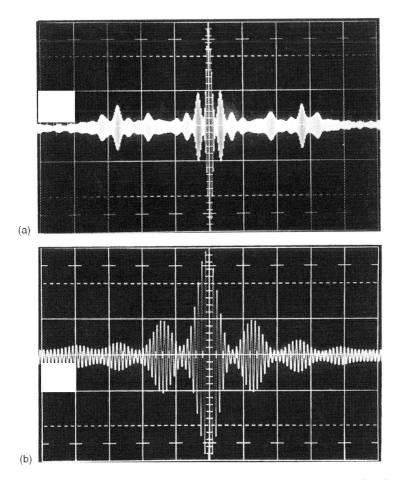

(a)

(b)

Figure 8.6 Autocorrelogram taken in a reverberation chamber by the play-back method. The room was excited by a filtered impulse with about 1 ms duration and a centre frequency of 2000 Hz: (a) abscissa unit corresponding to 20 ms; (b) same as (a) but abscissa unit 5 ms.

1 ms. The central peak of this function is nearly a replica of the exciting impulse.

Since any time function is related to a frequency function by the Fourier transformation, all relations and operations mentioned above can be expressed in the frequency domain as well. Table 8.1 lists some of these correspondences. So the autocorrelation functions (second line) correspond to power spectra, according to eqns (1.37) and (1.39), and convolutions in the time domain (fourth line) correspond to multiplications in the frequency domain, according to eqns (1.44) and (1.45). Therefore a useful alternative to the direct correlation of time functions as described before may be to transform these functions into frequency functions, to perform the required

Table 8.1 Corresponding time and frequency functions

Time domain	Frequency domain
$g(t)$	$G(f)$
$\Phi_{11}(\tau)$	$G_1(f) \cdot G_1^*(f) = \lvert G_1(f) \rvert^2$
$\Phi_{12}(\tau)$	$G_1(f) \cdot G_2^*(f)$
$\Phi_{11}^{mod}(\tau) = \Phi_{11}(\tau) * \Phi_{FF}(\tau)$	$\lvert H_1(f) \rvert^2_{mod} = \lvert H_1(f) \rvert^2 \cdot \lvert S(f) \rvert^2$

multiplications with them and to transform the result back into the time domain. Which method is preferable depends on the time needed to perform it.

8.4 Examination of the time structure of the impulse response

After this digression into correlation analysis we return now to the impulse response of a room or, more precisely, to the impulse response of a particular transmission path within a room. Some of the information it contains on the acoustics of the room can be found directly by inspection of a 'reflectogram', by which term we mean the graphical representation of the impulse response or another time function which is closely related to it. Futhermore, certain parameters which have been discussed in the preceding chapter may be extracted from the impulse response. (The measurement of reverberation time will be postponed to a separate section below.) In any case, however, some further processing of the measured impulse response is useful or necessary.

From the visual inspection of a reflectogram the experienced acoustician may learn quite a bit about the acoustical merits and faults of the place for which it has been measured. One important question is, for instance, to what extent the direct sound will be supported by shortly delayed reflections, and how these are distributed in time. Furthermore, strong and isolated peaks with long delays which hint at the danger of echoes are easily detected.

The direct examination of a reflectogram is greatly facilitated – especially that of a band-limited reflectogram – if insignificant details of it are removed beforehand. In principle, this can be effected by rectifying and smoothing the impulse response. This process, however, introduces some arbitrariness into the obtained reflectogram with regard to the applied time constant: if it is too short, the smoothing effect may be insufficient; if it is too long, important details of the reflectogram will be suppressed. One way to avoid this uncertainty is to apply a mathematically well-defined procedure to the impulse response, namely to form its 'envelope'. Let $s(t)$ denote any signal, then its envelope is defined as

$$e(t) = \sqrt{\{[s(t)]^2 + [\check{s}(t)]^2\}} \qquad (8.18)$$

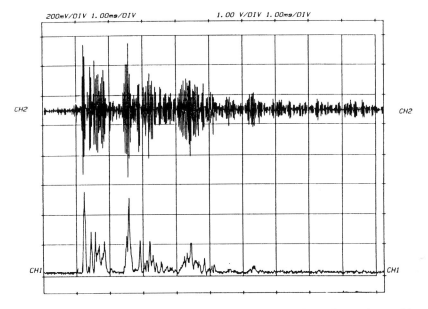

Figure 8.7 Impulse response (upper part) and its squared envelope, obtained by means of an analogue Hilbert transformer. Total range of abscissa in 400 ms.

Here $\check{s}(t)$ denotes the Hilbert transform of $s(t)$:

$$\check{s}(t) = \frac{1}{\pi} \int_{-\infty}^{+\infty} \frac{s(t - t')}{t'} \, dt' \equiv \mathcal{H}[s(t)] \tag{8.19}$$

which has quite a number of interesting properties and applications (*see* Ref. 4 of Chapter 5, for instance). Probably the most convenient way to calculate the Hilbert transform is by exploiting its spectral properties. Let $S(f)$ denote the Fourier transform of $s(t)$, then the Fourier transform of $\check{s}(t)$ is

$$\check{S}(f) = -iS(f)\, \mathrm{sign}(f) \tag{8.20}$$

Hence, a function $s(t)$ may be Hilbert transformed by computing its spectral function S, modifying it according to eqn (8.20) and transforming it back into the time domain. There are also other efficient methods to compute the Hilbert transform in the time domain.

Figure 8.7 illustrates how an experimental reflectogram is modified by forming its squared envelope $[e(t)]^2$. It is obvious that the latter exhibits the significant components much more clearly.

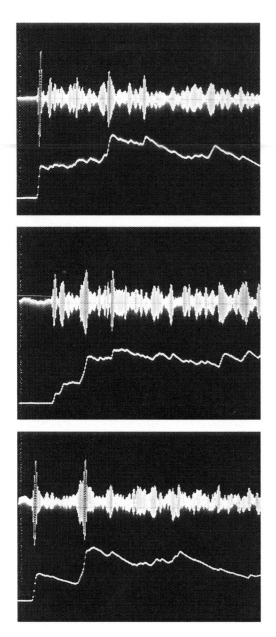

Figure 8.8 Reflectograms of a lecture room at different places (centre frequency 3000 Hz, impulse duration about 1 ms). Upper traces: original impulse response. Lower traces: after rectifying and smoothing with time constant $\tau = 25$ ms.

The visual examination of reflectograms may further be facilitated by smoothing their envelope in order to simulate the integrating properties of our hearing. For this purpose the envelope $e(t)$ (or the rectified impulse response $|g(t)|$) is convolved with $\exp(-t/\tau)$. This corresponds to applying the signal $|g(t)|$ or $e(t)$ to a simple RC network with the time constant τ. A reasonable choice of the time constant τ is 25 ms.

In Fig. 8.8 a few experimental 'reflectograms' are shown as an example, obtained at several places in a lecture room which was excited by short impulses with a centre frequency of 3000 Hz and a duration of about 1 ms; the frequency bandwidth was about 500 Hz. The lower trace of each registration shows the result of the smoothing described above. The total length of an oscillogram corresponds to a time interval of 190 ms. The uppermost reflectogram was taken at a place close to the sound source, consequently the direct sound is relatively strong. The most outstanding feature in the lowest oscillogram is the strong reflection delayed by about 40 ms with regard to the direct sound. It is not heard as an echo, since it still lies within the integration time of our ear (*see* Section 7.3).

Although the visual inspection of reflectograms is very suggestive it does not permit a safe decision whether a reflection will be heard as an echo or not. This can only be achieved by applying one of the echo criteria discussed in Section 7.3. About the same holds for a periodic train of reflections which can cause quite undesirable subjective effects even when the periodic components are obscured by other non-periodically distributed reflections and therefore cannot be detected simply by visual examination of a reflectogram. Usually the periodic components are caused by repeated reflections of sound rays between parallel walls, or generally in rooms with a very regular shape, as for instance in rooms which are circular or regularly polygonal in cross-section. At relatively short repetition times they are perceived as colouration, at least under certain conditions (*see* Section 7.3). But even a single dominating reflection may cause audible colouration, especially of music, since the corresponding transmission function has a regular structure or substructure.

The most adequate technique for testing the randomness or pseudorandomness of an impulse response is the autocorrelation analysis. In this procedure all the irregularly distributed components are swept together into a single central peak (*see* Fig. 8.6), whereas the remaining reflections will form side components and satellite maxima in the autocorrelogram. In order to decide the question of whether or not a certain side maximum indicates audible colouration, we at first form, from the experimental autocorrelation function ϕ_{gg} (in the preceding section referred to as Φ_{11}), a 'weighted auto-correlation function':[7]

$$\phi'_{gg}(\tau) = b(\tau)\phi_{gg}(\tau) \qquad (8.21)$$

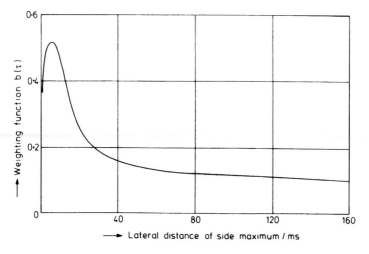

Figure 8.9 Weighting function for autocorrelation functions with respect to colouration.[7]

The weighting function $b(\tau)$ can be calculated from the thresholds represented in Fig. 7.11 and is shown in Fig. 8.9.

Let us denote by τ_0 the value of the argument at which the side maximum second to the central maximum (at $t = 0$) appears. Then we have to expect audible colouration if

$$\phi'_{gg}(\tau_0) > 0.06\phi'_{gg}(0) \tag{8.22}$$

no matter if this side maximum is caused by a single strong reflection or by a periodic succession of reflections.[8]

The temporal structure of a room's impulse response determines not only the shape of the autocorrelation function obtained in this room but also its modulation transfer function (MTF), which was introduced in Section 5.5. Indeed, as was shown by M.R. Schroeder,[9] the complex MTF for white noise as a primary sound signal is related to the impulse response by

$$\overline{m}(\Omega) = \frac{\int_0^\infty [g(t)]^2 \exp(i\Omega t)\, dt}{\int_0^\infty [g(t)]^2\, dt} \tag{8.23}$$

This means, the complex modulation transfer is the Fourier transform of the squared room impulse response $[g(t)]^2$ divided by the integral over $[g(t)]^2$.

Of course, this procedure can also be applied to an impulse response $g'(t)$ which has been confined to a suitable frequency band by bandpass filtering.

As described in Section 7.4, a reliable criterion for the intelligibility of speech in auditoria, the 'speech transmission index' (STI), can be deduced from the magnitude of the complex MTF, $m = |\overline{m}|$. Unfortunately the experimental determination of the modulation transfer function and the evaluation of the speech transmission index is a relatively time-consuming and complicated process. For this reason Houtgast and Steeneken[10] have developed a simplified version of the STI, called 'RApid Speech Transmission Index' (RASTI). It is obtained by measuring m for four modulation frequencies $\Omega/2\pi$ in the octave band centred at 500 Hz, and for five modulation frequencies in the 2000 Hz octave band. The applied modulation frequencies range from 0.7 to 11.2 Hz. Each of the nine values of m is converted into an 'apparent signal-to-noise ratio':

$$(S/N)_{app} = 10 \log_{10}\left(\frac{m}{1-m}\right) \tag{8.24}$$

These figures are averaged after truncating any which exceeds the range of ± 15. The final parameter is obtained by normalising the average $(\overline{S/N})_{app}$ into the range from 0 to 1:

$$RASTI = \tfrac{1}{30}[(\overline{S/N})_{app} + 15] \tag{8.25}$$

For practical RASTI measurements both octave bands are emitted simultaneously, each with a complex power envelope containing five modulation frequencies. Likewise, the automated analysis of the received sound signal is performed in parallel. With these provisions it is possible to keep the duration of one measurement as low as about 12 s. By extensive investigations on the validity of RASTI, carried out in several countries (i.e. languages), the abovementioned authors were able to show that there is good agreement between the results of RASTI and the more elaborate STI, and furthermore that the RASTI method is well suited to rate the speech intelligibility in auditoria. Table 8.2 shows the relation between five classes of speech quality and certain intervals of RASTI values.

Table 8.2 Relation between scores of speech transmission quality and RASTI

Quality score	RASTI
Bad	<0.32
Poor	0.32–0.45
Fair	0.45–0.60
Good	0.60–0.75
Excellent	>0.75

Table 8.3 Criteria for the assessment of acoustical qualities of rooms

Name of criterion	Symbol	Defined by equation
Definition ('Deutlichkeit')	D	7.9
Clarity index ('Klarheitsmaß')	C, C_{80}	7.10
Centre time	t_s	7.12
Echo coefficient ('Echograd')	ε	7.6
Echo criterion (Dietsch and Kraak)	EC	7.7, 7.8
Speech transmission index	STI	Ref. 19 of Ch. 7
Reverberation time and early decay time	T, EDT	see Section 8.5
Strength factor	G	7.15
Early lateral energy fraction	LEF	7.18
Late lateral energy	LG_{80}^{∞}	7.21
Interaural cross correlation	$IACC$	7.19

It goes without saying that all the parameters introduced in Chapter 7 can be evaluated from impulse responses by suitable operations. Table 8.3 lists these criteria along with the equations by which they are defined and which can be used to compute them.

The experimental determination of the 'early lateral energy fraction' (LEF) and the 'late lateral energy' (LG_{80}^{∞}) requires the use of a gradient microphone (figure-of-eight microphone) with its direction of minimum sensitivity directed towards the sound source. For measuring the 'early lateral energy fraction', an additional non-directional microphone placed at the same position as the gradient microphone is needed. In contrast, the normalising term of LG_{80}^{∞}, namely the denominator in eqn (7.21), is independent of the measuring position in the room and must be determined just once for a given sound source. The 'interaural cross correlation' (IACC) is obtained by cross-correlating the impulse responses describing the sound transmission from the sound source to both ears of a human head. This can be achieved by applying any of the methods described in Section 8.3. If such measurements are carried out only occasionally, the responses can be obtained with two small microphones fixed in the entrance of both ear channels of a person whose only function is to scatter the sound waves properly. For routine work it is certainly more convenient to replace the human head by an artificial head with built-in microphones.

8.5 Measurement of reverberation

For reasons which have been discussed earlier, Sabine's reverberation time is still the best known and most important quantity in room acoustics. This fact is the justification for describing the measurement of this important parameter in a separate section which includes that of its younger relative, the 'early decay time' (EDT).

Although both the reverberation time of a room as well as the 'early decay time' at a particular place in it can be derived from the corresponding

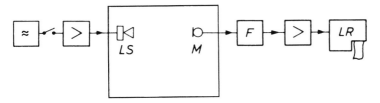

Figure 8.10 Reverberation measurement by steady state excitation of the room.

impulse responses, we start by describing the more traditional methods which still maintain their place in everyday practice. They are usually based on the analysis of the decay process and hence on the evaluation of decay curves. Accordingly, the first step of a decay measurement is to record decay curves over a sufficiently large range of the decaying sound level.

The standard equipment for this purpose (which can be modified in many ways) is depicted schematically in Fig. 8.10. A loudspeaker LS, driven by a signal generator, excites the room to steady state conditions. The output voltage of the microphone M is fed to an amplifier and filter F, and then to a logarithmic recorder LR, whose deflection is calibrated in decibels. At a given moment the excitation is interrupted by a switch, and at the same time the recorder is triggered and starts to record the decay process.

The signal from the generator is either a frequency modulated sinusoidal signal whose momentary frequency covers a narrow range or it is random noise filtered by an octave or a third octave filter. The range of mid-frequencies, for which reverberation time measurements are usually taken, extends from about 50 to 10 000 Hz; most frequently, however, the range from 100 to 5000 Hz is considered. As mentioned in Section 8.1, excitation by a pistol shot is often a practical alternative. Pure sinusoidal tones are used only occasionally, as for example to excite individual modes in the range well below the Schroeder frequency, eqn (3.32).

The loudspeaker, or more generally the sound source, is usually placed at the same location where, during normal use of the room, the natural sound source is located. This applies not only to reverberation measurements but also to other measurements. Because of the validity of the reciprocity principle, however (*see* Section 3.1), the location of sound source and microphone can be exchanged without altering the results, in cases where this is practical and provided that the sound source and the microphone have no directionality. In any case, it is important that the distance between the sound source and the microphone is much larger than the reverberation distance given by eqn (5.38), otherwise the direct sound would have an undue influence on the shape of the decay curve.

If the sound field were completely diffuse, the decay curves should be independent of the location of the sound source and the microphone. Since these ideal conditions hardly ever exist in normal rooms, it is advisable to carry out several measurements for each frequency at different microphone positions, as not only the reverberation time, which corresponds to the average slope of a decay curve, but also other details of the curve may be relevant to the acoustics of a hall or of a particular point in it. This is even more important if the quantity to be evaluated is the early decay time which may vary considerably from one place to the next within one hall.

The microphone is followed by a filter – usually an octave or third octave filter – largely to improve the signal-to-noise ratio, i.e. to reduce the disturbing effects of noise produced in the hall itself as well as that of the microphone and amplifier noise. If the room is excited by a pistol shot or another wide-band impulse, it is this filter which defines the frequency discrimination and hence yields the frequency dependence of the reverberation time.

For recording the decay curves the conventional electromechanical level recorder has been replaced nowadays by the digital computer, which converts the sound pressure amplitude of the received signal into the instantaneous level. Usually, the level $L(t)$ in the experimental decay curves does not fall in a strictly linear way but contains random fluctuations which are due, as explained in Section 3.5, to complicated interferences between decaying normal modes. If these fluctuations are not too strong, it is easy to approximate the decay within the desired section by a straight line. In many cases, this can be done visually. Any arbitrariness of evaluation is avoided, however, if a 'least square fit' is carried out. Let t_1 and t_2 denote the interval in which the decay curve is to be approximated (*see* Fig. 8.11), then the following integrations must be performed:

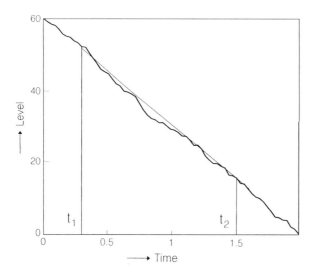

Figure 8.11 Approximation of a logarithmic decay curve by a straight line within limits t_1 and t_2.

$$L_1 = \int_{t_1}^{t_2} L(t)\,\mathrm{d}t \quad L_2 = \int_{t_1}^{t_2} L(t)\,t\,\mathrm{d}t$$

With the further abbreviations $I_1 = t_2 - t_1$, $I_2 = (t_2^2 - t_1^2)/2$ and $I_3 = (t_2^3 - t_1^3)/3$, the slope of the straight line is given by:

$$-\left(\frac{\Delta L}{\Delta t}\right) = \frac{I_1 L_2 - I_2 L_1}{I_1 I_3 - I_2^2} \tag{8.26}$$

This procedure is particularly recommended for the evaluation of the 'early decay time'.

In any case, the slope of the decay curve (or its approximation) is related to the reverberation time by

$$T = 60\left(\frac{\Delta L}{\Delta t}\right)^{-1} \tag{8.27}$$

The quasi-random fluctuations of decay level and the associated uncertainties about the true shape of a decay curve can be avoided, in principle, by averaging over a great number of individual reverberation curves, each of which was obtained by random noise excitation of the room. Fortunately this very time-consuming procedure will lead to the same result as another much more elegant method, called 'backward integration', which was proposed and first applied by Schroeder.[11] It is based on the following relationship between the ensemble average $\langle h^2(t) \rangle$ of all possible decay curves (for a certain place and bandwidth of exciting noise) and the corresponding impulse response $g(t)$:

$$\langle h^2(t) \rangle = \int_t^{\infty} [g(x)]^2\,\mathrm{d}x = \int_0^{\infty} [g(x)]^2\,\mathrm{d}x - \int_0^t [g(x)]^2\,\mathrm{d}x \tag{8.28}$$

The proof of this relation is similar to that of eqn (8.15). Suppose the room is excited by white noise $r(t)$, which is switched off at the time $t = 0$. According to eqn (1.44), the sound decay is given by

$$h(t) = \int_{-\infty}^{0} r(x)g(t - x)\,\mathrm{d}x = \int_t^{\infty} g(x)r(t - x)\,\mathrm{d}x \quad \text{for } t \geq 0$$

Squaring the latter expression yields a double integral, which after averaging reads

$$\langle h^2(t) \rangle = \int g(x)\,\mathrm{d}x \int g(y)\langle r(t - x)r(t - y) \rangle\,\mathrm{d}y$$

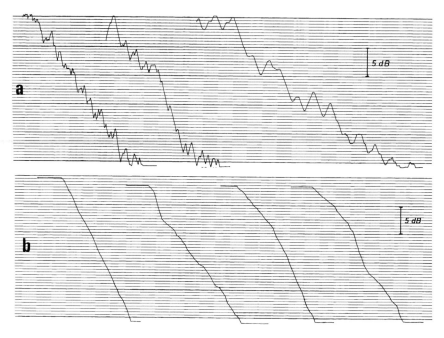

Figure 8.12 Examples of experimentally obtained reverberation curves: (a) recorded according to Fig. 8.10; (b) recorded by application of eqn (8.28).

The brackets $\langle \rangle$ on the right-hand side indicate that an ensemble average is to be formed which is identical with the autocorrelation function of $r(t)$ with the argument $x - y$. Now the autocorrelation function of white noise is a delta function. Invoking eqn (1.42) shows immediately that the double integral is reduced to the single integral of eqn (8.28). This derivation is valid no matter whether the impulse response is that measured for the full frequency range or only of a part of it.

The merits of this method may be underlined by the examples shown in Fig. 8.12. The upper decay curves have been measured with the traditional method, i.e. with random noise excitation, according to Fig. 8.10. They exhibit strong fluctuations of the decaying level which do not reflect any acoustical properties of the transmission path and hence of the room, but are due to the random character of the exciting signal; if one of these recordings were repeated, each new decay curve would differ from the preceding one in many details. In contrast, the lower curves, obtained for different conditions by processing the impulse responses according to eqn (8.28), are free of such confusing fluctuations and hence contain only significant information. Repeated measurements for one situation yield identical results,[12] which is not too surprising since these decay curves are based on an exactly reproducible characteristic, namely the impulse response. It is clear that the reverberation time can be obtained from such curves with

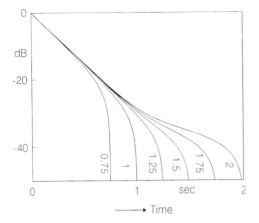

Figure 8.13 Effect of noise (*T* = 2 s) processed with backward integration method. The noise level is −41.4 dB. Parameter: upper integration limit t_∞.

much greater accuracy than from those recorded in the traditional way, which is even more true for the 'early decay time'. Furthermore, any characteristic deviations of the sound decay from exponential behaviour are much more obvious (*see*, for instance, the third curve in Fig. 8.12).

For the practical execution of the integration in eqn (8.28), the upper limit ∞ must be replaced with a suitable finite value, say t_∞, which, however, is not uncritical because in every experimental set-up there is some acoustical or electrical background noise. Its effect on basically linear decay curves corresponding to a reverberation time T = 2s is demonstrated by Fig. 8.13. If the limit t_∞ is too long, the decay curve will have a tail which limits the useful dynamic range, too short an integration time will cause an early downward bend of the curve, which is also awkward. Obviously, there exists an optimum for t_∞ which depends on the relative noise level and the decay time.

For evaluating the reverberation time, the slope of the decay curve is frequently determined in the level range from −5 to −35 dB relative to the initial level. This procedure is intended to improve the comparability and reproducibility of reverberation times in such cases where the fall in level does not occur linearly. It is doubtful, however, whether the evaluation of an average slope from curves which are noticeably bent is very meaningful, or whether the evaluation should rather be restricted to their initial parts, i.e. to the EDT which is anyway a more reliable indicator of the subjective impression of reverberance than Sabine's reverberation time. The same applies if the absorption coefficient of a test material is to be determined from reverberation measurements (Section 8.7) since the initial slope is closely related to the average damping constant of all excited normal modes (*see* eqn (3.44*a*)).

We conclude this section by mentioning that the absorption of a room and hence its reverberation time could be obtained, at least in principle, from the steady state sound level or energy density according to eqn (5.37). Likewise, the modulation transfer function could be used to determine the reverberation time (*see* eqn (5.36*a*)). In practice, however, these methods do not offer any advantages compared to those described above, since they are certainly more time consuming and less accurate.

8.6 Sound absorption – tube methods

The knowledge of sound absorption of typical building materials, etc., is indispensable for all tasks related to room acoustical design, i.e. for the prediction of reverberation times in the planning phase of auditoria and other rooms, for model experiments (*see* Section 9.5), for the acoustical computer simulation of environments and other purposes.

Basically, there are two standard methods of measuring absorption coefficients, namely by plane waves travelling in a rigid tube, and by employing a reverberation chamber. In this section the first one will be described. It is restricted to the examination of locally reacting materials with a plane or nearly plane surface, and also to normal wave incidence onto the test specimen.

A typical set-up is shown in Fig. 8.14. The tube is a pipe with a rigid wall and a rectangular or circular cross-section. At one of its ends, there is a loudspeaker which generates a sinusoidal sound signal. This signal travels along the tube as a plane wave towards the test specimen which terminates the other end of the tube and which must be arranged in the same way as it is to be used in practice, for example at some distance in front of a rigid wall. To reduce tube resonances it may be useful (although not essential for the principle of the method) to place an absorbing termination in front of

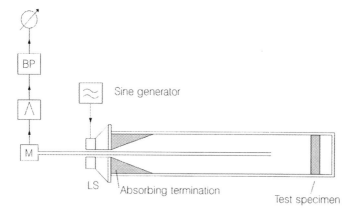

Figure 8.14 Conventional impedance tube, schematic.

the loudspeaker. The test sample reflects the incident wave more or less, leading to the formation of a partially standing wave as described in Section 2.2. The sound pressure maxima and minima of this wave are measured by a movable probe microphone, which must be small enough not to distort the sound field to any great extent. As an alternative to the arrangement shown, a miniature microphone mounted on the tip of a thin movable rod may be employed as well.

The tube should be long enough to permit the formation of at least one maximum and one minimum of the pressure distribution at the lowest frequency of interest. Its lateral dimensions have to be chosen in such a way that at the highest measuring frequency they are still smaller than a certain fraction of the wavelength λ_{min}. Or, more exactly, the following requirements must be met:

$$\text{Dimension of the wider side} < 0.5\lambda_{min} \quad \text{for rectangular tubes}$$
$$\text{Diameter} < 0.586\lambda_{min} \quad \text{for circular tubes} \qquad (8.29)$$

Otherwise, apart from the appearance of an essentially plane fundamental wave propagating at free field sound velocity of the medium, higher order wave types may occur with non-constant lateral pressure distributions and with different and frequency-dependent sound velocities. On the other hand, the cross-section of the tube must not be too small, since otherwise the wave attenuation due to losses at the wall surface would become too high. Generally at least two tubes of different dimensions are needed in order to cover the frequency range from about 100 to 5000 Hz.

For the determination of the absorption coefficient it is sufficient to measure the maximum and the minimum values of the sound pressure amplitudes, i.e. the pressures in the nodes and the anti-nodes of the standing wave. According to eqns (2.9) and (2.1), the absolute value of the reflection factor and the absorption coefficient are obtained by

$$|R| = \frac{\hat{p}_{max} - \hat{p}_{min}}{\hat{p}_{max} + \hat{p}_{min}} \qquad (8.30)$$

$$\alpha = \frac{4\hat{p}_{max}\hat{p}_{min}}{(\hat{p}_{max} + \hat{p}_{min})^2} \qquad (8.31)$$

If possible, the maxima and minima closest to the test specimen should be used for the evaluation of R and α since these values are influenced least by the attenuation of the waves. It is possible, however, to eliminate this influence by interpolation or by calculation, but in most cases it is hardly worthwhile doing this.

The absorption coefficient is not the only quantity which can be obtained by probing the standing wave; additional information can be derived from

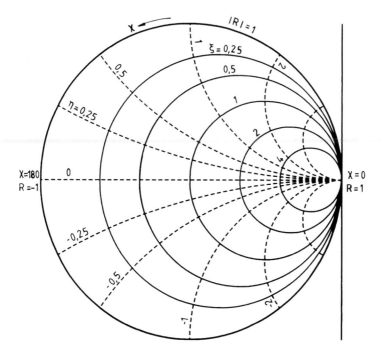

Figure 8.15 Smith chart (circles of constant real part ξ and imaginary part η of the specific impedance ζ represented in the complex R-plane).

the location of the pressure minimum (pressure node) which is next to the test specimen. According to eqn (2.9), the condition for the occurrence of a pressure node is $\cos(2kx + \chi) = -1$. If x_{min} is the distance of the nearest pressure node from the surface of the sample, this condition yields for the phase angle χ of the reflection factor

$$\chi = \pi\left(\frac{4x_{min}}{\lambda} - 1\right) \tag{8.32}$$

Once the complex reflection factor is known, the wall impedance Z or the specific impedance ζ of the material under test can be obtained by eqns (2.6) and (2.2a), for instance by applying a graphical representation of these relations known as a 'Smith chart' (*see* Fig. 8.15). Furthermore, the specific impedance of the sample can be used to determine its absorption coefficient α_{uni} for random sound incidence, either from Fig. 2.11 or by applying eqn (2.42). In many practical situations this latter absorption coefficient is more relevant than that for normal sound incidence. However, the result of this procedure will be correct only if the material under test can be assumed to be of the 'locally reacting' type (*see* Section 2.3).

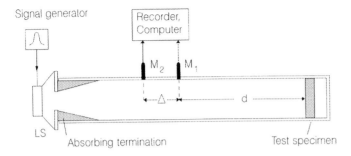

Figure 8.16 Impedance tube with two fixed microphones.

Several attempts have been made to replace the somewhat involved and time-consuming standing wave method by faster and more modern procedures using fixed microphone positions. For steady state test signals the separation of the reflected wave from the incident one can be achieved with microphones which may be mounted flush into the wall of the tube as shown in Fig. 8.16. Let $S(f)$ denote the spectrum of the signal emitted by the loudspeaker, for instance of random noise. Then the spectra of the sound signals received at both microphone positions are

$$S_1(f) = S(f)[\exp(ikd) + R(f)\exp(-ikd)]$$

$$S_2(f) = S(f)\{[\exp[ik(d + \Delta)] + R(f)\exp[(-ik(d + \Delta)])]\}$$

with $k = 2\pi f/c$. Here d is the distance of microphone 1 from the surface of the sample under test, and Δ denotes the distance between both microphones. From these equations, the complex reflection factor is easily obtained as

$$R(f) = \exp[ik(2d + \Delta)]\frac{S_2 - S_1\exp(ik\Delta)}{S_1 - S_2\exp(ik\Delta)} = \exp(2ikd)\frac{\exp(ik\Delta) - H_{12}}{H_{12} - \exp(-ik\Delta)}$$

$$(8.33)$$

with $H_{12} = S_2/S_1$ denoting the transfer function between both microphone positions. Critical are those frequencies for which $\exp(ik\Delta)$ is close to unity, i.e. the distance Δ is about an integer multiple of half the wavelength. In such regions the accuracy of measurement is not satisfactory. This problem can be circumvented by providing for a third microphone position. Of course, the relative sensitivities of all microphones must be taken into account, or the same microphone is used to measure S_1 and S_2 successively.

If a short impulse is used as a test signal, the measurement can be carried out with one microphone only since the incident and the reflected wave produce relatively short signals which can be separated by proper time

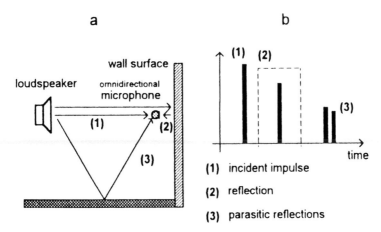

Figure 8.17 *In situ* measurement of acoustical wall properties: (a) experimental set-up; (b) sequence of reflections. Reflection 2 is separated by a time window (from Mommertz[12]).

windows. If $s(t)$ denotes the signal produced by the loudspeaker, the reflected signal is

$$s'(t) = r(t) * s(t - 2d/c) = \int_0^\infty r(t') s\left(t - t' - \frac{2d}{c}\right) dt' \qquad (8.34)$$

where d is the distance of the microphone from the surface of the test specimen, and $r(t)$ is the 'reflection response' of the test material as already introduced in Section 4.1. As explained in Section 8.2, the 'deconvolution' needed to remove the influence of the original signal in eqn (8.34) is most conveniently performed in the frequency domain. After Fourier transformation, eqn (8.34) reads:

$$S'(f) = R(f)S(f) \exp(-2ikd) \qquad (8.34a)$$

from which the complex reflection factor is easily obtained provided the signal spectrum $S(f)$ has no zeros in the considered frequency range. The signal-to-noise ratio is greatly improved by replacing the test impulse by a signal which can be deconvolved to an impulse, for instance by maximum length sequences as described in Section 8.2.

In order to separate safely the reflected signal from the primary one the latter must be sufficiently short, and the distance d of the microphone from the sample must be large enough. The same holds for any reflections from the loudspeker. This may lead to impractically long tubes. An alternative is to omit the tube, as depicted in Fig. 8.17 which can be used for remote measurement of acoustical wall and ceiling properties in existing enclosures, i.e. for *in situ* measurements. In this case, however, the waves are not plane but spherical. For this reason the results may be not too exact because the reflection of spherical waves is different from that of plane waves. Furthermore, the $1/r$ law of spherical wave propagation has to be accounted for by proper correction terms in eqn (8.34*a*). Further refinements of this useful method are described in Ref. 12.

8.7 Sound absorption – reverberation chamber

In a way, the reverberation method of absorption measurement is superior to the impedance tube method. First of all, the measurement is performed with a diffuse sound field, i.e. under conditions which are much more realistic for many practical applications than those encountered in a one-dimensional waveguide. Secondly, there are no limitations concerning the type and construction of the absorber. This means the reverberation method is well suited for measuring the absorption coefficient of almost any type of wall linings and of ceilings, but as well to determine the absorption of single or blocks of seats, unoccupied or occupied.

A so-called reverberation chamber is required for the method discussed here. This is a small room with a volume of at least 100 m³, better still 200 to 300 m³, whose walls are as smooth and rigid as possible. The absorption coefficient α_0 of the bare walls, which should be uniform in construction and finish, is determined by reverberation measurements in the empty chamber and by application of one of the reverberation formulae. (Usually the Sabine formula

$$T_0 = 0.163 \frac{V}{S\alpha_0} \tag{8.35}$$

(V = volume in m³, S = wall area in m²)

is sufficient for this purpose.) Then a certain amount of the material under investigation (or a certain number of absorbers) is brought into the chamber; the test material should be mounted in the same way as it would be applied in the practical case. The reverberation time is decreased by the test specimen and by applying once more the reverberation formula preferably in the Eyring version

$$T_0 = -0.163 \frac{V}{S \ln (1 - \bar{\alpha})} \tag{8.36}$$

with

$$\bar{\alpha} = \frac{1}{S}[S_s\alpha + (S - S_s)\alpha_0] \tag{8.36a}$$

the absorption coefficient α is easily calculated (S_s is the area of the test sample). In the case of single absorbers, the first term on the right-hand side of eqn (8.36a) is replaced by the number of absorbers times the absorption cross-section of one absorber (*see* Section 6.5), and S_s is set zero.

When applying the reverberation formulae, the air absorption term $4mV$ can usually be neglected, since it is contained in the absorption of the empty chamber as well as in that of the chamber containing the test material and therefore will almost cancel out. Because the chamber has a small volume the effect of air attenuation is low anyway.

The techniques of reverberation measurement itself have been described in detail in Section 8.5, and therefore no further discussion on this point is necessary. Usually, absorption measurements in the reverberation chamber are performed with frequency bands of third octave bandwidth.

The advantages of the reverberation method as mentioned at the beginning of this section are paid for by a considerable uncertainty concerning the reliability and accuracy of results obtained with it. In fact, several round robin tests[13,14] in which the same specimen of an absorbing material has been tested in different laboratories (and consequently with different reverberation chambers) have revealed a remarkable disagreement in the results. This must certainly be attributed to different degrees of sound field diffusion established in the various chambers and shows that increased attention must be paid to the methods of enforcing sufficient diffusion.

A first step towards sufficient sound field diffusion is to design the reverberation chamber without parallel pairs of walls and thus avoid sound waves which can be reflected repeatedly between two particular walls without being influenced by the remaining ones.

Among all further methods to achieve a diffuse sound field the introduction of volume scatterers as described in Section 5.1 seems to be most adequate for reverberation chambers, since an existing arrangement of scatterers can easily be changed if it does not prove satisfactory. Practically, such scatterers can be realised as bent shells of wood, plastics or metal which are suspended from the ceiling by cables in an irregular arrangement (*see*, for instance, Fig. 8.18). If necessary, bending resonances of these shells should be damped by applying layers of lossy material onto them. It should be noted, however, that too many diffusers may also affect the validity of the usual reverberation formulae and that therefore the density of scatterers has a certain optimum.[15] If H is the distance of the test specimen from the wall opposite to it, this optimum range is about

$$0.5 < \langle n \rangle Q_s H < 2 \qquad (8.37)$$

with $\langle n \rangle$ and Q_s denoting the density and the scattering cross-section of the diffusers introduced at the end of Section 5.1. This condition has also been proven experimentally.[16] For not too low frequencies the scattering cross-section Q_s is roughly half the geometrical area of one side of a shell.

Figure 8.18 Reverberation chamber fitted out with 25 diffusers of perspex (volume 324 m³; dimensions of one shell 1.54 m × 1.28 m).

Systematic errors of the reverberation method may also be caused by the so-called 'edge effect' of absorbing materials. If an absorbing area has free edges, it will usually absorb more sound energy per second than is proportional to its geometrical area, the difference being caused by diffraction of sound into the absorbing area. Formally, this effect can be accounted for by introducing an 'effective absorption coefficient':[17]

$$\alpha_{\text{eff}} = \alpha_\infty + \beta L' \tag{8.38}$$

α_∞ is the absorption coefficient of the unbounded test material and L' denotes the total length of the edges divided by the area of the actual sample. The factor β depends on the frequency and the type of material. It may be as high as 0.2 m or more and can be determined experimentally using test pieces of different sizes and shapes. In rare cases, β may even turn out slightly negative. A comprehensive treatment of the edge effect can be found in Ref. 1 of Chapter 6.

In principle, this kind of edge effect in absorption measurements can be avoided by covering one wall of the reverberation chamber completely with the material to be tested, since then there will be no free edges. However, the adjacent rigid or nearly rigid walls cause another, although less serious, edge effect, sometimes referred to as 'Waterhouse effect'.[18] According to eqn (2.38) (see also Fig. 2.10), the square of the sound pressure amplitude in front of a rigid wall exceeds its value far from the wall, and the same holds for the energy absorbed per unit time and area by the test specimen which perpendicularly adjoins that wall. This effect can be corrected for by replacing the geometrical area S of the test specimen with

$$S_{\text{eff}} = S(1 + \tfrac{1}{8}L'\lambda) \tag{8.39}$$

λ is the wavelength corresponding to the middle frequency of the selected frequency band, $\lambda = c/f_m$.

Finally, a remark may be appropriate on the frequency range in which a given reverberation chamber can be used. If the linear chamber dimensions are equal to a few wavelengths only, then statistical reverberation theories can no longer be applied to the decay process and hence to the process of sound absorption. Likewise, a diffuse sound field cannot be established when the number and density of eigenfrequencies (see Section 3.2) are small. It has been found experimentally that absorption measurements employing reverberation chambers are only meaningful for frequencies higher than

$$f_g \approx \frac{1000}{(V)^{1/3}} \tag{8.40}$$

where the room volume V has to be expressed in m³ and the frequency in Hz.

8.8 Diffusion

As pointed out by the end of Section 5.1, the term 'diffusion' denotes two conceptually different things in acoustics: firstly a property of sound fields, namely the isotropy or directional uniformity of sound propagation, and secondly, a property of surfaces, namely their ability to scatter incident sound into non-specular directions as described in Section 2.6. Although sound field diffusion may be a consequence of diffusely reflecting boundaries, both items must be well distinguished.

The directional distribution of sound intensity in a sound field is characterised by a function $I(\varphi, \vartheta)$. This quantity can be measured by scanning all directions with a directional microphone of sufficiently high resolution. Let $\Gamma(\varphi, \vartheta)$ be the directivity function, i.e. the relative sensitivity of the microphone as a function of angles φ and ϑ, from which a plane wave reaches it, then the squared output voltage of the microphone in a complicated sound field is proportional to

$$I'(\varphi, \vartheta) = \int\int I(\varphi', \vartheta') |\Gamma(\varphi - \varphi', \vartheta - \vartheta')|^2 \sin \vartheta' \, d\vartheta' \, d\varphi' \qquad (8.41)$$

Only if the microphone has a high directionality, i.e. if $\Gamma(\varphi, \vartheta)$ has substantial values only within a very limited solid angle, is there a virtual agreement between the measured and the actual directional distribution; in all other cases irregularities of the distribution are more or less smoothed out.

The measurement is usually performed using a stationary sound source which emits filtered random noise or warble tones (frequency modulated sinusoidal tones). It is much more time consuming to determine experimentally the directional distribution in a decaying sound field by recording the same decay process at many different orientations of the directional microphone and to compare subsequently the intensities obtained at corresponding times relative to the arrival of the direct sound or to the moment at which the sound source was interrupted.

Quantitatively, the degree of approximation to perfectly diffuse conditions can be characterised by 'directional diffusion' defined according to Thiele[19] in the following way. Let $\langle I' \rangle$ be the measured quantity averaged over all directions and

$$m = \frac{1}{4\pi \langle I' \rangle} \int\int |I' - \langle I' \rangle| \, d\Omega \qquad (8.42)$$

the average of the absolute deviation from it. Furthermore, let m_0 be the quantity formed analogously to m by replacing I' in eqn (8.42) by $|\Gamma|^2$. Then the directional diffusion is

$$d = \left(1 - \frac{m}{m_0}\right) \times 100\% \qquad (8.43)$$

The introduction of m_0 effects a certain normalisation and consequently $d = 100\%$ in a perfectly diffuse sound field, whereas in the sound field

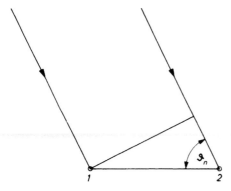

Figure 8.19 Derivation of eqns (8.45a–c).

consisting of one single plane wave the directional diffusion becomes zero. This procedure, however, does not eliminate the fact that the result still depends on the directional characteristics of the microphone. Therefore such results can only be compared if they have been gained by means of similar microphones. Numerous results on the directional distribution measured in this way can be found in papers published by Meyer and Thiele[20] and by Junius.[21]

If one is not interested in all the details of the directional distribution but only in a measure for its uniformity, more indirect methods can be applied, i.e. one can measure a quantity whose value depends on diffusion. One of these quantities is the correlation of the steady state sound pressure at two different points, which yields characteristic values in a diffuse sound field. Or more precisely: we consider the correlation coefficient Ψ of two sound pressures p_1 and p_2, defined by eqn (7.17)

$$\Psi = \frac{\overline{p_1 p_2}}{(\overline{p_1^2} \cdot \overline{p_2^2})^{1/2}} \tag{8.44}$$

To calculate the correlation coefficient in the case of a diffuse sound field we assume that the room is excited by random noise with a very small bandwidth. The sound field can be considered to be composed of plane waves with equal amplitudes and randomly distributed phase angles ψ_n. The sound pressures due to one such wave at points 1 and 2 at distance x (*see* Fig. 8.19), is

$$p_1(t) = A \cos (\omega t - \psi_n), \quad p_2(t) = A \cos (\omega t - \psi_n - kx \cos \vartheta_n)$$

Hence

$$\overline{p_1^2} = \overline{p_2^2} = \tfrac{1}{2} A^2$$

Furthermore, we obtain for the time average of the product of both pressures

$$\overline{p_1 p_2} = A^2 \cos(kx \cos \vartheta_n) \overline{\cos^2(\omega t - \psi_n)}$$
$$+ A^2 \sin(kx \cos \vartheta_n) \overline{\cos(\omega t - \psi_n) \sin(\omega t - \psi_n)}$$
$$= \tfrac{1}{2} A^2 \cos(kx \cos \vartheta_n)$$

Inserting these expressions into eqn (8.44) leads to a direction-dependent correlation coefficient, which has to be averaged subsequently with constant weight (corresponding to complete diffusion) over all possible directions of incidence. This yields

$$\Psi(x) = \frac{\sin kx}{kx} \tag{8.45a}$$

If, however, the directions of incident sound waves are not uniformly distributed over the entire solid angle but only in a plane containing both points, we obtain, instead of eqn (8.45a),

$$\Psi(x) = J_0(kx) \tag{8.45b}$$

(J_0 = Bessel function of order zero).

If the connection between both points is perpendicular to the plane of two-dimensional diffusion, the result is

$$\Psi(x) = 1 \tag{8.45c}$$

The functions given by eqns (8.45a) to (8.45c) are plotted in Fig. 8.20. The most important is curve a; each deviation of the measured correlation coefficient Ψ from this curve hints at a lack of diffusion. To avoid any ambiguity Ψ should be measured for three substantially different orientations of the axis connecting points 1 and 2 in Fig. 8.19.

The derivation presented above is strictly valid only for signals with vanishing frequency bandwidths. Practically, however, its result can be applied with sufficient accuracy to signals with bandwidths of up to a third octave. For wider frequency bands an additional frequency averaging of eqn (8.45a) is necessary.

The correlation coefficient Ψ is the cross-correlation function $\phi_{p_1 p_2}(\tau)$ at $\tau = 0$ (*see* eqn (1.40)), divided by the root-mean-square values of p_1 and p_2. In practical situations the maximum of $\phi_{p_1 p_2}$ may occur at a slightly different value of τ, due to delays in the signal paths. Therefore it is advisable to observe the cross-correlation function in the vicinity of $\tau = 0$ in order to catch its maximum. This can be achieved by one of the methods discussed in Section 8.3.

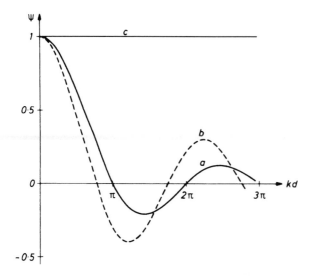

Figure 8.20 Theoretical dependence of correlation coefficient Ψ on the distance between both measuring points: (a) in a three-dimensional diffuse sound field; (b) in a two-dimensional diffuse sound field, measuring axis in plane of directions of sound incidence; (c) same as (b) but measuring axis perpendicular to sound propagation.

An even simpler method is to measure the squared sound pressure amplitude in front of a sufficiently rigid wall as a function of the distance as discussed in Section 2.5. In fact, eqn (8.45a) agrees – apart from a factor 2 in the argument – with the second term of eqn (2.38) which describes the pressure fluctuations in front of a rigid wall at random sound incidence. This similarity is not merely accidental, since these fluctuations are caused by interference of the incident and the reflected waves which become less distinct with increasing distance from the wall according to the decreasing coherence of those waves. On the other hand, it is just the correlation factor of eqn (8.44) which characterises the degree of coherence of two signals. The additional factor of 2 in the argument of eqn (2.38) is due to the fact that the distance of both observation points here is equivalent to the distance of the point from its image, the rigid wall being considered as a mirror.

Now we turn to the second subject of this section, the diffuse reflectivity of surfaces. The direct way to measure it is to irradiate a test specimen of the considered surface with a sound wave under a certain angle of incidence and to record the sound reflected (or scattered) into the various directions by swivelling a microphone at fixed distance around the specimen. In many cases, of course, this measurement must be carried out with scale models of the surfaces under investigation. Its result is a scattering diagram or a collection of scattering diagrams in which the scattered sound components can

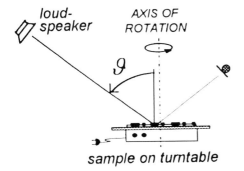

sample on turntable

Figure 8.21 Experimental set-up for measuring scattering from rough surfaces.

be separated from the specular one. It seems that Meyer and Bohn[22] were the first to employ this time consuming procedure to investigate the scattering of surfaces with regular corrugations. The scattering characteristics from another object, namely an irregularly structured ceiling, are shown in Fig. 2.14.

Very often one is interested not so much in scattering diagrams but in a figure which characterises the diffuse reflectivity of a wall. For this purpose, in Section 5.1 the total reflected energy was split up into the fractions s and $1 - s$ denoting relative energies of the specularly and the diffusely reflected components, respectively. Our present goal is to describe procedures for measuring the quantity

$$s = \frac{I_{\text{spec}}}{I_0(1 - \alpha)} \tag{8.46}$$

where I_0 and I_{spec} denote the intensities of the incident and the specularly reflected wave, respectively. α is the absorption coefficient of the test specimen.

Vorländer and his co-workers[23,24] have developed an efficient method to determine s. A sound source and a microphone are adjusted in such a way that the latter picks up the specular reflection from the test specimen which is placed on a turntable (Fig. 8.21). Then the complex reflection factor of the sample is measured at many different positions of the turntable, each result being different from the preceding one since different amounts of energy are scattered into non-specular directions. These individual differences can be suppressed by averaging all these results. This average, $\langle R(f) \rangle$, is the specular reflection factor and hence

$$\langle R(f) \rangle^2 = s(1 - \alpha) \tag{8.47}$$

In a second method which is due to Mommertz and Vorländer[25] the test specimen on its turntable is placed in an otherwise empty reverberation chamber. Now n impulse responses $g_1(t)$, $g_2(t)$, ... $g_n(t)$ are measured at slightly different positions of the sample. Each of them consists of an invariable part g_0 and a part g' which differs from one measurement to the other, $g_i(t) = g_0(t) + g'_i(t)$. Hence the sum of all these impulse responses is

$$h(t) = \sum_{i=1}^{n} g_i(t) = ng_0(t) + \sum_{i=1}^{n} g'_i(t)$$

The last term on the right-hand side is a random variable being itself composed of n independent random variables. Hence its variance is n times the variance of g', while its mean value is zero. As a consequence, the expectation value $\langle h \rangle$ of h is ng_0, and its variance reads

$$\langle h^2 \rangle - \langle h \rangle^2 = n \langle g'^2 \rangle$$

from which follows

$$\langle h^2 \rangle = n^2 [g_0(t)]^2 + n \langle [g'(t)]^2 \rangle \tag{8.48}$$

This function describes the decay of the energy contained in the sum of all impulse responses. It consists of two parts with different decay constants and which depend in a different manner on the number of measurements n:

$$\langle h^2 \rangle \propto n \exp(-2\delta_1 t) + \exp(-2\delta_2 t) \tag{8.49}$$

The decay of the variable part of the impulse responses, i.e. of the second term in eqn (8.48), is determined by the sound absorption present in the reverberation chamber, hence

$$\delta_2 = \frac{c}{4V} A_2 = \frac{c}{4V} [(S - S_s)\alpha_0 + S_s \alpha_s] \tag{8.50a}$$

where V denotes the volume of the chamber and S is the area of its boundary with the absorption coefficient α_0; S_s and α_s are the area and the absorption coefficient of the sample, respectively. The first term of eqn (8.48) decays faster because the scattering sample removes additional energy in an irreversible way:

$$\delta_1 = \frac{c}{4V} A_1 = \delta_2 + \frac{cS_s}{4V}(1 - s)(1 - \alpha_s) \tag{8.50b}$$

In Fig. 8.22 several logarithmic decay curves are plotted. The parameter is n, the number of individual decays from which the averaged decay has been

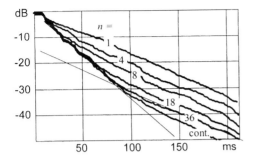

Figure 8.22 Averaged decay curves. Here *n* is the number of individual decays from which the average has been formed (measurement performed in a model reverberation chamber, *see* Vorländer and Mommertz[26]).

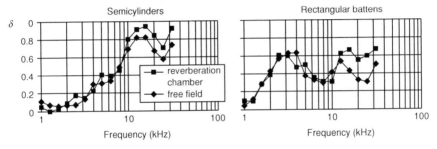

Figure 8.23 Scattering coefficients $d = 1 - s$ of irregular arrangements of battens on a plane panel as a function of frequency. —♦—, free field method; —■—, reverberation method. Left side: rectangular cross-section (side length 2 cm). Right side: semicircular cross-section (diameter 2 cm) (after Mommertz and Vorländer[25]).

formed. With increasing *n*, the initial slope corresponding to the average decay constant

$$\bar{\delta} = \frac{n\delta_1 + \delta_2}{n + 1} \approx \delta_1 \quad \text{for n} \gg 1$$

becomes more prominent. If the number *n* of decays is high enough both decay constants δ_1 and δ_2 can be unambiguously evaluated, particularly if the backward integration technique (*see* Section 8.5) is applied. From their difference the 'specular reflection ratio' *s* is easily calculated.

As an example, Fig. 8.23 represents experimental data of the 'scattering coefficient' $1 - s$ obtained with the direct method (averaged over all directions of incidence) and with the reverberation method. The objects were battens with quadratic or semicylindrical cross-section (side length or diameter 2 cm) irregularly mounted on a plane panel. The agreement of both results is obvious.

References

1 Sabine, W.C., *Collected Papers on Acoustics*, Dover, 1964 (first published 1922).
2 Klug, H. and Radek, U., in *Fortschr. d. Akustik – DAGA '87*, DPG-GmbH, Bad Honnef, 1987.
3 Fasbender, J. and Günzel, D., *Acustica*, **45** (1980) 151.
4 Golomb, S.W., *Shift Register Sequences*, Holden Day, San Francisco, 1967.
5 Alrutz, H. and Schroeder, M.R., Proceedings of the 11th International Congress on Acoustics, Paris, 1983, Vol. 6, p. 235.
6 Borish, J., *J. Audio Eng. Soc.*, **33** (1985) 888.
7 Bilsen, F.A., *Acustica*, **19** (1967) 27.
8 Kuttruff, H., Proceedings of the Sixth International Congress on Acoustics, Tokyo, 1968, Paper GP-4-1.
9 Schroeder, M.R., *Acustica*, **49** (1981) 179.
10 Houtgast, T. and Steeneken, H.J.M., *Acustica*, **54** (1984) 186.
11 Schroeder, M.R., *J. Acoust. Soc. America*, **37** (1965) 409.
12 Mommertz, E., *Appl. Acoustics*, **46** (1995) 251.
13 Kosten, C.W., *Acustica*, **10** (1960) 400.
14 Myncke, H., Cops, A. & de Vries, D. Proceedings of the 3rd Symposium of FASE on Building Acoustics, Dubrovnik, 1979, p. 259.
15 Kuttruff, H., *J. Acoust. Soc. America*, **69** (1981) 1716.
16 Kuhl, W. and Kuttruff, H., *Acustica*, **54** (1983) 41.
17 de Brujin, A., Calculation of the edge effect of sound absorbing structures. Dissertation, Delft, The Netherlands, 1967.
18 Waterhouse, R.V., *J. Acoust. Soc. America*, **27** (1955) 247.
19 Thiele, R., *Acustica*, **3** (1953) 291.
20 Meyer, E. and Thiele, R., *Acustica*, **6** (1956) 425.
21 Junius, W., *Acustica*, **9** (1959) 289.
22 Meyer, E. and Bohn, L., *Acustica*, **2** (1952) (Akustische Beihefte) 195.
23 Vorländer, M., in *Fortschr. d. Akustik – DAGA '88*, DPG-GmbH, Bad Honnef, 1988.
24 Vorländer, M. and Schaufelberger, T., in *Fortschr. d. Akustik – DAGA '90*, DPG-GmbH, Bad Honnef, 1990.
25 Mommertz, E. and Vorländer, M., Proceedings of the 15th International Congress on Acoustics, Trondheim, 1995, p. 577.
26 Vorländer, M. and Mommertz, E., *Appl. Acoustics*, **60** (2000) 187.

9 Design considerations and design procedures

The purpose of this chapter is to describe and to discuss some more practical aspects of room acoustics, namely the acoustical design of auditoria in which some kind of performance (lectures, music, theatre, etc.) is to be presented to an audience, or of spaces in which the reduction of noise levels is of most interest. Its contents are not just an extension of fundamental laws and scientific insights towards the practical world, nor are they a collection of guidelines and rules deduced from them. In fact, the reader should be aware that the art of room acoustical design is only partially based on theoretical considerations, and that it cannot be learned from this or any other book but that successful work in this field requires considerable practical experience. On the other hand, mere experience without at least some insight into the physics of sound fields and without certain knowledge of psychoacoustic facts is of little worth, or is even dangerous in that it may lead to unacceptable generalisations.

Usually the practical work of an acoustic consultant starts with drawings being presented to him which show the details of a hall or some other room which is at the planning stage or under construction, or even one which is already in existence and in full use. First of all, he must ascertain the purpose for which the hall is to be used, i.e. which type of performances or presentations are to take place in it. This is more difficult than appears at first sight, as the economic necessities sometimes clash with the original ideas of the owner or the architects. Secondly, he must gain some idea of the objective structure of the sound field to be expected, for instance the values of the parameters characterising the acoustical behaviour of the room. Thirdly, he must decide whether or not the result of his investigations favours the intended use of the room; and finally, if necessary, he must work out proposals for changes or measures which are aimed at improving the acoustics, keeping in mind that these may be very costly or may substantially modify the architect's original ideas and therefore have to be given very careful consideration.

In order to solve these tasks there is so far no generally accepted procedure which would lead with absolute certainty to a good result. Perhaps it is too much to expect there ever to be the possibility of such a 'recipe', since one project is usually different from the next due to the efforts of architects and owners to create something quite new and original in each theatre or concert hall.

Nevertheless, a few standard methods of acoustical design have been evolved which have proven useful and which can be applied in virtually every case. The importance which the acoustic consultant will attribute to one or the other, the practical consequences which he will draw from his examination, whether he favours reverberation calculations more than geometrical considerations or vice versa – all this is left entirely to him, to his skill and to his experience. It is a fact, however, that an excellent result requires close and trustful cooperation with the architect – and a certain amount of luck too.

As we have seen in preceding chapters, there are a few objective, sound field properties which are beyond question regarding their importance for what we call good or poor acoustics of a hall, namely the strength of the direct sound, the temporal and directional distribution of the early sound energy, and the duration of reverberation processes. These properties depend on constructional data, in particular on the

(a) shape of the room;
(b) volume of the room;
(c) number of seats and their arrangement;
(d) materials of walls, ceiling, floor, seats, etc.

While the reverberation time is determined by factors (b) to (d) and not significantly by the room shape, the latter influences strongly the number, directions, delays and strengths of the early reflections received at a given position or seat. The strength of the direct sound depends on the distances to be covered, and also on the arrangement of the audience.

In the following discussion we shall start with the last point, namely with factors which determine the strength of the direct sound in a hall.

9.1 Direct sound

The direct sound signal arriving from the sound source to a listener along a straight line is not influenced at all by the walls or the ceiling of a room. Nevertheless, its strength depends on the geometrical data of the hall, namely on the (average) length of paths which it has to travel, and on the height at which it propagates over the audience until it reaches a particular listener.

Of course the direct sound intensity under otherwise constant conditions is higher, the closer the listener is seated to the sound source. Different plans of halls can be compared in this respect by a dimensionless figure of merit, which is the average distance of all listeners from the sound source divided by the square root of the area occupied by audience. For illustration, in Fig. 9.1 a few types of floor plans are shown; the numbers indicate this

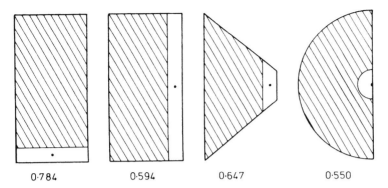

Figure 9.1 Normalised average distance from listeners to source for various room shapes.

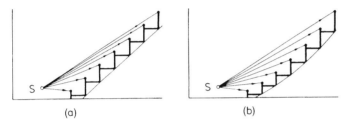

Figure 9.2 Reduction of direct sound attenuation by sloping the seating area: (a) constant slope; (b) increasing slope.

normalised average distance. The audience areas are shaded and the sound source is denoted by a point.

It is seen that a long rectangular room with the sound source on its short side seats the listeners relatively far from the source, whereas a room with a semicircular floor plan provides particularly short direct sound paths. For the same reason, many large lecture theatres and session halls of parliaments are of this type. This is probably the reason why most ancient amphitheatres have been given this shape by their builders. (The same figure holds for any circular sector i.e. also for the full circle.) However, for a closed room this shape has specific acoustical risks in that it concentrates the sound reflected from the rear wall toward certain regions. Generally considerations of this sort should not be given too much weight since they are only concerned with one aspect of acoustics which may conflict with other ones.

Attenuation of the direct sound due to grazing propagation over the heads of the audience (*see* Section 6.7) can be reduced or avoided by sloping the audience area upwardly instead of arranging the seats on a horizontal floor. This holds also for the attenuation of side or front wall reflections. A constant slope (*see* Fig. 9.2a) is less favourable than an increasing ascent of the audience area. The optimum slope (which is optimal as well with respect to the listeners' visual contact with the stage) is reached if all sound rays originating from the sound source S strike the audience area at the same incidence angle ϑ (*see* Fig. 9.2b). The mathematical expression for this condition, which can be strictly fulfilled only for one particular source position, is

$$r(\varphi) = r_0 \exp (\varphi \tan \vartheta) \tag{9.1}$$

In this formula $r(\varphi)$ is the length of the sound ray leaving the source under an elevation angle φ and r_0 is a constant. The curve it describes is a logarithmic spiral. The requirement of constant angle of incidence is roughly equivalent to that of constant 'sight-line distance', by which term we mean the vertical distance of a ray from the end of the ray beneath it. A reasonable value for this distance is about 10 cm, of course higher values are even more favourable. However, a gradually increasing slope of the seating area has certain practical disadvantages. They can be circumvented by approximating the sloping function of eqn (9.1) by a few straight sections, i.e. by subdividing the audience area in a few blocks with uniform seating rake within each of them.

Front seats on galleries or balconies are generally well supplied with direct sound since they do not suffer at all from sound attenuation due to listeners sitting immediately in front. This is one of the reasons why seats on galleries or in elevated boxes are often known for excellent listening conditions.

9.2 Examination of the room shape with regard to reflections

As already mentioned, the delay times, the strengths and the directions of incidence of the reflections – and in particular of early reflections – are determined by the position and the orientation of reflecting areas, i.e. by the shape of a room. Since these properties of reflected sound portions are to a high degree responsible for good or poor acoustics, it is indispensable to investigate the shape of a room carefully in order to get a survey on the reflections produced by the enclosure.

A simple way to obtain this survey is to trace the paths of sound rays which emerge from an assumed sound source, using drawings of the room under consideration. In most cases the assumption of specular reflections is more or less justified.

The sound rays after reflection from a wall portion can be found very easily if the enclosure is made up of plane boundaries; then the concept of image sound sources as described in Chapter 4 can be applied with advantage. This procedure, however, is feasible for first-order or at

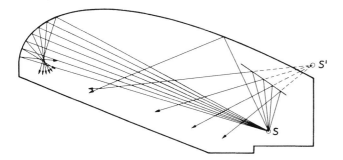

Figure 9.3 Construction of sound ray paths in the longitudinal section of a hypothetical hall.

best for second-order reflections only, which on the other hand is often sufficient.

For curved walls the method of image sources cannot be applied. Here we have to determine the tangential plane (or the normal) of each element-ary area of interest and to consider the reflection from this plane. A schem-atic example of sound ray construction is presented in Fig. 9.3.

From the constructed sound paths one can usually establish very quickly whether the reflected sound rays are being concentrated on some point or in a limited region, and where a focal point or a caustic is to be expected. If a sufficiently large portion of a wall or the ceiling has a circular shape in the sectional drawing or can be approximated by a circle, the location of the focus associated with it may be found from eqn (4.18). Furthermore, the directions of incidence onto various seats can be seen immediately, whereas the delay time between a reflection with respect to the direct sound is determined from the difference in path lengths after dividing the latter by the sound velocity.

The decision whether a particular reflection will be perceivable at all, whether it will contribute to speech intelligibility, to 'clarity' or to 'spacious-ness', or whether it will be heard as a disturbing echo requires knowledge of its relative intensity (*see* Chapter 7). Unfortunately the determination of the intensities of reflected signals is affected by greater uncertainties than that of their time delays. If the reflection occurs on a plane boundary with dimensions large compared to acoustical wavelengths, the $1/r$ law of spher-ical wave propagation can be applied. Eqns (2.44) or (2.45) represent criteria to decide whether this condition is met or not by a particular wall portion, for instance by a balcony face or a suspended reflector. Let r_0 and r_i be the path length of the direct sound ray and that of a particular reflec-tion, measured from the sound source to the listener, then

$$\Delta L = 20 \log_{10}(r_0/r_i) \ \text{dB} \qquad (9.2)$$

is the pressure level of that reflection relative to the direct sound pressure. If the reflecting boundary has an absorption coefficient α, the level of first-order reflections is lower by another $10 \log (1/\alpha)$ decibels. Irregularities on walls and ceiling can be neglected as long as their dimensions are small compared to the wavelength; this requirement may impose restrictions on the frequency range for which the results obtained with the formula above are valid. The strengths or intensities of reflections from a curved wall section can be estimated by comparing the density of the reflected rays in the observation point with the ray density which would be obtained if that wall section were plane. For spherical or cylindrical wall portions the ratio of the reflected and the incident energy can be calculated from eqn (4.19) which is equivalent to

$$\Delta L = 10 \log_{10} \left| \frac{1 + x/a}{1 - x/b} \right| \tag{9.3}$$

The techniques of ray tracing with pencil and ruler takes into account only such sound paths which are situated in the plane of the drawing to hand. Sound paths in different planes can be found by applying the methods of constructive geometry. This, of course, involves considerably more time and labour, and it is questionable whether this effort is justified in every case considering the rather qualitative character of the information gained by it. For rooms of more complicated geometry it may be more practical to investigate the reflections experimentally using a room model at a reduced scale (*see* Section 9.5) or by applying computerised ray tracing techniques (*see* Section 9.6).

So far we have described methods to investigate the effects of a given enclosure upon sound reflections. Beyond the particular case, there are some general conclusions which can be drawn from geometrical considerations, and experiences collected from existing halls or from basic investigations. They shall be summarised briefly below.

If a room is to be used for speech, the direct sound should be supported by as many strong reflections as possible with delay times not exceeding about 50 ms. Reflecting areas (wall portions, screens) placed very close to the sound source are especially favourable, since they can collect a great deal of the emitted sound energy and reflect it in the direction of the audience. For this reason it is wrong to have heavy curtains of fabric behind the speaker. On the contrary, the speaker should be surrounded by hard and properly orientated surfaces, which can even be in the form of portable screens, for instance. Similarly, reflecting surfaces above the speaker have a favourable effect. If the ceiling over the speaker is too high to produce strong and early reflections, the installation of suspended and suitably tilted reflectors should be taken into consideration (*see* Fig. 9.3). An old and familiar example of a special sound reflector is the canopy above the pulpits in churches. The acoustical advantage of these canopies can be observed very clearly when it is removed during modern restoration.

Unfortunately these principles can only be applied to a limited extent to theatres, where such measures could in fact be particularly useful. This is because the stage is the realm of the stage designer, of the stage manager and of the actors; in short, of people who sometimes complain bitterly about the acoustics but who are not ready to sacrifice one iota of their artistic intentions in favour of acoustical requirements. It is all the more important to shape the wall and ceiling portions which are close to the stage in such a way as to direct the incident sound immediately onto the audience.

In conference rooms, school classrooms, lecture halls, etc., at least the front and central parts of the ceiling should be made reflecting since, in most cases, the ceiling is low enough to produce reflections which support the direct sound. Absorbent materials required for the reduction of the reverberation time can thus only be mounted on more remote ceiling portions (and on the rear wall).

In the design of concert halls, it is advisable to make only moderate use of areas projecting the sound energy immediately towards the audience. This would result in a high fraction of early energy and – in severe cases – to subjective masking of the sound decay in the hall. The effect would be dry acoustics even if the objective reverberation time has correct values. As with lecture halls, etc., the sound sources on the stage should be surrounded by reflecting areas which collect the sound without directing it towards special locations and directions.

As we have seen in Section 7.7, it is the fraction of lateral reflections in the early energy which is responsible for the 'spatial impression' or 'spaciousness' in a concert hall. For this reason particular attention must be given to the design of the side walls, especially to their distance and to the angle which they include with the longitudinal axis of the plan.

This may be illustrated by Fig. 9.4, which shows the spatial distribution of early lateral energy computed for three differently shaped two-dimensional enclosures,[1] the area of which was assumed to be 600 m^2. The position of the sound source is marked by a cross; the densities of shading of the various areas correspond to the following intervals of the 'early lateral energy fraction' *LEF* (*see* eqn 7.18): 0–0.06, 0.06–0.12, 0.12–0.25, 0.25–0.5 and >0.5. In all examples the *LEF* is very low at locations next to the sound source, but it is highest in the vicinity of the side walls. Accordingly the largest areas with high *LEF* and hence with satisfactory 'spaciousness' are to be expected in long and narrow rectangular halls. On the other hand, particular large areas with low 'early lateral energy fraction' appear in fan-shaped halls, a fact which can easily be verified by a simple construction of the first-order image sources. These findings explain – at least partially – why so many concert halls with excellent acoustics (for instance Boston Symphony Hall or Großer Musikvereinssaal in Vienna; *see* Table 7.3) have

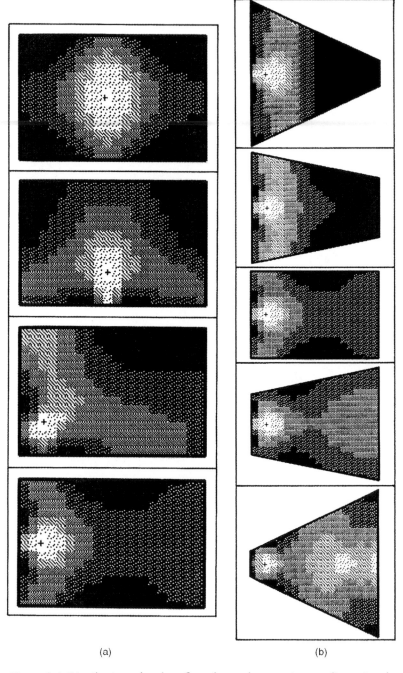

(a)   (b)

Figure 9.4 Distribution of early reflected sound energy in two-dimensional enclosures of 600 m²: (a) rectangular, different source positions; (b) fan shaped.

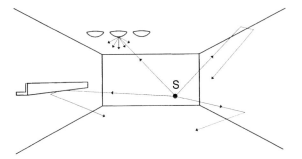

Figure 9.5 Origin of lateral or partially lateral reflections (S = sound source).

rectangular floor plans with relatively narrow side walls. It may be noted, by the way, that the requirement of strong lateral sound reflections favours quite different room shapes than the requirement of strong direct sound (*see* Section 9.1).

In real, i.e. in three-dimensional halls, additional lateral energy is provided by the double reflection from the edges formed by a side wall and horizontal surfaces such as the ceiling or the underfaces of galleries or balconies (Fig. 9.5). These contributions are especially useful since they are less attenuated by the audience below than reflections from the side walls alone. If no balconies are planned the beneficial effect of underfaces can be achieved as well by properly arranged surfaces or bodies protruding from the side walls.

With regard to the performance of orchestral music one should remember that various instruments have quite different directivity of sound radiation which depends also on the frequency. Accordingly sounds from certain instruments or groups of instruments are predominantly reflected by particular wall or ceiling portions. Since every concert hall is expected to house orchestras of varying composition and arrangement, only some general conclusions can be drawn from this fact, however. Thus the high frequency components, especially from string instruments, which are responsible for the brilliance of the sound, are reflected mainly from the ceiling overhead and in front of the stage, whereas the side walls are very important for the reflection of components in the range of about 1000 Hz and hence for the volume and sonority of the orchestral sounds.[2]

Some further comments may be appropriate on the acoustical design of the stage of concert halls, which has been a neglected subject for many years but recently has attracted the attention of several researchers. From the acoustical point of view, the stage enclosure of a concert hall has the purpose of collecting sounds produced by the musical instruments, to blend them and finally to project them towards the auditorium, but also to reflect part of the sound energy back to the performers. This is necessary to establish the mutual auditory contact they need to maintain ensemble, i.e. proper intonation and synchronism.

At first glance platforms arranged in a recess of the hall seem to serve these purposes better in that their walls can be designed in such a way as to direct the sound in the desired way. As a matter of fact, however, several famous concert halls have more exposed stages which form just one end of the hall. From this it may be concluded that the height and inclination of the ceiling over the platform deserves particular attention.

Marshall *et al.*[3] have found by systematic experimental work that the surfaces of a stage enclosure should be far enough away from the performers to delay the reflected sound by more than 15 ms but not more than 35 ms. This agrees roughly with the observation that the optimum height of the ceiling (or of overhead reflectors) is somewhere between 5 and 10 m. With regard to the side walls, this guideline can be followed only for small performing groups, since a large orchestra will usually occupy the whole platform. In any case, however, the side walls should be surfaces which reflect well.

Another important aspect of stage design is raking of the platform,[4] which is often achieved with adjustable or movable risers. It has, of course, the effect of improving the sightlines between listeners and performers. From the acoustical standpoint it increases the strength of the direct sound and reduces the obstruction of sound propagation by intervening players. It seems, however, that this kind of exposure can be carried too far; probably the optimum rake has to be determined by some experimentation.

The inspection of room geometry can lead to the result that some wall areas, particularly if they are curved, will give rise to very delayed reflections with relatively high energy, which will neither support the direct sound nor be masked by other reflections, but instead these reflections will be heard as echoes. The simplest way of avoiding such effects is to cover these wall portions with highly absorbent material. If this precaution would cause an intolerable drop in reverberation time or is impossible for other reasons, a reorientation of those surfaces could be suggested or they could be split up into irregularly shaped surfaces so that the sound is scattered in all directions. Of course the size of these irregularities must at least be comparable with the wavelength in order to be effective. If desired, any treatment of these walls can be concealed behind acoustically transparent screens, consisting of grids, nets or perforated panels, whose transmission properties were discussed in Section 6.3.

9.3 Reverberation time

Among all significant room acoustical parameters and indices the reverberation time is the only one which is related to constructional data of the room and to the absorptivity of its walls by relatively reliable and tractable formulae. Their application permits us to lay down practical procedures, provided we have certain ideas on the desired values of the reverberation times at various frequencies, which in turn requires knowledge of the purposes for which the room is intended.

For an exact prediction of the reverberation time quite a few room data are needed: the volume of the room, the materials and the surface treatment of the walls and of the ceiling, the number, the arrangement and the type of seats. Many of these details are often only finally settled at a later stage. This is an advantage as it enables the acoustician to exercise his influence to a considerable extent in the direction he desires. On the other hand, he must at first be content with a rough assumption about the properties of the walls. Therefore it is sound reasoning not to carry out a detailed reverberation calculation at this first stage but instead to predict or estimate the reverberation approximately.

An upper limit of the attainable reverberation time can be obtained from Sabine's formula (5.24) with $m = 0$, by attributing an absorption coefficient of 1 to the areas covered by an audience and an absorption coefficient of 0.05–0.1 to the remaining areas, which need not be known too exactly for this purpose.

For halls with a full audience and without any additional sound absorbing materials, i.e. in particular for concert halls, a few rules-of-thumb for estimating the reverberation time are in use. The simplest one is

$$T \approx \frac{V}{4N} \tag{9.4}$$

with N denoting the number of occupied seats. Another one is based on the 'effective seating area' S_a,

$$T \approx 0.15 \frac{V}{S_a} \tag{9.5}$$

Here S_a includes a strip of 0.5 m around each block of seats; aisles are added into to S_a if they are narrower than 1 m (*see* Section 6.7). In order to give an idea of how reliable these formula are, the mid-frequency reverberation times (500–1000 Hz) of numerous concert halls are plotted in Fig. 9.6 as a function of the 'specific volume' V/N (Fig 9.6a) and of volume per square metre audience V/S_a (Fig 9.6b). Both are based on data from Ref. 6 of Chapter 6; each point corresponds to one hall. In both cases, the points show considerable scatter, and the straight lines representing eqns (9.4) and (9.5) can be considered as upper limits for the reverberation time at best.

Probably more reliable is an estimate which involves two sorts of areas, namely the audience area S_a as before, and the remaining area S_r:

$$T \approx 0.163 \frac{V}{S_a \alpha_a + S_r \alpha_r} \tag{9.6}$$

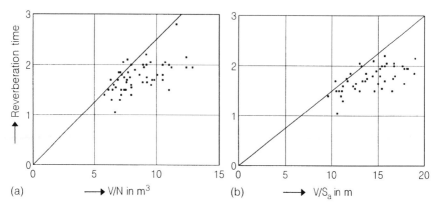

Figure 9.6 Reverberation times of occupied concert halls: (a) as a function of the volume per seat; (b) as a function of the volume per effective audience area (data from Ref. 6 of Chapter 6). The straight lines represent eqns (9.4) and (9.5).

The absorption coefficients attributed to those areas, namely the absorption coefficient of various types of seats, both occupied and empty, and the 'residual absorption coefficient' α_r may be found in Tables 6.4 and 6.5 which have been collected by Beranek and Hidaka (*see* Ref. 7 of Chapter 6).

In any case, a more detailed reverberation calculation should definitely be carried out at a more advanced phase of planning, during which it is still possible to make changes in the interior finish of the hall without incurring extra expense. The most critical aspect is the absorption by the audience. The factors which influence this phenomenon have already been discussed in Section 6.7. The uncertainties caused by audience absorption are so great that it is almost meaningless to try to decide whether Sabine's formula (5.24) would be sufficient or whether the more accurate Eyring equation (5.23) should be applied. Therefore the simpler Sabine formula is preferable with the term $4mV$ taking into account the sound attenuation in air. If the auditorium under design is a concert hall which is to be equipped with pseudorandom diffusors their absorption should be accounted for as well. The same holds for an organ (*see* Section 6.8).

It is frequently observed that the actual reverberation time of a hall is found to be lower than predicted. This fact is usually attributed to the impossibility of taking into account all possible causes of absorption. The variation will, however, scarcely exceed 0.1 s, provided that there are no substantial errors in the applied absorption data and in the evaluation of the reverberation time.

As regards the absorption coefficients of the various materials and wall linings, use can be made of compilations which have been published by several authors (*see*, for instance, Ref. 5). It should be emphasised that the actual absorption, especially of highly absorptive materials, may vary considerably from one sample to the other and depends strongly on the par-

Table 9.1 Typical absorption coefficients of various types of wall materials

Material	Centre frequency of octave band (Hz)					
	125	250	500	1000	2000	4000
Hard surfaces (brick walls, plaster, hard floors, etc.)	0.02	0.02	0.03	0.03	0.04	0.05
Slightly vibrating walls (suspended ceilings, etc.)	0.10	0.07	0.05	0.04	0.04	0.05
Strongly vibrating surfaces (wooden panelling over air space, etc.)	0.40	0.20	0.12	0.07	0.05	0.05
Carpet, 5 mm thick, on hard floor	0.02	0.03	0.05	0.10	0.30	0.50
Plush curtain, flow resistance 450 Ns/m^3, deeply folded	0.15	0.45	0.90	0.92	0.95	0.95
Polyurethane foam, 27 kg/m^3, 15 mm thick on solid wall	0.08	0.22	0.55	0.70	0.85	0.75
Acoustic plaster, 10 mm thick, sprayed on solid wall	0.08	0.15	0.30	0.50	0.60	0.70

ticular way in which they are mounted. Likewise, the coefficients presented in Table 9.1 are to be considered as average values only. In many cases it will be necessary to test actual materials and the influence of their mounting by *ad hoc* measurements of their absorption coefficient which can be carried out in the impedance tube (*see* Section 8.6) or, more reliably, in a reverberation chamber (*see* Section 8.7). This applies particularly to chairs whose acoustical properties can vary considerably depending on the material and the quantity and quality of the fabric used for the upholstery. If possible the chair should be constructed in such a way that, when it is unoccupied, its absorption is not substantially lower than when it is occupied. This has the favourable effect that the reverberation time of the hall does not depend too strongly on the degree of occupation. With tip-up chairs this can be achieved by perforating the underside of the plywood or hardboard seats and backing them with rock wool. Likewise, an absorbent treatment of the rear of the backrests could be advantageous. In any event the effectiveness of such treatment should be checked by absorption measurements.

According to Table 9.1, light partitions such as suspended ceilings or wall linings have their maximum absorption at low frequencies. Therefore, such constructions can make up for the low absorptivity of an audience and thus to achieve a more uniform frequency dependence of the reverberation time.

For large and prestigious objects, it is recommended that reverberation measurements in the hall itself be performed during several stages of the hall's construction. This allows the reverberation calculations to be checked and to be corrected if necessary. Even during later stages in the construction there is often an opportunity of taking corrective measures if suggested by the results of these measurements.

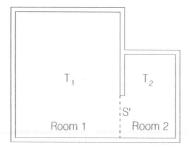

Figure 9.7 Coupled rooms.

In practice it is not uncommon to find that a room actually consists of several partial rooms which are coupled to each other. Examples of coupled rooms are theatres with boxes which communicate with the main room through relatively small apertures only, or the stage (including the stage house which may by quite voluminous) of a theatre or opera house which is coupled to the auditorium by the proscenium, or churches with several naves or chapels. Cremer[6] was the first to point out the necessity of considering coupling effects when calculating the reverberation time of such a room. This necessity arises if eqn (5.54) is fulfilled, i.e. if the area of the coupling aperture is substantially smaller than the total wall area of a partial room.

Let us denote the partial room in which the listener finds himself by number 1 and the other partial room by 2 (*see* Fig. 9.7). Now we must distinguish between two different cases, depending on whether Room 1 on its own has a longer or a shorter reverberation time than Room 2. In the first case the reverberation of Room 2 will not be noticed in Room 1 as the coupling area acts merely as an 'open window' with respect to Room 1 and can be taken as having an absorption coefficient 1. Therefore, whenever an auditorium has deep balcony overhangs, it is advisable to carry out an alternative calculation of decay time in this way, i.e. by treating the 'mouths' of the overhangs as completely absorbing wall portions. Likewise, instead of including the whole stage with all its uncertainties into the calculation, its opening can be treated as an absorbing area with an absorption coefficient rising from about 0.4 at 125 Hz to about 0.8 at 4 kHz.

Matters are more complicated if Room 2 has the longer decay time. The listener can hear this longer reverberation through the coupling aperture, but will not perceive it as a part of the decay of the room which he is occupying. How strongly this 'separate reverberation' will be perceived depends on how the room is excited and on the location of the listener. If the sound source excites Room 1 predominantly, then the longer decay from Room 2 will only be heard, if at all, with impulsive sound signals (loud cries, isolated chords of a piece of music, etc.) or if the listener is close to the coupling aperture. If, on the contrary, the location of the sound source

Table 9.2 Coupled rooms

Relation between decay times	Character of reverberation	
$T_1 > T_2$	Reverberation of Room 2 is not perceived	
$T_1 < T_2$	Source in Room 1	Reverberation of Room 2 is not perceived except for locations next to the coupling aperture
	Both partial rooms excited by the source	Reverberation of Room 2 is clearly audible

is such that it excites both rooms almost equally well, as may be the case with actors performing on the stage of a theatre, then the longer reverberation from Room 2 is heard continually or it may even be the only reverberation to appear. In any event it is useful to calculate the reverberation times of both partial rooms separately. Strictly speaking, for this purpose the eigenvalues δ_i' of Section 5.7 should be known. For practical purposes, however, it is sufficient to increase the total absorption $\Sigma S_i \alpha_i$ for each partial room by the coupling area and to insert the result into Sabine's reverberation formula. Table 9.2 presents an overview of the most extreme situations to be distinguished.

Coupling phenomena can also occur in enclosures lacking sound field diffusion, in particular. This is sometimes observed in rooms having simple geometrical shapes and extremely non-uniform distribution of absorption on the walls. A rectangular room, for instance, whose ceiling is not too low and which has smooth and reflecting side walls will, when the room is fully occupied, often build up a two-dimensional reverberating sound field in the upper part with a substantially longer decay time than corresponds to the average absorption coefficient. The sound field consists of horizontal or nearly horizontal sound paths and is influenced only slightly by the audience absorption. Similarly, an absorbent or scattering ceiling treatment will not change this condition noticeably. This effect may also occur with other ground plans. Whether the listeners will perceive this separate reverberation at all again depends on the strength of its excitation.

For lecture halls, theatre foyers, etc., this relatively long reverberation is of course undesirable. In a concert hall, however, it can lead to a badly needed increase in reverberation time beyond the Sabine or Eyring value, namely in those cases where the volume per seat is too small to yield a sufficiently long decay time in diffuse conditions. An example of this is the Stadthalle in Göttingen, which has an exactly hexagonal ground plan and in fact has a reverberation time of about 2 s, although calculations had predicted a value of 1.6–1.7 s only (both for medium frequencies and for the fully occupied hall). Model experiments carried out afterwards had demonstrated very clearly that it was a sound field of the described type which was responsible for this unexpected, but highly desirable, increase in reverberation time. This particular lack of diffusion in itself does not cause specific acoustical deficiencies in that case.

But even if the enclosure of a hall can be assumed to mix and thus to redistribute the impinging sound by diffuse reflections, the diffusion of the sound field and hence the validity of the simple reverberation formulae may be impaired merely by non-uniform distribution of the absorption. Since this is typical for occupied auditoria, it may be advisable to check the reliability of reverberation prediction by tentatively applying the more exact eqn (5.48).

Sometimes the acoustical consultant is faced with the task of designing a room which is capable of presenting different kinds of performances, such as speech on one occasion and music on another. This is typical for multi-purpose halls; the same thing is frequently demanded of broadcasting or television studios. As far as the reverberation time is concerned, some variability can be achieved by installing movable or revolving walls or ceiling elements which produce some acoustical variability by exhibiting reflecting surfaces in one position (long reverberation time) and absorbent ones in the other (short reverberation time). The resulting difference in reverberation time depends on the fraction of area treated in this way and on the difference in absorption coefficients of those elements. Installations of this type are usually quite costly and sometimes give rise to considerable mechanical problems. A relatively simple way of changing the reverberation time in the abovementioned manner was described by Kath.[7] In a broadcasting studio with a volume of 726 m³ the walls were fitted with strips of glass wool tissue which can be rolled up and unrolled electrically. Behind the fabric there is an air space with an average depth of 20 cm, subdivided laterally in 'boxes' of 0.5 m × 0.6 m. The reverberation times of the studio for the two extreme situations (glass wool rolled up and glass wool completely unrolled) are shown in Fig. 9.8 as a function of the frequency. It is clearly seen

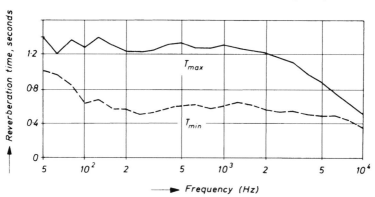

Figure 9.8 Maximum and minimum reverberation times in a broadcasting studio with changeable acoustics.

that the reverberation time at medium frequencies can be changed from 0.6 to 1.25 s and that a considerable degree of variability in reverberation time has also been achieved at other frequencies. Other methods which make use of electroacoustical installations will be described in Chapter 10.

9.4 Prediction of noise level

There are many spaces which are not intended for any acoustical presentations but where some acoustical treatment is nevertheless desirable or necessary. Although they show wide variations in character and structural details, they all fall into the category of rooms in which people are present and in which noise is produced, for instance by noisy machinery or by the people themselves. Examples of this are staircases, concourses of railway stations and airports, entrance halls and foyers of concert halls and theatres, etc. Most important, however, are working spaces such as open-plan offices, workshops and factories. Here room acoustics has the relatively prosaic task of reducing the noise level.

Traditionally acoustics does not play any important role in the design of a factory or an open-plan office, to say the least; usually quite different aspects, as for instance those of efficient organisation, of the economical use of space or of safety, are predominant. Therefore the term 'acoustics' applied to such spaces does not have the meaning it has with respect to a lecture room or a theatre. Nevertheless, it is obvious that the way in which the noise produced by any kind of machinery propagates in such a room and hence the noise level in it depends highly on the acoustical properties even of such a room, and further that any measures which are to be taken to reduce the noise exposure of the personnel must take into account the acoustical conditions of the room.

A first idea of the steady state sound pressure level a sound source with power output P produces in a room with wall area S and average absorption coefficient $\bar{\alpha}$ is obtained from eqn (5.37). Converting it in a logarithmic scale with PL denoting the sound power level (*see* eqn (1.48)) yields

$$SPL^{\infty} = PL - 10 \log_{10}\left(\frac{\bar{\alpha}S}{1m^2}\right) + 6\,\mathrm{dB} \tag{9.7}$$

This relation holds for distances from the sound source which are significantly larger than the 'reverberation distance' as given by eqn (5.38) or eqn (5.40), i.e. it describes the sound pressure level of the reverberant field. For observation points at distances comparable to or smaller than r_h the sound pressure level is, according to the more general eqn (5.41):

$$SPL = SPL^{\infty} + 10 \log_{10}\left(1 + \frac{r_h^2}{r^2}\right) \tag{9.7a}$$

Both equations are valid under the assumption that the sound field in the room is diffuse.

Numerous measurements in real spaces have shown, however, that the reverberant sound pressure level decreases more or less with increasing distance, in contrast to eqn (9.7). Obviously sound fields in such spaces are not completely diffuse, and the lack of diffusion seems to affect the validity of eqn (9.7) much more than that of reverberation formulae. This lack of diffusion may be accounted for in several ways. Often one dimension of a working space is much larger (very long rooms) or smaller (very flat rooms) than the remaining ones. Another possible reason is non-uniform distribution of absorption. In all these cases a different approach is needed to calculate the sound pressure level.

For enclosures made up of plane walls the method of image sources could be employed, which has been discussed at some length in Section 4.1. It must be noted, however, that real working spaces are not empty, and that there are machines, piles of material, furniture, benches, etc., in them; in short, numerous obstacles which scatter the sound and may also partially absorb it.

One way to account for the scattering of sound in fitted working spaces is to replace the sound propagation in the free space by that in an 'opaque' medium as explained at the end of Section 5.1. If we restrict the discussion to the steady state condition, the energy density of the unscattered component, i.e. of the direct sound, is

$$w_0(r, t) = \frac{P}{4\pi c r^2} \exp(-r/\bar{r}) \tag{9.8}$$

with P as before denoting the power output of the source. Now it is assumed that the mean free path is so small that virtually all sound particles will hit at least one scatterer before reaching one wall of the enclosure. Then we need not consider any reflections of the direct sound. On the other hand, the scattered sound particles will uniformly fill the whole enclosure due to the equalizing effect of multiple scattering. Since the scattered sound particles propagate in all directions they constitute a diffuse sound field with its well-known properties. In particular, its energy density is $w_s = 4P/cS\bar{\alpha}$ with the same source power as in eqn (9.8). The steady state level can be calculated from eqn (9.7) or (9.7a). In the latter case, however, the modified 'reverberation distance' $r_h = (A/16\pi)^{1/2}$ has to be replaced with a modified value r'_h which is smaller than r_h. In fact, equating w_s and w_0 from eqn (9.8) yields

$$r'_h = r_h \exp(-r'_h/\bar{r}) \tag{9.9}$$

Solving this transcendental equation yields $r'_h/r_h = 0.7035$ for $r_h/\bar{r} = 1$, while this fraction becomes as small as 0.2653 for $r_h/\bar{r} = 10$, i.e. when a sound particle undergoes 10 collisions on average per distance r_h). However, there remains some uncertainty on the scattering cross-sections Q_s of machinery or other pieces of equipment; obviously there is no practical way to calculate them exactly from geometric data. Several authors (*see* Ref. 8) identify Q_s with one quarter of the scatterer's surface. This procedure agrees with the rule given at the end of Section 5.1.

The transient sound propagation in enclosures containing sound scattering obstacles is much more complicated than the steady state case. It has been treated successfully by several authors, for instance by M. Hodgson.[9]

In a different approach, the scatterers are imagined as being projected onto the walls, so to speak, i.e. it is assumed that the walls produce diffuse sound reflections rather than specular ones. Then the problem can be treated by application of the integral equation (4.24). As already mentioned in Section 4.5, this equation has a closed solution for the stationary sound propagation between two parallel planes, i.e. in an infinite flat room. This is of considerable practical interest since this kind of 'enclosure' may serve as a model for many working spaces in which the ceiling height h is very small compared with the lateral dimensions (factories, or open-plan bureaus). Therefore, sound reflections from the ceiling are absolutely predominant over those from the side walls, and hence the latter can be neglected unless the source and/or the observation point are located next to them.

Equation (4.27) represents this solution for both planes having the same, constant absorption coefficient α or 'reflection coefficient' ρ, and for both the sound source and the observation point being located in the middle between both planes. Fortunately, the awkward evaluation of eqn (4.27) can be circumvented by using the following approximation (see Ref. 6 of Chapter 4):

$$w(r) \approx \frac{P}{4\pi c} \left\{ \frac{1}{r^2} + \frac{4\rho}{h^2} \left[\left(1 + \frac{r^2}{h^2}\right)^{-3/2} + \frac{b\rho}{1-\rho}\left(b^2 + \frac{r^2}{h^2}\right)^{-3/2} \right] \right\} \quad (9.10)$$

The constant b depends on the absorption coefficient of the floor and the ceiling. Some of its values are listed in Table 9.3. Equation (9.10) may also

Table 9.3 Values of the constant b in eqn (9.10)

α	ρ	b
0.7	0.3	1.806
0.6	0.4	1.840
0.5	0.5	1.903
0.4	0.6	2.002
0.3	0.7	2.154
0.2	0.8	2.425
0.1	0.9	3.052

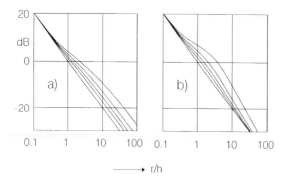

Figure 9.9 Sound pressure level in an infinite flat room as a function of distance *r* divided by the room height *h*. The absorption coefficient α of the walls is (from bottom to top): 1, 0.7, 0.5, 0.3, and 0.1. (a) smooth walls; (b) diffusely reflecting walls.

be used if both boundaries have different absorptivities, in this case α is the average absorption coefficient.

Figure 9.9b shows how the sound pressure level, calculated with this formula depends on the distance from an omnidirectional sound source for various values of the (average) absorption coefficient $\alpha = 1 - \rho$ of the walls. For comparison, the corresponding curves for specularly reflecting planes, computed with eqn (4.2) are presented in Fig. 9.9a. The plotted quantity is ten times the logarithm of the energy density divided by $P/4\pi ch^2$. Both diagrams show characteristic differences: smooth boundaries direct all the reflected energy away from the source, this results in a level increase which remains constant at large distances. In contrast, diffusely reflecting boundaries reflect some energy back towards the source, accordingly the level difference – compared to that of free field propagation ($\alpha = 1$) – reaches a maximum at a certain distance and vanishes in large distances from the source. This behaviour is typical for enclosures containing scattering objects and was experimentally confirmed by numerous measurements carried out by Hodgson[9,10] in factories as well as in models.

Both aforementioned methods are well suited to predicting noise levels in working spaces and estimating the reduction which can be achieved by an absorbing treatment of the ceiling, for instance. Other possible methods are measurements in a scale model of the space under investigation (Section 9.5) or computer simulation as described in the following sections.

Absorbing treatment of walls or the ceiling has a beneficial effect on the noise level, not only in working spaces such as factories or large offices but also in many other rooms where many people gather together, e.g. in theatre foyers. A noise level reduction of only a few decibels can increase the acoustical comfort to an amazing degree. If the sound level is too high due to insufficient boundary absorption, people will talk more loudly than in a quieter environment. This in turn again increases the general noise level and so it continues until finally people must shout and still do not achieve satisfactory intelligibility. In contrast, an acoustically damped environment usually makes people behave in a 'damped' manner too – for reasons which are not primarily acoustical – and it makes them talk no louder than necessary.

There is still another psychologically favourable effect of an acoustically damped theatre or concert hall foyer: when a visitor leaves the foyer and enters the hall, he will suddenly find himself in a more reverberating environment, which gives him the impression of solemnity and raises his expectations.

The extensive application of absorbing materials in a room, however, is accompanied by an oppressive atmosphere, an effect which can be observed quite clearly when entering an anechoic room. Furthermore, since the level of the background noise is reduced too by the absorbing areas, a conversation held in a low voice can be understood at relatively great distances and can be irritating to unintentional listeners. Since this is more or less the opposite of what should be achieved in an open-plan office, masking by background noise is sometimes increased in a controlled way by loudspeakers fed with random white or 'coloured' noise, i.e. with a 'signal' which has no time or spectral structure. The level of this noise should not exceed 50 dB(A). Even so it is still contested whether the advantages of such methods surpass their disadvantages.

9.5 Acoustical scale models

A well tried method which has been used over a long period of time for the acoustical design of large halls is to build a smaller model of the hall under consideration which is similar to the original room, at least geometrically, and to study the propagation of waves in this model. This method has the advantage that, with little expenditure, a great number of variations can be tried out: from the choice of various wall materials to major changes in the shape of the room.

Since several properties of propagation are common to all sorts of waves, it is not absolutely necessary to use sound waves for the model measurements. This was an important point particularly during earlier times when acoustical measuring techniques were not yet at the advanced stage they have reached nowadays. So waves on water surfaces were sometimes applied in 'ripple tanks'. The propagation of these waves can be studied visually with great ease. The use of them, however, is restricted to an examination of plane sections of the hall. More profitable is the use of light as a substitute for sound. In this case absorbent areas are painted black or covered with black paper or fabric, whereas reflecting areas are made of polished sheet metal. Likewise, diffusely reflecting areas can be quite well simulated by white matt paper. The detection of the energy distribution can be carried out by photocells or by photography. However, because of the high speed of light this method is restricted to the investigation of the steady state energy distribution. Furthermore, all diffraction phenomena are neglected since the optical wavelengths are very small compared to the dimensions of all those objects which would diffract the sound waves in a real hall. In spite of these limitations, optical models are still considered a useful tool to get an idea of the steady state distribution of energy in an auditorium.

On the other hand, the techniques of electroacoustical transducers have reached a sufficiently high state of the art nowadays to permit the use of acoustical waves for investigating sound propagation in a scale model. For this purpose a few geometrical and acoustical modelling rules have to be observed. In the following, all quantities referring to the model are denoted by a prime. Then the scale factor σ is introduced by

$$l' = \frac{l}{\sigma} \tag{9.11}$$

where l and l' are corresponding lengths. For the time intervals in which waves with velocities c or c' travel along corresponding distances we obtain

$$t' = \frac{l'}{c'} = \frac{l}{c'\sigma} = \frac{c}{c'}\frac{t}{\sigma} \tag{9.12}$$

The ratios between the wavelengths and frequencies are

$$\lambda' = \frac{\lambda}{\sigma} \tag{9.13}$$

and

$$f' = \sigma\frac{c'}{c}f \tag{9.14}$$

According to the last relation, the sound frequencies applied in a scale model may well reach into the ultrasonic range. Suppose the model is filled with air ($c' = c$) and the model is scaled down by 1:10 ($\sigma = 10$), then the frequency range from 100 to 5000 Hz in the original room would correspond to 1–50 kHz in its model.

Since the model is intended to be not only a geometrical replica of the original hall but an acoustical one as well, the wall absorption should be modelled with care. This means that any surface in the model should have the same absorption coefficient at frequency f' as that of the corresponding surface in the original at frequency f:

$$\alpha_i'(f') = \alpha_i(f) \tag{9.15}$$

a condition which is not easy to fulfil. Even more problematic is the modelling rule for the attenuation of the medium. According to eqn (1.16a), $2/m$ is the travelling distance along which the sound pressure amplitude of a plane wave is attenuated by a factor $e = 2.718. . . .$ From this we conclude that

$$m'(f') = \sigma m(f) \tag{9.16}$$

Of course these requirements can be fulfilled only approximately, and the required degree of approximation depends on the kind of information we wish to obtain from the model experiment. If only the initial part of the impulse response or 'reflectogram' is to be studied (over, say, the first 100 or 200 ms in the original time scale), it is sufficient to provide for only two different kinds of surfaces in the model, namely reflecting ones (made of metal, glass, gypsum, etc.) and absorbing ones (for instance felt or plastic foam). The air absorption can be neglected in this case or its effect can be numerically compensated.

Matters are different if much longer reflectograms are to be observed, for instance to create listening impressions from the auditorium as was first proposed by Spandöck.[11] According to this idea music or speech signals which have been recorded without any reverberation are replayed in the model at frequencies elevated by the factor σ given in eqn (9.14). At a point under investigation within the model, the sound signal is picked up with a miniaturised artificial head which has the same directionality and transfer function at the model frequencies as the human head in the normal audio range. After transforming the re-recorded signals back to the original time and frequency domain it can be presented directly to a listener who can judge subjectively the 'acoustics' of the hall and the effects of any modifications to be studied. Nowadays this technique is known as 'auralisation'. More will be said about this matter in Section 9.7.

Concerning the instrumentation for measuring the impulse response in scale models, the omnidirectional impulse excitation of the model is more difficult the higher the scale factor and hence the frequency range to be covered. Small spark gaps can be successfully used for this purpose, but in any case it is advisable to check their directivity and frequency spectrum beforehand. Furthermore, electrostatic[12] or piezoelectric[13] transducers have been developed for this purpose; they have the advantage that they can be fed with any desired electrical signal and therefore allow the application of the more sophisticated methods described in Section 8.2. Since it is virtually impossible to combine in such transducers high efficiency with very small dimensions, they must have (at least approximate) spherical symmetry. For piezoelectric transducers this can be achieved with foils of certain high polymers which are formed in spherical shape and which can be made piezoelectric by special treatment.

Likewise, the microphone should be non-directional. Fortunately sufficiently small condensor microphones are commercially available ($\frac{1}{4}$- or $\frac{1}{8}$-in microphones). Any further processing, including the evaluation of the various sound field parameters as discussed in Chapters 7 and 8, is nowadays carried out, as in full scale measurements, by means of a digital computer.

9.6 Computer simulation

Although physical models of enclosures have proven to be a very useful tool for the acoustical design of large halls they are being superseded gradually by a cheaper, faster and more efficient method, namely by digital simulation of sound propagation in enclosures. The introduction of the digital computer into room acoustics is probably due to M.R. Schroeder[14] and his co-workers. Since then this method has been employed by many authors to investigate various problems in room acoustics; examples have been presented in Sections 5.6 and 9.2 of this book. The first authors who applied digital simulation to concert hall acoustics were Krokstad *et al.*,[15] who evaluated a variety of parameters from impulse responses obtained by digital ray tracing techniques. Meanwhile digital computer simulation has been applied not only to all kinds of auditoria but to factories and other working spaces as well.[8]

Basically, there are two methods of sound field simulation in use nowadays, namely ray tracing and the method of image sources. Both are based on geometrical acoustics, i.e. they rely on the validity and application of the law of specular or diffuse reflection. So far no practical way has been found to include typical wave phenomena such as diffraction into these algorithms.

The principle of digital ray tracing is illustrated in Fig. 9.10. A sound source at a given position is imagined to release numerous sound particles in all directions at time $t = 0$. Each sound particle travels on a straight path until it hits a wall which we assume to be plane for the sake of simplicity. The point where this occurs is obtained by first calculating the intersections of the particle path with all planes in which the walls are contained, and then selecting the nearest of them in the forward direction. Provided this

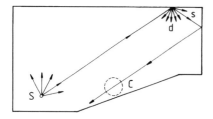

Figure 9.10 Principle of digital ray tracing. S = sound sorce, C = counting sphere, s = specular reflection and d = diffuse reflection.

intersection is located within the real wall, it is the point where the particle will be reflected, either specularly or diffusely. In the first case its new direction is calculated from the law of geometrical reflection; however, if diffuse reflection is assumed to occur, the computer generates two random numbers from which the azimuth angle φ and the polar angle ϑ of the new direction are calculated in such a way that the latter angle is distributed according to eqn (4.22) (ϑ is the angle between the scattered particle path and the local wall normal). After its reflection the particle continues on its way along the new direction towards the next wall, etc. The absorption coefficient of a wall can be accounted for in two ways: either by reducing the energy of the particle by a factor of $1 - \alpha$ after each reflection or by interpreting α as 'absorption probability', i.e. by generating another random number which decides whether the particle will proceed or whether it has been absorbed. In a similar way the effect of air attenuation can be taken into account. As soon as the energy of the particle has fallen below a prescribed value or the particle has been absorbed, the path of another particle will be 'traced'. This procedure is repeated until all the particles emitted by the sound source at $t = 0$ have been followed up.

The results of this procedure are collected by means of 'counters', i.e. of counting areas or counting volumes which must be assigned previously. Whenever a particle crosses such a counter its energy and arrival time are stored, if needed also the direction from which it arrived. After the process has finished, i.e. the last particle has been followed up, the energies of all particles received in a certain counter within prescribed time intervals are added; the result is a histogram (*see* Fig. 9.11), which can be considered as a short-time averaged energetic impulse response. The selection of these

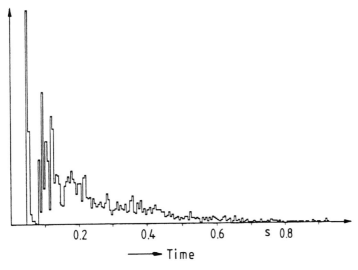

Figure 9.11 Time histogram of received particle energy (the interval width is 5 ms).

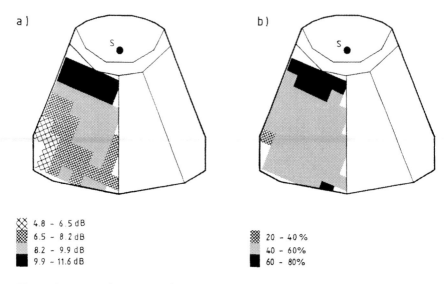

a)

b)

S

S

⊠ 4.8 - 6.5 dB
▦ 6.5 - 8.2 dB
▨ 8.2 - 9.9 dB
■ 9.9 - 11.6 dB

▦ 20 - 40 %
▨ 40 - 60%
■ 60 - 80%

Figure 9.12 Distribution (a) of the stationary sound pressure level and (b) of the 'definition' in a large lecture hall (after Vorländer[16]).

intervals is not uncritical: if they are chosen to be too long, the histogram will be only a crude approximation to the true impulse response since significant details are lost by averaging; too short intervals, on the other hand, will afflict the results by strong random fluctuations superimposed on them. As a practical rule, the interval should be in the range 5–10 ms, since this figure corresponds roughly to the time resolution achieved by our hearing.

The problem of properly selecting the time intervals in which the arrival times are classified does not apply if only parameters listed in Table 8.3, for instance the 'definition' D, the 'centre time' t_s or the lateral energy parameters LEF and LG_{80}^{∞} are to be determined, since the calculation of these quantities involves integrations over the whole impulse response or large parts of it. The same holds for the steady state energy or the 'strength factor' G which are just proportional to the integral over the whole energetic impulse response (*see* eqn (7.15)). As an example, Fig. 9.12 depicts the distribution of the stationary sound pressure level and definition obtained by application of ray tracing techniques to a lecture hall with a volume of 3750 m³ and 775 seats.[16]

In any case, however, the achieved accuracy of the results depends on the number of sound particles counted with a particular counter. For this reason the counting area or volume must be chosen so that it is not too small; furthermore, the total number of particles which the original sound impulse is thought to consist of must be sufficiently large. As a practical guideline, a total of 10^5–10^6 sound particles will yield sufficiently precise results if the dimensions of the counters are of the order of 1 m. With a good personal computer the time required for one run is somewhere between minutes and one hour, depending on the number of counters, the complexity of the room to be investigated and the efficiency of the algorithm employed.

The most tedious and time consuming part of the whole process is the collection and input of room data such as the positions and orientations of the walls and their acoustic properties. If the enclosure contains curved portions these may be approximated by planes unless their shape is very simple, for instance spherical or cylindrical. The degree of approximation is left to the intuition and experience of the operator. It should be noted, however, that this approximation will cause systematic and sometimes intolerably large errors.[17] These are avoided by calculating the path of direction of the reflected particle directly from the curved wall applying eqn (4.1) which is relatively easy if the wall section is spherical or cylindrical.

The process described can be modified and refined in many ways. Thus the sound radiation need not necessarily be omnidirectional, instead the sound source can be given any desired directionality. Likewise, one can study the combined effect of more than one sound source, for instance of a real speaker and several loudspeakers with specified directional characteristics, amplifications and delays. This permits the designer to determine the optimal configuration of an electroacoustic installation in a hall. Furthermore, any mixture of purely specular or ideally diffuse wall reflections can be taken into consideration; the same holds for the directional dependence of absorption coefficients.

The second basic method exploits the notion of image sources as has been described at some length in Section 4.1. In principle, this method is very old but its practical application started only with the advent of the digital computer by which constructing numerous image sources and collecting their contributions to the sound field has become very easy, at least in principle.

However, there is the problem of 'inaudible' or invalid image sources already addressed in Section 4.1. It is illustrated in Fig. 9.13 which shows two plane walls adjacent at an obtuse angle, along with a sound source A, both its first order images A_1 and A_2 and the second order images A_{12} and A_{21}. The latter one is inaudible since the line connecting it with the receiving point R does not intersect the plane (2) within the extension of the actual wall.

Unfortunately, most of all higher-order source images are invalid. As an example, consider an enclosure made up of six plane walls with a total area of 3600 m^2, the volume of the room being 12 000 m^3. According to eqn (4.8) a sound ray or sound particle would undergo 25.5 reflections per second on average. To compute only the first 400 ms of the impulse response, image sources of up to the 10th order (at least!) must be considered. With this figure and $N = 6$, eqn (4.2) tells us that about 1.46×10^7 (!) image sources must be constructed. However, if the considered enclosure were rectangular it is easy to see that there are only

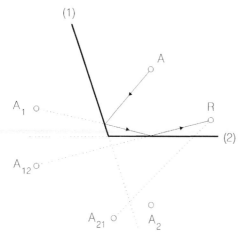

Figure 9.13 Valid and invalid image sources. Image source A_{21} is invalid, i.e. 'invisible' from the given receiver position R.

$$N_r(i_0) = 4i_0^2 + 2 \qquad\qquad (9.17)$$

different image sources of order $\leq i_0$ (neglecting their multiplicity), and all of them are valid. For our example this formula yields $N_r(i_0) = 402$. This consideration shows that the fraction of valid image sources is very small in general. And the set of valid image sources differs from one receiving point to another.

Fortunately, Vian and van Maercke[18] and independently Vorländer[19] have found a way to facilitate the validity checks. This is done by performing an abbreviated ray tracing process which precedes the actual simulation. Each sound path detected in this way is associated with a particular sequence of valid image sources, for instance $A \to A_1 \to A_{12} \to R$ in Fig. 9.13, which is identified by backtracing the path of the sound particle. The next particle which hits the counting volume at the same time can be omitted since it would yield no new image sources. After running the ray tracing for a certain period one can be sure that all significant image sources – up to a certain maximum order – have been found, including their relative strengths which depend on the absorption coefficients of the walls involved in the mirroring process.

Now the energy impulse response can be formed by adding the contributions of all image sources as was done in deriving eqn (4.3). Suppose the original sound source produces a short power impulse at time $t = 0$ represented by a Dirac function $\delta(t)$, then the contribution of a particular image source of order i to the energetic impulse response is

$$\frac{P}{4\pi c r^2_{m_1 m_2 \ldots m_i}} \rho_{m_1} \rho_{m_2} \cdots \rho_{m_i} \delta\left(t - \frac{r_{m_1 m_2 \ldots m_i}}{c}\right)$$

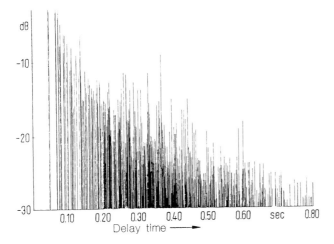

Figure 9.14 Impulse response of a room computed from image sources.

$m_1, m_2, \ldots m_i$ are the numbers of the walls involved in the particular sound path, $\rho_k = 1 - \alpha_k$ are their reflection coefficients, and $r_{m_1 m_2 \ldots m_i}$ denotes the distance of the considered image from the assumed receiving point. Figure 9.14 depicts an impulse response obtained in this way. For frequency-dependent absorptivities this computation must be repeated for a sufficient number of frequency bands.

But the image model permits the determination not only of the energetic impulse response of an enclosure, but that of the sound-pressure related impulse response as well. Suppose the original sound source would produce at free propagation a short pressure impulse $A\delta(t - r_0/c)$ at distance r_0, then the image source considered above contributes the component

$$(g_p)_{m_1 m_2 \ldots m_i} = A \frac{r_0}{r_{m_1 m_2 \ldots m_i}} r_{m_1}(t) * r_{m_2}(t) * \ldots * r_{m_{i_1}}(t) * \delta\left(t - \frac{r_{m_1 m_2 \ldots m_i}}{c}\right)$$

(9.18)

to the pressure impulse response. In this equation the function $r_{m_k}(t)$ is the 'reflection response' of the kth wall as already introduced in Section 4.1, i.e. the Fourier transform of its complex reflection factor $R_{m_k}(f)$. Each asterisk symbolizes one convolution operation. (As described in Chapter 8, it may turn out easier to compute the Fourier transform of eqn (9.18), namely

$$(G_p)_{m_1 m_2 \ldots m_i} = A \frac{r_0}{r_{m_1 m_2 \ldots m_i}} R_{m_1}(f) R_{m_2}(f) \ldots r_{m_{i_1}}(f) \exp\left(-2\pi i f r_{m_1 m_2 \ldots m_i}/c\right)$$

(9.18a)

and to calculate $(g_p)_{m_1 m_2 \ldots m_i}$ as the inverse Fourier transform of $(G_p)_{m_1 m_2 \ldots m_i}$.)

Hence the image model is in a certain way more 'powerful' than ray tracing. On the other hand it cannot be applied to model the effect of curved or diffusely reflecting surfaces.

Several successful attempts[20,21] have been made to develop hybrid procedures in order to combine the advantages of ray tracing and the image model. Typically, the latter is used to build up the early part of the impulse response, whereas the later parts of the response are computed by ray tracing in one of its various versions.

9.7 Auralisation

The term auralisation was coined to signify all techniques which intend to create audible impressions from enclosures not existing in reality but in the form of design data only. Its principle is outlined in Fig. 9.15. Music or speech signal originally recorded in an anechoic environment is fed to a transmission system which modifies the input signal in the same way as its real propagation in the considered room would do. This system is either a physical scale model of the room (*see* Section 9.5), equipped with a suitable sound source and receiver, or it is a digital filter which has the same impulse response as the room under investigation. The impulse response may have been measured beforehand in a real room or in its scale model, or it has been obtained by simulation as described in the preceding section. In any case, the room simulator must produce a binaural output signal, otherwise no realistic, i.e. spatial, impressions can be conveyed to the listener. The output signal is presented to the listener by headphones or, preferably, by two loudspeakers in an anechoic room fed via a cross-talk cancellation system as described in the beginning of Chapter 7.

The first experiments of auralisation with scale models were started by Spandöck's group in Karlsruhe/Germany in the early 1950s; a comprehensive report may be found in Ref. 22. Auralisation based on a purely digital room model was first carried out by Allen and Berkley.[23]

Since auralisation requires a frequency range of at least eight octaves the transducers used in a scale model have to meet very high standards. For the same reason the requirements concerning the acoustical similarity between an original room and its model are very stringent if realistic auditive impressions are expected. The absorption of the various walls materials and of the audience must be modelled quite correctly, including their frequency

Figure 9.15 Principle of auralisation. The input signal is 'dry' speech or music.

dependence, a condition which must be carefully checked by separate measurements. Even more difficult to model is the attenuation by the medium according to eqn (9.16). Several groups[22,24] have tried to meet this requirement by filling the model either with air of very low humidity or with nitrogen. If at all, by such measures the frequency dependence of air attenuation can be modelled only approximately, and only for a limited frequency range and a particular scale factor σ.

These problems do not exist for digital room models since both the acoustical data of the medium and the enclosure's geometrical data are fed into the computer from its keyboard or from a database. Furthermore, the binaural impulse responses can be made to include the listener's individual head transfer functions (*see* Section 1.6) or at least an average which is representative of many individuals. Generally, digital models are much more flexible because the shape and the acoustical properties of the room under investigation can be changed quite easily. Therefore it is expected that nearly all future auralisation experiments will be based on computer models. On the other hand, auralisation is the most fascinating application of room acoustical simulation.

Pressure-related impulse responses computed with the image source model according to eqn (9.18) or eqn (9.18a) can be immediately used for auralisation, provided they are rendered binaural. This is achieved by properly amending eqn (9.18). Let $L(f, \varphi, \vartheta)$ and $R(f, \varphi, \vartheta)$ denote the head transfer functions for the left and the right ear, respectively, and the angles ϑ and ϑ signify the direction of incidence in a head-related coordinate system. Their inverse Fourier transforms are $l(t, \varphi, \vartheta)$ and $r(t, \varphi, \vartheta)$. Then the modified contributions to the binaural impulse response are

$$(g_{pl})_{m_1 m_2 \ldots m_i} = (g_p)_{m_1 m_2 \ldots m_i} * l(t, \varphi, \vartheta) \tag{9.19a}$$

and

$$(g_{pr})_{m_1 m_2 \ldots m_i} = (g_p)_{m_1 m_2 \ldots m_i} * r(t, \varphi, \vartheta) \tag{9.19b}$$

In most cases, however, results obtained from room simulation are in the form of a set of energy impulse responses, namely one for each frequency band (octave band, for instance). This holds especially for ray tracing results. Let us denote these results by $E(f_i, t_k)$; f_i is the mid-frequency of the ith frequency band, while t_k denotes the kth time interval. Considered as a function of frequency, $E(f_i, t_k)$ approximates a short-time power spectrum valid for the time interval around t_k. By properly smoothing, this spectrum will become a steady function of frequency, $E_k(f)$. To convert it into a pressure-related transmission function $G_k(f)$ the square root of $E_k(f)$ is taken and a suitable phase spectrum $\psi_k(f)$ must be 'invented'. Then

$$G_k(f) = \sqrt{[E_k(f)]} \exp[i\psi_k(f)] \tag{9.20}$$

According to R. Heinz[20] the phase spectrum is not critical at all since all phases are anyway randomised by propagation in a room. Therefore any odd random phase function $\psi_k(f) = -\psi_k(-f)$ could be used for this purpose, provided it corrsponds to a system with causal behaviour, i.e. to a system the impulse response of which vanishes for $t < 0$. A particular possibility is to derive $\psi_k(f)$ from $E_k(f)$ as the minimum phase function. This is achieved by applying the Hilbert transform, eqn (8.19), to $E_k(f)$:

$$\Psi_k(f) = \frac{1}{2\pi} \int_{-\infty}^{\infty} \frac{\ln[E_k(f - f')]}{f'} \, df' \tag{9.21}$$

The Fourier transforms of the spectra $G_k(f)$ computed in this way are 'short-time impulse responses' which are subsequently combined into the impulse response of the auralisation filter in Fig. 9.15. In order to permit direct comparisons of several impulse responses (i.e. rooms) it may be practical to realise the auralisation filter in form of a real-time convolver.

If all steps – including the simulation process – are carefully carried out, the listener to whom the ultimate result is being presented will experience an excellent and quite realistic impression. To what extent this impression is identical with that which the listener would have if he were present in the actual room is a question which is still to be investigated. In fact, there are many details which are open to improvement and further development. In any case, however, an old dream of the acoustician is going to come true through the techniques of auralisation. Many new insights into room acoustics are expected from its application. Furthermore, it permits an acoustical consultant to convince the architect, the user of a hall (and himself as well) on the effectivity of the measures he proposes to reach the original design goal.

References

1 Vorländer, M. and Kuttruff, H., *Acustica*, **58** (1985) 118.
2 Meyer, J., *Acustica*, **36** (1976) 147.
3 Marshall, A.H., Gottlob, D. and Alrutz, H., *J. Acoust. Soc. America*, **64** (1978) 1428.
4 Allen, W.A., *J. Sound Vibr.*, **69** (1980) 143.
5 Crocker, M.J. (ed.), *Encyclopedia of Acoustics*, Vol. 3, Chapters 92 and 94, John Wiley, New York, 1997.
6 Cremer, L., *Die wissenschaftlichen Grundlagen der Raumakustik*, Band II., S. Hirzel Verlag, Stuttgart, 1961.
7 Kath, U., Proceedings of the Seventh International Congress on Acoustics, Budapest, 1961, Paper 25 A 8.
8 Ondet, A.M. and Barbry, J.L., *J. Acoust. Soc. America*, **85** (1989) 787.
9 Hodgson, M., Theoretical and physical models as tools for the study of factory sound fields, PhD thesis, University of Southampton, 1983.

10 Hodgson, M., *Appl. Acoustics*, **16** (1983) 369.

11 Spandöck, F., *Ann. d. Physik V.*, **20** (1934) 345.

12 Els, H. and Blauert, J., Proceedings of the Vancouver Symposium: Acoustics and Theatres for the Performing Arts, The Canadian Acoustical Association, Ottawa, Canada, 1986, p. 65.

13 Kuttruff, H., *Appl. Acoustics*, **27** (1989) 27.

14 Schroeder, M.R., Proceedings of the Fourth International Congress on Acoustics, Copenhagen, 1962, Paper M21.

15 Krokstad, A., Strøm, S. and Sørsdal, S., *J. Sound Vibr.*, **8** (1968) 118.

16 Vorländer, M., *Acustica*, **65** (1988) 138.

17 Kuttruff, H., *Acustica*, **77** (1992) 176.

18 Vian, S.P. and van Maercke, D., Proceedings of the Vancouver Symposium: Acoustics and Theatres for the Performing Arts, The Canadian Acoustical Association, Ottawa, Canada, 1986, p. 74.

19 Vorländer, M., *J. Acoust. Soc. America*, **86** (1989) 172.

20 Heinz, R., Entwicklung und Beurteilung von computergestützten Methoden zur binauralen Raumsimulation. Dissertation Aachen, Germany, 1994.

21 Dahlenbäck, B.-I., *J. Acoust. Soc. America*, **100** (1996) 899.

22 Brebeck, P., Bücklein, R., Krauth, E. and Spandöck, F., *Acustica*, **18** (1967) 213.

23 Allen, J.B. and Berkley, D.A., *J. Acoust. Soc. America*, **65** (1979) 943.

24 Xiang, N. and Blauert, J., *Appl. Acoustics*, **33** (1991) 123.

10 Electroacoustic installations in rooms

Nowadays there are many points of contact between room acoustics and electroacoustics even if we neglect the fact that modern measuring techniques in room acoustics could not exist without the aid of electroacoustics (loudspeakers, microphones, recorders). Thus we shall hardly ever find a meeting room of medium or large size which is not provided with a public address system for speech amplification; it matters not whether such a room is a church, a council chamber or a multi-purpose hall. We could dispute whether such an acoustical 'prothesis' is really necessary for all these cases or whether sometimes they are more a misuse of technical aids; it is a fact that many speakers and singers are not only unable but also unwilling to exert themselves to such an extent and to articulate so distinctly that they can make themselves clearly heard even in a hall of moderate size. Instead they prefer to rely on the microphone which is readily offered to them. But the listeners are also demanding, to an increasing extent, a loudness which will make listening as effortless as it is in broadcasting, television or cinemas. Acousticians have to come to terms with this trend and they are well advised to try to make the best of it and to contribute to an optimum design of such installations.

But electroacoustic systems in rooms are by far more than a necessary evil. They open acoustical design possibilities which would be inconceivable with traditional means of room acoustical treatment. For one thing, there is a trend to build halls and performance spaces of increasing size, thus giving large audiences the opportunity to witness personally important cultural, entertainment or sports events. This would not be possible without electroacoustic sound reinforcement since the human voice or a musical instrument alone would be unable to produce an adequate loudness at most listeners' ears. Furthermore, large halls are often used – largely for economic reasons – for very different kinds of presentations.

In this situation it is a great advantage that electroacoustic systems permit the adaptation of the acoustical conditions in a hall to different kinds of presentations, at least to some extent. A sound reinforcement system which is optimally designed for speech transmission in a particular hall can provide for satisfactory speech intelligibility even if the reverberation time of the room is considerably longer than the optimum for speech. This fact can be used to adapt the 'natural' acoustics of the hall for musical performances.

The reverse way is even more versatile, but also more difficult technically: to render the natural reverberation of the hall relatively short in order to match the needs of optimum speech transmission. For the performance of music, the reverberation is enhanced by electroacoustical means to a suitable and adjustable value. The particular circumstances will decide which of the two possibilities is more favourable.

Electroacoustic systems for reverberation enhancement can be used to simulate acoustical conditions which we are used to from halls with purely 'natural' sound. At the same time, they can be considered as a first step towards producing new artificial effects which are not encountered in halls without any electroacoustical system. In the latter respect we are just at the beginning of a development whose progress cannot yet be predicted.

Whatever is the type and purpose of an electroacoustic system, there is a close interaction between the system and the room in which it is operated in that its performance to a high degree depends on the acoustical properties of the enclosure itself. Therefore, the installation and use of such a system does not dispense with careful acoustical planning. Furthermore, without the knowledge of the acoustical factors responsible for speech intelligibility and of the way in which these factors are influenced by sound reflections, reverberation and other acoustical effects, it would hardly be possible to plan, to install and to operate electroacoustical sytems with optimal performance.

10.1 Loudspeaker directivity

In the simplest case, a sound reinforcement system consists of a microphone, an amplifier and one or several loudpeakers. If the sounds of musical ensembles are to be reinforced several microphones may be used, the output signals of which are electrically mixed.

The most critical component in this chain is the loudspeaker because it must handle high power without causing linear and non-linear distortions, and should at the same time radiate with a suitable directivity.

As a model of a loudspeaker we consider first a plane circular piston mounted flush in an infinite rigid baffle as shown in Fig. 10.1. Each of its area elements contributes to the sound pressure at some point. At higher frequencies when the radius a of the piston is not small compared with the wavelength of the radiated sound signal there may be noticeable phase differences between these contributions, leading to partial or total cancellation depending on the sound wave directions at the receiving point (not

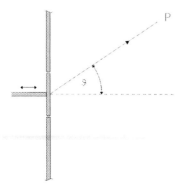

Figure 10.1 Piston radiator, schematic.

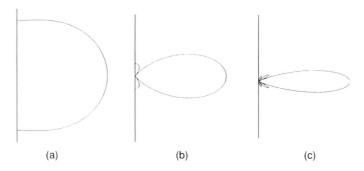

(a)   (b)   (c)

Figure 10.2 Directivity function of the circular piston: (a) $ka = 2$; (b) $ka = 5$; (c) $ka = 10$.

shown in the figure). As a result the sound pressure at a given distance depends in a typical way on the angle of radiation:

$$\Gamma(\vartheta) = \frac{2J_1(ka \sin \vartheta)}{ka \sin \vartheta} \tag{10.1}$$

Here $\Gamma(\vartheta)$ is the directivity function of the piston as already defined in Section 1.2, J_1 is the first-order Bessel function, and ka is the so-called Helmholtz number, in this case it is just the circumference of the piston divided by the acoustical wavelength. Figure 10.2 depicts a few directional patterns of the circular piston, i.e. polar representations of the directivity function $|\Gamma|$ for various numbers $ka = 2\pi a/\lambda$. (The three-dimensional directivity functions are obtained by rotating these diagrams around their horizontal axis.) For $ka = 2$ the radiation is nearly uniform, but with increasing ka the lobe becomes more and more narrow. For $ka > 3.83$, additional lobes appear in the diagrams.

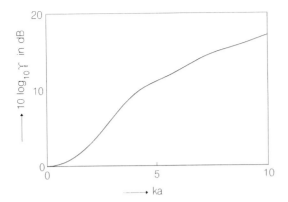

Figure 10.3 Directional factor γ (in dB) of the circular piston as a function of ka.

The 'narrowness' of the main lobe of a radiator's directional diagram can be characterised by its half-width, i.e. the angular distance $2\Delta\vartheta$ of the points for which $|\Gamma|^2 = 0.5$ as shown in Fig. 10.5. For the circular piston with $ka \gg 1$ this figure is approximately

$$2\Delta\vartheta \approx \frac{\lambda}{a} 30° \tag{10.2}$$

Another important 'figure of merit' is the gain or directivity factor γ defined as the ratio of the maximum and the average intensity, both at the same distance from the source (see eqn (5.39)). For the circular piston it is given by

$$\gamma = \frac{(ka)^2}{2} \left(1 - \frac{2J_1(2ka)}{2ka} \right)^{-1} \tag{10.3}$$

This function is plotted in Fig. 10.3 as a function of ka.

Real loudspeakers do not have a plane and rigid piston, and in most cases they are not mounted in a plane baffle but in a box. Hence their directivity differs from that described by eqns (10.1) to (10.3). Nevertheless, these relations yield at least a guideline for the directivity of real loudspeakers.

Another type of loudspeaker which is commonly used in public address systems is the horn loudspeaker. It consists of a tube with steadily increasing cross-sectional area, called a horn, and of an electrodynamically driven membrane at the narrow end (the throat) of the horn (*see* Fig. 10.4). Its main advantage is its high efficiency because the horn improves the acoustical match between the membrane and the free field. Furthermore, by combining several horns a wide variety of directional characteristics can

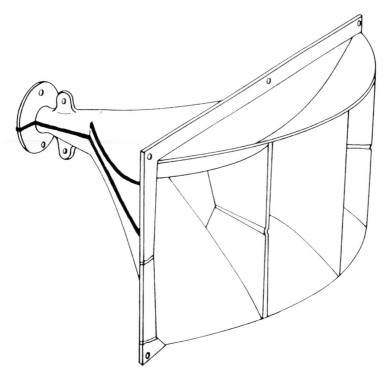

Figure 10.4 Horn loudspeaker (multi-cellular horn).

be obtained. For these reasons, horn loudspeakers are often employed for large-scale sound reproduction. Common horn shapes are based on an exponential growth of the cross-sectional area. Such horns have a marked cut-off frequency which depends on their flare and below which they cannot efficiently radiate sound.

The directional characteristics of a horn loudspeaker depends on the shape and the opening area of the horn and, of course, on the frequency. As long as the acoustical wavelength is larger than all lateral dimensions of the opening, i.e. at relatively low frequencies, its directivity pattern is similar to that of a plane piston with the same shape (*see* eqn (10.1)). At higher frequencies, the directional characteristics of horn loudspeakers are broader than those of the corresponding piston. Since they do not depend only on the size and shape of the opening but also on the shape of the whole horn, they cannot be expressed in simple terms, instead the reader is referred, for instance, to Olson's book.[1]

As mentioned, the directivity pattern can be shaped in a desired way by combining several or many horn loudspeakers. The most straightforward solution of this kind is the multi-cellular horn consisting of many single

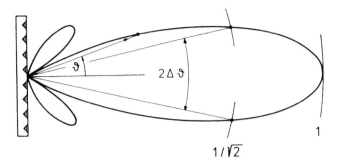

Figure 10.5 Directivity function $|\Gamma(\theta)|$ of a linear loudspeaker array with $N = 8$ elements for $kd = \pi/2$.

horns the openings of which approximate a portion of a sphere and yield nearly uniform radiation into the solid angle subtended by this portion.

If an electroacoustic sound source consists of several closely arranged loudspeakers with each of them generating the same acoustical signal their contributions may interfere with each other. As a consequence, the entire sound source has a directivity which may greatly differ from that of the single loudspeaker.

As a simple example we consider first a linear array of N point sources which are arranged along a straight line with equal spacing d. The sources are assumed to emit equal acoustical signals. The directivity function of this array reads

$$\Gamma_a(\vartheta) = \frac{\sin\left(\frac{1}{2}Nkd\sin\vartheta\right)}{N\sin\left(\frac{1}{2}kd\sin\vartheta\right)} \tag{10.4}$$

where ϑ is the angle which the considered direction includes with the normal of the array. This is illustrated in Fig. 10.5 which plots $|\Gamma(\vartheta)|$ as a polar diagram for $kd = \pi/2$ and $N = 8$. The three-dimensional directivity can be imagined by rotating this diagram around the (vertical) axis of the array. As in the case of the circular piston, the directivity function contains a main lobe which becomes narrower with increasing frequency. Furthermore, for $f > c/Nd$ it shows smaller satellite lobes, the number of which grows with increasing number of elements and with the frequency. For $N > 3$, the largest of these side lobes is at least 10 dB lower than the maximum of the main lobe. The angular half-width of the main lobe is

$$2\Delta\vartheta \approx \frac{\lambda}{Nd}50° \tag{10.5}$$

This relation, however, holds only if the resulting $2\Delta\vartheta$ is less than 30°.

If the point sources in this array are replaced with similar loudspeakers fed with identical electrical signals, the total directivity function is simply obtained by multiplying the directivity function of the array Γ_a with that of its elements Γ.

Linear loudspeaker arrays are widely used in sound reinforcement systems. In order to achieve uniform sound supply to an audience they must be mounted with their axes in a vertical direction, of course.

10.2 Design of electroacoustic systems for speech transmission

This section deals with some factors influencing the performance of systems for speech reinforcement, namely with the acoustical power to be supplied by the loudspeakers, with their directionality and with the reverberation time of the room where the system is operated.

If speech intelligibility were a function merely of the loudness, i.e. of the average energy density w_r at a listener's position, we could use eqn (5.37) for estimating the necessary acoustical power of the loudspeaker:

$$P = \frac{c}{4}Aw_r = 13.8\frac{V}{T}w_r \tag{10.6}$$

with

$$A = \sum_i S_i \alpha_i$$

denoting the total absorbing area in the room.

We know, however, from the discussions in Chapter 7, that the intelligibility of speech depends not only on its loudness but even more on the structure of the impulse response characterising the sound transmission from a sound source to a listener. In particular, the classification of the total energy conveyed by the impulse response into useful and detrimental energy is of great importance.

To derive practical conclusions from this latter fact, we idealise the impulse responses of individual transmission paths by an exponential decay of sound energy with a decay constant $\delta = 6.91/T$:

$$E(t) = E_0 \exp(-2\delta t)$$

Now suppose there is a sound source supplying an average power P to the room under consideration. We regard as detrimental those contributions to the resulting energy which are conveyed by the 'tail' of the energetic impulse response and which are due to reflections being delayed by more than 100 ms with respect to the direct sound. The corresponding modification of eqn (5.34) (second version) reads

$$w'_r = \frac{P}{V} \int_{0.1\,s}^{\infty} \exp\left(-2\delta t\right) dt$$

and leads to the detrimental part of the reverberant energy density

$$w'_r = \frac{P}{2V\delta} \exp\left(-0.2\delta\right) \tag{10.7}$$

On the other hand, the direct sound energy supplied by the loudspeaker is regarded as useful energy, taking into account, however, the directivity of the loudspeaker and eventually including the contributions made by reflecting surfaces close to the loudspeaker. We assume that the loudspeaker or the loudspeaker array has a gain γ and points with its main lobe towards the most remote parts of the audience which are at a distance r_{max} from it. Then the density of the useful energy in that most critical region is, according to eqn (5.39):

$$w_d = \frac{\gamma P}{4\pi c r_{max}^2} \tag{10.8}$$

On the assumption that the level L_d of the speech signal, undistorted by decaying sound energy, is about 70–80 dB, satisfactory intelligibility is achieved if

$$w_d \approx w'_r$$

or, after insertion of eqns (10.7) and (10.8):

$$\frac{\gamma}{2\pi r_{max}^2} \approx \frac{c}{V\delta} \exp\left(-0.2\delta\right)$$

By introducing the reverberation time $T = 3 \ln 10/\delta$ and solving for r_{max}, we obtain an expression for the range which can be supplied with amplified speech at good intelligibility

$$r_{max} \approx 0.057 \left(\frac{\gamma V}{T}\right)^{1/2} 2^{1/T} \tag{10.9}$$

(r_{max} in metres, V in cubic metres).

This critical distance is plotted in Fig. 10.6 as a function of the reverberation time; the product γV of the loudspeaker gain and the room volume is the parameter of the curves.

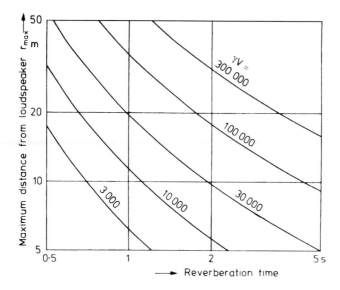

Figure 10.6 Allowed maximum distance of listeners from loudspeaker as a function of the reverberation time for various values of $\gamma V(V$ in m^3).

It should be noted that eqn (10.9) indicates the order of magnitude of the allowed r_{max} than an exact limit. Furthermore, its predictions are somewhat too pessimistic in that its derivation neglects the fact that the main lobe is usually directed towards the audience area, which is highly absorbing at mid and high frequencies. This reduces the power available for the excitation of the reverberant field roughly by a factor

$$\frac{1}{\gamma'} = \frac{1 - \alpha_a}{1 - \alpha_r}$$

with α_a and α_r denoting the absorption coefficient of the audience and the residual absorption coefficient, respectively (*see* Section 6.7). Consequently, the gain γ in eqn (10.9) and Fig. 10.6 can be replaced with $\gamma\gamma' \geq \gamma$. In any case, however, the reach of the loudspeaker is limited by the reverberant sound field and cannot be extended just by increasing the loudspeaker power.

As an example let us consider a hall with a volume of 15 000 m^3 and a reverberation time of 2 s. If the product $\gamma\gamma'$ can be made as high as 16, the maximum distance to a listener will be $r_{\text{max}} \cong 28$ m.

So it seems that the condition of eqn (10.9) is not too difficult to fulfil. This is indeed the case for medium and high frequencies. At low frequencies, however, γ as well as γ' are close to unity. As a consequence, most of the low frequency energy supplied by the loudspeaker will feed the reverberant part of the energy density where it is not of any use. This is the reason why so many halls equipped with a sound reinforcement system suffer from a low frequency background which is unrelated to the transmitted signal. The only remedy against this evil is to suppress the low frequency components of the signal by a suitable electrical filter since in any case they do not contribute to speech intelligibility.

The acoustical power to be emitted by the loudspeaker is determined by the requirement that the directly transmitted sound portion leads to a sufficiently high sound pressure p_d or pressure level L_d even at the most remote seats:

$$P = \frac{4\pi r_{max}^2}{\gamma} \frac{p_d^2}{\rho_0 c} \approx \frac{12}{\gamma} r_{max}^2 10^{0.1 L_d - 12} \qquad (10.10)$$

This is the same formula as that to be applied to outdoor sound amplification since it does not include any room properties. This equation suggests that the power which the loudspeaker supplies should be made particularly high at low frequencies where the gain γ is relatively small. However, for the reason discussed above just the opposite is true.

In a large hall there is usually a certain noise level, which is due to a restless audience, to the air-conditioning system or to insufficient insulation against exterior noise sources. If this level is 40 dB or less it can be left out of consideration as far as the required loudspeaker power is concerned. This is not so at higher noise levels, of course. To be prepared for all eventualities it is advisable to increase the acoustical power given by eqn (10.10) by a substantial safety factor. In any case, it should be clear that good speech intelligibility is not achieved just with sheer power.

10.3 A few remarks on the selection of loudspeaker positions

The amplified microphone signal can be supplied to the room either by one central loudspeaker, or by several or many loudspeakers distributed throughout the room. (The term 'central loudspeaker' includes of course the possibility of combining several loudspeakers closely together in order to achieve a suitable directivity, for instance in a linear array.) This section will deal with several factors which should be considered when a suitable loudspeaker location is to be selected in a room.

In each case the loudspeakers should ensure that all the listeners receive a uniform supply of sound energy; furthermore, for speech installations, a satisfactory speech intelligibility is required. We have already seen in the preceding section that this is not only a matter of applied acoustical power but also a question of a suitable loudspeaker arrangement and directionality.

In addition a sound reinforcement system should, in most cases, yield a natural sound impression. In the ideal case (possibly with the exception of the presentation of electronic music) the listener would be unable to notice

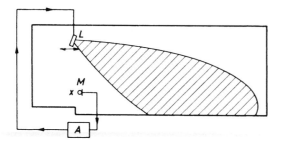

Figure 10.7 Central loudspeaker system (schematic representation).
L = loudspeaker, M = microphone, A = amplifier, x = source.

the electroacoustical aids at all. To achieve this, it would at least be necessary, apart from using high quality microphones, loudspeakers and amplifiers, for the sound radiated by the loudspeakers to reach, or appear to reach, the listener from the same direction from which he sees the actual speaker or natural sound source.

In most cases, the sound signal emitted by the loudspeaker is picked up by a microphone close to the natural sound source. If the loudspeakers as well as the microphone are in the same hall, the microphone will inevitably pick up sound arriving from the loudspeaker as well. This phenomenon, known as 'acoustical feedback', can result in instability of the whole equipment and can lead to howling or whistling sounds. However, even with stable operation, the quality of the amplified sound signals may be reduced substantially by acoustical feedback. A suitably selected loudspeaker location can minimise this effect. We shall discuss acoustical feedback in a more detailed manner in the next section.

With a central loudspeaker installation, the irradiation of the room is achieved by a single loudspeaker or loudspeaker combination with the desired directionality, and if necessary there is additional support from subsidiary loudspeakers in the more remote parts of the room (boxes, balconies, spaces behind corners, etc.). A simple central installation is depicted schematically in Fig. 10.7. The location of the loudspeaker, its directionality and its orientation have to be chosen in such a way that the audience is supplied with direct sound as uniformly as possible. This can be checked experimentally, not by stationary measurements, but by impulse measurements or using correlation techniques. In most cases, the loudspeaker will be mounted above the natural sound source; its actual position must be so chosen that feedback becomes as little as possible. This way of mounting has the advantage that the direct sound, coming from the loudspeaker, will always arrive from roughly the same direction (with regard to a horizontal plane) as the sound arriving directly from the sound source. The vertical deviation of directions is not very critical, since our ability to discriminate sound directions is not as sensitive in a vertical plane as in a horizontal one. The subjective impression is even more natural if care is taken that the loudspeaker sound reaches the listener simultaneously with the natural sound or a bit later. In the latter case the listener benefits from the law of the first wave front which raises the illusion that all the sound he hears is produced by the natural sound source, i.e. that no electroacoustic system is in operation. This illusion can be maintained even if the level of the loudspeaker signal at the listener's position surpasses that produced by the natural source by 5–10 dB, provided the latter precedes the loudspeaker signal by about 10–15 ms (Haas effect, *see* Section 7.3).

The simultaneous or delayed arrival of the loudspeaker's signals at the listener's seat can be achieved by increasing the distance between the loudspeaker and the audience. The application of this simple measure is limited, however, by the increasing risk of acoustical feedback, since the microphone will lie more and more in the range of the main lobe of the loudspeaker's directional characteristics. Thus, a compromise must be found. Another way is to employ electrical methods for effecting the desired time delay. They are described below.

Very good results in sound amplification, even in large halls, have been obtained by using a speaker's desk which has loudspeakers built into the front facing panel; these loudspeakers were arranged in properly inclined, vertical columns with suitable directionality. With this arrangement, the sound from the loudspeakers will take almost the same direction as the sound from the speaker himself. It reduces problems due to feedback provided that the propagation of structure-born sound is prevented by resiliently mounting the loudspeakers and the microphone.

In very large or long halls, or in halls consisting of several sections, the supply of sound energy by one single loudspeaker only will usually not be possible, for one thing because condition (10.9) cannot be met without unreasonable expenditure. The use of several loudspeakers at different positions has the consequence that each loudspeaker must only reach a smaller maximum distance r_{max} which makes it easier to satisfy eqn (10.9). Simple examples are shown in Fig. 10.8. If all loudspeakers are fed with identical electrical signals, however, confusion areas will be created in which listeners are irritated by hearing sound from more than one source. In these areas it is not only the natural localisation of the sound source which is impaired but the intelligibility will also be significantly diminished. This undesirable effect is avoided by electrically delaying the signals applied to the auxiliary loudspeakers. The delay time should at least compensate the distances between the auxiliary loudspeaker(s) and the main loudspeaker. Furthermore, the power of the subsidiary loudspeakers must not be too high since this again would make the listener aware of it and hence destroy his illusion that all the sound he receives is arriving from the stage.

The delay times needed in sound reinforcement systems are typically in the range 10–100 ms, sometimes even more. In the past, tape recorders

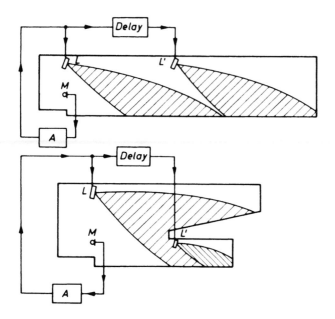

Figure 10.8 Public address systems with more than one loudspeaker unit.
L, L' = loudspeakers, M = microphone, A = amplifier.

with endless magnetic tapes or wheels with a magnetic track on their periphery have been used for this purpose. They were equipped with one recording head and several playback heads at distances proportional to the desired delay times. Nowadays these electromechanical devices have been superseded by digital delay units.

In halls where a high noise level is to be expected, but where nevertheless announcements or other information must be clearly understood by those present, the ideal of a natural-sounding sound transmission, which preserves or simulates the original direction of sound propagation, must be sacrificed. Accordingly, the amplified signals are reproduced by many loudspeakers which are distributed fairly uniformly and are fed by identical electrical signals. In this case it is important to ensure that all the loudspeakers which can be mounted on the ceiling or suspended from it are supplied with equally phased signals. The listeners are then, so to speak, in the near field of a vibrating piston. Sound signals of opposite phases would be noticed in the region of superposition in a very peculiar and unpleasant manner.

If the sound irradiation is effected by directional loudspeakers from the stage towards the back of the room, the main lobe of one loudspeaker will inevitably project sound towards the rear wall of the room, as we particularly wish to reach those listeners who are seated the furthest away immediately in front of the rear wall. Thus, a substantial fraction of the sound energy is reflected from the rear wall and can cause echoes in other parts of the room, which can irritate or disturb listeners as well as speakers. For this reason it is recommended that the remote portions of wall being irradiated by the loudspeakers are rendered highly absorbent. In principle, an echo could also be avoided by a diffusely reflecting wall treatment which scatters the sound in all possible directions. But then the scattered sound would excite the reverberation of the room, which, as was explained earlier, is not favoured for speech intelligibility.

The preceding discussions refer mainly to the transmission of speech. The electroacoustical amplification of music – apart from entertainment or dance music – is firmly rejected by many musicians and music lovers for reasons which are partly irrational. Furthermore, many of them have the suspicion that the music could be manipulated in a way which is outside the artists' influence. And finally, almost everybody has experienced the poor performance of technically imperfect reinforcement systems. If, in spite of objections, electroacoustical amplification is mandatory in a performance hall, the installation must be carefully designed and constructed with first class components and it must preserve, under all circumstances, the natural direction of sound incidence. Care must be taken to avoid linear as well as non-linear distortions and the amplification should be kept at a moderate level only. A particular problem is to comply with the large dynamical range of symphonic music. For entertainment music, the requirements are not as stringent; in this case people have long been accustomed to the fact that a singer has a microphone in his or her hand and the audience will more readily accept that it will be conscious of the sound amplification.

These remarks have no significance whatsoever for the presentation of electronic music; here the acoustician can safely leave the arrangement of loudspeakers and the operation of the whole equipment to the performers.

10.4 Acoustical feedback and its suppression

Acoustical feedback of sound reinforcement systems in rooms has already been mentioned in the last section. In principle, feedback will occur whenever the loudspeaker is in the same room as the microphone which inevitably will pick up a portion of the loudspeaker signal. Only if this portion is sufficiently small are the effects of feedback negligibly faint; in other cases, it may cause substantial linear distortions, ringing effects and finally self-sustained oscillations of the whole system which are heard as howling or whistling.

Before discussing measures for the reduction or suppression of feedback effects, we shall deal with its mechanism in a somewhat more detailed manner.

We assume that the original sound source, for instance a speaker, will produce at the microphone a sound signal whose spectrum is denoted by

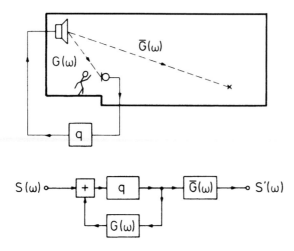

Figure 10.9 Acoustical feedback in a room. In the lower part the transmission paths in a room and the loudspeakers are represented by 'black boxes'.

$S(\omega)$ (*see* Fig. 10.9). Its output voltage is amplified with a frequency independent amplifier gain q and is fed to the loudspeaker. The loudspeaker signal will reach the listener by passing along a transmission path in the room with a complex transfer function $\bar{G}(\omega)$; at the same time, it will reach the microphone by a path with the transmission function $G(\omega)$. The latter path, together with the microphone, the amplifier and the loudspeaker, constitutes a closed loop through which the signal passes repeatedly.

The lower part of Fig. 10.9 shows the mechanism of acoustical feedback in a more schematic form. The complex amplitude spectrum of the output signal (i.e. of the signal at the listener's seat) is given by

$$S'(\omega) = q\bar{G}(\omega)\left[S(\omega) + G(\omega)\frac{S'(\omega)}{\bar{G}(\omega)} \right]$$

From this expression we calculate the transfer function of the whole system including the effects of acoustical feedback, $G'(\omega) = S'(\omega)/S(\omega)$:

$$G'(\omega) = \frac{q\bar{G}(\omega)}{1 - qG(\omega)} = q\bar{G}(\omega)\sum_{n=0}^{\infty}[qG(\omega)]^n \qquad (10.11)$$

The latter expression clearly shows that acoustical feedback is brought about by the signal repeatedly passing through the same loop. The factor $qG(\omega)$, which is characteristic for the amount of feedback, is called the 'open loop gain' of the system. Depending on its magnitude, the spectrum $S'(\omega)$ of the received signal and hence the signal itself may be quite different from the original signal with the spectrum $S(\omega)$.

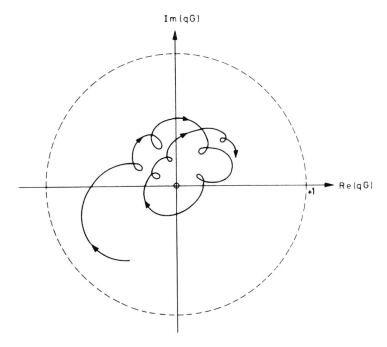

Figure 10.10 Nyquist diagram illustrating stability of acoustical feedback.

A general idea of the properties of the 'effective transfer function' G' can easily be given by means of the Nyquist diagram in which the locus of the complex open loop gain is represented in the complex plane (*see* Fig. 10.10). Each point of this curve corresponds to a particular frequency, abscissa and ordinate are the real part and the imaginary part of qG respectively. The whole system will remain stable if this curve does not include the point +1, which is certainly not the case if $|qG| < 1$ is true for all frequencies.

Now let us suppose that the amplifier gain and thus qG is at first very small. If we increase the gain gradually, the curve in Fig. 10.10 is inflated, keeping its shape. In the course of this process, the distance between the curve and the point +1, i.e. the quantity $|1 - qG|$, could become very small for certain frequencies. At these frequencies, the absolute value of the transfer function G' will consequently become very large. Then the signal received by the listener will sound 'coloured' or, if the system is excited by an impulsive signal, ringing effects are heard. With a further increase of q, $|qG|$ will exceed unity somewhere, namely for a frequency close to that of the absolute maximum of $|G(\omega)|$. Then the system becomes unstable and performs self-excited oscillation at that frequency.

The effect of feedback on the performance of a public address system can also be illustrated by plotting $|G'(\omega)|$ on a logarithmic scale as a function of the frequency. This leads to 'frequency curves' similar to that shown in

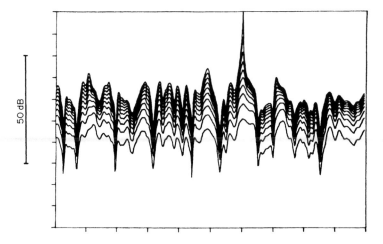

Figure 10.11 Simulated frequency curves of a sound reinforcement system operated in a hall at various amplifier gains. The latter range from −20 dB to 0 dB with respect to the critical gain q_0. The total frequency range is $90/T$ Hz.

Fig. 3.7b). Figure 10.11 represents several such curves for various values of the open loop gain qG, obtained by simulation with a digital computer.[2] With increasing gain one particular maximum starts growing more rapidly than the other maxima and becomes more and more dominating. This is the condition of audible colouration. When a critical value q_0 of the amplifier gain is reached, this leading maximum becomes infinite which means that the system carries out self-sustained oscillations. (In real systems, the amplitude of these oscillations remains finite because of inevitable non-linearities of its components.)

A question of great practical importance concerns the amplifier gain q which must not be exceeded if colouration is to be avoided or to be kept within tolerable limits. According to listening tests as well as to theoretical considerations[2] colouration remains imperceptible as long as

$$20 \log(q/q_0) \lesssim -12 \text{ dB} \tag{10.12}$$

For speech transmission, it is sufficient to keep the relative amplification 5 dB below the instability threshold to avoid audible colouration.

Another effect of acoustical feedback is the increase of reverberance which is again restricted to those frequencies for which $G'(\omega)$ is particularly high. To show this, we simplify eqn (10.11) by putting $\bar{G} = G$. Then the second version of this equation reads

$$G'(\omega) = \sum_{n=1}^{\infty} [qG(\omega)]^n \tag{10.13}$$

The corresponding impulse response is obtained as the (inverse) Fourier transform of that expression (*see* eqn (1.33*a*)):

$$g'(t) = \frac{1}{2\pi} \int_{-\infty}^{+\infty} G'(\omega) \exp(i\omega t) \, d\omega = \sum_{n=1}^{\infty} q^n g^{(n)}(t) \qquad (10.14)$$

In the latter formula $g^{(n)}$ denotes the *n*-fold convolution of the impulse response $g(t)$ with itself, defined by the recursion

$$g^{(n+1)}(t) = \int_{0}^{t} g^{(n)}(t')g(t-t') \, dt'$$

and

$$g^{(1)}(t) = g(t)$$

For our present purpose it is sufficient to use $g(t) = A \exp(-\delta t)$ as a model response. It yields $g^{(n)}(t) = A(At)^{n-1} \exp(-\delta t)/(n-1)!$. If this is inserted into eqn (10.14), the sum turns out to be the series expansion of the exponential function, hence

$$g'(t) = Aq \exp[-(\delta - Aq)t] \qquad (10.15)$$

Evidently, the decay constant of the exponential is reduced to $\delta' = \delta - Aq$, and the reverberation time is increased by a factor

$$\frac{T'}{T} = \frac{\delta}{\delta'} = \frac{1}{1 - Aq/\delta} \qquad (10.16)$$

When q approaches the critical value δ/A, the reverberation time becomes infinite. On account of our oversimplified assumption of $g(t)$, eqns (10.15) and (10.16) do not show that the increase of reverberation time is limited to one or a few discrete frequencies, and that therefore the reverberation sounds coloured as does a steady state signal of wide bandwidth.

Acoustical feedback can be avoided by selecting a sufficiently small amplifier gain. This, however, makes the loudness of the loudspeaker signal at the listener's seat so low that eventually the system will become virtually useless. The loudspeaker system can be rendered much more effective, however, by making the mean absolute value of $\bar{G}(\omega)$ in the frequency range of interest as high as possible, but that of $G(\omega)$ as low as possible (*see* Fig. 10.9). This in turn is achieved by carefully selecting the directivity of the loudspeaker with its main lobe pointing towards the listeners, whilst the microphone is located in a direction of weak radiation. Likewise, a microphone with some directivity should be used, for instance a cardiod microphone, which favours the original sound source but not the signal arriving and is arranged close to it. With these rather simple methods, which are very effective when applied carefully, acoustical feedback cannot be completely eliminated, but the point of instability can be shifted far enough away so that it will never be reached during normal operation.

A further increase of feedback stability would be attainable if the absolute value of the transfer function $G(\omega)$ could be replaced by its average, leading to an all-pass function:

$$G_a(\omega) = G_0 \exp\left[i\psi(\omega)\right]$$

Then the curve shown in Fig. 10.10 would be a circle with its radius depending on the amplifier gain q. The curves in Fig. 10.11 would not be smooth, to be sure, but they would contain many smaller peaks instead of one high maximum: a peak would occur for each frequency where the phase function $\psi(\omega)$ is an integer multiple of 2π. Hence the signal colouration caused by acoustical feedback would be much less severe, and instability would onset at many frequencies simultaneously and not at just one. Thus the important question is how the frequency curve can be levelled out.

This cannot be achieved just by using several loudspeakers fed by the same signal: the resultant transfer function would be the vector sum of single transfer functions, hence its general properties would be the same as those of a single room transfer function which itself is the vector sum of numerous components superimposed with random phases (*see* Section 3.4). In particular its squared absolute values are again exponentially distributed according to eqn (3.34).

In an early attempt to flatten or to average the frequency curve of a room the microphone was moved on a circular path during its operation.[3] Since each point of the path has its own transmission characteristics, the maximum and minimum or the phase relation between several components which make up the resulting sound pressure at the microphone, are averaged out to some degree provided that the diameter of the circle is substantially larger than all the wavelengths of interest. The use of a gradient microphone rotating around an axis which is perpendicular to the direction of maximum sensitivity has also been proposed and this has an effect which is similar to a moving microphone. These methods have the disadvantage that they require mechanical movements and they also produce some amplitude modulation which can be detected subjectively.

A more practical method of virtually flattening the frequency characteristics of the open loop gain has been proposed and applied in practice by Schroeder.[4,5] As we saw, acoustical feedback is brought about by particular spectral components which always experience the same 'favourable' amplitude and phase conditions when circulating along the closed loop in Fig. 10.9. If, however, at the beginning of each roundtrip, the frequencies of all spectral components are shifted by a small amount, then a particular component will experience favourable as well as unfavourable phase conditions, which, in effect, is the same as averaging the frequency curve. Let us suppose a sinusoidal signal has originally the angular frequency ω. After each roundtrip in the feedback loop its angular frequency has been increased by $\Delta\omega$, whereas its level has been increased or diminished by $L = 20 \log_{10} |qG(\omega')|$ with ω' denoting the actual frequency. Hence, after having performed N roundtrips, the angular frequency of the signal is $\omega + N\Delta\omega$ and its total change in level is

$$L(\omega + \Delta\omega) + L(\omega + 2\Delta\omega) + \ldots + L(\omega + N\Delta\omega) \approx N\langle L \rangle$$

where $\langle L \rangle$ is the average of the logarithmic frequency curve from ω to $\omega + N\Delta\omega$. The system will remain stable if $N\langle L \rangle \to -\infty$ as N approaches infinity, i.e. if $\langle L \rangle$ is negative. In any event, it is no longer the absolute maximum of the frequency curve which determines the onset of instability, but a certain average value. Since the difference between the absolute maximum and the mean value is about 10–12 dB for most large rooms, as we saw in Section 3.4, it is this level difference by which the amplifier gain theoretically may be increased without the danger of instability, compared with the operation without frequency shifting. Note that $\Delta\omega$ must be small enough on the one hand that the frequency shift will not be heard and, on the other hand, it must be high enough to yield an effective averaging after a few roundtrips. The latter will be the case if $\Delta\omega$ corresponds roughly to the mean spacing of frequency curve maxima, i.e. if according to eqn (3.36b) the frequency shift is chosen to be

$$\Delta\omega > 2\pi\langle \Delta f_{max} \rangle = \frac{8\pi}{T} \tag{10.17}$$

Both conditions can be fulfilled quite well in the case of speech; with music, however, even very small frequency shifts are audible, since they change the musical intervals. Therefore, this method is applicable to speech only. In practice the total increase in amplification of about 10–12 dB, which is possible theoretically, cannot be used; if the increase exceeds 5–6 dB, speech begins to sound unnatural and finally becomes unintelligible, even with stable conditions. In practice, the frequency shift is achieved by inserting a suitable electronic device into the amplifier branch.

A similar method of reducing the danger of acoustical feedback was proposed by Guelke and Broadhurst[6] who replaced the frequency shifting device by a phase modulator. The effect of phase modulation is to add side lines to each spectral line lying symmetrically with respect to the centre line. By suitably choosing the width of phase variations, the centre line can be removed altogether. In this case, the authors were able to obtain an additional gain of 4 dB. They stated that the modulation is not noticeable even in music if the modulation frequency is as low as 1 Hz.

10.5 Reverberation enhancement with external reverberators

As pointed out earlier, many large halls have to serve several quite different purposes such as meetings, lectures, performance of concerts, theatre and opera pieces, and sometimes even sports events, banquets and balls. It is obvious that the acoustical design of such a multipurpose hall cannot create optimum conditions for each type of presentation. At best some compromise can be reached which necessarily will not satisfy all expectations.

Great progress could be made if at least the reverberation time of such a hall could be varied within reasonable limits, thus adapting it to the different requirements for speech and for music. This can be achieved by movable or rotatable wall or ceiling sections which exhibit either its reflecting or its absorbing side to the arriving sound, or by thick curtains, as described in Section 9.3. Such devices, however, are costly and subject to mechanical wear. An alternative solution to this problem is offered by electroacoustic systems designed for the control of reverberation. These are expected to be more versatile and perhaps less expensive than mechanical devices.

A first step in this direction is a carefully designed speech reinforcement system. If the loudspeaker sounds are projected mainly towards the audience, i.e. towards absorbent areas, if care is taken to avoid acoustical feedback during normal operation, and if the low frequency components which are not very important to the intelligibility of speech are suppressed rather than enhanced by the amplifier, then the system will perform satisfactorily even if the reverberation time of the room is longer than is optimum for speech. This is because the reverberating sound field is only slightly excited by the loudspeakers. Hence a fairly good intelligibility can be obtained in a hall which was originally designed for musical events.

According to Fig. 9.6, the long reverberation time needed for orchestral music generally requires a high specific volume of a hall, i.e. high volume per seat, or high volume per square metre of audience. Since, on the other hand, volume is expensive, clients and designers have a natural tendency to cut costs by reducing the enclosed volume, and sometimes the acoustical consultant will find it hard to win through against this tendency. Another common situation is that of an existing hall which is to be used for orchestral performances although it was originally intended for other purposes and therefore has relatively short reverberation. In any event, a consultant is sometimes faced with the problem of too short a reverberation time which is more difficult to handle than the reverse problem.

The 'natural' solution, namely to increase the volume of the hall, is almost impossible because the costs of this measure are prohibitive. Therefore, it is not unreasonable to ask whether the same goal could be reached at less expense by employing electroacoustical aids. In fact, several types of electroacoustical systems for raising the reverberation time have been developed and applied.

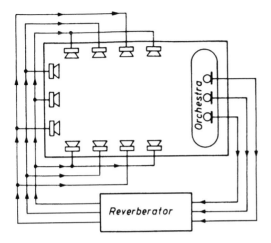

Figure 10.12 Principle of electroacoustic reverberation system employing separate reverberator.

The principle of one of them is depicted in Fig. 10.12. The sounds produced by the orchestra are picked up by microphones which are as close as possible to the musicians. The electrical signals are fed into a so-called 'reverberator'. This is a linear system with an impulse response which is more or less similar to that of an enclosure and which therefore adds reverberation to the signals. After this modification, they are re-radiated in the original room by loudspeakers. In addition, delaying devices must usually be inserted into the electrical circuit in order to ensure that the reverberated loudspeaker signals will not reach any listener's place earlier than the direct sound signal from the natural sound source, at the same time taking into account the various sound paths in the room.

It should be noted that the location of the loudspeakers has a great influence on the effectiveness of the system and on the quality of the reverberated sound. The obvious supposition that a great number of loudspeakers are required is not necessarily correct. The reverberating sound field must indeed be diffuse, not in an objective sense but in a subjective one, i.e. the listener should have the impression of 'spaciousness'. According to Section 7.7, this is not a question of numerous directions of sound incidence but a question of incoherence between the various components. Therefore, the reverberator should have several output terminals yielding mutually incoherent signals which are all derived from the same input signal. In order to provide each listener with sound incident from several substantially different directions, it may be necessary to use far more loudspeakers than incoherent signals. Nevertheless, the primary requirement is the use of incoherent signals, whereas the number of loudspeakers is a secondary question.

It is quite obvious that all the loudspeakers must be sufficiently distant from all the listeners in order to prevent one particular loudspeaker being heard much louder than the others. Finally, care must be taken to prevent significant acoustical feedback. Even when the amplification is low enough to exclude self-excitation, feedback can impair the quality of the loud-speaker sounds, since reiteration of the signal in the feedback loop causes the exaggeration of certain spectral components and the suppression of others. This was discussed in Section 10.4. The resulting colouration of the sound can be intolerable for music at a gain at which it would still be unnoticeable for speech.

A system of this type was installed for permanent use with music in the 'Jahrhunderthalle' of the Farbwerke Hoechst AG at Hoechst near Frank-furt am Main.[7] This hall, the volume of which is 75 000 m^3, has a cylindri-cal side wall with a diameter of 76 m, its roof is a spherical dome. In order to avoid echoes, the dome as well as the side wall were treated with highly absorbing materials. In this state it has a natural reverberation time of about one second. To increase the reverberation time, the sound signals are picked up by several microphones on the stage, passed through a reverber-ator and finally fed to a total of 90 loudspeakers which are distributed in a suspended ceiling and along the cylindrical side and rear wall. With this system, which underwent several modifications in the course of time, the reverberation time can be raised to about 2 s.

Adding reverberation to an electrical signal by a 'reverberator' can be effected in various ways. The most natural is to apply the microphone signal(s) to one or several loudspeakers in a separate reverberation chamber which has the desired reverberation time including the proper frequency dependence. The sound signal in the chamber is again picked up by micro-phones which are far apart from each other to guarantee the incoherence of the output signals (*see* Section 8.8). The reverberation chamber should be free of flutter echoes and may be as small as about 200 m^3.

Other reverberators which have found wide application in the past employed bending waves propagating in metal plates[8] or torsional waves travelling along helical springs, excited and picked up with suitable electro-acoustic transducers. The reverberation was brought about by repeated reflections of the waves from the boundary of these waveguides.

The essential thing about these devices is the finite travelling time be-tween successive reflections. Therefore, in order to produce some kind of reverberation, we only require, in principle, a delaying device and a suitable feedback path by which the delayed signal is transferred again and again from the output to the input of the delay unit (*see* Fig. 10.13a). If q denotes the open loop gain in the feedback loop, which must be smaller than unity for stable conditions, and t_0 denotes the delay time, the impulse response of the circuit is given by eqn (7.4). With each roundtrip, the signal is attenu-ated by $-20 \log q$ dB, and hence after $-60/(20 \log q)$ roundtrips, the level has fallen by 60 dB. The associated total delay is the reverberation time of the reverberator and is given by

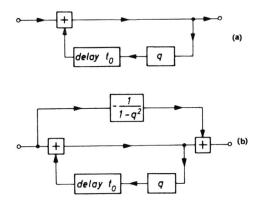

Figure 10.13 Reverberators employing one delay unit only: (a) comb filter type reverberator; (b) all-pass type reverberator.

$$T = -\frac{3t_0}{\log q} \tag{10.18}$$

It can be controlled by varying the open loop gain or the delay time t_0.

In order to reach a realistic reverberation time, either q must be fairly close to unity, which makes the adjustment of the open loop gain very critical, or t_0 must have a relatively large value. In both cases, the reverberation has an undesirable tonal quality. In the first case the reverberator produces 'coloured' sounds due to the regularly spaced maxima and minima of its transfer function as shown in Fig 7.10 (central part, right hand side). In the second case the regular succession of 'reflections' is heard as a flutter echo.

The quality of such a reverberator can be improved to a certain degree, according to Schroeder and Logan[9,10] by giving it all-pass characteristics. For this purpose, the fraction $1/(1 - q^2)$ is subtracted from its output (*see* Fig. 10.13b). The impulse response of the modified reverberator is

$$g(t) = -\frac{\delta(t)}{1 - q^2} + \sum_{n=0}^{\infty} q^n \delta(t - nt_0) \tag{10.19}$$

Its Fourier transform, i.e. the transfer function of the reverberator, is given by

$$
\begin{aligned}
G(f) &= \frac{1}{1 - q \exp(-2\pi i f t_0)} - \frac{1}{1 - q^2} \\
&= \frac{q \exp(-2\pi i f t_0)}{1 - q^2} \frac{1 - q \exp(2\pi i f t_0)}{1 - q \exp(-2\pi i f t_0)}
\end{aligned} \tag{10.20}
$$

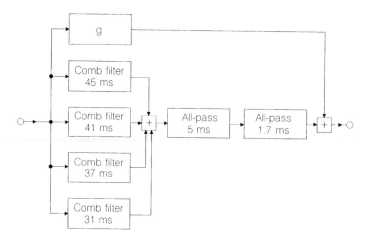

Figure 10.14 Electrical reverberator consisting of four comb filter units and two all-pass units. The numbers indicate the delay time of each unit. Additionally, the unreverberated signal can be added to the output signal attenuated by a factor *g* (after Schroeder[9]).

Since the second factor in eqn (10.20) has the absolute value 1, $G(f)$ has all-pass characteristics; there are no longer maxima and minima. Subjectively, however, the undesirable properties of the reverberation produced in this way have not completely disappeared at all, since our ear does not perform a Fourier analysis in the mathematical sense, but rather a 'short-time frequency analysis', thus also being sensitive to the temporal structure of a signal. A substantial improvement can be effected, however, by combining several reverberation units with and without all-pass characteristics and with different delay times. These units are connected partly in parallel, partly in series. An example is presented in Fig. 10.14. Of course it is important to avoid simple ratios between the various delay times as well as long pronounced fundamental repetition periods in the impulse response of the reverberator. As far as the practical implementation is concerned, time delays are produced with digital circuits nowadays.

More recently, a sophisticated system has been developed by Berkhout *et al.*[11,12] which tries to modify the original signals in such a way that they contain and hence transplant not only the reverberation but the complete wave field from a fictive hall (of course one with excellent acoustics) into the actual environment. This system, called Acoustic Control System (ACS), is based on Huygens' principle according to which each point hit by a wave may be considered as the origin of a secondary wave which effects the propagation to the next points. The ACS is intended to simulate this process by hardware components, i.e. by loudspeakers. In the following explanation of 'wave front synthesis', we describe all signals in the frequency domain, i.e. as functions of the angular frequency ω.

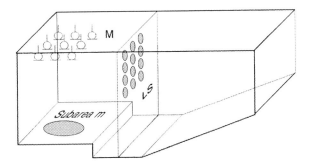

Figure 10.15 Principle of wavefront synthesis.

Let us consider, as shown in Fig. 10.15, an auditorium in which a plane and regular array of N loudspeakers is installed. If properly fed these loudspeakers should synthesise the wave fronts originating from the sound sources. For this purpose, the sounds produced in the stage area are picked up by M microphones regulary arranged next to the stage (for example, in the ceiling above the stage). These microphones have some directional characteristics, each of them covering a subarea of the stage with one 'notional sound source' in its centre which is at r_m. Accordingly, the signal picked up by the mth microphone at location r'_m is

$$M(r'_m, \omega) = W(r_m, r'_m)S(r_m, \omega) \tag{10.21}$$

W is a 'propagator' describing the propagation of a spherical wave from r_m to r'_m:

$$W(r_m, r'_m) = \frac{\exp(-ik|r_m - r'_m|)}{|r_m - r'_m|} \tag{10.22}$$

Each of these propagators involves an amplitude change and a delay:

$$W(r_m, r'_m) = A \exp(-i\omega\tau) \tag{10.23}$$

with $\tau = |r_m - r'_m|/c$.

The microphone signals $M(r'_m, \omega)$ will be fed to the loudspeakers after processing them as if the source signals $S(r_m, \omega)$ had reached the loudspeaker locations directly, i.e. as sound waves. Hence we have to undo the effect of the propagator $W(r_m, r'_m)$ and to replace it with another one connecting the mth notional source with the nth loudspeaker. Finally the input signal of this loudspeaker is obtained by adding the contributions of all sources:

$$P(r_n) = \sum_{m=1}^{M} W^{-1}(r_m, r'_m)W(r_m, r_n)M(r'_m, \omega) \tag{10.24}$$

The loudspeakers will correctly synthesise the original wave fronts if their mutual distances are small enough and if they have dipole characteristics. (The latter follows from Kirchhoff's formula which is the mathematical expression of Huygens' principle but will not be discussed here.) For a practical application it is sufficient to substitute the planar loudspeaker array by a linear one in horizontal orientation since our ability to localise sound sources in vertical directions is rather limited.

This relatively simple version of an ACS can be used not only for enhancing the sounds produced on stage but also for improving the balance between different sources, for instance between singers and an orchestra. It has the advantage that it preserves the natural localisation of the sound sources. Although the derivation presented above neglects all reflections from the boundary of the auditorium, the system works well if the reverberation time of the hall is not too long.

Sound reflections from the boundaries could be accounted for by constructing the mirror images of the notional sources at $\mathbf{r}_m$ and including their contributions into the loudspeaker input signals. At this point, however, it is much more interesting to construct image sources not with respect to the actual auditorium but to a virtual hall with desired acoustical conditions, and hence to transplant these conditions into the actual hall. This process is illustrated in Fig. 10.16. It shows the actual auditorium (assumed as fan-shaped) drawn in the system of image sources of a virtual rectangular hall. Suppose the positions and the relative strengths of the image sources are numbered in some way,

$$\mathbf{r}_m^{(1)}, \mathbf{r}_m^{(2)}, \mathbf{r}_m^{(3)}, \ldots, \quad \text{and} \quad B_m^{(1)}, B_m^{(2)}, B_m^{(3)}, \ldots$$

Then the propagator $W(\mathbf{r}_m, \mathbf{r}_n)$ in eqn (10.24) has to be replaced with

$$W(\mathbf{r}_m, \mathbf{r}_n) + B_m^{(1)} W(\mathbf{r}_m^{(1)}, \mathbf{r}_n) + B_m^{(2)} W(\mathbf{r}_m^{(2)}, \mathbf{r}_n) + \ldots$$

which leads to the following loudspeaker input signal

$$P(\mathbf{r}_n) = \sum_{m=1}^{M} \left[W(\mathbf{r}_m, \mathbf{r}_n) + \sum_k B_m^{(k)} W(\mathbf{r}_m^{(k)}, \mathbf{r}_n) \right] S(\mathbf{r}_m, \omega) \tag{10.25}$$

In practical situations it is useful to arrange loudspeaker arrays along the side walls of the actual auditorium and to assign each of them to the right-hand and the left-hand image sources, respectively, as indicated in Fig. 10.16.

Since the coefficients $B_m^{(k)}$ contain in a cumulative way the absorption coefficients of all walls involved in the formation of a particular image source (*see* Section 4.1), the reverberation time and the reverberation level in it, both in dependence of frequency, are easily controlled by varying these coefficients. Similarly, the shape and the volume of the virtual hall can

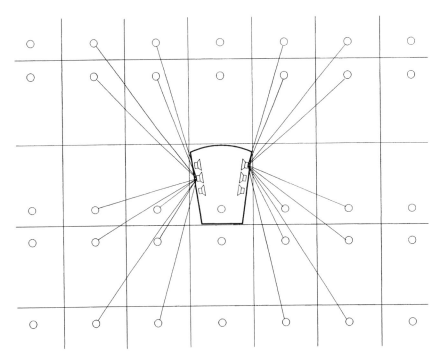

Figure 10.16 Actual hall and image sources of a rectangular virtual hall
(after Berkhout *et al.*[13]).

be changed. Thus, an ACS permits the simulation of a great number of
different acoustical conditions in a given environment, at least in principle.

Since the number of image sources increases rapidly with increasing
order, a vast number of amplitude-delay units as in eqn (10.23) would be
required to synthesise the whole impulse response of the virtual room.
Therefore this treatment is restricted to the first part of the impulse
response. The later parts, i.e. those corresponding to reverberation, can be
synthesized in a more statistical way because the auditive impression conveyed by them does not depend on individual reflections. More can be
found on this matter in Ref. 13.

Systems of this kind have been installed in many halls, theatres etc. and
are successfully used for natural sound reinforcement and for reverberation
enhancement. If carefully installed and adjusted even experienced listeners
will not be aware that any electroacoustic system is being operated during
the performance.

10.6 Reverberation enhancement by controlled feedback

So far electroacoustic systems for reverberation enhancement have been
described which are more or less different versions of the scheme in

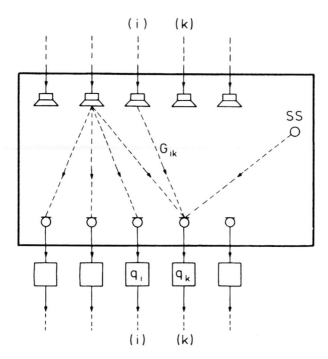

Figure 10.17 Multi-channel system after Franssen.[14]

Fig. 10.12, i.e. with some reverberation generating device outside the enclosure under consideration. In this last section we shall deal with systems which employ sound paths inside the room for increasing the reverberation time.

As discussed in Section 10.3, any acoustical feedback between a loudspeaker and a microphone is associated with additional reverberation increasing with the open loop gain. Unfortunately, this effect is restricted to one frequency only. In order to avoid ringing effects and poor tonal quality, many different channels operated in the same enclosure have to be employed. Figure 10.17 depicts the multichannel system invented by Franssen.[14] It consists of N ($\gg 1$) independent transmission channels with each microphone arranged outside the reverberation distance (*see* eqn (5.38) or (5.40)) of any loudspeaker. Electrically, the kth microphone is connected to the kth loudspeaker via an amplifier with gain q_k. Its output voltage contains the contribution $S_0(\omega)$ made by the sound source SS as well as the contributions of all loudspeakers. Therefore, its amplitude spectrum is given by

$$S_k(\omega) = S_0(\omega) + \sum_{i=1}^{N} q_i G_{ik}(\omega) S_i(\omega) \tag{10.26}$$

where G_{ik} characterises the acoustic transmission path from the ith loud-speaker to the kth microphone, including the properties of both transducers.

The expression above represents a system of N linear equations from which the unknown signal spectra $S_k(\omega)$ can be determined, at least in principle. To get a basic idea of what the solution of this system is like we can neglect all phase relations and hence replace all complex quantities by their squared magnitudes averaged over a small frequency range, i.e. S_k by the real quantity s_k and likewise G_{ik} by g_{ik} and S_0 by s_0. This is tantamount to superimposing energies instead of complex amplitudes and seems to be justified if the number N of channels is sufficiently high. Furthermore, we assume equal amplifier gains and also $g_{ik} \equiv g$ for all i and k. Then we obtain immediately from eqn (10.26):

$$s_k = s = \frac{s_0}{1 - Nq^2g} \quad \text{for all } k \tag{10.27}$$

The ratio s/s_0 characterises the increase of the energy density at a particular microphone caused by the electroacoustic system. On the other hand, under certain assumptions the reverberation time may be taken proportional to the steady state energy density in a reverberant space (*see* eqn (5.37)). Therefore the ratio of reverberation times with and without the system is with $\delta = 6.91/T$

$$\frac{T'}{T} = \frac{1}{1 - Nq^2g} \tag{10.28}$$

This formula is similar to eqn (10.16), but in the present case, one can afford to keep the open loop gain of each channel low enough to exclude the risk of sound colouration by feedback, due to the large number N of channels. Franssen[14] recommended making q^2g as low as 0.01; then 50 independent channels would be needed to double the reverberation time.

However, more recent investigations by Behler[15] and by Ohsmann[16] into the properties of such multi-channel systems have shown that eqn (10.28) is too optimistic in that the actual gain of reverberation time is lower. According to the latter author, a system consisting of 100 amplifier channels will increase the reverberation time by slightly more than 50% if all channels are operated with gains 3 dB below instability.

For the performance of a multi-channel system of this type it is of crucial importance that all open loop gains are virtually frequency independent within a wide frequency range. To a certain degree, this can be achieved by carefully adjusted equalisers which are inserted into the electrical paths. In any case there remains the problem that such a system comprises N^2 feedback channels, but only N amplifiers gains and equalisers to influence them.

Nevertheless, systems of this kind have been successfully installed and operated at several places, for instance in the Concert House at Stockholm.[17] This hall has a volume of 16 000 m³ and seats 2000 listeners. The electroacoustical system consists of 54 dynamic microphones and 104 loudspeakers. That means there are microphones which are connected to more than one loudspeaker. It increases the reverberation time from 2.1 s (without audience) to about 2.9 s. The tonal quality is reportedly so good that unbiased listeners do not become aware of the fact that an electroacoustical system is in operation.

An electroacoustical multi-channel system of quite a different kind, but to be used for the same purpose, has been developed by Parkin and Morgan[18] and has become known as 'assisted resonance system'. But unlike Franssen's system, each channel has to handle only a very narrow frequency band. Since the amplification and the phase shift occurring in each channel can be adjusted independently (or almost independently), all unpleasant colouration effects can be avoided. Furthermore, electroacoustical components, i.e. the microphones and loudspeakers, need not meet high fidelity standards.

The 'assisted resonance system' was originally developed for the Royal Festival Hall in London. This hall, which was designed and constructed to be used solely as a concert hall, has a volume of 22 000 m³ and a seating capacity of 3000 persons. It has been felt, since its opening in 1951, that the reverberation time is not as long as it should have been for optimum conditions, especially at low frequencies.[19] For this reason, an electroacoustical system for increasing the reverberation time was installed in 1964; at first this was on an experimental basis, but in the ensuing years several aspects of the installation have been improved and it has been made a permanent fixture.

In the final state of the system, each channel consists of a condenser microphone, tuned by an acoustical resonator to a certain narrow frequency band, a phase shifter, a very stable 20 W amplifier, a broad band frequency filter and a 10- or 12-inch loudspeaker, which is tuned by a quarter wavelength tube to its particular operating frequency at frequencies lower than 100 Hz. (For higher frequencies, each loudspeaker must be used for two different frequency bands in order to save space and therefore has to be left untuned.) The feedback loop is completed by the acoustical path between the loudspeaker and the microphone. For tuning the microphone, Helmholtz resonators with a Q factor of 30 are used for frequencies up to 300 Hz; at higher frequencies they are replaced by quarter wave tubes. The loudspeaker and the microphone of each channel are positioned in the ceiling in such a way that they are situated at the antinodes of a particular room mode.

There are 172 channels altogether, covering a frequency range 58–700 Hz. The spacing of operating frequencies is 2 Hz from 58 Hz to 150 Hz, 3 Hz for the range 150–180 Hz, 4 Hz up to 300 Hz, and 5 Hz for all higher frequencies.

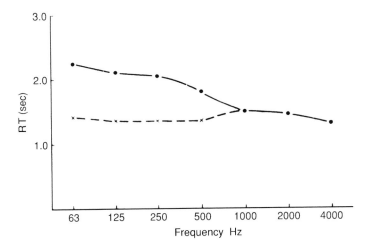

Figure 10.18 Reverberation time of occupied Royal Festival Hall, London, as a function of frequency both with (•————•) and without (×— — —×) 'assisted resonance system'.[20]

In Fig. 10.18 the reverberation time of the occupied hall is plotted as a function of frequency, again with both system on and system off. These results were obtained by evaluating recordings of suitable pieces of music which were taken in the hall. The difference in reverberation time below 700 Hz is quite obvious. Apart from this, the system has the very desirable effect of increasing the overall loudness of the sounds perceived by the listeners and of increasing the diffusion, i.e. the number of directions from which sound reaches the listeners' ears. In fact, from a subjective point of view, the acoustics of the hall seems to be greatly improved by the system and well-known musicians have commented enthusiastically on the achievements.[20]

During the past years, assisted resonance systems have been installed successfully in several other places. These more recent experiences seem to indicate that the number of independent channels need not be as high as was chosen for the Royal Festival Hall.[21]

The foregoing discussions should have made clear that there is a great potential in sophisticated electroacoustic systems for creating acoustical environments which can be adapted to nearly any type of performance. Their widespread and successful application depends, of course, on the technical perfection of their components and on further technical progresses, and equally on the skill and experience of the persons who operate them.

In the future, however, the 'human factor' will certainly be reduced by more sophisticated systems, allowing application also in places where no specially trained personnel are available.

References

1 Olson, H.F., *Acoustical Engineering*, D. van Nostrand, Princeton, 1960.
2 Kuttruff, H. and Hesselmann, N., *Acustica*, **36** (1976) 105.
3 Zwikker, C. French Patent No. 712 588.
4 Schroeder, M.R., Proceedings of the Third International Congress on Acoustics, Stuttgart, Elsevier, Amsterdam, 1959, p. 771.
5 Schroeder, M.R., *J. Acoust. Soc. America*, **36** (1964) 1718.
6 Guelke, R.W. and Broadhurst, A.D., *Acustica*, **24** (1971) 33.
7 Meyer, E. and Kuttruff, H., *Acustica*, **14** (1964) 138.
8 Kuhl, W., *Rundfunktechn. Mitteilungen*, **2** (1958) 111.
9 Schroeder, M.R., *J. Acoust. Soc. America*, **33** (1961) 1064.
10 Schroeder, M.R. and Logan, B.F., *J. Audio Eng. Soc.*, **9** (1961) 192.
11 Berkhout, A.J., *J. Audio Eng. Soc.*, **36** (1988) 977.
12 Berkhout, A.J., de Vries, D. and Vogel, P., *J. Acoust. Soc. America*, **93** (1993) 2764.
13 Berkhout, A.J., de Vries, D. and Boone, M.M., Proceedings of the 15th International Congress on Acoustics, Vol. II, p. 377, Trondheim, 1995.
14 Franssen, N.V., *Acustica*, **20** (1968) 315.
15 Behler, G., *Acustica*, **69** (1989) 95.
16 Ohsmann, M., *Acustica*, **70** (1990) 233.
17 Dahlstedt, S., *J. Audio Eng. Soc.*, **22** (1974) 626.
18 Parkin, P.H. and Morgan, K., *J. Sound Vibr.*, **2** (1965) 74.
19 Parkin, P.H., Allen, W.A., Purkis, H.J. and Scholes, W.E., *Acustica*, **3** (1953) 1.
20 Parkin, P.H. and Morgan, K., *J. Acoust. Soc. America*, **48** (1970) 1025.
21 Berry, G. and Crouse, G.L., 52nd Convention of the Audio Eng. Soc., 1975, Preprint No. 1070.

Index